"*The Social Studies Teacher's Toolbox* is a must-read for every soci[...] strategies in this book will engage students across the country, add to their analytical skills, and make stronger teachers out of any reader."

Michelle Voelker
ELA/History Teacher
Area 3 Writing Project Teacher Consultant

"As I read *The Social Studies Teacher's Toolbox* I thought to myself, "This is a book that any teacher could use, regardless of the content." The emphasis on literacy and culturally responsive teaching strategies as well as the inclusion of ideas for meeting *all* students' needs set this book apart. Ramos and Johnson's book is a must for every social studies teacher."

Karen Smith
Director, Area 3 Writing Project
UC Davis

"This piece is foundational and exceptionally written for social science teachers and beyond. It lays the groundwork and provides the tools that really capture the essence of this powerful profession in the social sciences in preparing and setting up our students for success."

Karina Figueroa-Ramírez, M.Ed.
Educational Equity Coordinator
Faculty Student Mentor Program Coordinator
College of Education | Sacramento State

"This welcome addition to the Toolbox Series draws on the author's own experiences and the experiences of their students. *The Social Studies Teacher's Toolbox* has a coherent and well-organized approach for teachers who want to implement proven practices and effective strategies for learning social studies, in particular teachers serving culturally and linguistically diverse youth and their communities."

Janet I Hecsh, PhD
College of Education
California State University, Sacramento

"Elizabeth and Evelyn, current veteran teachers, provide a well-organized, easy-to-follow, research-based resource full of classroom-tested instructional strategies and lessons that can be used tomorrow. A must-have practical toolkit that will become a well-tabbed, go-back-to resource for any teacher or instructional coach looking for ways to make social studies curriculum accessible and come alive for all students with the use of low-prep, move-beyond-the-textbook ideas that engage and foster effective student-centered learning."

Linda Biewer-Elstob
Instructional Coach Davis Joint Unified School District

"*The Social Studies Teacher's Toolbox* is a must-read for the social science teachers striving to teach more inclusive and accessible content. The chapters detail the research behind the strategies, ways to successfully engage students, support for English language learners, and extensions for advanced learners that make any worthwhile subject both intriguing and rigorous."

Dominique Williams
Social Science Teacher
Contributing author of "The Struggle for Ethnic Studies in the Golden State: Capitol City Organizers and Activists" in the book *Rethinking Ethnic Studies*

"Ramos and Johnson's book masterfully weaves discipline-specific strategies for any social studies classroom with straightforward, plainspoken, classroom-tested examples teachers can immediately use. It's a must for any new or seasoned social studies teacher."

Jed Larsen
Middle/High School Social Studies Teacher
Gilder Lehrman California History Teacher of the Year (2011)
Social Studies Teacher, Contributor to the UC Davis History Project

The Social Studies Teacher's Toolbox

Social Studies Teachers Will Find Classroom-Tested Lessons and Strategies That Can Be Easily Implemented in the Classroom

The *Teacher's Toolbox* series is an innovative, research-based resource providing teachers with instructional strategies for students of all levels and abilities. Each book in the collection focuses on a specific content area. Clear, concise guidance enables teachers to quickly integrate low-prep, high-value lessons and strategies in their middle school and high school classrooms. Every strategy follows a practical, how-to format established by the series editors.

The Social Studies Teacher's Toolbox contains hundreds of student-friendly classroom lessons and teaching strategies. Clear and concise chapters, fully aligned to Common Core Social Studies standards and National Council for the Social Studies standards, cover the underlying research, technology-based options, practical classroom use, and modification of each high-value lesson and strategy.

This book employs a hands-on approach to help educators quickly learn and apply proven methods and techniques in their social studies courses. Topics range from reading and writing in social studies and tools for analysis, to conducting formative and summative assessments, differentiating instruction, motivating students, incorporating social and emotional learning and culturally responsive teaching. Easy-to-read content shows how and why social studies should be taught and how to make connections across history, geography, political science, and beyond. Designed to reduce instructor preparation time and increase relevance, student engagement, and comprehension, this book:

- Explains the usefulness, application, and potential drawbacks of each instructional strategy
- Provides fresh activities applicable to *all* classrooms
- Helps social studies teachers work with English language learners (ELLs), advanced students, and students with learning differences
- Offers real-world guidance for addressing current events while covering standards and working with textbooks

The Social Studies Teacher's Toolbox is an invaluable source of real-world lessons, strategies, and techniques for general education teachers and social studies specialists, as well as resource specialists/special education teachers, elementary and secondary educators, and teacher educators.

The Social Studies Teacher's Toolbox

Hundreds of Practical Ideas to Support Your Students

ELISABETH JOHNSON
EVELYN RAMOS LAMARR
LARRY FERLAZZO
KATIE HULL SYPNIESKI

The Teacher's Toolbox Series

JB JOSSEY-BASS™
A Wiley Brand

Published by Jossey-Bass
A Wiley Brand
111 River Street, Hoboken NJ 07030
www.josseybass.com

Jossey-Bass books and products are available through most bookstores. To contact Jossey-Bass directly call our Customer Care Department within the U.S. at 800-956-7739, outside the U.S. at 317-572-3986, or fax 317-572-4002.

Wiley also publishes its books in a variety of electronic formats and by print-on-demand. Some material included with standard print versions of this book may not be included in e-books or in print-on-demand. For more information about Wiley products, visit www.wiley.com.

Library of Congress Cataloging-in-Publication Data

Names: Johnson, Elisabeth, 1984- author.
Title: The social studies teacher's toolbox : hundreds of practical ideas
   to support your students / Elisabeth Johnson, Evelyn Ramos LaMarr, Larry
   Ferlazzo, Katie Hull Sypnieski.
Description: First edition. | Hoboken, NJ : Jossey-Bass, [2020] | Series:
   The teacher's toolbox series | Includes bibliographical references and
   index.
Identifiers: LCCN 2020001747 (print) | LCCN 2020001748 (ebook) | ISBN
   9781119572053 (paperback) | ISBN 9781119572145 (adobe pdf) | ISBN
   9781119572091 (epub)
Subjects: LCSH: Social sciences—Study and teaching (Elementary)—United
   States. | Social sciences—Study and teaching (Middle school)—United
   States. | Social sciences—Study and teaching (Secondary)—United
   States. | Curriculum planning—United States.
Classification: LCC H62.5.U5 J56 2020 (print) | LCC H62.5.U5 (ebook) |
   DDC 300.71/2—dc23
LC record available at https://lccn.loc.gov/2020001747
LC ebook record available at https://lccn.loc.gov/2020001748

Cover Design: Wiley
Cover Image: © malerapaso/Getty Images

Printed in the United States of America
FIRST EDITION

PB Printing   V10018205_032320

Contents

About the Authors xxi
About the Editors of the Toolbox Series xxiii
Acknowledgments xxv
Letter from the Editors xxvii
Introduction xxix

I   Reading and Writing   1

1. A Fresh Look at Vocabulary 3
What Is It? 3
Why We Like It 3
Supporting Research 4
Common Core Connections 4
Social Studies Connections 4
Application 5
    Building a Word List 5
    Accessing Prior Knowledge 6
    Building Understanding 10
    Revising and Formalizing Definitions 11
    Differentiation 13
    Advanced Extensions 14
Student Handouts and Examples 15
What Could Go Wrong? 15
Technology Connections 15

Figures 16
    Figure 1.1   Splashed Vocabulary 16
    Figure 1.2   Word Card Example A 17
    Figure 1.3   Word Card Example B 17

2. Reading Strategies... **19**
What Is It? 19
Why We Like It 19
Supporting Research 20
Common Core Connections 20
Social Studies Connections 20
Application 21
    Text Selection 22
    Pre-reading 22
    Predicting 22
    Connecting 23
    Key Ideas 24
    Summarizing 24
    Questioning 25
    Visualizing 26
    Clarifying 27
    Differentiation 28
    Advanced Extensions 29
Student Handouts and Examples 29
What Could Go Wrong? 29
Technology Connections 30
Attribution 31
Figures 32
    Figure 2.1   Reading Strategies Sentence Starters 32
    Figure 2.2   Annotation Examples A 33
    Figure 2.3   Summarizing Examples 34
    Figure 2.4   Annotation Examples B 35

3. Read-Aloud Protocol **37**
What Is It? 37
Why We Like It 37
Supporting Research 37
Common Core Connections 38
Social Studies Connections 38
Application 38
    Finding and Preparing Authentic Texts 39
    Read-Aloud Protocol 41

Student-Created Read-Alouds 45

Differentiation 48

Advanced Extensions 48

Student Handouts and Examples 49

What Could Go Wrong? 49

Technology Connections 49

Attribution 49

Figures 50

    Figure 3.1   Bastille Soldier 50

    Figure 3.2   Guillotine 51

    Figure 3.3   Reign of Terror 52

    Figure 3.4   Annotation and Reading Strategy Prompts 52

    Figure 3.5   Attributes of a Good Read-Aloud 53

4. Thematic Data Sets 55

What Is It? 55

Why We Like It 55

Supporting Research 56

Common Core Connections 56

Social Studies Connections 56

Application 57

    Building a Data Set 57

    Teaching Protocol for Using Data Sets 59

    Differentiation 64

    Advanced Extensions 65

Student Handouts and Examples 65

What Could Go Wrong? 66

Technology Connections 66

Attribution 66

Figures 67

    Figure 4.1   Indigeneity Data Set 67

    Figure 4.2   France Headlines Data Set 70

    Figure 4.3   Types of Government Data Set 75

    Figure 4.4   Cut-Up Data Set Examples 77

    Figure 4.5   Student-Created Data Sets 78

5. Writing in Social Studies 79

What Is It? 79

Why We Like It 79

Supporting Research 79

Common Core Connections 80

Social Studies Connections 80

Application 80
    Golden Lines – Kick-Starting Writing 81
    Writing Frames 82
    Writing Structures 84
    Extended Argument Writing 88
    Other Social Studies Writing Activities 89
    Differentiation 90
    Advanced Extensions 91
Student Handouts and Examples 92
What Could Go Wrong? 92
Technology Connections 92
Attribution 93
Figures 94
    Figure 5.1   Letter Frame 94
    Figure 5.2   Letter Frame Example 95
    Figure 5.3   ABC Answering Strategy Guide 96
    Figure 5.4   ABC Model Questions and Responses 97
    Figure 5.5   Student Sample of ABC Strategy 98
    Figure 5.6   PEE Answering Strategy Guide 99
    Figure 5.7   Argument Organizer 100
    Figure 5.8   Sentence Starters for Argument Writing ... 101
    Figure 5.9   Teacher Argument Model Response 102
    Figure 5.10 Word Bank Paragraph 103

6. Mnemonics 105

What Is It? 105
Why We Like It 105
Supporting Research 106
Common Core Connections 106
Social Studies Connections 106
Application 107
    Story Mnemonics 107
    Differentiation 111
    Advanced Extensions 111
Student Handouts and Examples 112
What Could Go Wrong? 112
Technology Connections 112
Attribution 113
Figures 114
    Figure 6.1   Map Story Guide, South America 114
    Figure 6.2   Student Examples of Map Visual for Practice A 115
    Figure 6.3   Student Examples of Map Visual for Practice B 116

7. Timelines Revisited 117

What Is It? 117
Why We Like It 117
Supporting Research 118
Common Core Connections 118
Social Studies Connections 118
Application 118
    Identity Timelines 119
    Additional Timeline Activities 128
    Differentiation 129
    Advanced Extensions 130
Student Handouts and Examples 130
What Could Go Wrong? 131
Technology Connections 131
Attribution 131
Figures 132
    Figure 7.1   Identity Timeline – Teacher Model 132
    Figure 7.2   Student Example: Identity Timeline 133

8. Current Event Case Study 135

What Is It? 135
Why We Like It 135
Supporting Research 136
Common Core Connections 136
Social Studies Connections 136
Application 136
    Sequencing of Events 137
    Developing Questions 139
    Bias Awareness and Research 141
    Written Analysis 145
    Additional Ideas for Including Current Events in the Classroom 146
    Differentiation 147
    Advanced Extensions 148
Student Handouts and Examples 148
What Could Go Wrong? 148
Technology Connections 149
Figures 150
    Figure 8.1   Timeline Example 150
    Figure 8.2   Media Bias Chart Example 150

9. Genre Study 151

What Is It? 151
Why We Like It 151
Supporting Research 152
Common Core Connections 152
Social Studies Connections 152
    Application 152
    Student Choice Genre Project 159
    Differentiation 164
    Advanced Extensions 165
Student Handouts and Examples 165
What Could Go Wrong? 165
Technology Connections 166
Attribution 166
Figures 167
    Figure 9.1   Bollywood Movie Script Starter 167
    Figure 9.2   Annotated Bollywood Movie Script Starter 169
    Figure 9.3   Student Example: China Poem 170
    Figure 9.4   Student Example: Social Media 171
    Figure 9.5   Genre Cheat Sheet 172
    Figure 9.6   Scene Diagram Example 173

10. Concept Attainment 175

What Is It? 175
Why We Like It 176
Supporting Research 176
Common Core Connections 176
Social Studies Connections 176
Application 176
    Democracy Concept Attainment 177
    Concept Attainment to Improve Writing 180
    Differentiation 183
    Advanced Extensions 183
Student Handouts and Examples 184
What Could Go Wrong? 184
Technology Connections 184
Figures 184
    Figure 10.1   Dictatorship Paragraph Example 184

II   Analysis Tools   185

11. Questions for Learning 187
What Is It? 187
Why We Like It 187
Supporting Research 188
Common Core Connections 188
Social Studies Connections 188
Application 189
    Teacher-Generated Questions 190
    Student-Generated Questions 194
    Differentiation 197
    Advanced Extensions 197
Student Handouts and Examples 198
What Could Go Wrong? 198
Technology Connections 198

12. Image Analysis 199
What Is It? 199
Why We Like It 199
Supporting Research 200
Common Core Connections 200
Social Studies Connections 200
Application 201
    Photographs 201
    Paintings 207
    Political Cartoons 210
    Video 213
    Differentiation 218
    Advanced Extensions 219
Student Handouts and Examples 219
What Could Go Wrong? 219
Technology Connections 220
Figures 221
    Figure 12.1   Image Analysis Chart 221
    Figure 12.2   Japanese American Evacuation Photo 222
    Figure 12.3   Teacher Model – Photo Analysis Chart 223

Figure 12.4   DuBois and Washington Images – WordCloud 224
Figure 12.5   Political Cartoon – Analysis Chart 225
Figure 12.6   "Election Day!" – Political Cartoon 226
Figure 12.7   Teacher Model – Political Cartoon 227

13. Analysis of Primary Sources 229

What Is It? 229
Why We Like It 229
Supporting Research 230
Common Core Connections 230
Social Studies Connections 230
Application 230
    Primary Source Engagement Activity 230
    At a Glance Primary Source Analysis 232
    In-Depth Analysis of Source 234
    Additional Key Strategies 238
    Differentiation 243
    Advanced Extensions 243
Student Handouts and Examples 244
What Could Go Wrong? 244
Technology Connections 245
Attribution 245
Figures 246
    Figure 13.1   At a Glance Analysis of Source 246
    Figure 13.2   Hernán Cortés' Account of Tenochtitlan 247
    Figure 13.3   At a Glance – Student Example 248
    Figure 13.4   At a Glance – Teacher Copy 249
    Figure 13.5   In-Depth Analysis of a Written Source 250
    Figure 13.6   Cortés' Letter – Teacher Copy 251
    Figure 13.7   Roots of Slavery: Primary Source Data Set 252

14. Synthesis Charts 257

What Is It? 257
Why We Like It 257
Supporting Research 258
Common Core Connections 258
Social Studies Connections 258
Application 258
    Creating a Synthesis Chart 259
    Implementing Synthesis Charts with Students 266
    Differentiation 273
    Advanced Extensions 273

Student Handouts and Examples 274
What Could Go Wrong? 274
Technology Connections 274
Attribution 274

III   Speaking and Listening   275

15. Listening and Speaking Activities 277
What Is It? 277
Why We Like It 277
Supporting Research 278
Common Core Connections 278
   Social Studies Connections 278
Application 278
   Active Listening Mini-Lesson 278
   Guest Speakers 280
   Podcasts 283
   Student Presentations 285
   Differentiation 288
   Advanced Extensions 288
Student Handouts and Examples 288
What Could Go Wrong? 289
Technology Connections 289
Attribution 290
Figures 291
   Figure 15.1   Suggestions for a Guest Speaker 291
   Figure 15.2   Guest Speaker Thank-You Template 292
   Figure 15.3   Guest Speaker Thank-You Example 293

16. Discussions 295
What Is It? 295
Why We Like It 295
Supporting Research 296
Common Core Connections 296
Social Studies Connections 296
Application 296
   Informal Discussion Strategies 297
   Formal Discussion Strategies 300
   Additional Key Strategies 313
   Differentiation 315
   Advanced Extensions 315

Student Handouts and Examples 316
What Could Go Wrong? 316
Technology Connections 316
Attribution 317
Figures 317
  Figure 16.1   Question Strips – Terrorism in Paris 317
  Figure 16.2   Facilitator Card 318
  Figure 16.3   Small-Group Discussion Materials 319
  Figure 16.4   Group Discussion Norms 320
  Figure 16.5   Discussion "Cheat Sheet" for Teachers 320

IV   Additional Key Strategies   321

17. Project-Based Learning 323

What Is It? 323
Why We Like It 323
Supporting Research 324
Common Core Connections 324
Social Studies Connections 324
Application 324
  Key Steps in PBL 325
  Textbook Insert Project 334
  Other Ideas for Project-Based Learning 344
  Differentiation 345
  Advanced Extensions 346
Student Handouts and Examples 346
What Could Go Wrong? 347
Technology Connections 347
Figures 348
  Figure 17.1   Group Discussion Starters 348
  Figure 17.2   Email Template 349
  Figure 17.3   Textbook Insert Structure 350

18. Culturally Responsive Teaching 353

What Is It? 353
Why We like It 353
Supporting Research 354
Common Core Connections 354
Social Studies Connections 354
Application 354
  Reflective Questions 355
  Differentiation 369

Advanced Modifications 370
Student Handouts and Examples 370
What Could Go Wrong? 370
Technology Connections 371
Attribution 371
Figures 372
    Figure 18.1   Beginning of Year Questionnaire 372
    Figure 18.2   Senior Year History Community Circle 373
    Figure 18.3   Community Circle Template 374

19. Social and Emotional Learning **375**
What Is It? 375
Why We Like It 375
Supporting Research 376
Common Core Connections 376
Social Studies Connections 376
Application 377
    Growth Mindset Mini-Lesson 377
    Empathy Mini-Lesson 380
    Tips for Reinforcing SEL 383
    Differentiation 385
    Advanced Extensions 385
Student Handouts and Examples 386
What Could Go Wrong? 386
Technology Connections 386
Attribution 387
Figures 388
    Figure 19.1   Overcoming Adversity Matching Activity 388
    Figure 19.2   Brain Graphic Organizer 389
    Figure 19.3   Mindsets Graphic Organizer 390
    Figure 19.4   Ellis Island 1913 391
    Figure 19.5   Ellis Island 1913 Example 392
    Figure 19.6   Empathy Graphic Organizer 393
    Figure 19.7   Personal Empathy Map 394
    Figure 19.8   Personal Empathy Map Teacher Model 395
    Figure 19.9   Ellis Island Empathy Map 396

20. Assessment **397**
What Is It? 397
Why We Like It 397
Supporting Research 398
Common Core Connections 398
Social Studies Connections 398

Application 398

    Diagnostic 399

    Formative 403

    Summative 406

    Student Self-Assessment 411

    Differentiation 412

    Advanced Extensions 413

Student Handouts and Examples 413

What Could Go Wrong? 413

Technology Connections 414

Figures 416

    Figure 20.1 Scientific Revolution Concept Web 416

21. Getting the Most from Your Textbook 417

What Is It? 417

Why We Like It 417

Supporting Research 418

Common Core Connections 418

Social Studies Connections 418

Application 418

    Using Images 418

    Using Textbook Excerpts 419

    Discussions 420

    Timelines 421

    Vocabulary 422

    Reading Strategies 423

    Student-Created Tests 423

    Primary Sources 423

    Mnemonics 424

    Anticipatory Sets 425

    Scavenger Hunts 425

    Jigsaws 425

    Analyzing What's Missing in the Textbook 427

    Differentiation 427

    Advanced Extensions 427

Student Handouts and Examples 427

What Could Go Wrong? 428

Technology Connections 428

References 429

Index 455

List of Tables

Table 1.1   Unit Vocabulary Graphic Organizer 7
Table 1.2   Modified Vocabulary Graphic Organizer 13
Table 1.3   Answer Sheet for Modified Vocabulary Graphic Organizer 14
Table 2.1   Reading Strategies Handout 21
Table 4.1   Category Graphic Organizer 61
Table 4.2   Category Graphic Organizer Example 63
Table 6.1   Map Story Guide 109
Table 7.1   Timeline Grading Rubric 120
Table 7.2   Timeline Brainstorm 121
Table 7.3   Historical Figure Research 125
Table 7.4   Personal Connections 127
Table 8.1   Timeline Organizer 139
Table 8.2   Timeline Organizer Example 139
Table 8.3   Current Event Research Guide 143
Table 8.4   Current Event Research Guide Example 144
Table 9.1   Taking Apart a Scene 155
Table 9.2   Bollywood Script Assessment Rubric 157
Table 9.3   China Response – Teacher Model 161
Table 9.4   Student Choice Genre Assessment Rubric 161
Table 9.5   Genre Rating 163
Table 10.1 Democracy Concept Attainment 177
Table 10.2 Concept Attainment for Citing Sources 180
Table 10.3 Resumé Concept Attainment 181
Table 10.4 "Hooks" Concept Attainment 182
Table 11.1 Types of Questions Examples 190
Table 11.2 Essential and Guiding Question Example 193

Table 12.1   Image Slideshow – Graphic Organizer 206

Table 12.2   Video Analysis Chart 213

Table 12.3   Video – Teacher Model 215

Table 13.1   In-Depth Analysis – Teacher Copy 236

Table 13.2   Scaffolding Strategies for Analyzing Primary Sources 237

Table 13.3   Data Set Analysis Chart 239

Table 13.4   Categorization Chart 241

Table 14.1   Synthesis Chart Template 260

Table 14.2   Brazil Synthesis Chart 261

Table 14.3   Brazil Synthesis Chart Example 263

Table 14.4   Identity Synthesis Chart 265

Table 14.5   Identity Synthesis Chart Teacher Model 270

Table 15.1   Active Listening Graphic Organizer 279

Table 15.2   *Serial* Podcast Listening Graphic Organizer 284

Table 15.3   Jigsaw Presentations 287

Table 16.1   Response Frames 299

Table 16.2   Evidence for Fishbowl 308

Table 16.3   Evidence for Fishbowl Example (Prison Reform) 309

Table 16.4   New Insights Chart 311

Table 16.5   Evidence for Debate 314

Table 17.1   PBL Teacher Planning Form and Checklist 326

Table 17.2   Planning and Progress Form – General 328

Table 17.3   Research Chart 329

Table 17.4   General PBL Rubric 332

Table 17.5   PBL Teacher Planning Form and Checklist - Textbook Insert 334

Table 17.6   Planning and Progress Form - Textbook 338

Table 17.7   Textbook Insert Project Rubric 341

Table 20.1   Types of Assessment 398

Table 21.1   Multiphase Vocabulary – Bill of Rights 422

Table 21.2   Textbook Jigsaw Organizer Example 426

About the Authors

*E*lisabeth Johnson has taught social studies to both mainstream and English language learners at Luther Burbank High School in Sacramento, California for the past 13 years. She is a National Board Certified teacher with a master's degree in education.

She has contributed a chapter on social studies in *Navigating the Common Core with English Language Learners* written by Larry Ferlazzo and Katie Hull Sypnieski, as well as an article for the weekly teacher advice column *Education Week Teacher*, "'Doing' Geography Instead of 'Studying' It."

She is a teacher consultant with the Area 3 Writing Project through the University of California, Davis, and has led teacher development training through the San Joaquin County Office of Education.

Elisabeth lives in Sacramento with her husband and their twin daughters.

Evelyn Ramos LaMarr has taught at the secondary level for 12 years at Luther Burbank High School in Sacramento, California. She is currently teaching social studies to mainstream and International Baccalaureate students. She has taken an active role in creating curriculum and piloting the Ethnic Studies course newly adopted in the Sacramento City Unified School District. She has contributed to Larry Ferlazzo's weekly teacher advice column *Education Week Teacher*, "Response: 'Education Suffers Without More Teachers of Color.'"

She is a teacher consultant with the Area 3 Writing Project at the University of California, Davis, and has a master's degree in education. Evelyn is a proud daughter of immigrant parents who worked in the River Delta as farmworkers. Currently, she resides in Sacramento with her husband Todd and their young daughter, Belen.

About the Editors of the Toolbox Series

Larry Ferlazzo teaches English, social studies, and International Baccalaureate classes to English language learners and others at Luther Burbank High School in Sacramento, California.

He's written nine books: *The ELL Teacher's Toolbox* (with coauthor Katie Hull Sypnieski); *Navigating the Common Core with English Language Learners* (with coauthor Katie Hull Sypnieski); *The ESL/ELL Teacher's Survival Guide* (with coauthor Katie Hull Sypnieski); *Building a Community of Self-Motivated Learners: Strategies to Help Students Thrive in School and Beyond*; *Classroom Management Q&As: Expert Strategies for Teaching*; *Self-Driven Learning: Teaching Strategies for Student Motivation*; *Helping Students Motivate Themselves: Practical Answers to Classroom Challenges*; *English Language Learners: Teaching Strategies That Work*; and *Building Parent Engagement in Schools* (with coauthor Lorie Hammond).

He has won several awards, including the Leadership for a Changing World Award from the Ford Foundation, and was the Grand Prize Winner of the International Reading Association Award for Technology and Reading.

He writes a popular education blog at http://larryferlazzo.edublogs.org, a weekly teacher advice column for *Education Week Teacher*, and posts for the *New York Times* and the *Washington Post*. He also hosts a weekly radio show on BAM! Education Radio.

He was a community organizer for 19 years prior to becoming a public school teacher.

Larry is married and has three children and two grandchildren.

A basketball team he played for came in last place every year from 2012 to 2017. He retired from league play after that year, and the team then played for the championship. These results might indicate that Larry made a wise career choice in not pursuing a basketball career.

Katie Hull Sypnieski has taught English language learners and others at the secondary level for over 20 years. She currently teaches middle school English language arts and social studies at Fern Bacon Middle School in Sacramento, California.

She leads professional development for educators as a teaching consultant with the Area 3 Writing Project at the University of California, Davis.

She is coauthor (with Larry Ferlazzo) of *The ESL/ELL Teacher's Survival Guide, Navigating the Common Core with English Language Learners,* and *The ELL Teacher's Toolbox.* She has written articles for the *Washington Post, ASCD Educational Leadership,* and *Edutopia.* She and Larry have developed two video series with *Education Week* on differentiation and student motivation.

Katie lives in Sacramento with her husband and their three children.

Acknowledgments

Elisabeth Johnson: I would like to thank my family – especially Ella, Grace, and my husband, Jeff – for their constant support. Thank you to my coauthor, Evelyn Ramos LaMarr, for being an amazing partner on this incredible journey with me. I would also like to thank Larry Ferlazzo and Katie Hull Sypnieski for inviting us to be a part of the *Teachers' Toolbox* series and for their editing and guidance with writing this book. I'd like to thank the staff and administrative team at Luther Burbank High School, including former principal and mentor Ted Appel, current principal Jim Peterson, and our department leadership – especially Victoria Stolinski. Finally, to the students who I have been so lucky to work with through the years, thank you for all that you have taught me.

Evelyn Ramos LaMarr: I would like to thank my familia, especialmente mi Mami, for always supporting my professional endeavors. To my husband, Todd, thank you, for being the most unselfish support system for me and our daughter, Belen. Thank you, Elisabeth Johnson, my coauthor, for giving me the best professional compliment by asking me to write this book with you. A very special thanks to Larry Ferlazzo and Katie Hull Sypnieski for not only your crucial editorial expertise, but for sharing your skills and passion for teaching with so many of us (teachers and students). To Luther Burbank High School staff, especially my first principal, Ted Appel, Jim Peterson, Victoria Stolinski, Richard Godnick, and all of the students I have had the honor to teach: thank you for challenging and guiding me to create a career full of purpose.

We would like to thank Amy Fandrei and Pete Gaughan at Jossey-Bass for their guidance in preparing this book. A big thank-you to David Powell for his patience in formatting the manuscript. We also want to thank all the educators we have learned from and whose ideas have influenced our practice and this book.

Letter from the Editors

We have known Elisabeth and Evelyn for a very long time.

In fact, they were both student teachers in Larry's class when the two of us taught in adjoining classrooms many years ago, and they subsequently joined our school's faculty.

We have seen their teaching "magic" blossom, and feel lucky to be able to help bring some of it to the world through this book.

English language learners, students from diverse backgrounds, International Baccalaureate Diploma candidates, students who learn differently — it doesn't matter. Elisabeth and Evelyn are able to reach, connect, and teach them all.

The *Social Studies Teacher's Toolbox* does an excellent job of sharing some of their exceptional lessons, methodology, and instructional strategies. Their work combining social studies instruction with literacy development, social-emotional learning, and culturally responsive pedagogy stands above the crowd.

We've all been part of the same teaching family for years.

We're happy to now welcome them to the Teacher's Toolbox family!

Larry Ferlazzo and Katie Hull Sypnieski

Introduction

When series editors Larry Ferlazzo and Katie Hull Sypnieski approached us about putting together a collection of our best social studies teaching strategies, we jumped at the chance. Considering we have found their books and mentorship to have been so impactful to our own teaching, we were honored to have the opportunity. We were excited to share what we have accumulated from so many great educators (and students!) throughout our careers.

In building this collection of hundreds of practical ideas, two questions stayed consistent in our minds: "How is this strategy helping students improve their knowledge and skills?" and "Why should students care about this social studies topic?" The best thing we have ever done in our career is to never stray far from these questions.

As social studies teachers, we know firsthand that the love of the subject can overshadow the experience students are actually having in our classrooms. When we were new teachers, we struggled with this: our passion did not automatically translate into effective facilitation of social studies learning. In other words, we needed strategies that developed lifelong social studies learners.

For these reasons, we put this book together with a focus on relevance and skill building to create lifelong social studies learners. This type of learner is someone who is curious about the world around them, seeks information, and – most importantly – is actively developing the skills needed to process information. Furthermore, lifelong social studies learners recognize injustice and see their role as an agent of change. To this end, as the strategies in this book promote, our students should be engaged, inquiring, and competent.

The book is divided into four sections. The first focuses on strategies to support reading and writing in social studies, followed by a section on analysis tools.

Then, in our third section, we share strategies for speaking and listening. The fourth and final section of the book shares additional key strategies and serves as a catchall for those chapters that didn't easily fit into the first three sections.

We begin each chapter by describing each strategy, followed by an explanation of why we like it – simply put, how we have found the strategy useful in our social studies classrooms.

Next, we provide supporting research for the effectiveness of the strategy followed by an explanation of how both Common Core and the National Council for the Social Studies (NCSS) standards and themes are addressed. When appropriate, we refer to the NCSS Curriculum Standards, which are organized by 10 themes. We also refer to the College, Career, and Civic Life (C3) Framework created by the NCSS. This framework was added in 2010 to better align social studies with Common Core standards and is focused on inquiry, also an important theme in our book.

From there, each chapter moves into the Application section, which describes how to implement each strategy in detail, as well as ideas about how to apply the strategy in different ways within a variety of social studies classes.

Next, we provide ideas to differentiate each strategy. We share suggestions for both English language learners and students who learn differently. Having said that, we are acutely aware that these two groups of students are not the same. However, the scaffolds we share in this section exemplify good teaching that can help make social studies more accessible for a variety of students.

Following this section, we share Advanced Extensions, which include ways to provide extra challenges for students. Then, we share what could go wrong – some of our most common mistakes – in order to help readers avoid them.

We conclude each chapter with a variety of technology connections, frequently from Larry Ferlazzo's blog, due to its overall comprehensiveness. Seriously, we're not kidding! The blog has almost everything. Lastly, we share related figures. You can also access portions of this book online! All the Technology Connection URLs are collected in a hyperlinked PDF for easy clicking. Many of the figures from the book are provided as PDF files for copying and handouts. They can be found at www.wiley.com/go/socialstudiesteacherstoolbox.

Though we put this book together with secondary students in mind, the strategies are applicable to social studies learners of all grades. We hope you will find these strategies as effective as we have in our own practice.

SECTION 1

Reading and Writing

CHAPTER 1

A Fresh Look at Vocabulary

What Is It?

Vocabulary instruction must be part of any social studies class. The words themselves can be looked at through the lens of the Three Tiers concept developed by Isabel L. Beck, Margaret G. McKeown, and Linda Kucan (2013, p. 9). Tier 1 words are common, everyday words that children pick up in daily conversation (happy, book, see). Tier 2 words are referred to in the Common Core Standards as "general academic words" that are found in readings across content areas, but not typically in conversation (contrast, summarize, consequence) (Common Core, 2010a, p. 42). Tier 3 words are content specific vocabulary (capitalism, infrastructure, longitude) (McKeown & Beck, 2004).

In addition to the Tier 3 content words that are usually included in instruction, we incorporate general academic words or Tier 2 words as well as social and emotional learning (SEL) terms (these SEL words are related to the social studies content, such as *agency* when teaching about the French Revolution).

We break down the process of teaching new vocabulary into three phases: accessing prior knowledge, seeking new information to build understanding, and practicing revision of definitions. We also cover how to build a strong list of terms for units of study that will push students beyond a traditional vocabulary list.

Why We Like It

Teaching vocabulary has often meant giving students a list of words and telling them to copy down the definitions provided by the teacher, dictionary, or textbook. This kind of activity tends to generate little student interest or lasting understanding of words. Vocabulary presented in this way often lacks needed context and background (Hedrick, Harmon, & Linerode, 2004, p. 105).

We like how our three-phase approach to vocabulary places the primary responsibility for creating definitions on the students and not the teacher. In this way, students develop more ownership of their learning as they work to create their own understandings of terms. Instead of being the *source* of knowledge, the teacher works as a *facilitator* of learning. This style of teaching is inclusive of diverse learners by providing space for students to share their own experiences and ideas as a way to help them understand new words.

Supporting Research

Beginning a study of words by encouraging students to consider their prior knowledge – or what is known – before transitioning to new learning – what is unknown – can help to develop word comprehension. Research shows that when students link new information to what they already know, they can better retain the new material (Radboud University Nijmegen, 2014).

Additionally, repeated exposure to vocabulary, along with seeing these words in context, has been shown to improve student comprehension (Biemiller & Boote, 2006).

As we mentioned earlier, a common practice of teaching vocabulary is to give students a list of words, direct them to copy their definitions, and use the words in a sentence. However, researchers Douglas Fisher and Nancy Frey state, "This limited exposure to words and phrases in decontextualized situations has not proven to be effective, nor is it of a sufficient intensity" (Fisher & Frey, 2014a, p. 595). They add, "All learning is social; vocabulary instruction should leverage interactions between teacher, student, and text..." (Fisher & Frey, 2014a, p. 598). The interactive activities described in this chapter can support this kind of instruction.

Common Core Connections

The Craft and Structure strand of the Common Core Standards for Social Studies and History describes the importance of acquiring vocabulary. Students are asked to "determine the meaning of words and phrases in the text" (Common Core, 2010b).

The Text Type and Purpose strand of the Writing Standards provides guidelines for students to use content-specific language to make and explain written arguments (Common Core, 2010c). The activities in this chapter can help build a thorough understanding of content area language.

Social Studies Connections

According to the National Council for the Social Studies, vocabulary instruction is especially important because an education without it "can lead to lower literacy levels and . . . increase the achievement gap" (National Council for the Social Studies, 2017, "rationale"). We prefer the term *opportunity gap* to *achievement gap* (Wells, 2016) since we believe all students have the ability to achieve, but may face socioeconomic challenges or other barriers beyond their control.

Application

Instead of a single lesson plan, this chapter begins by explaining the process we use to build a word list for a unit of study. Then, we share how to divide the teaching of vocabulary into three phases that can be applied to build comprehension: Accessing Prior Knowledge, Building Understanding, and Revising Definitions. We include variations for each of the three phases in this chapter.

It's important to remember that we don't use every variation every time. Depending on time restraints and learning objectives, each step could take a few minutes or a whole period. We ensure, however, that we do utilize at least one instructional strategy from each phase during a unit of study.

BUILDING A WORD LIST

In our experience, developing a good word list is the critical first step of successful vocabulary instruction. This is not a list we give to students – rather, this is a list that we use to develop our lessons. This section focuses on *identifying* the words for this list. The next section will discuss different ways to *introduce* these terms to students.

We tend to keep our vocabulary list for any given unit to around 15 words. We choose this number of words based on research showing that working memory, which is discussed more in Chapter 6: Mnemonics, has an upper limit of between 10 and 20 items (Bick & Rabinovich, 2009, pp. 218101–218103). These 15 words are broken down into three different categories – Tier 3 (content words), Tier 2 (general academic words), and our bonus words, which are SEL terms (see Chapter 19: Social and Emotional Learning).

The first 8–10 words on our list are content focused, or Tier 3. For example, we include content terms like *tropical* and *deforestation* when studying Brazil. Another five or six are Tier 2 vocabulary or general academic words. These terms don't often come up in conversation, but appear frequently in academic texts across many domains. They are important to include because students need to understand them to be able to complete social studies thinking and writing tasks. Examples of these words include *analysis* and *culture*. After uploading our unit texts, we often use the Academic Word Finder feature on the Achieve the Core website, https:// achievethecore.org. This tool helps to locate and choose appropriately leveled Tier 2 words that exist in our unit texts. It's also easy to find lists of Tier 2 words online.

The third category of words we include in our vocabulary lists relate to SEL and also connect to the unit. We put one or two of these words on each list in an effort to integrate the "soft skills" that our students need to succeed in school and other aspects of life. We have discovered connections between most social studies units and SEL terms. For example, the French Revolution vocabulary list we discuss later in this chapter contains the terms *growth mindset* and *agency*. We use the term *growth mindset* to point out that many of the French had to adopt this type of thinking in order to believe that their lives could improve through effort. The term *agency* is the concept of feeling like you have the power to make change and impact the decisions that affect your life. This perspective was obviously another important conviction held by many participants in the French Revolution. For more information on these concepts and their importance to our students, see Chapter 19: Social and Emotional Learning.

ACCESSING PRIOR KNOWLEDGE

This section will discuss three different ways teachers can facilitate accessing prior knowledge in order to acquire new vocabulary. Typically, these Accessing Prior Knowledge activities are done before exposing students to unit texts.

Accessing prior knowledge is an important learning strategy in itself (Alber, 2011) and is especially helpful when used to jump-start the process of learning a word. We start our vocabulary instruction by having students think about any connections they can make to the word. For example, the word *tropical* is seen in Table 1.1: Unit Vocabulary Graphic Organizer. Often, when students see this word, they think of tropical fruit punch or tropical-flavored candy. We ask them to consider what makes these items tropical. Students can, through questioning, determine that *tropical* refers to the types of fruits used as flavors in these items. We push students to consider what these fruits may have in common or what is different about them compared to fruit that is not tropical. In this way, they are much closer to determining the definition for this term and often come up with something about the warm weather required to grow these types of fruits.

This practice is inclusive – all ideas are treated equally. We make clear to students this process is about engaging in the thinking process and not guessing the right answer. This point is important because we want students to build confidence and practice a growth mindset. However, we do highlight when students get a right answer or are on the right path. We may say something like, "That sounds really good, how did you come up with that?" We aren't overly focused on the answer, but instead on the use of context clues and the process of prediction. When students share guesses that are clearly incorrect we might say, "Maybe, let's do some more reading to see if that's right." The focus at this point is on intellectually grappling with the word, not on "nailing" a definition.

Vocabulary Graphic Organizer

One way we help students access prior knowledge is by giving them a list of words with space for writing as shown in Table 1.1 Unit Vocabulary Graphic Organizer. The graphic organizer has three columns. The first column lists the vocabulary words. The second is titled "First Look" and the third is "More Information." We begin by reading each word aloud and pausing to give students time to write any ideas they might have about the word in the "First Look" column.

Table 1.1 Unit Vocabulary Graphic Organizer

Unit – Brazil

Word	First Look	More Information
Carnival		
Amazon		
tropical		
deforestation		
analysis		
Favela		
melting pot		
compare/ contrast		
Rio de Janeiro		
culture		
samba		
Pelé		
Copacabana		
identity		

Students may need some gentle encouragement with taking risks to write an idea they aren't sure is accurate. If you have already taught lessons on practicing a growth mindset, it can be helpful to remind your students of the tenets behind the concept – the idea that knowledge can be improved and intelligence isn't fixed. If you haven't taught it, this would be a good time to do a brief lesson (see Chapter 19: Social and Emotional Learning for lesson ideas). We share that taking a risk by writing a definition they aren't sure is correct *is* practicing a growth mindset. After all, research has shown that our brains derive significant learning benefits in moments of struggle (Boaler & Lamar, 2019).

In addition to encouraging students to practice a growth mindset to make predictions, we also employ other scaffolds to support this phase of the activity. For example, we may say to students, "Write what you know or *think* you know about the word." Giving students a sentence starter like "I think it has to do with . . ." may help them get started. We also allow students to include a quick sketch or to write other words they think might be related to the vocabulary terms.

We model how there may be clues to a word's meaning within the word itself. For example, the teacher may point out root words or similar terms to help guide students toward a meaning. In a World History class during the study of World War II, students often encounter the word *genocide* for the first time. We begin by reading the word aloud. Next, we direct students to think about any portion of the word they may have seen before by asking, "What words have you seen that have the root *cide*?" Students usually are able to come up with both *homicide* and *suicide*. We then prompt students to consider what those words have in common and, based on this, encourage predictions for the term *genocide*.

After students have completed the "First Look" column of their graphic organizer, we review what they have written as a class. When students clearly have a wrong answer, we try to avoid crushing their spirit and respond in a few different ways. We might say something like, "maybe" or "hmm, I'm wondering how you came up with that idea?" We may also call on other students to share out an idea that is closer to the actual definition, or ask a student who is struggling to compare with their neighbor.

Ultimately, this initial phase is not about nailing an accurate definition. Instead, it is focused on cultivating student engagement and curiosity. When students are engaged in their work, they are more likely to stick with a challenging task and gain satisfaction from accomplishing it (Strong, Silver, & Robinson, 1995). Developing curiosity has also been shown to improve learning outcomes by strengthening memory (Sample, 2014). Both engagement and curiosity can make the learning experience more enjoyable and productive for both teachers and students.

Splashed Vocabulary

A second way we can help students learn new vocabulary by accessing prior knowledge involves giving them a handout like Figure 1.1: Splashed Vocabulary. In this figure, the vocabulary words are "splashed" all over the page. First, we ask students to write down thoughtful guesses about what any of the words might mean underneath each one and quickly share these predictions with a partner. Next, we ask students to draw a line between words they think may be related. After connecting a few words, we ask them to write *how* the words are related. We allow students to make *any* connections since there are no right answers. For example, *peasant* and *dictator* from Figure 1.1: Splashed Vocabulary may be connected because they are both types of people or economic or political classes of people. Another connection could be the terms *Reign of Terror* and *execute* based on the morbid connotation, or "scary sounding" quality of both. Students may also make connections based on the spelling of words (some words may begin with capital letters denoting a proper noun, whereas others do not). The key is having *students* provide evidence behind their connections and not whether *we* consider those connections to be particularly valuable. We want students to be motivated to make "multiple touches" on the word and remember its importance for when they see it later on in context.

Once students have had time to analyze their words and possible connections, we ask them to share and compare what they wrote with partners. We then call on a few students to share their findings with the whole class. This is a good moment to explicitly point out and validate the different thinking processes of various students. This process can help foster an inclusive classroom as students from all backgrounds and language levels are prompted to contribute their reasoning behind linking words together.

Stations Activity

A third variation on accessing prior knowledge gets students out of their seats as they participate in a "stations" activity. We divide students into partners or triads. In our experience, larger groupings for this activity tend to struggle with staying on task. At each station, we write one of the words from the vocabulary list onto a sheet of large paper. We do this for each of the words from the list and hang them spaced around the classroom. They should be written in fairly large print, but still have plenty of empty space around the word for student writing.

We give students a set amount of time at each station to write predictions, related words, or draw a quick sketch on the poster. We then give a signal to rotate to the next station. For accountability purposes, we have students write their initials next to their ideas. We also ask students to make sure they are writing down their own ideas, not simply copying down a previous group's idea. They may have similar thoughts, but they need to be written, or drawn, differently. After rotating through enough stations to generate several ideas on each poster (not every group has to go to every station), we ask students to go back to their seats. We then pass out one of two sheets – Table 1.1: Unit Vocabulary Graphic Organizer or Figure 1.1: Splashed Vocabulary. We share what students have written on the posters and ask them to copy down ideas from peers onto their own papers. This step could also be done as a stations activity by having students rotate through the stations again, this time writing down ideas from the posters onto their own papers. We ask that students copy down at least two ideas for each term.

Note: We want to re-emphasize that we only use one of these three "Accessing Prior Knowledge" variations when beginning a unit. We encourage you to choose the one that fits your style, the content of your unit, and time limitations.

BUILDING UNDERSTANDING

After students have made thoughtful guesses in one of the "Accessing Prior Knowledge" activities, we move to the next stage. In this phase, we assist them in building more accurate word understandings through viewing the words in context and by analyzing related images. This step may occur directly after the accessing prior knowledge phase or within the next few days as students begin to read unit materials.

In this phase, students build their own definitions for the words based on the information they encounter in the unit. This practice enhances a sense of student ownership because *they* are in charge of creating a more precise definition. We also use this process to again point out that knowledge isn't fixed – our understanding of terms is constantly growing and changing.

When students encounter the unit vocabulary words in class texts, we have them stop and look for context clues. Based on this analysis, students add new ideas about the words' meanings to the "More Information" section in Table 1.1: Unit Vocabulary Graphic Organizer.

Prior to having students read a text as a class, with a partner, or independently, we model our thinking process when we come across a term within the text. For example, students come across the vocabulary word *Carnival* in a unit about Brazil. The text may describe Carnival participants dressing in costumes and parading down the streets. We might say something like, "This reminds me of Halloween or Mardi Gras. I think Carnival might be some kind of celebration. I'm going to write that down on my graphic organizer."

After modeling using context clues to build an understanding of a term, students practice this process with most class materials within a unit. We remind students to have their vocabulary lists, like Table 1.1: Unit Vocabulary Graphic Organizer or Figure 1.1: Splashed Vocabulary, out on their desks while working with any class texts, pictures, or videos to help them keep the words in mind. When a word comes up in the text, we all circle it. This helps highlight the vocabulary term so students can easily return to it later. Depending on the text, we might immediately pause or wait until the end of a section to add new information to our handouts. We say to students, "Look at what is already written on your graphic organizers. What new information can be added from our reading?" We might also add, "Is there anything we want to remove because we now know it's not accurate?" Another option is to have students read in pairs, take turns with each paragraph, and use the same process themselves to clarify the vocabulary and add new understandings to their graphic organizers. Pairs can then share with the entire class and add new information to their papers.

Another simple – though more time-consuming – way to get students to address the third column – "More Information" – in Table 1.1: Unit Vocabulary Graphic

Organizer is to have them analyze pictures. In this strategy, we use a collection of images, generally one or two for every word, to create a presentation for students. If there is online access, a digital slideshow works well. You could also do this by collecting hard copies of images and having students pass them around.

For this picture analysis, we first project the image and word for a set period of time, usually 30 seconds. For example, we might show an image of land that's been razed when teaching *deforestation*. We limit our teacher explanation, and instruct students to analyze the picture for clues to develop a deeper understanding of the word. We ask questions to prompt student thinking: "What should we add to our definition based on what we see?" or "Based on what you see, how might this word connect to our unit?"

This phase often generates many student ideas and comments. For example, students may shout "All the trees are gone!" or "Everything got burned down!" We respond by telling them, "Great! Write that down!" Another option could be showing the picture for a set amount of time and then calling on a few people to share, or directing all students to share with their partners. We typically have students stop and pair share every three or four images. This process of periodically stopping to compare with a neighbor helps to build a collaborative environment. Students may find their partners noticed, or interpreted, different information from the same images. We ask that they write down at least one idea from their partner and mark it with a star for accountability purposes.

For this "Building Understanding" phase, students are constantly adding to and modifying their ideas about the words based on what they are reading and/or learning from their partners. We share with students that this continual process of modifying and building our understanding is a natural model of effective learning. We talk about how this process unfolds over time and with much practice. For example, initial images depicting *civil war* and *revolution* may be similar. However, it's through reading texts that contain these words and studying context clues that help us understand the difference.

REVISING AND FORMALIZING DEFINITIONS

The first phase of this strategy, "Accessing Prior Knowledge," encourages student engagement and curiosity and is less concerned with precise definitions. The second phase, "Building Understanding," sharpens the focus on accuracy as students build their own meanings throughout the unit. In this third phase, "Revising and Formalizing Definitions," we share how we develop class-wide understandings of each vocabulary word and make these definitions public.

During multiple points of the unit, we have students work individually or in pairs to create more formalized definitions for our vocabulary words that are then made public on a "word wall." This word wall serves as a constant visual reminder of the learning process – our definitions grow and change over time and students can build from one another's ideas. It also makes it easy to quickly reference definitions without having to wait for students to look through their papers.

If you don't have the wall space because of multiple classes, you can create word-wall posters that are hung up and taken down during different class periods – ideally by a student volunteer. We have also done a digital version that we display when feasible, which students can access electronically at anytime.

One way we have students add to the wall is by making what we call a "word card." These cards have three required elements – the word itself, a definition, and a visual to represent it (see Figure 1.2: Word Card Example A). Research has shown that drawing pictures can be especially helpful in remembering meanings (University of Waterloo, 2016).

We explain the cards should only include ideas from their graphic organizers and class notes. We don't want students to simply look up the definition and write it on the card. Instead, we ask students to include their "best definition of the word so far." By using this terminology, we show that we aren't expecting students to be a dictionary. Instead, we're asking them to show their *current* understanding of the term.

Another variation is to have students create a card that has a quote from the unit materials where the word was used (Figure 1.3: Word Card Example B). After putting the quote on the card, we have students add information they learned about the word based on this quote. We often give students the sentence starter, "What I learned about the word from this quote was . . ."

Students can modify the content on the wall as more is learned during the unit. In this way, as students add more word cards, the interpretations evolve into more specific and detailed definitions for all to see.

Again, the use of word cards and a word wall depend on teacher and student time and energy. An important element of this phase is to have students generate more precise definitions and communicate them publicly. In some units, this may be as simple as stopping two-thirds of the way through a unit and assigning students individual words. Then, challenge them to write down their very best definition on a sheet or card with a drawn image. Students can then stand up and quickly share what they wrote with the entire class.

Note: Do we use this three-phase process for every important word in a unit? No! Do we always use this three-phase process in every unit? No! Do we sometimes just tell students what a word means? Yes! Do we try to use these three phases as often as we realistically can in light of content we have to cover, time available, and our own energy levels and those of our students? Yes!

DIFFERENTIATION

One way to scaffold vocabulary for English language learners is to provide a graphic organizer that includes partial definitions or visuals to help jump-start the learning process. See Table 1.2: Modified Vocabulary Graphic Organizer for an example and Table 1.3: Answer Sheet for Modified Vocabulary Graphic Organizer. ELLs often need more support with specialized vocabulary, especially at the higher levels of social studies where terms are often very complex.

Table 1.2 Modified Vocabulary Graphic Organizer

Unit – Brazil

Word	Definition	Visual
Carnival	A huge _____ that happens every year in the Spring. Many people wear _____ and listen to _____ music.	
Amazon	The largest _____ in the world with the greatest variety of plants and _____. It is also a _____ that flows through South America.	
tropical	A type of climate where it is w_____ and r_____ most of the year.	
deforestation	The act of _____ down trees. This is a serious _____ in the Amazon.	
analysis	To study and _____ about something deeply.	
Favela	A _____ neighborhood where many people are struggling.	
melting pot	A phrase used to describe a place where people of _____ cultures live together.	
compare/contrast	To look at how things are s_____r and how things are d_____t.	
Rio de Janeiro	A very large __ __ __ __ in Brazil.	
culture	A group of people's way of life, including their l_____, arts, and religion.	
samba	A type of music and Brazilian d_____ with roots in A____.	
Pelé	Known as one of the best _____ players of all time. He grew up in the f_____ of Brazil.	
Copacabana	A famous _____ where people can relax, play v_____l in the sand, and _____ in the ocean.	
identity	How a person s_____s him/herself.	

Another option is encouraging ELLs to add definitions or synonyms in their home language, also known as L1, to their word lists. Depending on the language, this process might show similarities between the word in a student's L1 and the English version (also known as cognates).

Students who learn differently may benefit from using the same ELL-modified graphic organizers.

Table 1.3 Answer Sheet for Modified Vocabulary Graphic Organizer

Unit – Brazil
Please note that in some cases other words may also be correct

Word	Definition	Visual
Carnival	A huge <u>celebration</u> that happens every year in the Spring. Many people wear <u>costumes</u> and listen to <u>samba</u> music.	
Amazon	The largest <u>rainforest</u> in the world with the greatest variety of plants and <u>animals</u>. It is also a <u>river</u> that flows through South America.	
tropical	A type of climate where it is w<u>arm</u> and r<u>ainy</u> most of the year.	
deforestation	The act of <u>cutting</u> down trees. This is a serious <u>problem</u> in the Amazon.	
analysis	To study and <u>think</u> about something deeply.	
Favela	A <u>poor</u> neighborhood where many people are struggling.	
melting pot	A phrase used to describe a place where people of <u>many</u> cultures live together.	
compare/ contrast	To look at how things are s<u>imilar</u> and how things are <u>different</u>.	
Rio de Janeiro	A very large <u>c i t y</u> in Brazil.	
culture	A group of people's way of life, including their <u>language</u>, arts, and religion.	
samba	A type of music and Brazilian d<u>ance</u> with roots in <u>Africa</u>.	
Pelé	Known as one of the best <u>soccer</u> players of all time. He grew up in the <u>favelas</u> of Brazil.	
Copacabana	A famous <u>beach</u> where people can relax, play v<u>olleyball</u> in the sand, and <u>swim</u> in the ocean.	
identity	How a person s<u>ees</u> him/herself.	

ADVANCED EXTENSIONS

To increase the difficulty for more advanced learners, teachers can identify more challenging terms by reviewing the text. More difficult Tier 2 word lists can be found online by searching "Tier 2 words" and the grade level. Students can then teach their classmates these additional words and their definitions.

Another advanced variation is to have pairs of students create examples and non-examples of an assigned word on a poster. This is a "play" on concept attainment, which has been shown to deepen understanding of concepts in addition to creating lasting knowledge (Boulware & Crow, 2001, p. 5). This inductive learning strategy is explored further in Chapter 10: Concept Attainment.

For example, the term *dictator* from Figure 1.1: Splashed Vocabulary, may lead students to write things like *king, boss, master*, or *person with all the power*. Then, students generate a list of what a dictator is not, such as *elected leader, listener, or follower*. This poster containing examples and nonexamples of a "dictator" can be displayed on the word wall and added to throughout the unit.

Student Handouts and Examples

Table 1.1: Unit Vocabulary Graphic Organizer

Figure 1.1: Splashed Vocabulary

Figure 1.2: Word Card Example A

Figure 1.3: Word Card Example B

Table 1.2: Modified Vocabulary Graphic Organizer

Table 1.3: Answer Sheet for Modified Vocabulary Graphic Organizer

What Could Go Wrong?

Students may struggle with generating ideas during the first phase of accessing prior knowledge. We address this directly by talking about taking learning risks. However, students may still have a hard time practicing a growth mindset. In our experience, students get better as they repeat this process. It can also be helpful for the teacher to model making predictions that turn out to be incorrect and model a positive response when discovering the errors.

Vocabulary instruction, like most instructional strategies, can get boring if done the same way all the time. We try to avoid getting stuck in a rut by not using the same process over and over again. Mix-and-match the strategies that we offer in this chapter and create modifications of your own.

One way to make it a bit more interesting is to review words through a game! Students can be in pairs or small groups with mini whiteboards. A teacher can call out the word and give students a few seconds to write down the definition (after having covered up the word wall) or give the definition and have students write the correct word.

Technology Connections

An online presentation platform like Prezi or Google Slides allows students to create digital versions of "word cards." They can then be shared and modified by peers as a way to fuse technology and vocabulary acquisition.

Another helpful site, which is mentioned in Larry Ferlazzo's Websites of the Day, is called Dictionary Squared (http://larryferlazzo.edublogs.org/2018/01/09/dictionary-squared-looks-like-it-could-be-a-useful-vocabulary-development-tool-for-students). This site allows the teacher to track progress of students' vocabulary learning. More websites that support academic English and vocabulary can also be found at Larry Ferlazzo's website under "The Best Websites for Developing Academic English Skills and Vocabulary" (http://larryferlazzo.edublogs.org/2008/04/06/the-best-websites-for-developing-academic-english-skills-vocabulary).

Figures

representative

estate

Versailles

execute   Napoleon Bonaparte

<u>French Revolution</u>

Reign of Terror

peasants

Bastille

dictator

"Great Fear"   riot

deliberate

agency

growth mindset

Figure 1.1 Splashed Vocabulary

Figure 1.2 Word Card Example A

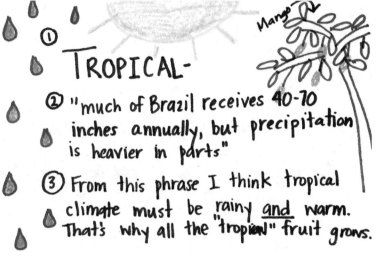

Figure 1.3 Word Card Example B

CHAPTER 2

Reading Strategies

What Is It?

Reading strategies are tools that students can use to help them understand a text. As they practice and become skilled at employing these strategies, their use can become automatic.

The instructional process begins with a heavy amount of guidance from the teacher unless students have often used these strategies in previous years. The high level of support can be reduced as students develop their abilities to use the strategies independently. Over time, the main strategies – summarizing, questioning, clarifying, connecting, visualizing, and predicting – can help students improve their reading comprehension while practicing metacognition ("thinking about one's thinking" – we discuss metacognition and its benefits in Chapter 11: Questions for Learning).

Students build and demonstrate their understanding of these strategies through text annotation. In some cases students can do this annotation directly on consumable texts. In other words, reading that can be written on (like copied articles). In other cases, such as when reading textbooks, students can use sticky notes to document their use of reading strategies. When reading online text, there are many tools for students to create virtual sticky notes. See the Technology Connections section for information on these types of tools.

Why We Like It

Reading strategies are inclusive and can be employed with any text and in any subject area. Teaching these strategies to students can set them up to be successful and independent readers. Instead of keeping what good readers do a secret from students, the teacher shares and models for students how they interact with complex text. Working together, students and teachers are able to build knowledge and comprehension. Practicing multiple reading strategies provides readers of all levels with the tools they need to access any challenging text.

Explicitly teaching students these strategies shows readers how to thoughtfully interact with complex texts and improve comprehension. This kind of direct instruction can be a prelude to students developing the "automatic" skills utilized by fluent readers. In addition, developing these reading skills can result in improved writing abilities.

Applying these reading strategies can also assist with accountability. We have found that some students are just more motivated to read the text if they also have to demonstrate assigned reading strategies at the same time.

Supporting Research

These strategies have been selected based on the needs of our students and evidence that shows the positive impact they can have on literacy (Fisher & Frey, 2014b, p. 347). The National Reading Panel found that teaching students strategies for reading and how to use them is an effective approach to reading instruction (National Institute of Child Health and Human Development, n.d., "findings").

Teaching students specific annotation strategies can improve comprehension as well as promote active reading (O'Donnell, 2004, pp. 85–87).

Common Core Connections

Improving text comprehension is one goal of the Common Core Initiative as seen in the Range of Reading and Level of Text Complexity strand. This standard says that students are expected to be able to comprehend complex history texts without assistance from the teacher at the end of their secondary schooling (Common Core, 2010d). Reading strategies can help students achieve this goal by supporting their development as independent readers.

Social Studies Connections

A student's ability to evaluate evidence and understand historical documents rests heavily on their literacy skills. For this reason, student text comprehension is an integral part of most social studies tasks. The College, Career, and Civic Life (C3) Framework from the National Council for the Social Studies acknowledges the overlapping literacy goals between the Common Core and the C3 Framework (National Council for the Social Studies, 2010).

Application

We teach reading strategies in our classroom by modeling and supporting students as they practice the following techniques: pre-reading, predicting, connecting, identifying key ideas, summarizing, questioning, visualizing, and clarifying.

At the beginning of the year we introduce these strategies and model each one several times prior to asking students to practice it independently. We give students Table 2.1: Reading Strategies Handout and Figure 2.1: Reading Strategies Sentence Starters. After reading through each description aloud, we ask students to create a quick sketch to help them remember the strategy – modeling this process can be helpful. We like students to keep these handouts close by to reference during reading and they sometimes glue them into their notebooks. Another way to keep these handouts accessible is to laminate a class set and pass them out during any reading activity.

Table 2.1 Reading Strategies Handout

Reading Strategy	Create a Sketch to Represent Each Strategy
Prereading Before reading the text, give it a quick scan to figure out what type of text/ writing it is. Look for clues about the purpose of the text and the topic.	
Prediction Predict/Guess/Wonder about what will happen next or as a result of the event.	
Connection Connect the text/news/map to your prior knowledge. Think about what you read/see and how it relates to what you already know.	
Key Ideas Who? What? When? Where? Why? And How? Where is the main idea?	
Summary Explain what you read in your own words. Using your own words, rewrite the main idea.	
Question Ask questions about the information in the text. Question unknown words or phrases in the text. Generate questions for further research.	
Visualize Imagine the words/story as pictures in your mind. Write about what you imagine while you read.	
Clarify Review or reread to make sure you understand. Revisit annotations to make corrections or add new information. Stop and think about what you have read so far.	

Source: Adapted from Jeffrey Wilhelm's Improving Comprehension with Think-Aloud Strategies *(2012). Used with permission.*

TEXT SELECTION

Before any reading occurs, it's our job to make sure the text we select is appropriate for applying reading strategies. This means the text needs to be suitably complex (text complexity is a metric that measures the difficulty of a text through various criteria) (Common Core, 2010e). An overly simple text may not allow for students to employ the multiple strategies needed to become a proficient reader. This does not mean, however, that we do an in-depth analysis of every text prior to using it in class. We use our professional judgment to determine if, as the Common Core Standards explain, the "structure, language conventionality and clarity, and knowledge demands" of the reading are appropriate for our students (Common Core, 2010e). In general, we choose shorter texts and keep in mind that this can mean different things in different classrooms. Longer texts might be chunked into shorter sections so that students get a portion at a time. Or, this could mean selecting only one or two paragraphs out of a longer document. These shorter selections can help students develop stamina so that they can experience success with breaking down a complex text while not feeling overwhelmed by the task.

PRE-READING

We first have students look over the text prior to reading – skimming the document, reading headings, and/or looking at any included images. We often have students label the different text features to help determine its genre. For example, when we use entire articles or clips from newspapers, we direct students' attention to the headline, byline, date, and publication. We might point to the headline on the page and say, "What is this? Based on this, what type of text do you think this is?" By pointing out these features, the teacher can help students note information that sets the stage for reading the text. Noticing these parts of the text helps students to realize that this particular writing is informational, nonfiction, and most likely about a current event. This familiarity may allow students to access related background knowledge and help them construct meaning while reading the text (Kelley & Clausen-Grace, 2010).

PREDICTING

Making a prediction means considering what you noticed during the initial viewing of a text in order to make an "educated guess" about what comes next. Predicting is a way to access prior knowledge because we all use the past to think about the future. Reflecting on prior knowledge can help build context, increase understanding of text ("New Information Is Easier," 2015), and enhance the accuracy of predictions.

Students can use the title, date, or author of a text to make predictions. For example, if the date of a text is near 1776, one might predict the text is related to, or influenced by, the American Revolution. The teacher could model this prediction process by pointing out the date and saying, "Notice the date. Based on this date, I predict that this may be related to American independence" and then writing that comment down in the margin near the date. If an image is included, students can use the content of the image to come up with a logical guess about the text.

When we teach students to predict, we often ask them to complete the sentence starter "I predict . . ." Another option is to have students write down a list of words, concepts, or ideas they predict might be related to the text. Readers can continue predicting during the reading of a text – it isn't limited to the beginning of the task. In fact, it's a good idea to have students continue to predict while reading so that they can *clarify* their predictions, a reading strategy discussed later in this chapter. That section provides examples of how students can revisit their predictions.

CONNECTING

When we ask students to make connections to the text, we are explicitly asking them to access their prior knowledge and experiences. To model this reading strategy, we read a portion of text aloud and demonstrate how we might use the sentence starter "This reminds me of . . ." This can be challenging for students to do at first because sometimes the connections may seem a little *dis*connected.

For example, in our geography class, after reading a headline about the increase of plant-eating bugs due to climate change, a student wrote, "This reminds me of a guy who burned down his house." This comment did not seem connected to either bugs, agriculture, or climate change. When asked to elaborate on his connection, the student shared that he heard a story about a man who was using a technique called "flaming" (where fire is used to get rid of pests and weeds) when he accidentally burned his house down. After sharing this, we were able to modify his connection to include the portion about different pest-control methods – not just the man's house burning down. In other words, the idea is not to connect for the sake of connecting, but to connect in order to gain a deeper understanding of the text.

At the same time, however, it is also possible that making a personal connection to the text can generate greater student engagement. For example, some of our Hmong students might be reminded of family members' deaths during the Vietnam War when they read about civilian casualties during the study of World War II. Although that connection might not help them have an increased historical understanding of World War II, it might make them more interested in learning about it. The resulting greater motivation can make a purely personal "connection" equally as useful as one that would help them understand the text.

KEY IDEAS

Proficient readers are able to recognize the main ideas in a text. In our experience, many secondary level students struggle with this task. One technique that can help students identify key ideas is highlighting (or underlining or circling) the text. We model the process by selecting a reading, going through it with them, and sharing aloud our thinking as we highlight the key information.

Teaching students *how* to highlight may seem unnecessary, but we have discovered that many students have been highlighting ineffectively for years. We take time at the beginning of the year to teach students this skill and regularly model it for them.

We first define what effective highlighting involves – carefully selecting words or short phrases that represent key ideas (Leutner, Leopold, & den Elzen-Rump, 2007, p. 179). We explain that if all of the other words on the page disappeared, what remains should communicate the most important information. We often set a word limit to encourage students to make their selections carefully.

In our experience, practicing effective highlighting with students and revealing our process can make a difference in comprehension, engagement, and accountability. Even if the act of highlighting itself may not dramatically improve comprehension (Baer, 2014), the requirement of highlighting increases the odds of students actually reading the text (Yue, Storm, Kornell, & Bjork, 2014, p. 2).

Another tip we give students is to look for information that answers the questions often addressed in informational text: "Who?" "What?" "When?" "Where?" "Why?" and "How?" We make clear that not *all* the answers will be there *all* the time, but being aware of these questions can help clarify the main idea when reading a text.

See Figure 2.2: Annotation Examples A for an example of what annotations for predicting, connecting, and identifying key ideas might look like on a text.

SUMMARIZING

Summarization can be a powerful strategy to increase student comprehension (Guthrie et al., 2004, p. 405). In addition, it can function as a useful formative assessment tool (see Chapter 20: Assessment for more information). We teach students how to summarize by asking them to reread what they highlighted and then use that information to form their own sentence illustrating the main idea.

Many students struggle with summarizing, especially in social studies classes when they are reading complex primary sources. We first help students by modeling the strategy. For example, in our US history class, we read aloud this phrase from The Declaration of Independence, and then talk through our thought process as we develop a summary:

He has endeavoured to prevent the population of these States; for that purpose obstructing the Laws for Naturalization of Foreigners . . .

We might say,

The declaration is a list of complaints, so what does the writer seem to be complaining about here? I highlighted the words prevent *and* obstructing *and I know they mean stopping something from happening. What is being stopped from happening?*

Students may chime in and say that "population of these states" or "naturalization" is what is being prevented. We then highlight those words and explain that naturalization is the process of becoming a citizen, so the author seems to be complaining that the King is blocking more people from becoming part of the colonies by not allowing them to be citizens. Then, we can pull the summary together by saying:

Basically, what the writer is saying here is that the American colonists want to increase the number of people in the colonies and the King isn't letting them.

We then model writing this main idea in the margin for students to see.

For more practice, we have students complete Figure 2.3: Summarizing Examples and then review it as a class.

Even with modeling and using the figure, there may be students who struggle when they are trying to summarize a text and say, "I just don't know what it's talking about." One way to help with this challenge is to ask them to orally explain their ideas: "If your classmate was absent and asked you what the reading was about, what would you say?" This kind of prompting can be helpful prior to writing a summary. When students are summarizing a complex text, or perhaps a longer text, make sure to stop multiple times and have them summarize each section. In this way, after completing the text, they can review their "smaller" ideas to write a larger overall summary.

QUESTIONING

Questioning is an especially inclusive strategy because students from all backgrounds and at all proficiency levels can often generate them fairly easily (especially with a list of "question-starters" posted on the classroom wall). There are suggestions for where to find question starters in the Technology Connections section of this chapter. This strategy invites students to be active participants in their learning process which, in turn, can increase engagement and motivation for reading

(Corley & Rauscher, 2013, p. 3). We start by breaking questions down into two different types, "right-there questions" and "think-about questions." The answer to a "right-there question" can be found directly in the text, something you could point to and say, "it's right there." The answer to a "think-about question" may not be obvious or included in the text – rather, it is something you have to "think about."

The right-there questions help us to see that students can comprehend the text, whereas the think-about ones help to extend the learning beyond the section of text currently in front of them. To help students develop an understanding of the two types, we have them create practice questions related to the content topic.

For example, in geography, if students are reading a set of statistics about Brazil, we can model asking both types of questions. We may say,

> *I just read the statistics about the literacy rate of Brazil. If I wanted to ask a right-there question I could ask, "What is the literacy rate in Brazil?" After reading what the literacy rate is, I'm also wondering, "What might be the impact of this literacy rate on economic development?" That would be an example of a think-about question for this part of the text.*

These questions help students develop a more complete picture of the topic and provide them with tools to more critically analyze future texts.

VISUALIZING

In this strategy, students draw or sketch the images that come to mind while reading. We see visualizing as a version of summarizing – just in a different format. Practicing visualizing can help set the foundation for other visually focused tasks in social studies like creating infographics or analyzing political cartoons (see Chapter 12: Image Analysis). In addition, researchers suggest that the act of consciously creating images of words helps readers understand and remember the text (National Reading Panel, 2000, pp. 4–42). Many of your students might already be doodlers (you know this from the sketches covering their papers when they turn them in). Utilizing this strategy can be another opportunity to build on student assets instead of looking at them through the lens of deficits.

To teach this strategy we first have students read a portion of a text and visualize it ("What does it make you see in your mind?"). We ask them to do a quick sketch of what they imagined on the page next to the passage. A key point is to emphasize *quick* sketch. This should take no longer than any other reading strategy.

For example, after reading the First Amendment in our government class, we model visualizing by pointing out that the amendment protects five basic freedoms. We can model the five freedoms by doing a quick sketch of symbols representing each one. For example, religion may be represented by one of the commonly seen religious symbols like a crucifix, Star of David, or Star and Crescent. Freedom of speech could be a stick figure with a speech bubble above its head, and freedom of the press is shown as a quick sketch of a newspaper. Freedom of assembly and petition could be shown together as a group of stick figures standing (assembly) holding picket signs (petition).

Some students may be initially resistant to sketching due to their lack of confidence with their art skills. We model our own drawing so that students can see it's not about the skill. Instead, it's about creating a visual summary of the text. Occasionally we will have a student who just refuses to draw images. In that case, we ask them to use the sentence starter "When I read this, I see . . ." and describe what they imagine while reading the text. In this way, the student is still developing their visualization skills.

See Figure 2.4: Annotation Examples B for an example of what annotations for summarizing, questioning, and visualizing might look like on a text.

CLARIFYING

When students clarify, we explicitly ask them to revisit their annotations by evaluating, modifying, and responding based on their developing understanding of the text. If a student made a prediction at the beginning of the text and discovers that prediction was incorrect, they can make a correction by adding new information and noting where they found it.

We model this strategy for students by showing them how we make corrections in our own reading. For example, in our study of World War II, we make a prediction about the relationship between Germany and the Soviets prior to reading about the the Molotov-Ribbentrop Pact. This was a nonaggression pact signed between Nazi Germany and the Soviet Union in 1939. We might say,

> *Based on prior knowledge, I know that Russia, which became the Soviet Union, was on the side of the Allies during World War I. Therefore, I predict that Germany and the Soviet Union are enemies during World War II.*

When we read through the text, students are surprised to find a nonaggression agreement between Germany and the Soviet Union. At the end of the text, we practice clarifying by going back to the original prediction.

> *After reading, I see that my prediction was not correct. In fact, I'm really surprised about the nonaggression agreement between the Soviet Union and Germany. I'm going to clarify by adding this information.*

We then add this new information to our previous prediction.

We use this as an opportunity to share about the learning gained from making corrections. We remind students that many famous athletes have missed numerous game-winning shots. These very same athletes find that growth and learning can come from making corrections. We want our students to take the shot and not walk off the court if they miss. The belief that mistakes are not obstacles and that you can use them to improve knowledge and skills, or "growth mindset," is what we want students to develop. Adopting this mindset can help improve achievement and motivation ("Dr. Dweck's Research," n.d.). This "clarify" strategy reinforces a growth mindset as students revisit and learn from potential errors in their thinking.

Summation is another good opportunity to practice clarifying. Students can reread and modify their summary as they pull more information from the text. As we said earlier, if students are summarizing smaller portions of the text as they go, they can revisit those to create larger main ideas. Students are clarifying when they revisit their ideas to determine which details should remain in the overall summary.

DIFFERENTIATION

Reading strategies can be inclusive for English language learners (ELLs). Students are able to apply and practice the strategies at their own levels of understanding. Teachers can allow students to write annotations in their home language first to capture their initial thinking processes and then translate them into English. Sentence frames and sentence starters (Figure 2.1: Reading Strategies Sentence Starters) can be particularly helpful to these students.

Another idea is for teachers to copy and paste a complex text on a website like Rewordify (http://rewordify.com/index.php), which can simplify the language so that the student can read it before exploring the original text in class.

Also, before asking students to share their strategy with the entire class, make sure you let ELL students know ahead of time when you are going to be calling on them. It might be helpful to practice their answer out loud with you or their partner before sharing with the whole class.

Depending on the challenges facing students who learn differently, they, too, can pre-read the complex text at a more simple level prior to tackling the original. Teachers can also make the simplified text their primary one. Letting students who learn differently know in advance you will be calling on them to contribute their thoughts to the entire class is an important modification for them, as well.

ADVANCED EXTENSIONS

Students can do independent research to learn more about the author of a text or find answers to questions raised during the reading. Of course, the highest level of practice with reading strategies is to let students practice independently, especially with more complex texts. Students can choose which strategies are best to apply to the text as they read without direction from the teacher. This independent ability to seamlessly apply different strategies to derive the deepest meaning from the text is our ultimate goal.

Once students are confident in their ability to practice the reading strategies fluidly, a fun twist may be to assign students historical figures as a lens through which to read and annotate a text. For example, ask them to read the Declaration of Independence as if they were King George III. Students can then comment as they think the King would while reading a list of complaints from his subjects. For example, when the colonists complained about taxes, the King may have responded by claiming that those taxes were needed to pay for the soldiers that protected the colonists from threats in the New World. Students can write this response as an annotation in the margin.

Student Handouts and Examples

Table 2.1: Reading Strategies Handout
Figure 2.1: Reading Strategies Sentence Starters
Figure 2.2: Annotation Examples A
Figure 2.3: Summarizing Examples
Figure 2.4: Annotation Examples B

What Could Go Wrong?

In our earliest days of teaching reading strategies, our biggest pitfall was to rely on an overly formulaic sequence of instruction. We now avoid a one-size-fits-all process. We want students to develop fluidity with the use of these strategies – moving between them seamlessly and being able to identify when it is best to use each one. For this reason, we wrote this section as a list of options rather than a step-by-step process. Students develop at different paces, and certain strategies may help some students more than others. Repeated practice using multiple strategies is an effective way to support the reading growth of all students.

Some students might refuse to employ the strategies while reading. They may have many reasons for their refusal, including "it's boring" and "this doesn't matter." This resistance is a good opportunity to bring up the relevance of this practice to their daily lives. We use several lessons to help students see the importance of improving literacy. One involves showing students the science behind how reading impacts the brain in positive ways. (See Technology Connections for more on lesson ideas on this topic.)

Teachers can also ask students themselves to think about and share reasons why *they* think class topics can be applicable to their present lives. For example, if we're reading about immigration, at least some students are likely to talk about its relevance to challenges going on in our world today and why it's worthwhile to delve deeply into its complexities.

To further address the importance of literacy, have students brainstorm jobs they think may not require much reading or writing. Then, point out where they do. Almost all jobs require reading and writing in some fashion, and the ability to do it well often determines one's success in professional life. Another option is to consider all the tasks adults have to deal with that *do* require literacy skills; taxes, job applications, drivers license test, and more. For more on the relevance of history, see our discussion in Chapter 8: Current Event Case Study.

Just having students sit in their seats and doing reading and writing tasks is not a recipe for engagement or learning. It's important to combine use of reading strategies with classroom collaboration and sharing. After students have spent several minutes doing text annotation, have them talk with a partner and then invite them to share particularly insightful thinking with the entire class. Students can work in groupings of two, three, or four; standing or sitting; and move to different sections of the classroom. They can also modify what they originally wrote based on what they learned from their classmates. The key is variety!

Technology Connections

Tools for annotating online text can be found in Larry Ferlazzo's blog post "The Best Applications for Annotating Websites" (http://larryferlazzo.edublogs.org/2008/12/18/best-applications-for-annotating-websites).

The web is full of ideas about reading; it can be overwhelming. A quick image search will show you many posters with different reading protocols or sentence starters to try out, but be careful of adhering too closely to any one in particular. Again, one-size-fits-all doesn't work with reading strategies. A good post about reading strategies can be found at Larry Ferlazzo's blog, "The Best Posts on Reading Strategies and Comprehension – Help Me Find More!" (http://larryferlazzo.edublogs.org/2015/03/19/the-best-posts-on-reading-strategies-comprehension-help-me-find-more). For the questioning strategy, it may help to have a variety of sentence starters posted in the classroom so that students have easy access. For numerous resources and examples of sentence starters, see "The Best Resources for Helping Teachers Use Bloom's Taxonomy in the Classroom" (http://larryferlazzo. edublogs.org/2009/05/25/the-best-resources-for-helping-teachers-use-blooms-tax-onomy-in-the-classroom).

To find resources – including lessons – for teaching students about the connections between their brains and learning, see Larry Ferlazzo's blog post "The Best Resources for Showing Students That They Make Their Brain Stronger By Learning" (http://larryferlazzo.edublogs.org/2011/11/26/the-best-resources-for-showing-students-that-they-make-their-brain-stronger-by-learning).

Attribution

The handouts in this chapter were adapted from sentence starters in Jeffrey D. Wilhelm's book *Improving Comprehension with Think-Aloud Strategies* (2012). Jeffrey Wilhelm is a distinguished professor at Boise State University, where he directs the Boise State Writing Project and is a prolific education and teaching author.

Figures

Pre-Reading
Based on the title of the text I think it's about. . .
Looking at the picture, I believe this may be about. . .
The topic of this text is probably. . .

Prediction
I predict. . .
In the next part/section I think. . . will happen, because. . .
The effect of this will be. . .

Connection
This reminds me of. . .
This is similar to. . .

Key Ideas
After reading the text, highlight or underline Who? What? When? Where? Why? and How?
(Who?) is/are the person(s) involved in this text
(What?) is/are the main event/action(s) of this text
This/These event(s) occurred (Where?/When?/Why?/How?)

Summary
The main idea is. . .
This text/photo/video is about. . .
The author's point is. . .

Question
I wonder. . .
What does the author mean by. . .
What does the word _____ mean?

Visualize
(Draw a quick sketch of what you imagined while reading the text)
When I read this I imagine. . .

Clarify
I really don't understand. . .
After rereading I changed my thinking about. . .
My earlier prediction was/was not correct because. . .

Figure 2.1 Reading Strategies Sentence Starters *Source:* Adapted from Jeffrey Wilhelm's *Improving Comprehension with Think-Aloud Strategies* (2012). Used with permission.

1. There are some common traits and values amongst indigenous peoples around the world. For example, although many people from other ethnicities care about the environment, all indigenous peoples have rituals and stories that remind them of their spiritual responsibility to the earth. This is accompanied by an in-depth understanding of the connections between all living things. Another example is the strong sense of teamwork amongst native peoples. The cooperation of various tribes has helped them survive immense adversity. (Source: https://www.culturalsurvival.org/publications/cultural-survival-quarterly/being-indigenous-21st-century page Unit-1, Chapter-1)

predict

I predict that Native Americans will be a big part of fighting climate change

2. The Sacramento region is considered the home to four Native American tribes: the Nisenan, Sierra Miwok, Northern Valley Yokuts, and the Patwin. Yet, other tribes have ties to the Sacramento region as well, even if their specific origin extends out of the area. The Wintu and the Konkow live to the north. Extending to the west of what is now Sacramento are the Pomo and the Wappo. (source: https://www.amazon.com/Our-Stories-Voices-MARK-GREGORY/dp/1524923478)

connect

This reminds me of a story I read about Miwok building a casino near us

3. There is great diversity amongst all indigenous peoples around the world. They exist in every continent and lead very unique lives. Some indigenous people are hunter gatherers while others are academics. Another trait that is considered to be shared amongst all Indigenous people is that they all have a history of cruel and unfair treatment. Largely thanks to colonization, the identity and dignity of natives has been threatened. (source: http://hrlibrary.umn.edu/edumat/studyguides/indigenous.html)

key ideas

Figure 2.2 Annotation Examples A

Methods of Allocation

1. One way to distribute a product for which there is a shortage is to randomly draw names or numbers. This method of allocation is called a lottery system. For example, in some states there is a high demand to be able to fish for salmon, but the government has a limit on the amount of permits it gives out. Often these areas have a lottery, and if you are lucky enough to get your name picked, you can try your luck at fishing and catching salmon during the season.

Circle the summary:

a. A lottery method allocates goods by randomly selecting numbers assigned to a person.

b. You can pull a number out of a hat.

c. "Limit on the amount of permits it gives out."

2. Another method for allocating a good or service is called "first come, first served." In this method of allocation, whoever gets there first gets the item. For example, when buying concert tickets, whoever gets in line first will get to buy the tickets until they are all sold out. Sometimes people also call this method the queue method because people are literally or figuratively lining up for something.

Circle the summary:

a. Sometimes you have to wait in line.

b. The first come, first served method of distribution gives the item to whoever is first.

c. "Another method for distributing a good or service"

3. Goods and services can be allocated by competition. For example, students may write essays to compete against each other for scholarship money. Whoever writes the best essay gets the money. This method requires judges to decide who "wins."

Circle the summary:

a. "Whoever writes the best essay gets the money."

b. People compete to win the good or service in the competition method.

c. Whoever wants the money the most gets it.

4. A common way goods are allocated in our economy is by price. The price on an item is raised until supply meets demand. This means that whoever can afford the item can purchase it. For example, if you want an airplane you can have one, if you have the money to purchase one.

Circle the summary:

a. The price system gives the items to whoever can afford them.

b. "If you want an airplane, you can have one."

c. You can pay a lot of money.

Figure 2.3 Summarizing Examples *Source:* Modified from Larry Ferlazzo's and Katie Hull Sypnieski's book *The ELL Teacher's Toolbox,* page 171, www.amazon.com/ELL-Teachers-Toolbox-Hundreds-Practical/dp/1119364965.

Summarize

7. Many Northern California locations have names given by the Native Americans who once controlled these lands. One is example is the word "Cosumnes" as in Cosumnes River or Cosumnes Community College. The word "Cosumnes" comes from the Miwok words for "salmon" which is "kosum." Other Northern California place names from Indigenous peoples include Lake Tahoe (Washo) and Natomas coming from the word "Natoma" (Maidu).
http://soda2.sou.edu/awdata/030731c1.pdf

The main idea is that many words come from Native Americans, especially place names

question

8. Not until 1978 did the United States government officially issue regulations to determine the Federal Acknowledgement Process for tribes in the United States. An Indian group may be federally recognized by an act of Congress, the administrative procedures under 25 C.F.R. Part 83, or the decision of a United States court. Federally recognized tribes are able to access some federal funding and services from the Bureau of Indian Affairs. Being federally recognized also allows for self government or tribal sovereignty. *Why did it take the federal gov't*
https://www.bia.gov/frequently-asked-questions *so long to recognize Native Americans?*

Visualize

9. Storytelling is an inherent part of Native American culture. Oral stories passed down from generation to generation were used to teach traditions and culture instead of written languages. These telling of these stories was/is often combined with dance and music creating an entire experience for those present.
https://prairieedge.com/tribe-scribe/native-american-tradition-storytelling/

Figure 2.4   Annotation Examples B

CHAPTER 3

Read-Aloud Protocol

What Is It?

The simple strategy of a teacher reading selections of short text out loud helps to engage students and is important for the development of student reading skills (Anderson, Hiebert, Scott, & Wilkinson, 1985, p. 23). Read-alouds can spark student curiosity, deepen understanding of targeted content, and create opportunities for students to respond to complex text orally and in writing.

Why We Like It

We like this strategy for multiple reasons. It allows teachers to model prosodic reading (reading with rhythm and feeling) and can pull the class together to work on one text. The short length of the texts makes them more accessible to students and creates opportunities for them to apply reading strategies (see Chapter 2: Reading Strategies). Teachers can provide accompanying speaking or writing prompts to deepen student thinking and writing skills.

Choosing compelling texts for this protocol can expose our students to complex ideas and sophisticated examples of writing. These types of readings are an excellent supplement to textbooks, which often lack first-person narratives. In addition, read-alouds present opportunities to include perspectives from those who are often underrepresented in traditional texts, including women, people of color, and the LGBTQ+ community.

Supporting Research

According to a US Department of Education report, "The single most important activity for building the knowledge required for eventual success in reading is reading aloud to children." In addition, the report states that "It is a practice that should continue throughout the grades" (Anderson et al., 1985, p. 23).

Research has also proven that teachers in the middle grades who utilize read-aloud protocols were able to use them to help students "make more meaningful connections between learning and their lives" (Albright & Ariail, 2005, p. 582).

Common Core Connections

Read-alouds and their related activities fall under multiple Common Core literacy standards.

Students can be asked to write evidence-based responses to prompts about certain texts. In other words, students need to "Cite specific textual evidence to support analysis of primary and secondary sources" as listed in *The Key Ideas and Details of the Common Core Standards for Social Studies and History* (Common Core, 2010f).

Social Studies Connections

In the Evaluating Sources and Using Evidence section of the College, Career, and Civic Life (C3) Framework from the National Council for the Social Studies, use of varied texts is a priority. It states that responding to a compelling question in social studies "demands that students draw evidence from more than one or two sources" (National Council for the Social Studies, 2010, p. 18). The read-aloud protocol described in this chapter utilizes three diverse sources on the same topic. Students must pull evidence from the texts in order to respond to prompts.

Application

This Application section explains how a teacher can use structured read-alouds and follow-up activities to build literacy in the social studies classroom. Literacy skills are modeled and practiced with a diverse set of reading strategies and other annotations applied to engaging texts (autobiographical excerpts, historical fiction). We typically use three to five separate reading selections about a similar topic. Generally, each of these readings range in length from one to four paragraphs.

The first part of this section gives guidance on how to find and prepare these readings. The second part explains the three elements of the read-aloud protocol we use in class: reading aloud, revisiting text with annotations, and supporting students with writing prompts that foster personal connections, reading comprehension, and improved evidence-based writing skills.

As an example in this chapter, we apply the read-aloud protocol to a series of readings about the French Revolution, but it is adaptable to any social studies topic.

We have used this protocol for overpopulation in India, the "brother versus brother" aspect of the American Civil War, daily life of immigrants during the industrial era, and countless other topics.

Lastly, we offer ideas on how students can create their own read-alouds and become "teachers" to their classmates.

FINDING AND PREPARING AUTHENTIC TEXTS

Before selecting and preparing texts, teachers have to decide on the content learning goal or goals. For example, we use the read-alouds in Figures 3.1–3.3 to build curiosity about the French Revolution.

Once a topic has been decided, the search begins for excerpts from novels or other non-textbook sources. Teachers can be intentional about including the perspectives of traditionally underrepresented groups.

We like to find short passages, usually between one to four paragraphs, from biographies, descriptive magazine articles, historical fiction, travel memoirs, and investigative articles or books. We often create a set of readings that consist of fiction and nonfiction.

It is important for students to be able to distinguish whether a source is fiction or nonfiction. We want students to know the difference between "real" and "realistic" history, especially for citation purposes. For example, when teaching about the effects of Nazism on everyday Germans, we use an excerpt from the World War II novel *The Book Thief* (Zusak, 2005). We make it clear that this text is fiction, but that we have chosen it for the description it provides of Germans during this time period. On the other hand, we often use nonfiction excerpts from articles in *National Geographic* to give students a taste of life from around the world.

A simple web search of your topic can result in an almost limitless list of sources, but you can make the search more specific by adding descriptors like "investigative journalism in _____" or "firsthand accounts of _____." The Library of Congress and many universities also have rich databases of primary sources (see Technology Connections for resources). Citing each source is an important step in modeling research integrity for our students.

One way to access excerpts of books is to search a title or author and look for a preview. These online previews usually consist of a chapter or smaller section of the whole text. Because only an excerpt is required, we often find exactly what we need from the samples, and a full citation is always included. There are also many online sites that have short texts on multiple subjects – with author permission – that can be used for free or very low cost. See the Technology Connections section for resources to learn about copyright issues and for links to free short texts.

Although each set of readings should be about the same topic, we purposely differentiate the styles, perspectives, and content of the texts. For example, Figure 3.1: Bastille Soldier is a first-person account of a French soldier who was shown murdered city officials before being asked of his own loyalty to the revolution. Figure 3.2: Guillotine is a seemingly unsympathetic account of the use of the guillotine by an English observer. Figure 3.3: Reign of Terror is a gruesome account of a crowd celebrating the murders of prisoners. We sometimes include not only primary sources, but also historical fiction or well-written excerpts from news articles.

In addition to the read-aloud text, it can be helpful to show images to help build context. For example, if we did not show an image of a guillotine prior to doing a read-aloud, many students would not have the prior knowledge needed to comprehend these texts. Furthermore, we must use good judgment when selecting read-alouds, because some students may be sensitive to graphic or highly emotional texts.

Once we have created a document with the text, we tend to enlarge the font to size 14–18. This can help make the text more accessible and reader-friendly. We sometimes add extra space between lines for annotations. We also leave the margins around the paper at 1 inch, or even a little wider, for further student notes. In other words, we "engineer the text" to make it more accessible to students (see the Differentiation section in Chapter 5: Writing in Social Studies for more details).

The last step in preparing read-alouds is to add a writing prompt. We typically place the prompt at the bottom of the reading, if there is room. If not, we place it on the back of the page. The purpose of these prompts can be to develop personal connections in order to enhance student engagement, to explore content-related information, and/or to practice making written arguments.

For example, in Figure 3.1: Bastille Soldier, one of the prompts reads "Briefly describe a time when you decided to make a change in your life, but you didn't really want to do it." This can encourage a personal connection to the text. In contrast, the prompt of Figure 3.2: Guillotine focuses on content by asking "According to the context clues, what is a guillotine for? Which quotes lead you to this response?" Other times, we ask students to create an argument, such as in the prompt for Figure 3.3: Reign of Terror: "Why do you think the witnesses of the violent scene considered the 'shouts of Vive la Nation! (long live our country!) a thousand times more horrifying . . . than the awful silence that preceded them?" We might also ask students to write an evidence-based response like the second prompt in Figure 3.1: "Quoting a minimum of two descriptive phrases, please describe the general mood of the French people."

Prompts should not *only* check for comprehension. Instead, aim for prompts that allow students to voice their opinions and encourage them to support their ideas with evidence from the text.

READ-ALOUD PROTOCOL

In this section we break down the three phases of our read-aloud protocol: reading aloud, revisiting text with annotations, and responding to prompts. In addition, we discuss how to facilitate the sharing of student responses. The described protocol tends to take about one hour for three readings or could be done one a day for three consecutive days.

Reading Aloud

We announce to students that we will be reading and writing about three short texts on the French Revolution. We explain that we will be cycling through the readings as a class and that students will have a job at all times.

We project the first reading on a screen and purposely withhold student copies of the passage at this time. In order to keep the whole class together and focused, we ask students to follow along on the screen while we read aloud and circulate around the room.

Here are some pointers for a successful read-aloud:

- Rehearse ahead of time.
- Slower is better than faster, calm is more powerful than frantic.
- Don't worry about overemphasizing text, just be natural.
- A simple pause can add tremendous effect, if needed. For example, in Figure 3.1: Bastille Soldier, a pause would be effective after the line "Already two of my soldiers had been assassinated behind me by the furious people..."
- *Do not* interrupt with clarification, lengthy definitions, or lecturing as it distracts students. Instead, address one or two terms that might lead to confusion in advance. Or, offer a quick synonym while reading aloud.

Of course, as with any effective instructional strategy, there are exceptions to some of these "rules." For example, we might have a bad computer projector, a window that shines right on the screen, or have no screen at all. In those instances, we would probably distribute the read-aloud text to everyone prior to a first reading. If we have ELLs in our class, we might quickly define three or four words instead of one or two.

Do we always have time to rehearse? Of course not! We try our best and plan to do better during the next class. Do our students *always* look at the screen when we are reading? No! Keeping it short, making sure our voice sounds prosodic, and carefully screening texts to make sure they're engaging increases the odds of everybody following along. We also need to make sure to balance maintaining continuity when reading with realistic classroom-management expectations.

Revisiting Text with Annotations

Once we are done reading the first text aloud, and prior to distributing it to students, we show annotation instructions on the board or screen. For example, "Reread the text and highlight or underline any two lines that stand out to you and note why they did." We review and clarify the tasks for students before passing out the reading. This way, students already have a task to begin as soon as they get their copy of the text. We also tell students that they can look at the writing prompt on the sheet now, but they won't be answering it until later. Depending on the needs of the class, it may be beneficial to first provide a model of this type of reading strategy prompt. For example, we might project Figure 3.1: Bastille Soldier and highlight the line "I was passed before the body of M. de Lorme [guardian of City Hall] who was on the ground in a bath of his own blood . . ." We explain that this stood out to us because of the striking visual elicited by the phrase "in a bath of his own blood."

Next, we pass out student copies of the reading.

We announce to students that they have three minutes to complete the task: "Reread the text and highlight or underline any two lines that stand out to you." A teacher could use a timer or follow the clock carefully to make sure three does not become seven. Timing is important because it creates a sense of urgency and encourages motivation. The teacher also circulates around the room to support students while they are working.

When the three minutes are up, we announce that students will be sharing their annotations with a partner. During this series of read-alouds, we "mix-up" these methods of sharing. One time, students might share to several students in a "speed-dating" style. Another time, we might have alternates move so they could share with several students who are next to them. Asking students to get up and pair-share with someone new has multiple benefits – our fidgeters get a chance to move, students work with students they may not know as well, and it can refresh the energy in the room. If time is short, we have them only share with a neighbor or two.

After they are done sharing with their partner, we call on one or two students to tell the entire class what they highlighted. Some students will see that their peers may have selected the same thing. Others may get new ideas from students who selected different phrases.

When you come back to this phase of the protocol for the other texts, provide a different task for each passage. For example, have students write questions, make predictions, or write a summary of a specific paragraph. We make it a priority to fight stagnation by choosing from a variety of annotations. Figure 3.4: Annotation and Reading Strategy Prompts has a list of additional ideas. Chapter 2: Reading Strategies describes additional ways to process text.

Answering Writing Prompts

Once students have reread, annotated, and "pair-shared," we have them answer one or two prompts. To get students started on the writing prompt, we project it and read it aloud. Here are some ways to help students be successful in writing their responses:

- Break down synonyms to clarify what the prompt is asking of students. For example, while projecting the second prompt from Figure 3.1: Bastille Soldier, we say the following:

   This prompt says, "Quoting a minimum of two descriptive phrases, please describe the general mood of the French people." Let's first underline the words "two descriptive phrases" because that is what we have to look for. Another way to say "descriptive phrases" is writing that gives a good visual. So right above "descriptive phrases" I am going to write "gives a good visual." Now I can look for text that gives a good visual or illustrates the "mood" or feelings of the French people.

- Give sentence starters to answer the question. For example, to respond to the prompt in Figure 3.3: Reign of Terror we would share the following think-aloud:

   *The prompt says, "Why do you think the witnesses of the violent scene considered the shouts of 'Vive la Nation!' (long live our country!) a thousand times more horrifying than the awful silence that preceded them?" I am going to re-use words from the prompt to help me get started. Let's write (make sure students can see and add emphasis to the words you are borrowing from the prompt), "I **think** the **witnesses of the violent scene** thought **the shouts** of the people were worse than the violence they were seeing because . . ."*

- Help students find evidence in the text that connects to the question, but leave it up to the students to utilize the evidence in their written response. We do this by saying:

   The prompt from Figure 3.2: Guillotine says, "According to the context clues, what is a guillotine for? Which quotes lead you to this response?" Let's take our pen and underline phrases that might help us answer the question. The first line says, "The process of execution," which this reading seems to be focusing on, so I am going to underline that. In the second paragraph, I am going to underline "the menacing instrument of death," "the polished axe," "the neck was secure and closed in," and "weighty knife was then dropped with a heavy fall." Now that we have underlined some quotes, please use them to figure out what a guillotine is and respond to the prompt.

- Create a model answer "frame" for students who seem to be struggling. For the prompt, "Briefly describe a time when you decided to make a change in your life, but you didn't really want to do it." from Figure 3.1: Bastille Soldier, we provide the following frame:

A time that I had to make a change in my life was

_____.

I did not want to make this change because _____

_____.

For more information on supporting evidence-based writing, please refer to Chapter 5: Writing in Social Studies.

After we scaffold the prompt, we give about three to five minutes for students to respond while we circulate and give support. When students are done, we instruct them to share responses with a partner. After they share, we call on one or two students to read their answers to the class.

Now that students have completed all three phases of the protocol, it is time to start again with the next text. A sense of rhythm is developed as students continue to practice the protocol with the next two readings. The repetition of this cycle with multiple texts on the same topic helps to build a deeper understanding of the content.

As we all know, unexpected events occur in classrooms. Some might be less than good (an altercation between students), others might be unexpected learning opportunities (particularly thoughtful questions connecting the content to a current event). When these occur and take up time, it might not be possible to complete all three read-alouds in one day. If that's the case – no worries. Just do the next one the following day. Or, just stop at two of them. We find that three read-alouds work very well, but there is nothing magical about the number three.

STUDENT-CREATED READ-ALOUDS

After the class has been exposed to the read-aloud protocol, we like to have students create their own read-alouds and teach them to their classmates. Creating and teaching their own read-alouds can help students practice autonomy over their learning, which can lead to higher engagement, less boredom, and the development of a stronger sense of self-efficacy (Wang et al., 2017).

We begin our student-created read-alouds activity by reviewing the criteria of a good read-aloud. Next, students choose a related topic and prepare and teach their own read-aloud to a classmate. A good time for this activity would be after concluding a series of read-alouds, because the protocol is fresh in their minds. After completing the protocol with the French Revolution series, we direct students to review the three readings on their desk. Then, we ask the following question: "What are the common attributes, or features, of the texts?"

Students title a blank piece of paper "Attributes of a Good Read-Aloud." We then project our version of this paper on the screen and say:

> *One thing I notice all these readings have in common is that they are short in length – just a couple paragraphs – and never more than a page. So, on my paper titled "Attributes of a Good Read-Aloud," I am going to write, "short in length, just a few paragraphs."*

Students copy this first attribute onto their papers. We provide one more example in the same manner, this time focusing on style of writing instead of just format. For example, we share with students that the readings about the French Revolution were very descriptive and make us feel like we can "see" what is happening.

We then assign students a partner and direct them to continue the list. After they finish their list of attributes, we have them share in small groups to compare.

Once all groups have had a chance to share, we call on students to contribute to a class list of attributes. We project this paper for all to see. Students are challenged to *only* share ideas not previously mentioned to prevent repetition and encourage active listening. They are also asked to copy down any attributes they don't have listed. After listing about five to six attributes, we then use our "cheat sheet," Figure 3.5: Attributes of a Good Read-Aloud. We add any other key attributes that students may have missed. Students copy these last few examples onto their paper.

We share with the class that now *they* will be creating and teaching a read-aloud to another student. Their read-aloud must incorporate all the criteria on their "Attributes of a Good Read-Aloud" paper.

Next, it is time to help students choose their topic and start their search for texts. To prevent students from getting off track in their research, it may be helpful for the teacher to choose one (or more) of the following questions. This will help students not become overwhelmed when searching for their read-aloud:

- What topics do you want to learn more about within the current unit of study?
- After considering our current series of read-alouds, what would you add? What is a perspective that has not been represented?
- What is a vocabulary word from the current unit that could serve as a topic?

We might select the first option: students identify a topic that they are wondering about. We ask, "What is something about the French Revolution that you would want to know more about, but has not been covered in the readings?" After students have had an opportunity to discuss their responses with a partner, we call on them to share with the class. Many express curiosity about the causes of all the bloodshed and gore in the readings. They wonder, "Why were the French people so angry?"

Once students have shared, a teacher can choose one of the following two options: Pick one or a few topics for the whole class OR let each student pick his or her own. The first choice can be easier to manage since the whole class can use the same resources. The second option, on the other hand, provides students with even more autonomy over their learning.

Regardless of whether the class is using the same topic or their individual choices, it is helpful to guide students' search for text. Using a digital platform like Google Classroom, we "post" sources that we think could be helpful. Newsela (https://newsela.com) has sets of texts about specific social studies topics. The Library of Congress (www.loc.gov) has a search function that helps students narrow primary sources to fit their specific topics. Other resources can be found in the Technology Connections section of this chapter and in Chapter 13: Analysis of Primary Sources.

Before students start searching for a source, it is helpful to have them review their "Attributes of a Good Read-Aloud" list. We also remind students that they will be teaching this read-aloud to a classmate, so it is important to be thoughtful in their text selection.

Once they find a suitable excerpt, students "copy and paste" their texts onto a word-processing document. Then, they create their read-aloud according to the format criteria. This includes citing the source at the bottom of the paper. We direct students to review how we cite the sources for Figures 3.1–3.3 and have them do the same for their read-aloud.

After students have selected their text, it is time to direct their attention to creating a prompt. We discuss the difference between two kinds of questions: "right-there" and "think-about" questions. We explain that a right-there question can be found directly in the text and can be pointed out in the passage. A think-about question may not be obvious in the reading, requiring more thought. Both types of questions can be helpful. Right-there questions are good to check comprehension. For example, a right-there question for Figure 3.1: Bastille Soldier would be, "How was the soldier, who is describing his experience, treated?" On the other hand, think-about questions push students to think beyond the text in front of them. Prompts like "Briefly describe a time when you decided to make a change in your life out of necessity" in Figure 3.1: Bastille Soldier make students extend their thinking by asking them to make a personal connection. Due to the nature of the assignment, we push students to develop think-about questions that will be engaging for their classmates to answer and interesting for our "student teachers" to read.

We explain how some of the prompts in the French Revolution readings are open-ended think-about questions. We encourage students to stylistically imitate the prompts in Figures 3.1–3.3 when creating their own. For example, students could use the phrase "According to the context clues" from the prompt in Figure 3.2: Guillotine, to start their own prompt. Once students have completed creating their prompt, we have them print two copies of their read-aloud and the writing prompt.

We spend a few minutes teaching students about prosodic reading to prepare them for the first part of the protocol, reading the text aloud. We explain that reading with prosody, or expression and phrasing while reading aloud, can make a big difference. To make our point, we read a section of a French Revolution reading in our most monotone, expressionless voice. "Why is it so awful?" we ask. They share things like "it makes it boring" or "it makes me want to stop paying attention." We give them a few pointers to help them improve their reading, such as:

- Rehearse ahead of time.
- Slower is better than faster; calm is usually more powerful than frantic.
- Don't be *too* dramatic with the text. Just be natural.
- A simple pause can add tremendous effect, if needed.
- *Do not* interrupt with clarification, definitions, or explanations. It is distracting.

We give students a few minutes to practice reading their text aloud to themselves. We circulate to offer assistance with pronunciation and any other concerns.

Then, we ask students to choose an annotation strategy (highlight two phrases you like, write a one- or two-word summary, draw an image of what the text makes you see in your mind, and so on) that we have used in class for the second phase of the protocol. We review the different choices and list them on the board. Then, we ask students to pick one that they think would be most helpful to their "students."

Everyone is assigned a partner. We keep the three phases of the protocol projected on the screen the entire time for reference. Each student begins teaching their read-aloud by first giving one copy of the text to their partner and keeping the other copy for themselves to read. We instruct students to teach their read-aloud following the three phases of the protocol: reading the text aloud with prosody, directing their partner to complete an annotation strategy, and giving their partner time to respond to the written prompt. Once one student is done facilitating his or her read-aloud, the other begins. For accountability, both students turn in their completed read-alouds, including prompt responses, to the teacher.

This student-created read-aloud activity can take two full class periods and can be repeated throughout the year.

DIFFERENTIATION

A simple way to support ELLs with more difficult texts is to identify and define three to four words that may support the understanding of the text. Providing these definitions to students ahead of time helps minimize roadblocks during the reading. In addition to identifying key terms, creating a context for the reading with either a picture or video clip can help as well – with ELLs and everyone else!

Another modification we sometimes make to support ELLs and students with learning differences is to shorten the text we are preparing as a read-aloud. Teachers can closely read the text and keep the lines or sections that are the essence of the reading. This process can ensure that students are still being exposed to good and relevant writing, but with a less-overwhelming reading task. For example, in Figure 3.2: Guillotine, leaving only the middle paragraph can provide students with enough detail to start to understand the morbid purpose of this device.

ADVANCED EXTENSIONS

Creating an encompassing prompt is a simple way to modify the activity for more advanced students. With this type of prompt, students are asked to reference all three readings to respond to an overarching question. For example, students can be encouraged to use evidence from all three readings (Figures 3.1–3.3) for the following prompt:

> One definition for the word revolution is "activity or movement designed to effect fundamental changes in the socioeconomic situation" (www.merriam-webster.com/dictionary/revolution). How do the readings connect to or illustrate this definition?

Student Handouts and Examples

Figure 3.1: Bastille Soldier

Figure 3.2: Guillotine

Figure 3.3: Reign of Terror

Figure 3.4: Annotation and Reading Strategy Prompts

Figure 3.5: Attributes of a Good Read-Aloud

What Could Go Wrong?

A common pitfall with this strategy is spending too long on one of the phases. For example, we have been guilty of lingering on a favorite reading by overexplaining. In addition, calling on too many students to share their ideas, reactions, or questions can lead to a lull in energy in the room. This can interrupt the ideal sense of rhythm during the protocol. Having a timer is one of the most helpful tools for this strategy.

Another mistake is choosing texts that are too difficult, long, or technical. To maintain the cyclical flow of this activity and to preserve engagement, ensure that texts are limited in length, highly engaging, and accessible.

Technology Connections

As mentioned in the Differentiation section, finding videos online with a simple Google search is a great way to give context to readings. For the readings about the French Revolution in this chapter, the following video from NutshellEdu on YouTube (www.youtube.com/watch?v=VEZqarUnVpo) provides a general summary of the event with visuals.

In addition, Teaching Tolerance (www.tolerance.org/classroom-resources/texts) offers free texts that provide perspectives typically under-represented in social studies. For a very low-cost annual subscription, Ed Helper (www.edhelper.com) also shares many texts that can be used as read-alouds.

For copyright issues see Larry Ferlazzo's blog post *The Best Resources to Learn About Copyright Issues* (http://larryferlazzo.edublogs.org/2009/08/10/the-best-resources-to-learn-about-copyright-issues).

Attribution

We were introduced to the read-aloud protocol by Kelly Young, former educator, curriculum consultant, and creator of Pebble Creek Labs (www.pebblecreeklabs.com).

Daniel Muth, our colleague at Luther Burbank High School in Sacramento California, created the prompt for Figure 3.3: Reign of Terror.

Figures

During the trip, the streets and the houses, even the roofs, were full of crowds who insulted me and cursed me. I was continually subject to swords, bayonets, and pistols pressed against my body. I did not know how I was going to die but I was sure I was at my final moment. Those without arms threw stones at me, and women grimaced their teeth at me and menaced me with their fists. Already two of my soldiers had been assassinated behind me by the furious people. . . .

I arrived finally to general cries that I should be hung and at several hundred paces from the City Hall, when a head on a pike was brought before me to consider and I was told that it was M. de Launay [governor of the Bastille]. Crossing the place de Greve, I was passed before the body of M. de Lorme [guardian of City Hall] who was on the ground in a bath of his own blood. . . .

I was brought inside the City Hall and presented to a committee seated there. I was accused of being one of those who had put up resistance at the Bastille and that I was also the cause of blood being spilled. I justified myself better than I thought possible, saying that I had been under orders. . . . Not seeing any other means of saving myself and . . . what remained of my troops, I declared my willingness to serve the City and the Nation. . . This appeared to them convincing; there was applause and a general cry of "bravo!" which I hoped would grant me a pardon. Instantly, I was brought wine and we had to drink to the health of the City and the Nation.

Prompts:

1. Briefly describe a time when you decided to make a change in your life, but you didn't really want to do it.

2. Quoting a minimum of two descriptive phrases, please describe the general mood of the French people.

Figure 3.1 Bastille Soldier *Source:* "A Defender of the Bastille Explains His Role" (n.d.).

The process of execution was also a sad and heart-rending spectacle. In the middle of the Place de la Révolution was erected a guillotine, in front of a colossal statue of Liberty. . . On one side of the scaffold were drawn out a sufficient number of carts, with large baskets painted red, to receive the heads and bodies of the victims. Those bearing the condemned moved on slowly to the foot of the guillotine; the culprits were led out in turn, and, if necessary, supported by two of the executioner's valets, as they were formerly called. . .

   Most of these unfortunates ascended the scaffold with a determined step—many of them looked up firmly on the menacing instrument of death, beholding for the last time the rays of the glorious sun, beaming on the polished axe; and I have seen some young men actually dance a few steps before they went up to be strapped to the perpendicular plane, which was then tilted to a horizontal plane in a moment, and ran on the grooves until the neck was secured and closed in by a moving board, when the head passed through what was called in derision, *la lunette republicaine* [the republican telescope]; the weighty knife was then dropped with a heavy fall; and, with incredible dexterity and rapidity, two executioners tossed the body into the basket, while another threw the head after it.

Prompt:

According to the context clues, what is a guillotine for? Which quotes lead you to this response?

Figure 3.2 Guillotine *Source:* "The Revolutionary Tribunal's Use of the Guillotine" (n.d.).

The piercing cries of a man whom they were hacking to pieces with a sabre, drew us to the window of the small tower, and we perceived opposite the gate of our prison, the body of a man extended upon the pavement; an instant after another was butchered, and so they went on with others. It is utterly impossible to express the horror of the profound and gloomy silence, which reigned during these executions; interrupted only by the cries of those whom the barbarians were immolating (burning), and by the blows which were inflicted on their heads by swords. At the moment the wretched victim fell, a dreadful murmur would arise, which was immediately drown by shouts of *Vive la Nation! (Long live our country!)* a thousand times more horrifying to us than the awful silence that preceded them.

Prompt:

Why do you think the witnesses of the violent scene considered the "shouts of 'Vive la Nation! (Long live our country!)' a thousand times more horrifying . . . than the awful silence that preceded them?"

Figure 3.3 Reign of Terror *Source:* Pinkerton and Ashworth (1898).

Annotation and Reading Strategy Prompts:

- Reread and highlight or underline any two lines that stand out to you and explain why.
- Reread and write a question and a comment about any part of the reading.
- Reread and choose a line you like and explain why you like it.
- Reread and choose a line you think is the main point, or idea. Then, use your own words to explain the main idea.
- Reread and highlight or underline any unfamiliar words. Pick one and use context clues to guess what it might be about.
- Reread and highlight or underline the most descriptive phrase. Circle the least descriptive phrase. Rewrite the phrase you circled as "least descriptive" to add in more details.
- Reread and highlight or underline the big ideas. How does this piece of text remind you of one of the other topics we have studied so far?

Figure 3.4 Annotation and Reading Strategy Prompts

Attributes of a Good Read-Aloud

1. Short passage, usually between one to four paragraphs from a longer piece of text.
2. The type size is larger, with extra space in between the lines for notes.
3. Unique, compelling writing. . . not boring.
4. Writing is very descriptive and visual. It makes you feel like you can "see" what is happening.
5. Can be fiction or nonfiction, just needs to communicate which one it is. Can also be a primary source.
6. Needs to be about the same topic being covered in class.
7. Needs a citation at the bottom for the source of the text.
8. A prompt at the bottom asks a "think-about" question.

Figure 3.5 Attributes of a Good Read-Aloud

CHAPTER 4

Thematic Data Sets

What Is It?

This chapter will explain how to use thematic data sets to teach about a topic or concept while applying the Inductive Model of learning. This model asks students to analyze pieces of specific information in order to find larger patterns. The "data sets" described in this chapter are collections of this type of short, detailed passage on a specific topic. Our data sets generally include 20 to 30 items and can be organized into five or six categories; however, there aren't any hard and fast rules. A "category" is a way to organize the passages by identifying the characteristics they have in common. The size of each item varies – items can be a one-line quote or a small paragraph of information. Items might fit into three categories or as many as six.

Due to the amount of information contained in a data set, they often serve as an anchor text for thematic units in our social studies classes. To guide students through the data sets, we use a multiphase protocol, which includes considering questions, reading for understanding, classifying, analyzing, and extending knowledge.

Why We Like It

We like the higher-order thinking involved with inductive learning because it reflects real-world skills needed in college and the workplace. Students can learn how to analyze data to build an overall understanding of a topic. This process encourages student-centered learning, moving away from the teacher as "sage on the stage." Students use a multiphase process with the data set to do the "heavy lifting" of analyzing the text for patterns and main ideas. This strategy can deepen student understanding of any concept or topic.

Another benefit of this strategy is that it's very adaptable and a good way to cover a lot of content. Creating data sets on different topics is easy (though it can be time-consuming) once a teacher understands the basics of how to build one. Teachers can create data sets to anchor any unit of study or supplement a textbook (or even convert the content in a textbook – see Chapter 21: Getting the Most from Your Textbook). Students can also create their own data sets and teach them to their classmates.

Supporting Research

Research on cognition has shown that using the inductive model of learning, like the one described in this chapter, helps students to develop their thinking. Using this model can encourage students to tap into prior knowledge, foster motivation, support the transfer of knowledge to real-world situations, and develop metacognition (Prince & Felder, 2006, p. 125).

The use of thematic data sets can also help students extend their learning on a particular topic. Applying our multiphase protocol helps to encourage student-generated questions that can lead to critical thinking and engaging class discussions (Bersh, 2013, p. 49).

Common Core Connections

While the standards leave the instructional decisions to the teacher, they have very clear goals about strengthening students' literacy skills (Common Core, 2010g). The multiphase process we use with thematic data sets builds these skills. Studying information using a data set and the inductive learning model can help students identify key ideas and details. It also encourages the integration of knowledge and ideas laid out by the Common Core (Common Core, 2010h).

Additionally, reading in this structured way can help students identify patterns that they can apply when learning complex concepts. This focus on recognizing patterns is brought up in a variety of ways in the Common Core including patterns of events, words, and sentences (Common Core, 2010i, 2010j, 2010k).

Social Studies Connections

The College, Career, and Civic Life (C3) Framework from the National Council for the Social Studies (2010) states, "Inquiry is at the heart of social studies." The process we use with thematic data sets *is* a process of inquiry. The framework recognizes the need to motivate students in social studies and advises that inquiry can spark curiosity and deepens understanding of the content while students engage with complex concepts. Teachers can create thematic data sets that relate to each of the 10 Themes of the NCSS standards.

Application

In our classrooms, a thematic data set is often the anchor text of a unit. Our students can develop their critical thinking skills as they do multiple reads of a data set, revisiting the information again and again in a variety of ways.

The *inductive* model involves students studying examples to develop generalizations about key concepts to organize them into categories – going from the specific to the general. In an inductive lesson, students could be given a series of vignettes about various aspects of an American Civil War soldier's life and then be asked to place them into categories such as weapons, hardships, and battle tactics. Subsequent activities can include summaries of the categories, adding additional information, and/or extended writing activities.

On the other hand, *deductive* learning involves first providing students with the concepts/rules and a few examples that fit into those guidelines. Then students would search for more reinforcing information/examples. In other words, deductive teaching is going from the general to the specific. It might mean first giving students an overview of what life was like for a soldier during the American Civil War and then having students look through documents from that time period for examples.

The inductive process, the focus of this chapter, mirrors what historians do. For example, to understand a battle during the American Civil War, a historian may collect primary source documents like letters, pictures, or military reports and then analyze them. From this analysis, the historian draws conclusions about the battle. Using the inductive model here allows the historian to develop key ideas about the battle based on evidence. While we can't expect our students to work at the same level as a college professor just yet, thematic data sets let us introduce the inductive-learning process to our students with a high level of support. Applying the inductive model to teaching was pioneered by educator Hilda Taba (1967) and then later by Bruce Joyce (Joyce, Weil, & Calhoun, 2017).

What follows is a description of the process we use to create our own data sets, as well as a breakdown of our multiphase teaching protocol: considering questions, reading for understanding, classifying, analyzing, and extending knowledge.

BUILDING A DATA SET

Before building a data set, it's important to understand that it isn't something you can throw together five minutes before class begins. Once you get the "hang" of creating data sets, however, you will be able to develop multiple types on any topic relatively quickly. They can be used to supplement any existing curriculum or textbooks. In fact, we often take information from chapters in our textbooks and create more accessible data sets (see Chapter 21: Getting the Most from Your Textbook).

The data sets we use in our classrooms range anywhere from 10 to 30 items depending on the topic and level of students. For less-experienced students, we may have shorter passages and fewer items. More advanced learners may do well with longer passages and/or as many as 30 items. We typically get through two pages of a data set in a one-hour class period with careful reading and annotating.

We always number our items so that we can clearly reference them in class. For example, if we ask students to read item number five, we don't want any confusion about which passage they are expected to read.

There are a variety of data sets we have used in our classrooms. The one we use most often is a "standard data set" (Figure 4.1: Indigeneity Data Set). Here, we use paraphrases from multiple nonfiction sources to give information about a topic. Another version of a data set is a "headlines data set" in which each example is the headline and lead of a news article (Figure 4.2: France Headlines Data Set). A third type is a "quotes data set" (Figure 4.3: Types of Government Data Set). These texts include quotes from different people on a given topic.

There are two different methods we use to create a data set. These methods are best explained as *deductively* building a data set and *inductively* building a data set. To build a data set deductively, first choose a topic and then come up with the five or six categories prior to finding examples. Next, do research to find pieces of text that can fit into each of the predetermined categories. For example, we might be studying Frederick Douglass and look specifically for items that would fit into the categories: life as an enslaved person, life as an abolitionist, personal life, and life after the civil war.

To build a data set inductively, you would begin by collecting research on a topic and then analyzing the information to see what categories arise. This process is closer to what historians practice – reviewing the work of previous historians, digging into primary-source documents, and determining their own interpretations backed by evidence ("Historians Defined," n.d.). Though both methods of building data sets work well, an inductive method mimics the experience our students have when working through the text in class. This exposure can help build empathy and understanding of the process we are asking our students to go through.

Practically speaking, most of our data sets are created through a combination of both processes. We might start with categories in mind and add to, or subtract from, them as we search through texts for examples.

For historical primary sources, the Library of Congress is an excellent resource (www.loc.gov). When making a headlines data set, visit a variety of newspaper web pages and use the search feature to locate stories on the selected topic or category. *National Geographic* articles are also often useful.

TEACHING PROTOCOL FOR USING DATA SETS

Phase One – Considering Questions

Thought-provoking questions are essential to the success of inductive learning because they can engage and motivate students.

Our units often begin with an essential or "big" question (or two) that students will be expected to answer when the unit is completed. See Chapter 11: Questions for Learning for more on essential questions. For example, in our Foundations of Government unit, we ask students, "Is the system of government in the United States the best? How does our system of government compare with others around the world?" As students review different data sets while progressing through the unit, they take notes that will help them answer these questions.

Phase Two – Reading for Understanding

In phase two of the data set protocol, students employ reading strategies (see Chapter 2: Reading Strategies) to help them interact with the text for a deeper understanding. In our classes, we rarely pass out the entire data set at once. Instead, we give students one page at a time to better control the pace of this phase. Students are then less likely to feel overwhelmed or to complain about the length of the data set.

Start by modeling the process for your students, especially if they are new to the thematic data-set protocol. Eventually, we want students to move through the data set, practicing and applying reading strategies as they see fit. However, it can be helpful to give more structure during the first few times students work through one. For example, we might direct students to write down the specific tasks that they are to complete while working through the page. These tasks could be:

1. Read passage
2. Highlight key ideas
3. Make a comment or a prediction

These assignments can be modified or reduced depending on students' experiences (please note the discussion about highlighting in Chapter 2: Reading Strategies). It may be wise to only give students two tasks per page during their first data set, or even just one. Other activities could include writing a summary, drawing a sketch, or making a connection between what they are reading and prior knowledge. We find that assigning different tasks to different pages increases student engagement. The key focus to keep in mind is that the tasks push students to examine the text more deeply.

After students copy down the instructions for the page, we model the assigned annotations with the first two or three passages. When students are new to data sets and reading strategies, we often explicitly tell them which reading strategy we want them to practice, like question or prediction. We do this to help students build their skills with a variety of reading strategies so that they don't rely on only one or two. When students become more skilled at working through thematic data sets, we reduce the specific tasks and simply tell them to "read like a scholar," which means they independently practice reading strategies of their choice (see Chapter 2: Reading Strategies).

Teachers may want to consider having students read the passages to each other for this phase of the data set. The act of reading the items aloud to one another has been shown to increase memory (Forrin, 2018, p. 4), which may help students with the classifying and analyzing phases of the data set. Additionally, reading aloud helps with word familiarity so that when these words appear in the future, they are more recognizable to students (Forrin, 2018, p. 4). This activity can also increase accountability by ensuring that everyone is actually doing the reading.

Giving students a set amount of time to work through a page can help increase the level of concern for students. This encourages them to dive into the text right away. We often err on the side of "less is more" with giving time for reading, finding that too much time can lead to some students finishing early and disrupting others who are still reading the page. Therefore, it may be a good idea to set a reasonable amount of time to complete the task and then move on without necessarily waiting for *all* students to have completed each page at the same time.

To ensure that each student gets to interact with all passages even if they haven't finished reading, we have students share their annotations with a partner. Sharing also provides accountability and an opportunity to practice good communication skills. While this sharing is going on, we circulate around the room to identify students to share their work with the entire class.

At the bottom of each page, we often have students write a final thought. A final thought could be what stood out most to them, what was surprising, or attempting to respond to a previously asked essential question.

All the tasks that are a part of phase two (reading, highlighting key ideas, commenting, sharing with partners, sharing with the class, end of page final thoughts, and so forth) give students multiple interactions with the text. By interacting in a variety of ways with each page of the text, students are more prepared for the next phase of the data-set process – classifying.

Phase Three – Classifying

In phase three of the thematic data set protocol, students revisit the passages and classify them into categories. They do this by identifying common characteristics shared by examples and grouping them together. Data-set categories may be consistent throughout a social studies course or they can change for each data set.

In geography, we typically have the same core categories for each of our data sets on different focus countries. Those categories include land and climate, people/population, economics, politics, culture, and challenges. When a topic becomes large enough that it needs its own category, like the Amazon in the Brazil unit or the Tour de France in the France unit, we just add it.

Categories might also be unique for different data sets. For example, in our US Government class, the Types of Government Data Set (Figure 4.3: Types of Government Data Set) categories are rule by one, rule by few, and rule by many. Or, in World History, a data set on religions can be categorized by the different religions themselves or by the different parts of religions like beliefs, practices, holidays, and texts. Sometimes, we ask students to create their own categories to push higher levels of thinking.

When teaching students how to categorize, we tell them to first reread the key ideas of the item. They can use their highlighting and annotations to help them determine the appropriate category for that passage. We also may ask students to circle the key evidence in the passage that would justify it being placed in that category.

After deciding the appropriate category for an item, we ask students to write each item number on a graphic organizer like Table 4.1: Category Graphic Organizer.

Table 4.1 Category Graphic Organizer

Category	Item Numbers	Main Ideas
Rule by One		
Rule by Few		
Rule by Many		

For example, if items 7, 4, 1, 8, and 9 of the Types of Government Data Set fit best in the rule-by-one category, we write the numbers in the box that says Item Numbers. We also tell them not to write anything in the column labeled Main Ideas because that will be a later step. When teaching categorizing, we avoid using the terms *correct* or *right*. Instead, we explain to students that as long as they can reasonably justify their placement, any category can be "correct." Our focus is on helping students understand the critical role that evidence plays in supporting their positions. We sometimes ask students to "show us their thinking" by highlighting the clue words they used to determine the category for a passage. They can also demonstrate their reasoning by writing a simple explanation of why an item fits into a certain category.

We also make sure to show students that sometimes an item could work in more than one category. If this happens while they are categorizing, we ask that students choose one category, but put a mark (circle/asterisk) next to the item number. The mark can be used later to adjust categories that become too large (or too small). We generally have five or six categories and limit each category to between three to six items. If students have over six items in a single category, we ask them to reread and consider which items might fit somewhere else or if a new category needs to be created. This rereading process prompts students to look for small details that set passages apart from each other and can help develop critical thinking skills.

Categorizing is another opportunity for collaboration. When working together, they often automatically begin justifying their choices to their partner(s). Students are encouraged to consider the thinking process they used when categorizing and finding evidence to support their choices. When students think about *how* they know something, they are practicing metacognition, which has been shown to be beneficial for comprehension (Boulware-Gooden, Carreker, Thornhill, & Joshi, 2007, p. 76). We discuss metacognition in more detail in Chapter 11: Questions for Learning.

The practice of metacognition, as explained by foundational researcher on the subject, J.H. Flavell, is "one's knowledge or beliefs about the factors that effect cognitive activities" (n.d., p. 2). The practice of using metacognitive strategies encourages students to consider the "why" and "how" they know something as well as "how well" they understand information. This has been shown to be connected to how well students perform academically (Dunlosky & Thiede, 1998, p. 54).

Phase Four – Analyzing

In phase four of the data set, students analyze the items they placed in each category to develop generalizations. These generalizations can help students understand the main ideas, themes, or "rules" for each category.

We begin this phase by modeling for students. We select one category as a focus, and talk students through our thought process as we review the passages in that category, pulling together repeated ideas and key concepts into short phrases. These become the main ideas or rules about this category. We have students write these down on Table 4.1: Category Graphic Organizer in the section "Main Ideas." For example, when reviewing the items for the category of rule-by-one in the Types of Government Data Set, students may repeatedly see that the leader of a nation feels they are chosen by a higher power. They may also notice that the leader feels they are "destined" to be in control. Students then note these concepts in the Main Ideas section of their graphic organizer. For an example of a student-completed graphic organizer see Table 4.2: Category Graphic Organizer Example.

We have found that students working through a data set can sometimes struggle with this analyzing phase because it requires them to remember information and big ideas as they flip through multiple pages. To support students with this step, it can be helpful to have them actually cut the passages into separate strips and glue them to a sheet of paper so they can look at one category at a time. Students can display all the categories on one large, poster-size paper and glue the items underneath each category title in columns, or they can use separate sheets of paper for each category (see Figure 4.4: Cut-Up Data Set Examples). Cutting up the data set and looking at one category at a time can help students focus on making generalizations and not get distracted by other information. This kind of organization can also be

Table 4.2 Category Graphic Organizer Example

Category	Item Numbers	Main Ideas
Rule by One	8 7 9 1 4	One leader chosen by a higher power See leader as a man Leader has strength and power and is never wrong
Rule by Few	12 2 6 3 13	A "high class" of people The elite share power between themselves, kept from most people Elite and high class seems to mean wealthy
Rule by Many	10 14 15 11 16 5	All men are equal and should be involved in government The leaders are chosen by the people To be free you need to have choices

helpful in the classifying phase to make categorizing more visual. When moving to the extending phase, it can be beneficial because students will quickly be able to see the information contained in a category and can more easily add new knowledge.

Phase Five – Extending

In the fifth phase of the data set, students extend their recently gained knowledge to add new information to their categories, explain a concept, or argue a position.

Students can research online, use a textbook, or even watch a video to add new information (for example, three new passages or pieces of information) to each of the categories.

Another idea is to have students create additional categories. Students can use their unit materials or outside research to find additional relevant information. Requiring students to use primary sources to create new items is another way to increase the challenge while encouraging the practice of a historian. For example, students could use the Declaration of Independence or the Constitution of the United States to add a category about republics to the Types of Government Data Set.

Students can also use their main ideas from phase four of the thematic data set process to write and/or draw about each of the categories. Students can turn each category into a paragraph, add an introduction and conclusion, and then "magically" have a simple research paper in their hands. Students could create visuals to show their understanding of the characteristics for each category.

In addition, students can answer the unit's essential question and support their responses with evidence. For example, after completing the other phases of the Types of Government Data Set, students would revisit the question, "What are the types of government and which one is best?" and use evidence from the text to respond to the question.

Of course, we might do one, two, three, or none of the actions explained in phase five because of time constraints.

DIFFERENTIATION

Data sets are excellent tools for English language learners (ELLs) because they can be modified in many different ways. The number of items that they can be asked to read could be shortened or the items themselves reduced in length. For example, we sometimes take a passage that is three or four sentences and cut it down to one or two sentences. An online text-simplifying tool like Rewordify (www.rewordify.com) can be used to help with this modification. These strategies increase the accessibility of the content for ELLs while maintaining the challenge of using higher-order thinking skills as they work through the classification, analysis, and extension phases of a data set.

Data sets for ELLs, and all students, could be image-based, with pictures and/or paintings reflecting a theme, historical event or time period, described, sorted, and analyzed.

Another idea is to take snippets from primary sources that are difficult to decipher. For example, instead of having students read the entire Declaration of Independence, select short passages and put them together into a data set.

These same differentiation strategies can be helpful to students who learn differently as they *amplify* and do not *simplify* class work (see Chapter 13: Analysis of Primary Sources for additional details on this idea).

ADVANCED EXTENSIONS

When working with advanced or more experienced students, the easiest way to add a layer of difficulty is to put students completely in charge of the categorization process. In other words, we don't give them any categories. Instead, they are challenged to develop their own. When doing this extension activity, we often circulate to identify good examples of categories and ask students to write them on the board for everyone's use. This process challenges everyone without penalizing those who, for whatever reason, are struggling that day to develop their own categories.

Once students have enough practice with the inductive method, they can be challenged to create their own data sets for content of interest to them. More detailed instructions about student-created data sets can be found on Figure 4.5: Student-Created Data Sets, which was modified from *The ELL Teacher's Toolbox* (Ferlazzo & Sypnieski, 2018b). We sometimes have had students then teach those data sets to their classmates following the multiphase protocol described in this chapter.

Student Handouts and Examples

Figure 4.1: Indigeneity Data Set
Figure 4.2: France Headlines Data Set
Figure 4.3: Types of Government Data Set
Table 4.1: Category Graphic Organizer
Table 4.2: Category Graphic Organizer Example
Figure 4.4: Cut-Up Data Set Examples
Figure 4.5: Student-Created Data Sets

What Could Go Wrong?

In our experience, the biggest challenge is getting students to engage in multiple readings of a text. We don't want them to treat the reading tasks as a checklist or worksheet to be completed, but instead, as tools for understanding. To address this challenge, we focus on building students' social and emotional skills as well as keeping things novel.

To build our students' social and emotional skills, sometimes called soft skills ("Soft Skills," n.d.), we teach lessons during the year on how the brain works, developing academic perseverance, and setting goals (Chapter 19: Social and Emotional Learning). This gives us a common language to help guide our learners during the year when they need to be reminded of our purpose.

There are several ways to keep things fresh when using data sets: make sure the unit question is engaging, the data sets contain interesting details about the topic, and the passages are well written. In addition, try to avoid doing the same set of reading tasks on each page and get students out of their seats by rotating partners.

Technology Connections

Using technology to have students build data sets, especially picture data sets, can be effective and engaging. One explanation of how to do this is located on Larry Ferlazzo's website, where students use Padlet to create picture data sets, "How My ELL Students Used Padlet to Create a Picture Data Set" (http://larryferlazzo.edublogs.org/2017/05/26/how-my-ell-students-used-padlet-to-create-a-picture-data-set).

Attribution

We were first introduced to inductive data sets through Pebble Creek Labs curriculum created by Kelly Young (www.pebblecreeklabs.com).

Figures

Categories:
- Common traits amongst most indigenous people
- Indigenous people of Sacramento/California
- Indigenous rights

1. There are some common traits and values amongst indigenous peoples around the world. For example, although many people from other ethnicities care about the environment, all indigenous peoples have rituals and stories that remind them of their spiritual responsibility to the earth. This is accompanied by an in-depth understanding of the connections between all living things. Another example is the strong sense of teamwork amongst native peoples. The cooperation of various tribes has helped them survive immense adversity (Mankiller, 2009).

2. The Sacramento region is considered the home to four Native American tribes: the Nisenan, Sierra Miwok, Northern Valley Yokuts, and the Patwin. Yet, other tribes have ties to the Sacramento region as well, even if their specific origin extends out of the area. The Wintu and the Konkow live to the north. Extending to the west of what is now Sacramento are the Pomo and the Wappo (Mark & Allender, 2017).

3. Another trait that is considered to be shared amongst all indigenous people is that they all have a history of cruel and unfair treatment. Largely thanks to colonization, the identity and dignity of natives has been threatened (Hymowitz, Dikkers, & Anderson, 2003).

4. In addition to fighting for land rights, indigenous people all over the world have been fighting for cultural rights. For example, there have been international legal efforts to protect cultural property in the form of music, prayers, motifs, etc. This effort is in response to the concern about the commercialization of these types of cultural items. In other words, many Indigenous groups are frustrated by the fact that their art and cultural items are turned into objects that can be sold for money (Chen, 2014).

5. Native American scholars are currently pushing for more representation of indigenous groups in California classrooms. The governor of California has signed laws that would require more inclusion of Native Americans in the state curriculum. Scholars have noted that because of the great diversity of Native groups, one lesson plan cannot completely cover the complexity and differences amongst indigenous people of California (Jones, 2018).

Figure 4.1 Indigeneity Data Set

6. In Native American society, the role of elders is important. It's the elders who teach the following generations about their history, culture, and customs. The elders of a tribe are often the keepers of knowledge about rituals, arts, music, and customs (National Museum of the American Indian, n.d.).

7. Many Northern California locations have names given by the Native Americans who once controlled these lands. One example is the word "Cosumnes" as in Cosumnes River or Cosumnes Community College. The word "Cosumnes" comes from the Miwok words for "salmon" which is "kosum." Other Northern California place names from indigenous peoples include Lake Tahoe (Washo) and Natomas coming from the word "Natoma" (Maidu) (Kroeber, 1916).

8. Not until 1978 did the US government officially issue regulations to determine the federal acknowledgment process for tribes in the United States. Federally recognized tribes are able to access some federal funding and services from the Bureau of Indian Affairs. Being federally recognized also allows for self government or tribal sovereignty ("Frequently Asked Questions," n.d.).

9. Storytelling is an inherent part of Native American culture. Oral stories passed down from generation to generation were used to teach traditions and culture instead of written languages. The telling of these stories was, and is, often combined with dance and music creating an entire experience for those present (Tracey, 2011).

10. The relationship between Native peoples and the land is special. The land is viewed as the creator from which all life originates. Native Americans see themselves as stewards, or caretakers of the earth. Man and earth are seen as equal and because of this, both parties should be considered when making choices. The earth and landscape make up a large portion of Native American origination stories, which connects the earth directly with the culture of Native Americans (Kirwan, n.d.).

11. After Spain outlawed slavery the Queen later allowed a practice which came to be known as the Encomienda System. In this system Spaniards were allowed to "protect" and Christianize indigenous peoples. "Protecting" the Natives usually consisted of forced labor. The Christianizing meant to strip Natives of all cultural practices and beliefs, including language, and replacing them with the preferred Spanish culture ("Parallel Histories," n.d.).

12. Sutter's Fort is a central landmark in Midtown Sacramento on 27th and L Streets. Now visited by many tourists and school groups, this fort was an important post for immigrants and people looking to buy supplies or find work. What many people don't recognize is that this fort was built on the lands belonging to both Nisenan-Maidu tribes and Mewuk. In fact, the entire fort was built by people belonging to these tribes (Dutschke, 1988).

Figure 4.1 (Continued)

13. After the discovery of gold in 1849, settlers rushed into the San Joaquin Valley in search of riches. Later, the fertile soil proved useful for farming. The Native tribes inhabiting these lands, mostly Northern Yokut tribes, were pushed out of the way. After signing treaties to turn over all Native lands, the treaties were not ratified by Congress, which meant the tribes effectively lost their homelands without the promised reservations in return. This is one of many examples of broken treaties that led to the loss of identity and culture of Native Americans (Santos, 2014).

14. Language revitalization of Native Americans has been supported by proposed legislation such as the Esther Martinez Native American Languages Preservation Act. Programs funded by this legislation would provide grants (government money) to help various tribal groups preserve the languages of their people. Without these kinds of programs, many Native groups may run the risk of losing their mother tongues forever (Linguistic Society of America, n.d.).

15. After the American Civil War, efforts were taken by the Federal Government to "Americanize" the Native populations. Children were taken and compelled to attend boarding schools, where they were divested of all cultural practices and re-educated to the American culture. Parents who refused to send their children to these schools faced jail or losing federal aid. Children in these schools often faced harsh conditions including physical punishment. Many children attempted to, or did, run away (Marr, n.d.).

16. From 1969 to 1971, a group known as Indians of All Nations occupied the former Alcatraz Prison located off the coast of San Francisco as an act of resistance. This act lasted two years and brought national attention to the concerns of Natives from California and across the United States. This led to the passage of some reforms to improve healthcare and education access as well as returning land that had been illegally taken from the Yakima Indians and Taos Pueblo (Clarke, 2016).

17. Sacramento area Natives from the Wintu tribe are working to protect and restore the winter-run Chinook Salmon. The local salmon which used to make up the majority of the Wintu diet are now regulated to only ceremonial events due to the reduced numbers. The salmon population has been drastically reduced since the 1960s following effects from the building of Shasta Dam in 1945 (Bland, 2016).

18. By appointing certain tribal leaders as chiefs, John Sutter ensured Indian labor via trade. To maintain a steady flow of Indian labor, he kidnapped the children of enemy tribes. These children became servants or slaves at the fort or were sent to friends of John Sutter around the country (Dutschke, 1988).

Figure 4.1 (Continued)

(Categories: land/climate, politics, challenges, economy, culture)

1. **Angry workers storm Air France meeting on job cuts**

   Liz Alderman, *New York Times*, October 5, 2015
   Air France executives, including the chief of human resources, Xavier Broseta, . . . , fled after angry workers broke into a meeting about mass job cuts. (www .nytimes.com/2015/10/06/business/international/angry-workers-stormair-france-meeting-on-job-cuts.html)

2. **France approves controversial immigration bill**

   Ian Traynor, *BBC*, April 23, 2018
   The bill shortens asylum application deadlines, doubles the time for which illegal migrants can be detained, and introduces a one-year prison sentence for entering France illegally. President Emmanuel Macron's governing centrist party says the bill will speed up the process of claiming asylum. (www.bbc .com/news/world-europe-43860880)

3. **An ode to tartiflette: The "most in demand recipe in France"**

   The Local, December 17, 2017
   The great God Google has revealed that the most searched for recipe in France this year was tartiflette. Here's what you need to know about the unctuous, heart-warming, stomach filling, waistline bursting Alpine dish, which everyone must have at least once this winter. (www.thelocal.fr/20171213/ an-ode-to-tartiflette-the-most-popular-recipe-in-france)

4. **Train shooting heroes: The men who helped avert a massacre in Europe**

   Faith Karimi, *CNN*, January 8, 2018
   Now the world knows them as heroes. Anthony Sadler, Spencer Stone and Alek Skarlatos were aboard a high-speed train en route to Paris from Amsterdam on Friday when a gunman opened fire. Along with two others – a French national and a Briton – they charged, tackled and subdued him, officials said. (www.cnn.com/2015/08/22/europe/france-train-shootingheroes/ index.html)

5. **France beat Croatia to win World Cup 2018**

   Al Jazeera and News Agencies, July 16, 2018
   France won the World Cup for the second time by ending hard-battling Croatia's dream of a first title with a 4-2 victory in an entertaining and action-packed final. (www.aljazeera.com/news/2018/07/world-cup-final-francebeat-croatia-win-russia-2018-180715160625847.html)

Figure 4.2   France Headlines Data Set

6. **Chris Froome: Anti-doping case against four-time Tour de France winner dropped**

Dan Roan, *BBC*, July 2, 2018
The four-time Tour de France winner, 33, was under investigation after more than the allowed level of legal asthma drug salbutamol was found in his urine. The World Anti-Doping Agency (WADA), which worked closely with the UCI, has accepted there was no breach and recommended the case is dropped. (www.bbc.com/sport/cycling/44679483)

7. **How Chanel's makeup artist prepped for the brand's New York show**

Laura Neilson, *New York Times Style Magazine*, December 6, 2018
On a recent morning, Lucia Pica, Chanel's global creative director for makeup and color, stops into Cafe Gitane in SoHo for a chamomile tea. In just a few hours, she will be consumed by all things Chanel, starting with its much-anticipated Métiers d'Art fashion show, which will take place the next evening. (www.nytimes.com/2018/12/06/t-magazine/lucia-pica-makeupartist-chanel.html?action=click&module=MoreInSection&pgtype=Article&region=Footer&contentCollection=T%20Magazine)

8. **Rioting engulfs Paris as anger grows over high taxes**

Elaine Ganley and John Leicester, *Chicago Tribune*, December 8
As tens of thousands of Syrians and Iraqis travel to Germany, they are largely passing France, where some are worried an influx of migrants could have a negative effect. (www.chicagotribune.com/news/nationworld/ct-franceparis-riots-macron-20181208-story.html)

9. **What is France doing in Syria? New U.S. military photos may have shown too much**

Tom O'Connor, *Newsweek*, September 18, 2018
The official Twitter account for the Special Ops Joint Task Force involved in the U.S.-led mission against the Islamic State (ISIS) in Iraq and Syria shared pictures Wednesday from the eastern Syrian province of Deir Ezzor featuring U.S. Marines loading a mortar and a French light armored vehicle in the background. While France has been involved in the U.S.-led fight against the jihadis since 2014, this was the first evidence of the country deploying troops in this part of Syria. (www.newsweek.com/what-france-doing-syria-new-usmilitary-photos-may-show-too-much-1120332)

10. **Paris's best new fall menus**

Alexander Lobrano, *The New York Times Style Magazine*, October 5, 2015
Fortuitously for the fashion set, currently in Paris to see the spring/summer 2016 collections, more restaurants make their debut during la rentrée (early Fall) than any other time of year in the City of Light. And many of the best new tables this season — including an old standby, with an updated menu — cater to healthier appetites with lighter fare. (www.nytimes.com/2015/10/05/t-magazine/paris-restaurants-new-fall-menus.html)

Figure 4.2 (Continued)

11. The Louvre launches Beyonce and Jay-Z tour

Francesca Street, *CNN*, July 11, 2018
(CNN) — Want to spend an afternoon following in the footsteps of Beyoncé and Jay Z? Now you can – thanks to the Louvre's new "Jay-Z and Beyoncé at the Louvre" self-guided tour, which spotlights 17 artworks used in the music video for "Apes**t," the super successful single the couple surprise-dropped in June. (www.cnn.com/travel/article/louvre-beyonce-jay-z-tour/index.html)

12. Eiffel Tower, Louvre close over "significant violence" during protests

Amanda Woods, *New York Post*, December 7, 2018
Dozens of famed Paris attractions — including the Eiffel Tower and the Louvre museum — are set to shutter on Saturday as local authorities warned of "significant violence" during an outbreak of anti-government protests. (https://nypost.com/2018/12/07/eiffel-tower-louvre-close-over-significantviolence-during-protests/)

13. On one Paris street, shopkeepers specialize in only one thing

Elaine Sciolino, *New York Times Style Magazine*, August 26, 2015
Here, on this narrow, half-mile stretch that moves upward into the base of Montmartre, the one-product shop is celebrated. Mesdemoiselles Madeleines makes only madeleines; Les Grands d'Espagne specializes in Spanish ham. (www.nytimes.com/2015/08/26/t-magazine/paris-shops-rue-des-martyrs.html)

14. String of Paris terrorist attacks leaves over 120 dead

Maura Judkis and Griff Witte, *Washington Post*, November 13, 2015
PARIS — France declared a state of emergency and secured its borders Friday night after attackers unleashed a coordinated wave of explosions, gunfire and hostage-taking in Paris that left more than 120 people dead and generated scenes of horror and carnage. (www.washingtonpost.com/world/europe/paris-rocked-by-explosions-andshootouts-leaving-dozens-dead/2015/11/13/133f5bc2-8a50-11e5-bd91-d385b244482f_story.html?utm_term=.b448011b7924)

15. France takes on cellphone addiction with a ban in schools

Schechner, *Wall Street Journal*, August 13, 2018
When school starts up in September, a new French law will ban students ranging roughly from ages 3 to 15 from using smartphones anywhere on school grounds, with only narrow exceptions. (www.wsj.com/articles/france-takeson-cellphone-addiction-with-a-ban-in-schools-1534152600)

Figure 4.2   (Continued)

16. **Dancers took over the runway at Dior's spring 2019 show**

Lauren Alexis Fisher, *Harper's BAZAAR*, September 24 2018
The Spring 2019 show opened with a theatrical routine choreographed by Israeli choreographer Sharon Eyal. As rose petals fell from the ceiling, the modern dance performance lasted the duration of the show, with dancers weaving in and out of models walking the runway in Dior's latest collection. (www.harpersbazaar.com/fashion/fashion-week/a23398506/dior-spring-2019-show-parisfashion-week/)

17. **Migrants bring cricket (and victory) to life in Northern France**

Elian Peltier, *New York Times*, November 3, 2018
ST.-OMER, France — The players erupted in joy, dancing and shouting in Pashto, celebrating their second victory in a regional cricket tournament. It might have been a familiar scene in parts of Afghanistan or Pakistan, but it was far less so here in northern France. (www.nytimes.com/2018/11/03/world/europe/france-cricket-refugees.html)

18. **French museum discovers more than half its collection is forged**

Jake Cigainero, NPR, April 29, 2018
A museum in Southern France has discovered more than half its collection of paintings thought to be by a celebrated local artist are counterfeit. And investigators say that works attributed to other regional artists could also be fakes. (www.npr.org/2018/04/29/606919098/french-museum-discoversmore-than-half-its-collection-is-forged)

19. **French Muslims say veil bans give cover to bias**

Suzanne Daley and Alissa J. Rubin, *New York Times*, May 27, 2015
The head coverings of observant Muslim women have become one of the most potent flash points in the nation's tense relations with its Muslim population. (www.nytimes.com/2015/05/27/world/europe/muslim-frenchwomen struggle-with-discrimination-as-bans-on-veils-expand.html)

20. **Tour de France 2018: Geraint Thomas wins to make sporting history**

Paul Gittings, *CNN*, July 29, 2018
Sporting history was made on the Champs-Elysees Sunday as Geraint Thomas became the first Welshman to win cycling's Tour de France. Arm-in-arm with 2017 champion and Team Sky teammate Chris Froome, the 32-year-old Thomas crossed the finishing line after the 21st and final stage in Paris in triumph. (https://edition.cnn.com/2018/07/29/sport/tour-de-france-geraintthomas-wins/index.html)

Figure 4.2 (Continued)

21. **Dopes, not doping, threaten to derail the Tour de France**

Matt Bonesteel, *Washington Post*, July 20, 2018
The Tour de France threatened to descend into chaos as the riders ascended the Alps during Thursday's Stage 12, with fans crowding the course and lighting flares, the smoke clouding the riders' view. It got so bad that Vincenzo Nibali, the 2014 champion, was knocked from his bike and out of the Tour entirely. (www.washingtonpost.com/news/early-lead/wp/2018/07/20/dopes-not-doping-threaten-to-derail-the-tour-de-france/?utm_term=.f91ec2a6edb0)

22. **Wine's pedigree faked**

Associated Press, *New York Times*, October 24, 2013
European authorities are pursuing a network of counterfeiters who passed off hundreds of bottles of mediocre wine as Romanée-Conti, often considered the best and most expensive wine in the world. (www.nytimes.com/2013/10/24/world/europe/wines-pedigree-faked.html)

23. **Paris killings mark escalation from Charlie Hebdo attack**

Gregory Viscusi, Bloomberg, November 15, 2015
Unlike the killings at the satirical magazine Charlie Hebdo – that often made the Prophet Muhammad a cartoon subject – and at a kosher grocery store, the attacks on Friday were meticulously prepared, were aimed at the entire nation and have greater international implications, terror analysts said. (www.bloomberg.com/news/articles/2015-11-16/paris-killings-markmajor-escalation-from-charlie-hebdo-attack)

24. **After a promise to return African artifacts, France moves toward a plan**

Annalisa Quinn, *New York Times*, March 6, 2018
President Emmanuel Macron of France announced on Monday his appointment of two experts to make plans for the repatriation of African artifacts held in French museums, following his pledge in November that "African heritage cannot be a prisoner of European museums." (https://www.nytimes.com/2018/03/06/arts/design/france-restitution-african-artifacts.html)

25. **"Spider-Man" of Paris to get French citizenship after child rescue**

Kim Willsher, *The Guardian*, May 29, 2018
As an undocumented migrant in France, Mamoudou Gassama knew it was best to keep his head down, to not draw attention to himself. But when he spotted a young child dangling from the balcony of a fourth-floor Paris flat he felt he had to act. (www.theguardian.com/world/2018/may/28/spider-man-of-paris-to-getfrench-citizenship-after-rescuing-child)

Figure 4.2 (Continued)

1. "The stronger must dominate and not blend with the weaker, thus sacrificing his own greatness."

   —Adolf Hitler

2. "Extremely wealthy families are hell-bent on destroying the democratic vision of a strong middle class which has made the United States the envy of the world. In its place they are determined to create an oligarchy in which a small number of families control the economic and political life of our country."

   —Bernie Sanders

3. "The rich and powerful now have new means to further enrich and empower themselves at the cost of the poorer and weaker, we have a responsibility to protest."

   —Nelson Mandela

4. "As all perfection and all strength are united in God, so all the power of individuals is united in the person of the [king]. What grandeur that a single man should embody so much!"

   —King Louis XIV

5. "Any law which the people has not ratified in person is void; it is not law at all."

   —Jean-Jacques Rousseau

6. "It is enough that the people know there was an election. The people who cast the votes decide nothing. The people who count the votes decide everything."

   —Joseph Stalin

7. "I am the state [government]."

   —King Louis XIV

8. "Surely every man will have advisers by his side, but the decision will be made by one man."

   —Adolf Hitler

9. "A monarchy conducted with infinite wisdom and infinite benevolence is the most perfect of all possible governments."

   —Ezra Stiles

Figure 4.3 Types of Government Data Set *Source: Navigating the Common Core with ELL (Ferlazzo & Sypnieski, 2016).*

10. "Educate and inform the whole mass of the people. . . . They are the only sure reliance for the preservation of our liberty."

—Thomas Jefferson

11. "We have learned from history we have reason to conclude that all peaceful beginnings of government have been laid in the consent of the people."

—John Locke

12. "Any constitution in which wealth confers the privileges of citizenship, whether the rulers are few or many, must be regarded as oligarchy."

—Aristotle

13. "There is danger from all men. The only maxim of a free government is to trust no man living with power to endanger the public liberty."

—John Adams

14. "The way to secure liberty is to place it in the people's hands, that is, to give them the power at all times to defend it in the legislature and in the courts of justice."

—Thomas Jefferson

15. "In a democracy, the people are sovereign."

—Montesquieu

16. "Men are equal; it is not birth but virtue that makes the difference."

—François-Marie Voltaire

Figure 4.3 (Continued)

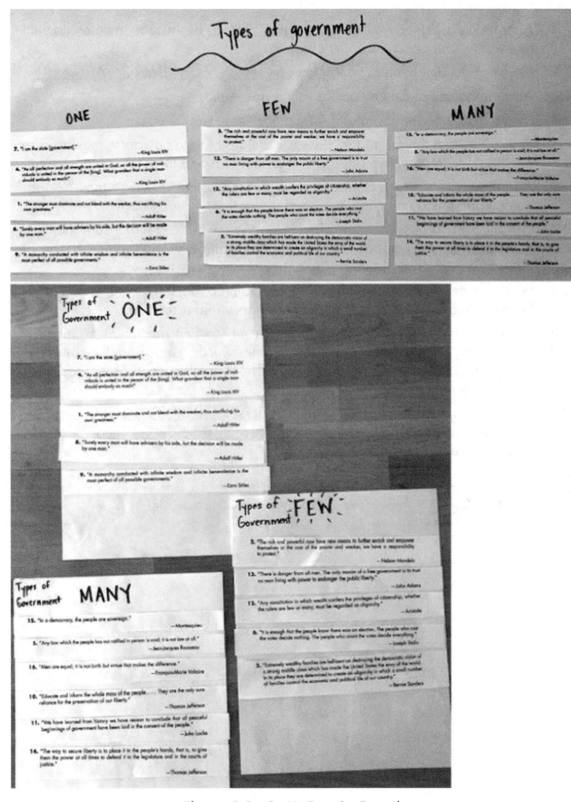

Figure 4.4 Cut-Up Data Set Examples

1. After being assigned a historical event or person, brainstorm to come up with four to five categories about your topic.

2. Create a document and title it <u>(name of person/event) Data Set Answer Key</u>.

3. Add the names of the categories to the document.

4. Look for information for one of the categories.

5. Select between three and five passages related to the category, making sure each is no more than five sentences in length and add them to your document.

6. Add the passages to your document under the category where they belong; you can do this by copying and pasting the text.

7. Continue this process for the other categories. Check to make sure that you have a balanced number of items in each category and a wide range of information covered about the topic.

8. Next, create a new document and title it <u>(name of person/event) Data Set for Students</u> and add the names of each category under the title.

9. Copy and paste each of the passages from the first document to this new one making sure they are mixed up. In other words, items from the same category should not be next to each other. Then, number each of the passages in the document.

10. Print out a single copy of the <u>(name of person/event) Data Set Answer Key</u> and four copies of the <u>(name of person/event) Data Set for Students</u>. Now, it's time to teach your data set.

Figure 4.5 Student-Created Data Sets *Source: Modified from The ELL Teacher's Toolbox: Hundreds of Practical Ideas to Support Your Students (Ferlazzo & Sypnieski, 2018b, p.134).*

CHAPTER 5

Writing in Social Studies

What Is It?

It is not unusual for writing in many social studies classes to consist of the teacher just giving students a prompt and telling them when it is due.

That strategy is not what this chapter is all about.

This chapter focuses on explicitly building students' writing skills in the context of studying social studies content. We want all our students to be successful writers. Toward that end, we provide scaffolding – both in assisting students to see themselves as writers and by providing a series of basic steps that will help them formulate well-developed arguments.

Why We Like It

We like the specific strategies we discuss in this chapter because they provide avenues toward success for all students. Feelings of competence are essential for any of us to be intrinsically motivated – students included (Ferlazzo, 2015a). By strategically providing key scaffolds along the way, student confidence and engagement in writing can increase and result in improved literacy skills.

We appreciate how these activities act as building blocks for the extended and more advanced writing demands our students might face in the future. These skills, once learned, can be put to use independently by students any time they have to respond to a prompt or question.

Supporting Research

In a study comparing how two social studies teachers approached historical evidence-based writing, researchers concluded, "The act of writing alone is not sufficient for growth in evidence-based historical writing" (Monte-Sano, 2017, p. 1045). Instead, the same research found that helping students through explicit teaching of writing strategies, along with guided practice, yielded the best results. Also, showing students models of good writing helps them identify what to emulate or avoid in their own writing (Graham et al., 2016, p. 19). We provide models for students throughout the application section.

Common Core Connections

Citing specific textual evidence and analyzing how it supports the authors' claims are both listed as goals in the Grades 6–12 Literacy in History/Social Studies Common Core Standards (Common Core, 2019). Additionally, the writing standards call for using "relevant and sufficient evidence" to write an argument (Common Core, 2019, Text Types and Purposes section, para. 1).

Social Studies Connections

The strategies in this chapter directly support the *College, Career, and Civic Life (C3) Framework* from the National Council for the Social Studies. In it, the NCSS lists specific skills that students are expected to master including "gathering relevant information" and "evaluating the credibility of a source" (Swan et al., 2017, p. 53). Argument writing in social studies, which requires analyzing information to draw a conclusion, is also foundational to the inquiry process (Swan et al., 2017).

Application

This application section includes extended explanations of five separate strategies to help support writing in social studies. The activities grow in sophistication to meet a variety of writing demands. We explain how, and when, we explicitly teach these strategies to our students. All can be applied to any social studies content.

We begin by confronting one key challenge: getting students to want to write *something* of value related to social studies. Toward this end, we begin the application section with an activity called Golden Lines. This lesson can be a low-stress and highly engaging way to bridge reading and writing.

Our second strategy, evidence-based writing structures, moves students to a more complex writing level. We discuss two writing structures that help students include, organize, and analyze evidence in their writing: ABC (Answer, Back-it-up, Commentary) and PEE (Point, Example, Explain). We explain how we model and guide students to use specific "moves" to build a well-written evidence-based paragraph.

The third activity shows how to utilize sentence frames to incorporate evidence in an argumentative letter. We explain how we guide students to write slightly longer pieces with these frames while providing help with organization of sources.

In the fourth strategy, we provide a protocol that involves teacher think-alouds and written examples to help students employ sentence starters with success. This activity can be utilized for one well-analyzed evidence-based paragraph or to help build multiple paragraphs for a longer written piece.

We conclude the application section with a list of additional strategies that any social studies teacher could employ to encourage and facilitate successful writing in their classrooms.

GOLDEN LINES – KICK-STARTING WRITING

In our experience, one of the biggest challenges about writing in social studies is getting students meaningfully engaged in the writing process. Golden Lines is a well-known reading-response and writing-to-learn strategy introduced to us by the WRITE Institute, a highly regarded writing curriculum for English language learners (ELLs) (Write Institute, 2019). It helps us "spark" student engagement. This strategy involves students identifying impactful phrases and writing about them. Finding golden lines is an open-ended and safe strategy because it is difficult to do incorrectly.

Golden lines can be used to highlight style and content in social studies texts. We look for highly engaging, stylized text that is likely to kick-start student writing. We often find these powerful excerpts in historical fiction, memoirs, novels, investigative journalism, and travel pieces. This golden lines activity can also be used when examining thematic data sets (see Chapter 4: Thematic Data Sets).

We define golden lines to students as "memorable sentences or phrases in a text." In other words, they are portions of the text that "jump out" to the reader. We share with students that these lines may resonate with us because they tend to fall into the following criteria:

- They get to the heart, or the main point of the text.
- Many times they are written in a creative or especially powerful way.
- Sometimes they reveal an unexpected detail that changes the entire text.
- They evoke genuine emotional responses such as laughter, sadness, or anger.

After we explain these criteria, we pass out a short reading (two to three paragraphs) that relates to a unit we are studying. In our US history class, we use an excerpt from the Vietnam War novel *The Things They Carried* by Tim O'Brien (1990).

This powerful excerpt about the soldier experience in the Vietnam War is read aloud while students are following along on the screen or on their copy of the reading (please refer to Chapter 3: Read-Aloud Protocol).

Afterward, we model our process for identifying a golden line:

> *There are many phrases in this text that make me respond emotionally, like "covered their heads and said Dear Jesus." However, for me, the golden line that brings out the strongest reaction is "They would repair the leaks of their eyes." I am going to highlight this line because all this violence has brought these soldiers to tears. To me, this communicates the trauma they are experiencing.*

Next, we ask students to select another line they think is worthy of golden-line status. We then ask them to explain, in writing, their rationale in the margin or on a sticky note. If needed, we provide sentence starters such as "This line makes me feel. . . because. . ." or "I like this line because. . ." After they discuss their selection and reasoning in partners, we call on a few students to share with the class.

We then encourage students to practice again on a second text about the same topic. Students repeat the sharing process. They have now highlighted two pieces of text and written about the reasons behind their choices.

Right after this practice, we ask students to respond to a prompt that encourages them to review their golden lines, along with their writing about them. In this case, "What does the reading help you realize about the Vietnam War? Please use one of your golden lines as evidence to support your answer." This final step can function as a simple introduction to the concept of evidence-based writing.

WRITING FRAMES

Sentence *starters*, like the ones mentioned in the golden-lines section ("I like this line because. . ."), are just that – sentences where the beginning words are provided so that students can complete them.

Sentence *frames* provide even more scaffolding for less-experienced writers. This strategy gives students sentences with blank spaces that help frame their entire writing response. (For example, "In addition, the statistics show that_____ _____, which means that_____.") Sentence starters and sentence frames can be combined into a longer fill-in-the-blank passage like the four-paragraph letter in Figure 5.1: Letter Frame. This scaffold is called a writing frame because it is a longer piece of writing that includes connecting words and an overall structure. This section will describe how we use this handout in class, and how it can be modified for many other social studies topics.

We start this activity after spending a few days learning about the local Sacramento area in our World Geography class. Readings, video clips, and demographic statistics provide students with background knowledge of the local area. We make sure to include materials on current challenges facing the community and actions being taken to respond to them. We have found that studying a place that students are familiar with serves as a relevant and engaging introduction to our unit about the United States. If there are negative narratives about a community, this investigation can counter them by highlighting the positive aspects. It can also serve as a case study for broader national issues – immigration, housing, and demographic trends are topics that often arise in our study.

The purpose of this activity is to have students apply content knowledge, in this case information about Sacramento, while practicing evidence-based writing. They do this by writing a letter using evidence from classwork arguing why Sacramento is the best city in the United States. Of course, this letter can be modified to identify your own community as the best in the country, the best in the state, or the best in your region. Though students seldom choose it, we do offer them the choice to explain why they don't believe it is the best city. We provide Figure 5.1: Letter Frame to support evidence inclusion and organization of ideas.

We distribute Figure 5.1: Letter Frame and read it as a class. We then assign students a partner and employ the think-pair-share format as described in Chapter 16: Discussions. Students converse about the following two questions: What is the main point or purpose of this letter? Which sources from the last few days would work best for this writing assignment?

Students are called on to share their answers. Most share that the letter is about Sacramento and, according to the greeting at the top of Figure 5.1: Letter Frame, it is trying to convince someone that Sacramento is the best city. They also typically note, sometimes with our guidance, that the top paragraph focuses on fun aspects of Sacramento, while the second paragraph seems to cover statistics about the city. The third paragraph shares possible negative aspects of the city and provides a counter-argument to them. The fourth paragraph serves as the letter's conclusion.

We ask students to open their class folders. They are directed to work with their same partner and identify which prior assignments have information that could be used for this letter. We then call on students to share which class assignments would help and why. We narrow down the sources to those that focus on the positive and recreational aspects of Sacramento, sources with demographic statistics about the city, and articles about current challenges facing the area.

After modeling how to fill out one or two sentence frames, or more if needed, students continue working on the template on their own. They are reminded that whatever they choose as evidence needs to make sense within the sentence frame.

We do allow students to make minor grammatical changes to the sentences, if necessary. We remind them, however, that the overall meaning of the sentence shouldn't change.

After the students are done filling out the first paragraph template, they share what they wrote with a partner. They read their paragraphs aloud to each other. This interaction allows them to hear how answers may vary greatly but can still be "correct." In addition, students may be reminded of content that they have read but forgotten.

We facilitate the same cycle for the second paragraph of the letter. In our example, we focus on the strengths conveyed in our demographic statistics. Together, we identify which class sources would be the best for this section. Students finish this paragraph while working with partners.

To complete the third paragraph, we encourage the class to brainstorm challenges facing our city that we have studied, as well as actions being taken to respond to them. For the sake of variety, everyone changes partners to complete the third paragraph and the closing section of the letter.

For a completed example see Figure 5.2: Letter Frame Example.

This kind of letter introduces the concept of evidence-based writing in an accessible format. Teachers can use this same process for many other topics. Students in another class at our school applied it by trying to convince city officials to support greater investment into our neighborhood. After studying the lives of Nelson Mandela and Malala Yousafzai, we had students write letters to a younger sibling or cousin explaining why they were each great leaders. After learning about climate change, students wrote this kind of letter to their congressional representatives urging them to take action on the issue.

Obviously, after the first or second use of this kind of writing frame, the scaffolding can be reduced or removed entirely. These frames can also be used as a differentiation tool; after they are used initially, some students may or may not need them any longer. Ultimately, we want students to be able to write these simple arguments without them.

WRITING STRUCTURES

As we explained, writing *frames* are fill-in-the-blanks. Writing *structures*, on the other hand, provide guiding prompts for students as they construct their own complete sentences and paragraphs (Ferlazzo, 2018). In this section, we provide simple supports to scaffold an evidence-based short response to a prompt.

The examples we use are from our world geography classes. However, the activities can be easily adapted for multiple units and subjects.

ABC Writing Structure

The ABC writing structure breaks down evidence-based responses into three steps: Answer the question, Back it up with evidence, Comment to explain how the evidence supports the answer. Figure 5.3: ABC Answering Strategy Guide includes easy-to-use sentence starters from the book *They Say, I Say: The Moves That Matter in Academic Writing* by Gerald Graff and Cathy Birkenstein (2014). Students can use the sentence starters to scaffold ABC responses.

We introduce this ABC acronym when students are answering prompts during a unit of study. Figure 5.3: ABC Answering Strategy Guide is distributed and is read through with students. Then, we show how to apply the structure with a model response. We don't always provide model responses. However, when students are first learning a writing strategy, we find it helpful to show them multiple examples. What follows is a *very* detailed explanation of how we introduce the ABC writing structure to our younger students. Depending on your grade level and student population, a less-guided sequence might or might not be more appropriate.

In a geography unit on Africa, we ask "What information did you find particularly interesting about Africa and why?" At this point, we pass out Figure 5.4: ABC Model Questions and Responses, which provides two sample responses to a similar prompt about South America. We don't want to provide model responses to the question about Africa because that would increase the likelihood of one or two students just copying a portion of them. Providing models of answers to exact questions students will be responding to also reduces the original ideas that they can choose from.

At this point, students should have both Figure 5.3: Answering Strategy Guide and Figure 5.4: ABC Model Questions and Responses on their desks. We begin by reading aloud the *first* sample response in Figure 5.4: ABC Model Questions and Responses. Then, we explain how the language in the question about South America can be converted into a sentence starter. We might say:

> *The prompt at the top of the page says "What information did you find particularly interesting about South America and why?" The opening sentence of the first example says "The information I found particularly interesting about South America is Brazil's population." What I notice is that the answer uses the same language as the prompt. Let's draw an arrow between the similar words in the prompt and in the answer. This will remind us how to start our answer, later.*

Once students have made this annotation, we begin breaking down the paragraph explaining how each sentence addresses the ABC strategy. After reading the first sentence, we ask students the following:

> *Look at the first sentence. What part in this sentence answers the question? Put your finger on it.*

We quickly go around the room checking to see where students have placed their finger. We then call on someone who has correctly identified "Brazil's population" on their paper as the answer. We then explain that in the ABC writing strategy we will be using, "Brazil's population" is our direct answer to "What did you find interesting?" This is why it is the "A" or *answer* portion of the model response.

Next, we need to explain to students how the sample response fulfills the "B" (back it up) portion of this writing structure. We read the next sentence of the sample answer aloud, "The statistical data set states that Brazil's population is 207,353,391." Then, we direct student attention to the "B" (back it up) section of Figure 5.3: ABC Answering Strategy Guide. We read and say the following:

> *In the Answering Strategy Guide, it lists "X states, '_____.'" as a way to introduce your quote. If we look at our example response, the second sentence uses the word "states" to introduce the statistic about Brazil's population. In this case "X," or the source, seems to be the statistical data set. The number 207,353,391 is the evidence that "backs up" the answer in the first sentence.*

For the final portion of this writing structure, "C" (commentary), we now explain how we analyze the evidence that supports their answer. We read the last sentence of the paragraph aloud:

> *In other words, the statistical data set shows that the population of Brazil is huge and makes me think Brazil is powerful in South America.*

Again, we point out the sentence starter used from the last section of Figure 5.3: ABC Answering Strategy Guide:

> *In other words, X shows that _____.*

We explain that "X" is the evidence we used and that the blank is where we comment to analyze or "break down" the evidence. We also share that this is an opportunity to show an opinion or incorporate student perspectives.

In order to give students more practice, we ask them to choose a partner. They then read through the second model response and discuss how it aligns with the ABC writing structure. During these student discussions, the teacher can circulate and assess if students have a firm enough grasp of the structure to independently practice. If needed, specific students could be called on to explain how a certain part of the strategy was fulfilled in the sample response. Further models can be provided, as well.

After going through the two teacher models, students practice their ABC response to a similar question: "What information did you find particularly interesting about Africa and why?" Figure 5.4: ABC Model Questions and Responses provides a section for them to practice their response while easily referring back to the sample paragraphs for guidance.

Before students complete this practice portion, we direct them to first circle one or two statistics they found interesting or stood out in their demographic analysis handouts for Africa. We remind them about borrowing language for "A" answering the question. In addition, students are directed to use the provided sentence starters from Figure 5.3: ABC Answering Strategy Guide for both introducing their evidence for "B" back it up and "C" commentary. Figure 5.5: Student Sample of ABC Strategy is a sample student response that follows the structure.

PEE Writing Structure

Another structure we use to help students build evidence-based paragraphs is PEE. It is important when introducing the PEE writing strategy to explain and model each part. In addition, Figure 5.6: PEE Answering Strategy Guide includes example responses. Students refer to these model responses when they are answering the following question in geography: "What demographic variables (population, per capita income, and so on) do you think have a cause-and-effect relationship? Explain with examples." This figure is a modified version of a handout our teaching colleague, Jeff Johnson, made for his students. Figure 5.6: PEE Answering Strategy Guide does not offer as many sentence starters, yet still places emphasis on evidence, explanation, and analysis. We like the way it pushes our students to add more detail to their explanation, by having them connect it back to the main point.

Keep in mind that students will probably laugh when you introduce the acronym PEE. The laughter may get you off-track for a minute or two, but this connection may make it more likely for students to remember the steps in the strategy!

Eventually, our young writers see that many of their writing assignments in school utilize these basic paragraph structures.

EXTENDED ARGUMENT WRITING

Practice with writing frames and structures can help build student confidence and competence in evidence-based writing. This practice also prepares students to better take on extended writing assignments independently.

After spending days or even weeks studying a topic through various activities discussed in Chapter 2: Reading Strategies, Chapter 4: Thematic Data Sets, and Chapter 13: Analysis of Primary Resources, we provide an opportunity for our students to write an extended evidence-based argument in response to a prompt. We create prompts that require students to develop a claim and support it with evidence from materials studied in class. We explain that a "claim" is an opinion in response to a question. We also note that other teachers might use the terms *thesis statement, main point,* or *position* as synonyms for *claim.*

Here are a few examples of argument prompts we use:

- What is an important lesson from the American Civil War that can be applied today? Support your point with evidence from our unit materials.

- What aspect of industrialization do you think had the greatest impact on society? Provide evidence to support your position.

- Which environmental concern do you think is going to have the greatest impact on the people of India? Support your argument with evidence from class work.

- Is raising the minimum wage ultimately beneficial or detrimental for the economy? Cite specific examples or research to support your claim.

- In your opinion, which amendment from the Bill of Rights has *not* been fully executed? Support your answer with both historical and modern examples.

We use Figure 5.7: Argument Organizer and teacher modeling to support students as they plan and write their responses. In our experience, the six sections in the handout represent the characteristics of a good written argument of any length: Stating Your Claim, Introducing a New Idea/Example, Introducing Evidence, Analyzing Evidence, Further Evidence Analysis, and Connecting Evidence and Analysis to Argument.

After we share Figure 5.7: Argument Organizer, we ask students to review their materials and develop a claim in response to the prompt. We ask them to refer to their responses to previous paragraphs they have written using writing structures like PEE and ABC. Depending on how much support is needed, we might write a sentence frame for the claim. For example, if the prompt asked "What was the worst impact of European colonialism on Native Americans?" we might write

"The worst impact European colonialism had on Native Americans was _____
_____." We instruct them to write their claim
in the first box of Figure 5.7: Argument Organizer.

Next, we have students look through their materials again to identify two
examples and evidence supporting them to write in the remaining boxes on
Figure 5.7: Argument Organizer. We want students to organize their ideas *first*
before they begin to write their draft response. This process takes time and obviously requires more support the first time students write an extended response.
This kind of assistance might include, in addition to the sentence frame for the
claim, providing a model for one example and its evidence. We would do this by
writing on our own projected copy of Figure 5.7. We also ask students to share
with partners and give them time to modify what they have written based on
those conversations.

Then, we tell students, "Now that you've done some thinking, it's time to put
your ideas in a draft form." We give students Figure 5.8: Sentence Starters for Argument Writing and explain that this sheet is a tool they can use while they are writing
their draft extended response. We then show them Figure 5.9: Teacher Argument
Model Response to demonstrate how we used the sentence starters in response to
a different argument prompt. We highlight how we used the different "levels" of
sentence starters to introduce our examples and the evidence supporting them, to
analyze the evidence, and then connect it to our claim.

After reviewing the teacher model, students begin writing their extended response.
Sometimes after a first draft is completed, we have students revise – perhaps based
on peer feedback or through teacher/student conferencing. We may even highlight
examples of exceptional writing or of mistakes through the use of the concept-
attainment strategy (see Chapter 10: Concept Attainment). We should note that we
always first ask permission of students prior to displaying those examples.

Once students become more familiar with the argument writing process, these
extended responses can become longer and more sophisticated.

OTHER SOCIAL STUDIES WRITING ACTIVITIES

Here are a few other ideas for incorporating writing into social studies classes.

- Quick Writes: A low-stakes writing-to-learn activity is useful for accessing
  prior knowledge, introducing a topic, or piquing student interest. Students
  can respond to an open-ended prompt like "Do you agree or disagree with
  the following statement? Slavery still exists today. Explain your answer."
  Everyone writes for about 5–10 minutes. Sentence starters can be provided
  to help students get started.

- Strip Stories: Students are asked to identify and write a chronological summary of a reading, video, or activity inside a graphic organizer. Typically, the strip story consists of five to eight sections organized as boxes. After students write in each box, they can add visuals. This activity can serve as a "change-of-pace" tool for reviewing important content.

- Word Bank: Students are provided with a set of teacher-selected terms from the current unit of study. Using these four to eight words, they write a paragraph that summarizes what they have learned while showing connections among terms. It is important to have a mix of words consisting of Tier-1 (basic, conversational language), Tier-2 (more academic language usually found in writing), and Tier-3 (content-area specific language) words. See Chapter 1: A Fresh Look at Vocabulary. See Figure 5.10: Word Bank Paragraph for an example.

- Historical Narrative: This writing-to-demonstrate-knowledge activity is a longer, creative-writing activity. Students can either create a character that lived during an important historical event or can pretend to have been there themselves. Using their content knowledge, students write a first-person account of the event or time period. Students can show content comprehension by including historical details along with an emotional perspective.

- Publishing Online: Thanks to the Internet, students can have the motivating experience of writing for an authentic audience. After obtaining the appropriate permission from guardians to publish work online, teachers can have their students build a website, create or contribute to a classroom blog, or even submit an article to a teen publishing website like TeenInk (www.teenink.com). Writing for an authentic audience online can encourage students to invest in their work because they know it will be read outside the classroom. Additional links are included in the Technology Connections section.

- Reflective Learning Logs: Asking students to write about the three most important things they learned in class that day can function as a useful self-reflection and formative assessment. It can also serve as a closing activity for the end of class.

DIFFERENTIATION

To help ELL students access challenging texts in preparation for responding to prompts, we "engineer the text." These changes can include leaving white space between paragraphs, giving each paragraph a heading, and including definitions of key vocabulary at the bottom of the page. Another way to "engineer text" is to prioritize the quality of content versus the quantity of text. This can be done by paring down a text to one or two paragraphs from the original reading that we feel most clearly communicate the content we want to address (Billings & Walqui, n.d.).

We always try to remember what our ELL students *can do* versus what they *can't do*. This activity can both challenge them and allow them to practice intellectual thought about complex ideas. ELL work, especially in social studies, does not have to consist of "watered down" versions of rich texts.

Despite increased support from the strategies in this chapter, one needs to remember that ELLs might not yet be well acquainted with basic grammatical conventions. Content-wise, the evidence that ELL students use might be accurate, but not clearly stated. The Common Core Standards for Writing state that it is more important to focus on the opportunity to communicate an evidence-based argument than place unhelpful attention on the mechanics (Bunch, Kibler, & Pimentel, n.d.).

As the saying goes, "Good ELL teaching is good teaching for everybody," the differentiation suggestions we offer for ELLs can also work well for students with learning differences. However, though those same modifications might be effective, it is always important to remember: *that the reason ELLs need this kind of support is different from why those with learning differences might need it (unless, of course, your student is an ELL who also has learning differences). ELLs are just not proficient in the English language – yet.*

ADVANCED EXTENSIONS

Including evidence from an opposing viewpoint (also known as a counterargument) can display a deeper understanding of issues (Argument, n.d.). Though we often ask all students to include counter-arguments in their responses, we don't always because of time constraints. Adding this requirement to the assignment can be a simple advanced modification. The Harvard College Writing Center (Harvey, 1999) uses two phrases to help students organize their counterclaims: "The Turn Against," challenging your own claim in your paper, and "The Turn Back," returning to your own argument to use the counterclaim to make your position stronger (Harvey, 1999). The following sentence frames can be helpful for students to structure their counterclaim:

- On the other hand, _____ may argue _____. However, _____.
- Opponents of _____ might object citing that_____. Nevertheless, _____. (Harvey 1999)

Student Handouts and Examples

Figure 5.1: Letter Frame

Figure 5.2: Letter Frame Example

Figure 5.3: ABC Answering Strategy Guide

Figure 5.4: ABC Model Questions and Responses

Figure 5.5: Student Sample of ABC Strategy

Figure 5.6: PEE Answering Strategy Guide

Figure 5.7: Argument Organizer

Figure 5.8: Sentence Starters for Argument Writing

Figure 5.9: Teacher Argument Model Response

Figure 5.10: Word Bank Paragraph

What Could Go Wrong?

Rushing to write prior to deep engagement with the text is often tempting because of time constraints. We have painfully learned that we cannot expect students to write if they do not first understand what they are reading. This may seem like an obvious statement, but helping students to understand text takes considerable practice and effort (both for teachers and students!). It may be helpful to employ reading strategies from Chapter 2: Reading Strategies to improve reading comprehension.

Passing out a writing frame or writing structure without modeling the thinking process aloud is not going to result in improved writing for all students. To truly build our students' skills, we must model the decision-making process undertaken by experienced writers. In other words, in addition to showing finished examples of writing to our students, we also need to periodically model the *process* we use when writing.

The evidence-gathering and writing processes may seem overwhelming if there is not a system for students to organize their sources (articles, class readings, textbook notes, film notes). To address this problem, we give all our students folders for each unit and a place to store them in the classroom. Using folders ensures all the readings and assignments are in one place. We also use paper clips, sticky notes, and synthesis charts (see Chapter 14: Synthesis Chart) to organize materials for writing tasks.

Technology Connections

Creating assignments in Google Classroom, or posting a document on a teaching platform like EdModo, allows the teacher to easily create writing frame templates.

Each student can then type in the frames and turn them in digitally. Having students work on a digital template also lets them easily reword the sentence frames as needed.

"The Best Scaffolded Writing Frames for Students" (http://larryferlazzo.edublogs.org/2016/12/01/the-best-scaffolded-writing-frames-for-students) is a post from Larry Ferlazzo's website with more examples, research, and general information about strategies to scaffold evidence-based writing. More examples of sentence starters and frames can be found at "Collections of Academic Sentence Starters" (http://larryferlazzo.edublogs.org/2017/07/21/collections-of-academic-sentence-starters).

Additional opportunities for authentic writing can be found at "The Best Places Where Students Can Write for an Authentic Audience" (http://larryferlazzo.edublogs.org/2009/04/01/the-best-places-where-students-can-write-for-an-authentic-audience).

Finally, resources for social studies–related argument prompts can be found at "The Best Resources for Writing in Social Studies" (http://larryferlazzo.edublogs.org/2016/10/16/the-best-resources-for-writing-in-social-studies-classes).

Attribution

Figure 5.6: PEE Answering Strategy Guide is an adapted version from Jeff Johnson, an English teacher at Luther Burbank High School in Sacramento, California. Kelly Young, former educator, curriculum consultant, and creator of Pebble Creek Labs (www.pebblecreeklabs.com) introduced us to the ABC writing structure.

Figures

<u>Welcome Letter Outline</u>

Dear Visitors,

Welcome to Sacramento, California, the best city in the United States! One of the reasons we believe Sacramento is the best city is because we have a long list of activities for residents, including _____, _____ _____, and_____. We also are known for _____ _____. Furthermore, we think you will appreciate that Sacramento _____ _____.

   Sacramento has all of the amazing things above, and more. The following demographic statistics for Sacramento prove the people here are _____ _____. The statistics also show that _____ _____.
In other words, this means that _____ _____.
In addition, the statistics show that_____ which means that_____ _____. Finally, the fact that Sacramento has_____ _____ means that _____ _____.

   You may have heard some negative things about Sacramento. For example, _____, _____, and _____. Those criticisms may be true. However, we believe they are offset by the positive attributes we have already shared, as well as some changes being made. For example, _____ _____, _____, and_____.

   We really hope that you find Sacramento, California an (a) _____ city. If you are considering moving, we hope that this letter will convince you that _____.

Sincerely,

_____

Figure 5.1 Letter Frame

<u>Welcome Letter Outline</u>

Dear Visitors,

Welcome to Sacramento, California, the best city in the United States! One of the reasons we believe Sacramento is the best city is because we have a long list of activities for residents, including *many walking and biking paths along the Sacramento River, parks with plenty of shade, festivals, and shopping venues for all ages.* We also are known for *our basketball team the Sacramento Kings who play at the Golden One Center.* Furthermore, we think you will appreciate that Sacramento *has a lot of different types of ethnic foods available to eat.*

Sacramento has all of the amazing things above, and more. The following demographic statistics for Sacramento prove the people here are *diverse.* The statistics also show that *37.2% of people speak a language other than English at home.* In other words, this means that *language is part of culture, so, because people are speaking other languages, it means we have many people with different cultures here.* In addition, the statistics show that *83.4% graduate from high school,* which means that *even though the number isn't 100%, most people who live here graduate with a diploma.* Finally, the fact that Sacramento has *6.2% population change* means that *Sacramento is growing and people want to live here.*

You may have heard some negative things about Sacramento. For example, *Stephon Clark was killed by police,* *the homeless population is growing* and *climate change is making it even hotter.* Those criticisms may be true. However, we believe they are offset by the positive attributes we have already shared, as well as some changes being made. For example, *community outcry has forced the police to change procedures and be more responsive to people of color,* *the city is putting millions of dollars more into supporting homeless people to find permanent shelter,* and *thousands of trees are being planted to provide shade and reduce energy use.*

We really hope that you find Sacramento, California an *interesting* city. If you are considering moving, we hope that this letter will convince you that *our city is a place of possibilities for all people.*

Sincerely,
Natalie D.

Figure 5.2 Letter Frame Example

Answer- answer the question

Back it up- use information to support your answer; often this is a quote from the text (make sure you introduce your quote AND explain it in your own words)

How to introduce your quote or evidence

X states, "_____."
As claimed by X, "_____."
In her article _____, X suggests that "_____."

Commentary- provide analysis; make a connection, explain why your quote supports your answer, or share your opinion

How to explain your quote or evidence

In other words, X shows that _____.
X is insisting that _____.
What X really means is that _____.

Figure 5.3   ABC Answering Strategy Guide *Source:* Graff and Birkenstein (2014).

Name_____Date_____Period_____

Question: *"What information did you find particularly interesting about South America and why?"*

1. The information I found particularly interesting about South America is Brazil's population. The statistical data set states that Brazil's population is 207,353,391. In other words, the statistical data set shows that the population of Brazil is huge and makes me think Brazil is powerful in South America.

2. Something that stood out to me about South America is their "school life expectancy." The statistical data set states that Brazil's "school life expectancy" is 15 years. In other words, the statistical data set shows that Brazil seems to provide decent access to education in their country despite high poverty rates.

Now you write an ABC paragraph answering the question:

What information did you find particularly interesting about Africa and why?

_____

_____

_____

_____

_____

_____

_____

Figure 5.4 ABC Model Questions and Responses

Name_____Date_____Period_____

Question: *"What information did you find particularly interesting about South America and why?"*

1. The information I found particularly interesting about South America is Brazil's population. The statistical data set states that Brazil's population is 207,353,391. In other words, the statistical data set shows that the population of Brazil is huge and makes me think Brazil is powerful in South America.

2. Something that stood out to me about South America is Brazil's school life expectancy. The statistical data set states that Brazil's school life expectancy is 15 years. In other words, the statistical data set shows that Brazil seems to provide decent access to education in their country which makes their poverty in the favelas hard to understand.

Now you write an ABC paragraph answering the question:

What information did you find particularly interesting about Africa and why?

Something that stood out to me about Africa is Kenya's education expenditures. The statistical data set states that Kenya's education expenditures is 5.2%. In other words, this shows that countries in Africa, like Kenya, are investing in the education of their country at rates similar to the USA (5%).

Figure 5.5 Student Sample of ABC Strategy

PEE Paragraph Structure

P = Point **E** = Example **E** = Explain

Prompt: What demographic variables (population, per capita income, and so on) do you think have a cause-and-effect relationship? Explain with examples.

Point = Topic + Opinion +Why

A country with a low per capita income is likely to have students complete fewer years of school because of a lack of funding for education.

OR

A country with a low per capita income is likely to have students complete fewer years of school because more have to drop out and work to support their families.

Example = X states, "..." OR For example, ...

The author states, "Poverty can be one indicator of low education levels because it may show that not enough revenue is produced in a country to pay for free and accessible schooling for all."

OR

For example, the data shows that a high percentage of workers are below the age of 17.

Explain = In other words ... OR When ....

In other words, schools tend to suffer when the communities they are in are struggling economically.

OR

When a high number of people don't make a lot of money in a country, this often means that children work to supplement a family's income instead of attending school.

Figure 5.6 PEE Answering Strategy Guide

Claim:

Idea/example that supports claim:
Details/evidence supporting idea/example (facts, research, quotes):

Idea/example that supports claim:
Details/evidence supporting idea/example (facts, research, quotes):

Figure 5.7 Argument Organizer

Stating Your Claim:

Introducing a New Idea/Example: *to introduce an example that supports your claim, usually a new paragraph*

1. The most effective way. . .
2. A strong example . . .
3. A major part of. . .
4. Another compelling way. . .
5. Another powerful example. . .

Introducing Evidence: *to introduce facts, research, quotes to support your idea/example*

1. For example, in_(source)_, it states that. . .
2. Research shows that. . .(cite).
3. For instance, (source) explains how. . .
4. As explained in (source). . .
5. A fact that supports. . .(cite).

Analyzing Evidence: *to break down your evidence for your readers*

1. This evidence shows that. . .
2. This research highlights how. . .
3. This. . .(evidence/quote/discovery) is proof that. . .
4. The fact that. . .(evidence). . . also demonstrates how. . .
5. The fact that. . .(evidence/quote/discovery), shows. . .

Further Evidence Analysis: *to go deeper into your analysis or commentary of your evidence*

1. Furthermore. . .
2. From this (evidence/quote/discovery), we can also infer that. . .
3. Another effect/outcome of. . .
4. Equally as important. . .
5. In addition. . .

Connecting Evidence and Analysis to Argument: *to make sure your evidence and analysis supports the thesis or main argument of your paper*

1. This evidence illustrates the point that. . .
2. The . . .(quick summary of evidence and/or analysis) shows how. . .
3. This information supports the fact. . .because it shows how. . .
4. Essentially, (quick summary of evidence and/or analysis) demonstrates. . .
5. For this/these reason(s), it can be concluded that. . .

Figure 5.8   Sentence Starters for Argument Writing *Source:* www.virtuallibrary.info/peel-paragraph-writing.html.

Prompt: *"What was the worst impact of European colonialism on Native Americans?"*

Claim: The worst impact European colonialism had on Native Americans was the illnesses and deaths caused by diseases that were brought to the Americas.

A strong example that proves that European diseases had the worst impact on Native Americans is the vast number of deaths they caused. **For instance,** the article "The Story of. . .Smallpox – and other Deadly Eurasian Germs" from the PBS "Guns, Germs, and Steel" website, **explains how** diseases like smallpox were most likely responsible for the deaths of up to 95% of the indigenous people in the Americas (https://www.pbs.org/gunsgermssteel/variables/smallpox.html). **This evidence shows that** despite other factors that may have contributed to the deaths of Natives, diseases like smallpox took the most lives. **In addition,** North and South America "were virtually emptied of their native inhabitants" because of the viruses brought by European colonists (https://www.pbs.org/gunsgermssteel/variables/smallpox.html). **This evidence illustrates the point that** unlike violence or war, diseases had the most catastrophic impact on indigenous populations.

Another powerful example of the terrible impact of European diseases is the way they were used as weapons. **For instance** the online article "Atrocities Against Native Americans" from the website "United to End Genocide" **explains how** British colonists used smallpox against Natives who had no immunity against the disease (http://endgenocide.org/learn/past-genocides/native-americans/). **The fact that** British military leaders like Sir Jeffrey Amherst were encouraging colonists to spread smallpox with blankets **shows** how diseases were considered an effective strategy to exterminate Natives (http://endgenocide.org/learn/past-genocides/native-americans/). **From this** use of contaminated blankets **we can also infer that** British colonists saw this spread of disease as an opportunity to either gain their land and/or eliminate indigenous people as a threat.

For these reasons, it can be concluded that the illness and death caused by diseases was the worst impact of colonization on Native Americans.

Figure 5.9 Teacher Argument Model Response

Unit - French Revolution

Please use the following words in a paragraph summarizing what you know so far about the French Revolution. Be sure to use the terms in a way that shows your understanding of them and how they relate to each other.

Reign of Terror
Bastille
representative
execute
agency

_____

_____

_____

_____

_____

_____

_____

_____

_____

_____

_____

_____

_____

Figure 5.10 Word Bank Paragraph

CHAPTER 6

Mnemonics

What Is It?

A mnemonic is a learning technique used to improve memory. In this strategy we will share how you can use acronyms, visuals, stories, or songs to help students remember content. Though there are many ways to create a mnemonic, we will share an example from a geography class, which uses a combination of a story, key words, and visuals to help students remember countries of the world. It could also be used in a world history class to help remember the Axis and Allied Powers, in a US government class to remember the Bill of Rights, or any other content where memorization is critical.

Why We Like It

We've found success using mnemonics to help students learn the names and locations of countries of the world, but mnemonics isn't limited to geography. This strategy can promote active learning and increase engagement by providing opportunities for students to get out of their seats, get creative, and often get a little silly in any social studies class.

Mnemonics help students remember information more easily, freeing up their mental bandwidth to achieve higher levels of learning (Shah, Mullainathan, & Shafir, 2012, p. 683). Mental bandwidth refers to your brain's ability to focus on incoming information while weighed down by other concerns. Teaching students an easy way to remember basic data frees up "bandwidth" that they can use to process, analyze, and evaluate other information.

Supporting Research

Research shows that mnemonic strategies can greatly improve memory, which, in turn, can improve student performance on tests (Mastropieri & Scruggs, 1998, p. 203). In addition, mnemonics help students recall information more efficiently so that they can focus on higher-level thinking tasks (Putnam, 2015, p. 133).

Furthermore, "Whenever students exhibit difficulties learning and retaining verbal information, mnemonics instruction represents an important component to a teacher's arsenal of instructional strategies" (Scruggs, Mastropieri, Berkeley, & Marshak, 2010, p. 84). Among these helpful strategies that teachers can employ is the keyword method, in which students use familiar words to remember unknown words. Another is the letter strategy, in which students use an acronym to remember important information (Scruggs et al., 2010, p. 84). Examples of how to use each of these strategies are provided in this chapter.

Common Core Connections

The goal of the reading standards in the Common Core is to increase text comprehension. To do this, students need to further develop reading skills and be able to build knowledge over time. Mnemonics helps students remember what they are reading *today* to apply as prior knowledge *tomorrow*, assisting them in building a more coherent understanding of concepts (Coleman & Pimentel, 2012, p. 8).

The Common Core requires integration of visual information (like maps) with other information (2010l). A discussion of current events involving multiple countries becomes more approachable when students remember their locations (the example used in this chapter). Additionally, by using a story for map memorization, students are incorporating narrative elements into informational text – two of the three required Common Core text types (2010m). Once students progress with this strategy, they will be more prepared to create these blended writing genres.

Social Studies Connections

The mnemonic example in this chapter helps students directly explore the theme "Global Connections" from the National Council for the Social Studies Curriculum Standards. In this chapter, students wind their way around the world developing stories which often include key information about the countries, their relationships to one another, and/or their historical importance. Mnemonics can also be applied to other themes such as culture or civic ideals and practices.

Application

This strategy can work with a variety of social studies content including remembering causes and consequences of different wars, types of governments, or amendments. In this chapter, we will explain how we use a mnemonic to teach the names of countries in a region of the world. We use an entire class period to introduce the mnemonic in depth, and then a few minutes daily to review it. In our experience, it takes students about two to three weeks to learn a set of 10 countries, and then it's time to add a new set of countries to our mnemonic practice. We continue this process throughout the year. We will also share a variation of an acronym mnemonic that can be used to teach countries and military alliances.

This mnemonic learning process can easily be adapted for any social studies class where a list of information needs to be remembered, such as important battles in a particular war or main points in a famous speech. What follows is an overview of the process for introducing the mnemonic device as well as some ideas for how to reinforce the concepts.

STORY MNEMONICS

The process of creating a story to help students learn and remember content (in the context of geography) begins with choosing an area of the world and then 7–10 countries from that region. Most research shows that seven items is typically the largest amount of data that can be successfully added to working memory by most people at one time, though some results suggest that an "upper bound of 10–20 is realistic" (Bick & Rabinovich, 2009, pp. 218101–218103). It is important to include pieces of factual or historical information when creating the story. At the same time, however, the story should also be fun. Students look forward to the stories because they are silly and make the daily practice more enjoyable.

After the countries are chosen, it's important to be strategic about the order in which they are placed in the story. Using them in a familiar pattern works best. In other words, moving across a given continent from left to right or in a clockwise direction. In this example, we share a mnemonic for South America, beginning in Brazil and then moving in a mostly clockwise pattern around the continent.

Introducing the Story

Story day is an exciting one in our classroom. We begin by telling the story, as dramatically as possible, and instructing students to listen to it the first time. We add that they may be able to figure out some of the country names if they listen carefully. The basics of the story are outlined in the "story" section of Figure 6.1: Map Story Guide, South America. It doesn't need to be repeated exactly, but we stick to the same basic storyline each time we tell it. The italicized words represent what we call "link words" for the countries. These are special words that help spark student memory and help them recall the name of the country. You can choose link words in multiple ways:

- Rhyme or sound similar to the name of the country – *aren't you Tina* as the link words for Argentina
- Shape/size of the country – *big* as the link word for Brazil, the largest South American country
- Connect to information about the country – *bowl* as the link word for Bolivia, known for their bowler hats

The story we tell, for 10 countries in South America, is as follows:

Our bus tour of South America began in a **big** way in the **big** country known for its **big** parties. After staying up all night, we headed to a place known for hats shaped like **bowls**. Seeing all the hats shaped like **bowls** made us think about eating so, in the next country, we asked a **pair of guys** for a good lunch recommendation. After lunch, we wanted to get out of the urban areas and headed for a smaller country full of **wide open space**. Exploring the rolling grasslands next to a beautiful coast made for a great memory. Later on, as we were getting back on the tour bus, we noticed a girl who looked really familiar. We asked her, "Hey, we know you, **aren't you Tina**?" Unfortunately, we were wrong, and she wasn't Tina. So embarrassing! We drove through winding mountain roads through a long country shaped like a **chili pepper** on our way to an ancient city. Once we reached our destination, we climbed as far as we could into the mountains to see the **view,** and what an amazing **view,** even if we couldn't make it to the top of Machu Picchu. When we loaded back onto the bus this time, we had some mechanical trouble. The air conditioner quit working, which was really unfortunate because we were so close to the **equator**. The bus was really hot and getting pretty stinky. To take a break from the bus, we stopped for a parade where the people waved the **colors** of their country; yellow, blue, and red. Finally, at our last stop of the tour, we relaxed on the beach and watched the palm trees **swaying** in the breeze. It was a magical journey, full of fun, and we'll never forget our trip to South America.

After telling the story, teachers can pass out a blank map of South America and ask students to label the following countries; Brazil, Bolivia, Paraguay, Uruguay, Argentina, Chile, Peru, Ecuador, Colombia, and Venezuela. We pass out the map after the story because we like to encourage students to listen to the story and see if they can figure out the link words and country names before we reveal the names of the countries. This challenge gives a secondary reason to engage in the story – beyond enjoyment. The teacher pronounces the name of each country twice during the labeling process and students repeat them. It is important everyone participates in the choral practice of the country names because many will not be familiar to them. They will need this repetition to be able to participate in review activities later. The teacher retells the story after students label the map. Students often begin to make connections between the story and the map at this point. They also enjoy the feeling of success from guessing the connections as the story is retold.

The next step is to pass out Table 6.1: Map Story Guide. Students go through the story again, one piece at a time, filling in the graphic organizer with the following: name of country, link word, line from the story, and a quick visual for that part of the story. We allow students to do a quick web search for images they may be unfamiliar with (for example, the wide open rolling plains or "spaces" of Uruguay). It may be a good idea to have some hard copies of images available if there is no web access. Once students fill in their graphic organizer, which will serve as their study guide, we have them create a full-page visual on a country of their choice. We avoid the problem of too many students choosing the same one by allowing no more than three students per country. We instruct students to create a visual that is based on the mnemonic story. They can include link words but *cannot* use the name of the country (see Figure 6.2: Student Example of Map Visual for Practice A and Figure 6.3: Student Examples of Map Visual for Practice B). These visuals will be used during subsequent practice of the map story.

Table 6.1 Map Story Guide

Number	Country	Link word(s)	Story	Illustration

Reviewing the Story

On story day, students interact with the map by listening, speaking, reading, writing, and visualizing, but regular review is key for long-term memory (Ericcson, Chase, & Faloon, 1980, p. 1181). We review the mnemonic in some way almost every day for two to three weeks and then learn a new set of countries using a different mnemonic. The review might be no more than five minutes and could be part of the warm-up, mid-class to inject some energy, or during the last five minutes of class when students are attempting to pack up. When reviewing the mnemonic in various ways, it is helpful to remind students that employing multiple senses (speaking, drawing, gestures, and so forth) enhances memory ("Learning with All the Senses," 2015, para. 2). There are a variety of ways to keep this practice novel and interesting. Here are a few we've used:

- Have multiple students tell the story, each taking one piece. In the beginning they can use their story guide, but as they become more proficient, we encourage students to use their memory. They need not tell it exactly, but must use the basic story idea and the link words.

- Say the link word out loud and have students verbally respond, either as a class or individually, with the name of the country that goes with the link word or vice versa.

- Say the name of country or link word, have students point to the matching country on a blank copy of the map, and then ask them to check their neighbor's work for accuracy.

- Show students a visual (from the ones they created earlier) and have them say aloud or write the name of the corresponding country or link word.

- Project a large blank map and give students a sticky note with a link word or country name. Students can come up to the map and place their sticky on the corresponding country.

- Play a form of "Pictionary" by having students draw a visual for a country and have members of their team guess the name of the country. This works better after students have had more than one set of countries.

- Create stations around the room that have a map with a few countries numbered. Students rotate through stations writing down the names of the numbered countries.

When it comes to review, just remember to mix it up, have fun, and keep it short.

Acronym Mnemonics

To mix things up, we occasionally use acronyms in place of stories when learning countries of the world. With an acronym mnemonic, we take the first letter of each word students are to remember and use that letter to start another word. These new words make up an easy-to-remember phrase or sentence. For example, we have used the acronym MATLE (Most Ants Taste Like Eggs) for Morocco, Algeria, Tunisia, Libya, and Egypt. Obviously, this has nothing to do with that particular area of the world, but it's fun and students remember the sentence.

Acronym mnemonics can work well for other topics in social studies as well. We have used the acronym GUCS (Gentle Unicorns Create Sparkles) for Great Britain, the United States, China, and the Soviet Union for remembering the Allied Powers during World War II. For the Axis Powers we use JIG (Jumbo Iguanas Glow) for Japan, Italy, and Germany.

When creating an acronym mnemonic we have found phrases that err on the side of ridiculous to be most memorable.

DIFFERENTIATION

This strategy is already crafted in a way that helps support English language learners (ELLs) and students with learning differences. Students will benefit from the different techniques used and regular opportunities to review with the teacher and their classmates. Partnering students up to practice saying the mnemonic can help to increase confidence.

Also, because ELL students might have background knowledge of other countries, this might be an opportunity for students to use their funds of knowledge and impress their peers and teach the entire class by sharing their personal experiences. These pieces of information will bring the countries to life for all of the students. It is important to make sure you are not making students feel uncomfortable by putting them on the spot or requiring them to share. Teachers should always check in with ELLs ahead of time.

When telling the mnemonic story, keep in mind that there could be words unfamiliar to your ELL students. If that is the case, define their meaning in simplified language while telling the story.

ADVANCED EXTENSIONS

To push students even further with this strategy, have them create their own stories after you have modeled one. Each student can have his or her own version, or you can have the class vote on the "best" to be the class story for practice purposes. Another idea is to give students a theme on which to base their stories.

Choose a topic or current event and have students write a mnemonic based on it. For example, when doing a mnemonic for a map in Europe, we instructed students to write about the conflict within the European Union. This required students to consider the current issues (e.g., Brexit or immigration) and weave them into their mnemonic story.

Student Handouts and Examples

Figure 6.1: Map Story Guide, South America
Table 6.1: Map Story Guide
Figure 6.2: Student Examples of Map Visual for Practice A
Figure 6.3: Student Examples of Map Visual for Practice B

What Could Go Wrong?

The travel story mnemonic is fun for learning country names and facts, but after several versions, both students and teachers can get tired of it. To change it up, in our study of Northern Africa, we wrote a themed mnemonic about building a house. Each country's link word was connected to a material that might be needed for construction. For example, Morocco became *more rocks*, as in "we needed *more rocks* to construct our house."

Be thoughtful when choosing a link word. For example, avoid using made-up words and other place names for link words like "Portland" for "Portugal." Try not to recycle old link words into new stories because this can lead to student confusion. Also, don't forget to continue reviewing prior stories as you build new mnemonics throughout the year.

In addition to these practical aspects of what could go wrong, there is the most important potential mistake: making the memorization of names the primary learning objective instead of using that memorization as a tool to make higher-order thinking activities more accessible. As Nobel Prize winner Richard Feynman pointed out, there is a difference between knowing the name of something and understanding it (Richard Feynman, n.d., 2014). For example, learning the names of countries should be a precursor to learning about their culture, their history, and the challenges they may face today.

Technology Connections

Students can turn their mnemonics into digital stories. Resources can be found at Larry Ferlazzo's blog post "The Best Digital Storytelling Resources" (http://larryferlazzo.edublogs.org/2009/04/15/the-best-digital-storytelling-resources).

Another website for students to visit is Flocabulary (www.flocabulary.com). This site has videos using rap to help students remember information on many different topics and may give students ideas about creating social studies raps using their mnemonics.

Attribution

We were first introduced to using mnemonics in the social studies classroom by Kelly Young, creator of Pebble Creek curriculum (www.pebblecreeklabs.com).

Figures

Number	Country	Link word(s)	Story	Illustration
1	Brazil	big	Our bus tour of South America began in a big way in a big country known for its big parties.	
2	Bolivia	bowl	After staying up all night, we headed to a place known for hats shaped like bowls.	
3	Paraguay	pair of guys	We asked a pair of guys for a good lunch recommendation.	
4	Uruguay	wide open spaces	After lunch, we wanted to get out of the urban areas and headed for a smaller country full of wide open spaces.	
5	Argentina	aren't you Tina?	We noticed a girl that looked really familiar, we asked her, "Hey, we know you, aren't you Tina?"	
6	Chile	shaped like a chili pepper	We drove through winding mountain roads through a long country shaped like a chili pepper.	
7	Peru	view	We drove into the mountains to see the view, and what an amazing view it was even if we couldn't make it to the top of Machu Picchu.	

Figure 6.1 Map Story Guide, South America

8	Ecuador	equator	We were so close to the equator that the bus was really hot and getting pretty stinky.	
9	Colombia	colors	We stopped for a parade where the people waved the colors of their country.	
10	Venezuela	swaying	We relaxed on the beach and watched the palm trees swaying in the breeze.	

Figure 6.1 (Continued)

Bowl Shaped Hat - Bolivia

Figure 6.2 Student Examples of Map Visual for Practice A

Big Party–Brazil

Figure 6.3 Student Examples of Map Visual for Practice B

CHAPTER 7

Timelines Revisited

What Is It?

Traditionally, timeline activities consist of listing events chronologically to help students understand the development of historical phenomena.

In a twist on timelines, this chapter shares how we modify them to move beyond a chronological order of events by adding a social-emotional learning (SEL) component to the study of inspiring historical figures. In this activity, students practice higher-order thinking and emotional intelligence by creating a timeline of the most significant events in *their* lives. Then, students create a timeline about the life of an inspiring historical figure of their choice. The activity concludes with students reflecting on connections between both timelines.

There are obviously many other ways to use timelines. We include a list of some of them, as well.

Why We Like It

Timelines serve as useful tools for students who need visual organizational structures to better understand content. In addition, they lend themselves to continual updating as students are learning new material.

In our ethnic studies courses, both students and teachers have been deeply moved by the SEL timeline activity. It not only helps students open up about themselves but also promotes a culture of emotional safety and belonging. When students (and teachers!) share about difficulties in their lives and/or moments of great joy, the class seems to fundamentally shift in the best of ways. There is a heightened sense of community and empathy after learning about similarities in each other's backgrounds.

Students tend to see history as more relevant when they create timelines for historical figures and are guided to make connections to their own lives. They can become more engaged in social studies when they identify hardships, struggles, and/or achievements they share with these figures.

Supporting Research

Timelines encourage students to visualize both historical events and the relationships between them (Fordham, Wellman, & Sandmann, 2010, p. 156).

The SEL timelines in this chapter also help students see connections between themselves and the people they are studying. This activity helps social studies teachers "develop classrooms that help students make sense of their own lives" (Ross, 2001, p. 135). In other words, inviting students to connect to their own experiences makes this activity more culturally relevant and can heighten overall engagement in the classroom (Willis, Faeth, & Immordino-Yang, in Sousa, 2010, p. 77).

Common Core Connections

The Integration of Knowledge and Ideas strand of the Common Core Standards for Social Studies and History encourages the use of primary and secondary sources to understand historical events (Common Core, 2010n). The strategies in this chapter direct students to use multiple sources such as class readings and digital resources to build a timeline about the life of a historical figure.

In addition, the Common Core Key Ideas and Details strand states that students need to "determine whether earlier events caused later ones or simply preceded them" (Common Core, 2010o). In a timeline, this is done by carefully analyzing a sequence of events and identifying the relationship between events.

Social Studies Connections

The Curriculum Standards from the National Council for the Social Studies lists "Individual Development and Identity" as one of the 10 themes of social studies. It asserts, "social studies programs should include experiences that provide for the study of individual development and identity" (National Council for the Social Studies, n.d.). The SEL timeline in this chapter directly addresses this theme. In addition, timelines can fit into the "Time, Continuity and Change" theme.

Application

Our primary activity, Identity Timelines, is a two-phase project. In the first phase, we build a personal identity timeline for students to explore events in their lives. This socially and emotionally based activity helps to build a positive classroom environment while helping students analyze their identities as well as those of others. Students who have this self-awareness, especially ethnic identity, tend to do better academically (Sleeter, 2011, p. vii).

The second phase of the project asks students to create another Identity Timeline, but this time for a historical figure. Students research both challenges and accomplishments of this person. After this timeline is completed, we bring the project full-circle by helping students identify connections between themselves and the historical figure.

We conclude this Application section with a list of simple and creative ways timelines can be used in any social studies course.

IDENTITY TIMELINES

The two-phase project described in this section tends to take about three to four days. In the first phase, the teacher uses events from his/her own life to model how to make an identity timeline. The teacher example provides guidance for both the structure and type of life events that might be added. Then, students create their own timeline based on the teacher's model.

We also incorporate a protocol for students to share their timelines as a community building exercise. Creating a sense of community in the classroom can lead to increased academic motivation (Solomon, Battistich, Watson, Schaps, & Lewis, 2000, p. 2).

The second phase asks them to create a timeline of a historical figure. Students practice making personal connections with this person, which can increase relevance (Willis, Faeth, & Immordino-Yang, in Sousa, 2010, p. 77).

We typically use this activity toward the beginning of our identity unit in our ethnic studies course, which can help students to further understand their own lives in order to make personal connections with content (Ross, 2001, p. 135).

This kind of tandem assignment can be used in any social studies class for the same purpose. In addition, using the process we describe for a historical figure timeline can be used on its own multiple times during the year in any class.

Teacher Identity Timeline

Creating a model timeline about *our* lives serves two major purposes: it models the basic components of the activity and, most importantly, the openness we want our students to bring to *their* timeline.

We make sure to have 8 to 10 items, including personal and professional triumphs and challenges on our teacher timeline. Based on our knowledge of our students' lives we try to be sensitive and avoid triggers that may relate to student trauma. For example, if one of our student's parents has recently died, we might think twice about sharing our experience of a similar tragedy. We do try to be as open as possible while still keeping the activity emotionally safe. This sharing shows our students that they can feel safe to do the same. We read aloud the items from our timeline. Here is one example from Figure 7.1: Identity Timeline – Teacher Model:

> 2017. My daughter was born. I was overjoyed but also very scared because she had many health problems. This is important because it showed me how my family and I can overcome anything.

After sharing, we point out the main features to students. We note how our items are listed from earliest to most recent. In addition, each event includes a short description along with its significance. We include visuals for several of the items.

After our example is complete, we announce that it is now the students' turn to create a timeline about themselves.

Student Identity Timeline

The student identity timeline, like the teacher model, should have 8 to 10 significant life events in chronological order. Each event should include a brief description, along with an explanation about its significance, and be accompanied by a visual. A more detailed list of requirements, such as legible writing and a creative title, is listed in Table 7.1: Timeline Grading Rubric. We typically share this rubric

Table 7.1 Timeline Grading Rubric

	Excellent 4	**Good 3**	**Satisfactory 2**	**Needs Improvement 0–1**
Title	The timeline has a creative title that accurately describes the material and is easy to locate.	The timeline has a title that describes the material and is easy to locate.	The timeline has a title that is easy to locate.	The title is missing or difficult to locate.
Documentation of Events	The timeline contains 10 significant events. This includes date (or age) and description.	The timeline contains at least 8–9 significant events. This includes date and description.	The timeline contains at least 5–7 significant events. This includes date and description.	The timeline contains less than 5 significant events. This includes date and description.
Significance of Events	Events described in timeline are descriptive and significance of event is well explained.	Description and significance are given with some detail.	Events are listed but little description given.	No description of events.
Visuals	All visuals clearly represent what was written and are balanced with text use.	All visuals clearly represent what was written, but there appear to be a few missing.	Some visuals clearly represent what was written, and there appear to be too few.	Several visuals are not effective or are missing.
Legibility	Legible handwriting, typing, or printing.	Marginally legible handwriting, typing, or printing.	Writing is not legible in places.	Writing is not legible.

with students right before they start building their identity timelines. In addition to our teacher model, students have found it helpful and motivating to view previous student examples.

Before students start their timelines, we have found it beneficial to scaffold the activity with Table 7.2: Timeline Brainstorm. This handout gives students the opportunity to list any events that they consider significant and why they are important. We advise everyone not to worry if they don't remember the exact year – they can just give the best estimate possible. In addition, there are extra rows so students can list multiple ideas and then choose their top 8 to 10.

Table 7.2 Timeline Brainstorm

Year (guess is fine)	Event *List important events in your life. Both the good and the bad.*
	This is significant because . . .
	This is significant because . . .
	This is significant because . . .
	This is significant because . . .
	This is significant because . . .
	This is significant because . . .

(Continued)

Table 7.2   (Continued)

Year (guess is fine)	Event *List important events in your life. Both the good and the bad.*
	This is significant because . . .
	This is significant because . . .
	This is significant because . . .
	This is significant because . . .
	This is significant because . . .
	This is significant because . . .

We project the following questions while students are working on Table 7.2: Timeline Brainstorm to help students reflect on their lives:

- When is a time that you have felt happy, sad, or mad?
- What is a memory or story that you and your family share?
- What is something that caused great change in your life, good or bad?

We also provide the following sentence starters to help students clearly describe their life events and their significance on their identity timeline:

- On this day . . .
- This is when . . .
- This event was important because . . .
- This day means a lot to me because . . .

Some students will want to create an unconventional timeline. For example, a winding path or a jagged line like a heartbeat monitor can be used to organize all the events. We welcome the creativity as long as there is a clear chronological order. See Figure 7.2: Student Example: Identity Timeline for a sample created by one of our students.

Sharing

After students are done working on their timelines, we put the classroom desks in a circle. We tell students that they have the power to decide what they feel comfortable sharing when responding to the following questions (which we post on the projector screen). We ask the first question, go around the circle, then ask the next one, and so on – depending on time:

1. What is an event on your timeline that makes you smile? Please read your description and explain why.
2. What is an event on your timeline that makes you sad or mad? Please read your description and explain why.
3. What is something you have realized about yourself or people in this class by taking part in this identity timeline activity?

We like to end with the last question about learning because it is an opportunity to remind students that what they share is being listened to and valued by others. In other words, the question helps build a sense of community and ensures a positive closing.

Another option is to invite students to share their entire timelines with each other either in small groups or through a "rotation" system. In this sharing structure, students in different rows move forward after they talk with the person next to them.

Historical Figure Timeline

Note: The activity in this section, making a timeline of a historical figure, can also be used (with minor modifications) as a stand-alone assignment without students having to make personal connections.

To connect the strategy back to the content, we ask students to create an identity timeline about a major historical figure. This activity serves two purposes. First, students learn social studies content through their research. Second, we increase relevancy by giving students an opportunity to make connections with people from history. Because we typically use this activity in ethnic studies, we tend to focus on activists who fought systematic racism or oppression in the United States like Cesar Chavez (Mexican American farm worker activist), Grace Lee Boggs (Asian American poverty activist), Diane Nash (African American Civil Rights Activist), or Ruth Bader Ginsburg (gender equality advocate and Supreme Court justice).

We purposely pick figures who have faced struggles in their lives. We make it a priority to include a variety of people to show diversity in race, gender, and/or personal backgrounds. We also try our best to not just pick well-known figures, but include people that don't get as much attention despite their great contributions. When selecting examples for other social studies subjects, we encourage the same criteria. For example, when teaching about westward expansion in US history, a teacher can have students make a timeline on a prominent Native American leader like Black Kettle, who worked to fight the encroachment of settlers on their land. In world history, a teacher could have students make a timeline about an activist like Beatrice Webb, who fought for factory workers' rights during the Industrial Revolution.

No matter the topic, we recommend giving students a choice of four to six historical figures. Students tend to feel more invested in their work if they have the power to choose the focus of their study. This sense of autonomy can lead to higher engagement (Patall, Cooper, & Robinson, 2008).

We usually give students a list of choices on either a handout or a slideshow. We like to include a picture of each figure along with a short biography (no more than two sentences). After students review the choices, they make their selections and begin their research. We often use Google Classroom and share links to at least two sites per historical figure that provide biographical information. A teacher can print out the information for students to use as well.

We like to use sites that we have reviewed and know will provide our students with the kinds of details that can foster personal connections down the road. In other words, we want sites that give information on both challenges *and* achievements. This way, students can make clear connections between themselves and the figures. For example, Ruth Bader Ginsburg lost her mother at a young age. The loss of a loved one is very relatable for many students. Please refer to our Technology Connections section for recommendations on sites to use.

Students use Table 7.3: Historical Figure Research to record 12 major life events as well as their significance. They are required to find at least *one* event for each box on the organizer. In addition to guiding students toward major accomplishments of their figure, we ask them to include moments of failure, tragedy, or influential

Table 7.3 Historical Figure Research

Events or Information to Look for When Researching Your Historical Figure
Fill-out the following chart with information about the historical figure you chose. Every box represents the different kinds of life events you need to include. Each box must include one specific event. It is up to you which sections have more than one fact so that you have a total of 12 on this paper.
A. Why is this person well known? Look for specific accomplishments.   These accomplishments are significant because . . .
B. What are the hardships they have had to endure and/or overcome? Include both personal and professional.   These hardships are significant because . . .
C. What events in their youth may have greatly impacted them?   These events in their youth are significant because . . .

(Continued)

Table 7.3   *(Continued)*

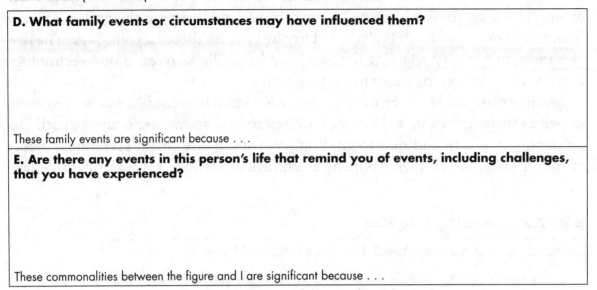

D. What family events or circumstances may have influenced them?
These family events are significant because . . .
E. Are there any events in this person's life that remind you of events, including challenges, that you have experienced?
These commonalities between the figure and I are significant because . . .

experiences from childhood to adulthood. Once students have completed their handouts, we have them choose 8 to 10 events to build a timeline using the same steps they used in their personal version.

Identifying Personal Connections

After students have completed both timelines, we pass out Table 7.4: Personal Connections. The first three questions ask students to reflect on aspects of their figure by posing questions like "What is an event in this person's life that surprised you?" These questions prime students to make connections in later writing tasks.

The last two boxes of the handout prompt students to find experiences they have in common with their historical figure such as loss, pain, and challenges. These questions are open-ended so students don't feel like they have to find an event that is exactly the same. For example, if students are researching Cesar Chavez, they might relate to dealing with poverty, even though they did not grow up in the Dust Bowl during the Great Depression, as his family did.

After students are done answering the analysis questions, we set them up in groups of three. Students select and share a response from one of the first three questions in Table 7.4: Personal Connections. Second, students share one commonality that they have with their historical figure. After the groups are done, we gather everyone back together and call on people to report to the class what stood out to their groups. This debriefing helps students see the universal human experience between these historical figures and themselves, despite obvious major differences.

Table 7.4   Personal Connections

1. What is an event in this person's life that surprised you?
2. What is an event in this person's life that you think required them to have grit or persist against great odds?
3. What is an event in this person's life where you think they felt very happy?
4. After reviewing your identity timeline and the timeline of your historical figure, describe an event where you both experienced pain and/or loss.
5. What is something else you and this figure have in common? For example, you could describe challenges that you both had to overcome. It does not have to be an exact similarity and it might not even be something in your Identity timeline.

Some additional follow-up writing activities can include the following prompts:

- After reviewing and reflecting on the items of your historical figure timeline, what do you think this person *should be* known for the most? Explain.

- If someone in the future were making a timeline about your life, what would you want to be known for? Explain.

- What would most people have in common with the person you researched? Explain.

ADDITIONAL TIMELINE ACTIVITIES

Here are some additional ideas for using timelines in any social studies class.

- Themed Timelines: Students create a timeline about a series of 10 to 15 major events (e.g., the effects of European colonization on Native Americans) by writing a short description of each event and its significance, along with drawing an illustration for each one. Afterward, students can share their timelines with classmates and use them for extended work.

  This work could include responding to the following questions in an ABC format (Answer the question, Back-it-up with evidence, Commentary on the evidence – please refer to Chapter 5: Writing in Social Studies for more ideas):

  1. Which of these events do you think had the biggest impact on our lives today? Why?

  2. Which of these events do you think had the biggest impact on people at that time? Why?

  3. What is a possible pattern in your timeline? In other words, what seems to keep repeating? Please share a possible reason why this type of event keeps happening.

  4. Rank the events on your timeline, in order, from least to most important. Explain your rationale.

- Group Timelines – Small groups can develop a timeline about an event or a person with 12 items each. Students can put each event on an index card with the title, a short description, and an explanation of its significance, along with a visual. These can be hung on a string or taped to poster paper. Groups can then share their creations with classmates and identify common and uncommon elements.

- Digital Timelines – The timeline from ReadWriteThink (www.readwriteth-ink.org/files/resources/interactives/timeline_2) is one of the easiest (and free!) applications available for use in the classroom. Students enter names, dates, and other information and a digital timeline is built for them. In addition, students can insert images from downloaded files. This tool can be especially helpful to ensure a neat and professional looking product. There are also many other online tools that can be used for this purpose – see the Technology Connections section for those links.

- Comparing Timelines – Selecting timelines from multiple sources on the same topic or person not only exposes students to content, but can also serve as a lesson about multiple perspectives or source bias. Students can use a Venn diagram to compare both. Guiding questions, like the following, can be provided to help with the analysis:

1. Look for an event mentioned on both timelines and compare the content. How is it similar? How is it different?

2. What is one event in one timeline that is not mentioned in the other? Why do you think the person creating the timeline decided to add that event? Why do you think the other left it out?

3. After reviewing all the items on the timelines, what seems to be the focus or the main point they are trying to communicate about this topic?

- Sequencing Activity – At the end of a unit, students can be given an out-of-order timeline of events (without specific dates). They can then be asked to put it in the correct chronological order. See Chapter 8: Current Event Case Study for specific instructions on how to create sequencing activities. That same chapter also shares research documenting their value as a learning tool.

- Progressive Classroom Timeline – Setting up a large classroom timeline that can be updated throughout the school year can provide a visual of chronological thinking and context for social studies. A teacher can mark the beginning of the class timeline with the year of the oldest topic or event. Students can take ownership of the timeline as the year progresses by adding visuals, specific events, historical figures, and key vocabulary to represent their learning.

- Alternative timelines – Students can work in pairs to identify a "point of divergence" – in other words, an event that could have happened differently (Washington dying at Valley Forge, Japan not attacking Pearl Harbor, etc.). Then, using research and critical thinking skills, they can create a timeline of what they imagine would then have happened after that change. See "The Best Resources for Teaching 'What If?' History Lessons" at Larry Ferlazzo's blog for examples and lesson plans (http://larryferlazzo.edublogs.org/2012/05/19/the-best-resources-for-teaching-what-if-history-lessons).

- Timeline Formats – Scores of different ways to physically represent timelines can easily be found online by searching "creative timelines."

DIFFERENTIATION

One way to assist ELL and other students with the writing aspect of all timeline activities is to provide sentence starters or sentence frames. For example, when students are brainstorming events in their own lives in the identity timeline, they might have an easier time putting pen to paper with sentence starters like "A big change in my life was when . . ." To provide even more support, a sentence frame can be help-ful. For example:

"In my life, I was the happiest when _____

because _____."

To assist students in their research, teachers can provide links to biographies that are particularly accessible to them. The Technology Connections section includes links to these resources.

ADVANCED EXTENSIONS

The linear format of a historical timeline lends itself to efficient pattern finding that is part of the inductive process (Silver, Dewing, & Perini, 2012). For example, at the end of our colonization of Native Americans unit, we review our timeline and have students write an essay explaining what they think are two or three major themes or patterns. We ask, "What keeps coming up in the history of Native Ameri-cans?" Students highlight ideas or actions that repeat on their timeline like forced assimilation tactics, widespread disease, and violence against Native Americans.

Another extension for this strategy is to assign individual students to further research a specific item on a timeline. For example, for a timeline about European colonization in North America, they can choose one of the European Conquista-dors, like Juan Ponce de León, to study more in depth. Students can then create an additional timeline about this individual and the outcomes of his actions after looking for additional resources. The same process can be followed for a specific event. For instance, if students have created a timeline about World War I, they can select an item like the Battle of the Somme and conduct further research to create an additional timeline.

Student Handouts and Examples

Figure 7.1: Identity Timeline – Teacher Model
Table 7.1: Timeline Grading Rubric
Table 7.2: Timeline Brainstorm
Figure 7.2: Student Example: Identity Timeline
Table 7.3: Historical Figure Research
Table 7.4: Personal Connections

What Could Go Wrong?

Some students may become emotional when sharing their identity timelines or listening to their peers. Other students may shut down or even refuse to participate. These reactions aren't wrong, but what can be wrong is if a teacher is unprepared for these kinds of responses. The best preparation is to have positive relationships with your students and know potential triggers in advance. Also, having a class protocol, like a signal, can provide students a safe way to step out of the activity if they need a break. Of course, another important rule is that students can always pass and not share if their events are too personal or sensitive.

Don't go overboard on using timelines. Don't have students create them every week! They can grow old and stale. Be strategic about when you use them – consider when having a hands-on activity could be useful to liven-up a classroom that has been focused on individual seat work for a while and/or when you are studying a topic that could be particularly beneficial for students to learn chronologically (a war, or the biography of a significant figure like Harriet Tubman, etc.).

Technology Connections

There are many online timeline generators that provide templates and helpful tools. In addition, Larry Ferlazzo's blog post "The Best Tools for Making Online Timelines" (http://larryferlazzo.edublogs.org/2008/08/06/the-best-tools-for-making-online-timelines) gives a list of resources to help teachers support the creation of digital timelines. Once students complete a digital timeline, they can post them on Google Classroom or a class blog for other students to view and make positive and thoughtful comments (modeling is important here).

The Biography Channel website (www.biography.com) is a good starting point for looking up influential historical figures. Also, there are thousands of biographies accessible to English Language Learners that can be found in Larry Ferlazzo's blog post "The Best Resources for Researching and Writing Biographical Essays" (http://larryferlazzo.edublogs.org/2009/03/18/the-best-resources-for-researching-writing-biographies).

Attribution

The student identity timeline portion of this strategy is an adapted version of Keoni Chock's activity. Keoni is a social studies teacher at Luther Burbank High School in Sacramento, California.

Figures

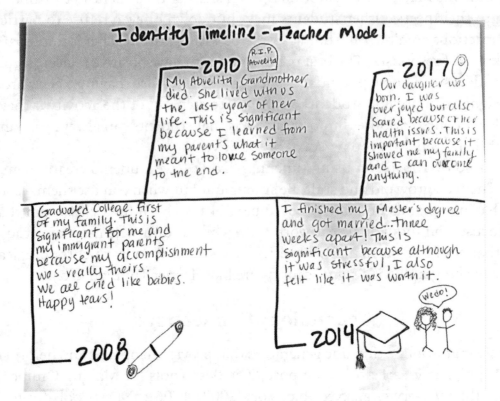

Figure 7.1 Identity Timeline – Teacher Model

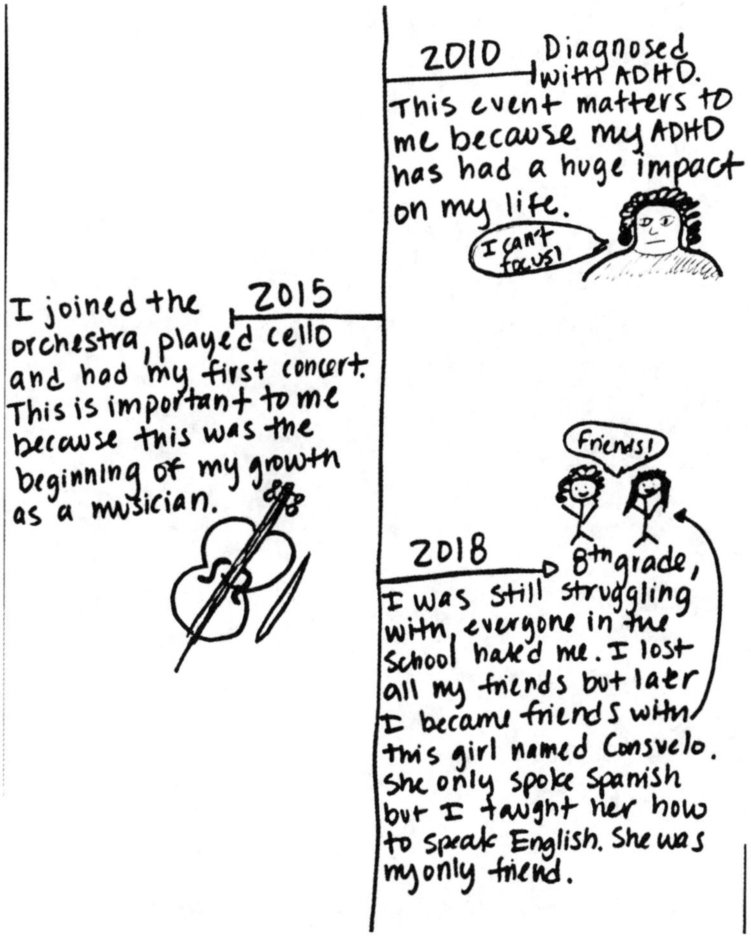

Figure 7.2 Student Example: Identity Timeline

CHAPTER 8

Current Event Case Study

What Is It?

The social studies classroom is an obvious place to study current events. We can help students understand the complexity of our modern world by recognizing that events don't occur in a vacuum and that there is a cause and effect that may be seen or unseen.

In this chapter, we describe a series of phases we use to guide students through the close examination of an individual current event. This process can help develop research skills and also creates opportunities to introduce bias awareness.

The process we use follows the basic outline of a traditional case study which, according to the National Council for the Social Studies, involves four steps: mapping out the facts, examining the issues involved, investigating the arguments of each side, and eventually making a decision about the case (McDonnell, 2002).

Why We Like It

The study of current events increases relevance. It helps students see connections between the content, themselves, and the world around them. This process can result in increased engagement, which can improve student motivation and academic performance (Frymier & Shulman, 2009, p. 46).

We like the way the study of current events can fit into any social studies course and, if chosen carefully, can help students connect to events of the past. Pictures and hashtags about current events flood our students' social media accounts. The abundance of information, however, does not equal deep understanding of issues. In our experience, a case study can help to develop the skills needed to properly analyze current events and determine the credibility of sources. Students must learn how to be careful consumers of news by questioning and utilizing many sources to form a more accurate picture.

Students become problem solvers during the inquiry process utilized in this strategy and teachers serve as facilitators. Acting in these roles can increase both engagement and critical thinking ("Concept to Classroom," n.d., para. 3).

Supporting Research

Research shows that case studies can be beneficial in deepening student understanding of a topic, as well as developing the skills used to study and learn information (Flyvbjerg, 2006, p. 222, para. 3). Additional studies support the student-centered learning model embedded in this process where students choose what interests them, ask their own questions, and direct their own investigations (McKenna, 2014).

Common Core Connections

A current event case study meets a major criteria of the Common Core Standards for Reading in History/Social Studies as seen in the Craft and Structure strand. It states that students should read multiple perspectives on the same topic (Common Core, 2010p). Additionally, students practice evidence-based writing, a touchstone of the Common Core Writing Standards as noted in the Text Types and Purposes strand. This standard requires students to write evidence-based arguments that "develop claim(s) and counterclaims fairly and thoroughly, supplying the most relevant data and evidence" (Common Core, 2010q).

Social Studies Connections

The College, Career, and Civic Life (C3) Framework developed by the National Council for the Social Studies (2010) was created for the purpose of increasing rigor and aligning social studies courses to the Common Core Standards. One of the main tenets of these standards is the use of inquiry, a type of structured investigation. With this method, teachers are able to engage students in a guided investigation of a real world topic. This process can help students to "become active and engaged citizens in the 21st century" (National Council for the Social Studies, 2010).

Application

In this section, we lay out a basic process that can be applied to almost any current event. It is scaffolded to meet varied needs by allowing the teacher and students to select texts at different levels of complexity. The four phases of our current event case study are sequencing of events, developing questions, bias awareness and research, and written analysis.

Of course, there are many other ways to tackle current events in the classroom. Following our discussion of the case study method, we also include a short section listing other strategies for teaching and learning about current events.

SEQUENCING OF EVENTS

The first phase of our case study process is called "sequencing." It involves teachers selecting a text, placing paragraphs out of order, and then having students read and reorder the text correctly based on context clues ("Story Sequence," n.d.). In other words, students are given the text out of order chronologically and have to use clues to discern the correct sequence. Having students practice sequencing can help them improve their understanding and memory of information (Moss, 2005, p. 52).

Selection and Preparation of the Text

We typically select a current event that can increase relevance for a concept students are studying in class. For example, we connected our study of the First Amendment to the August 2017 events in Charlottesville, Virginia. At this event, white supremacists gathered to protest the planned removal of a Confederate statue. A white supremacist subsequently murdered a counter-protester. Although some students were not particularly engaged with an overview of the First Amendment, many became "hooked" when we showed images or hashtags associated with the Charlottesville events.

Once a topic has been selected, the next step is to find a text that contains an overview and/or timeline of the topic or event. We have had success with doing an Internet search using the topic, plus the word *overview* or *timeline of events*. The website Newsela (https://newsela.com) is a good resource for news articles that are fairly short, cover the main points of a topic, and can be adjusted for different reading levels. Because this text will serve as the foundation for the case study, it is important to select an overview with minimal bias from a reputable news source. It may also be necessary to use selections from multiple sources and combine them into one document (of course, always providing attribution).

There are two ways (and probably more that we haven't thought of) to prepare the text for students to sequence.

1. Full Text Out of Order
   We copy and paste the selected text onto a new document so that paragraphs are out of order (making sure that we save a correct version for our answer sheet!). This out-of-order text will be given to students. After reading and

identifying context clues in the text and highlighting them (described in detail later on in this chapter), students then cut apart each paragraph. Next, students place the paragraphs in order by using the clues they previously identified. After determining the actual order of the text and having it reviewed by the teacher, students glue the passages down on a new sheet of paper.

2. Precut Passages

Alternatively, a teacher could precut all the sections of text and pass them out one at a time, out of order, for students to read and highlight sequence clues. This method allows for very careful control over the pace of the task since students only get a piece at a time. The teacher still does the modeling described in the next section for two passages prior to letting students work independently or in pairs.

Reading and Sequencing the Text

With either format chosen for sequencing, we begin the activity by asking students to clear their desks of everything except for a pen or highlighter and the document. We then model the process of locating context clues for two passages. To model, we display a passage on the document camera. We then highlight the context clues that may help identify the correct sequence. For example, in the article about the Charlottesville protests, we might underline dates, as well as phrases like, "Early in the day" and "hours after the state of emergency was declared." We explain that these clues help sequence the information because early gives us the sense that this passage likely occurs near the start of the text. On the other hand, information in the second phrase tells us that the passage will go *after* a declaration of a state of emergency.

If students are working with a full out-of-order text, we ask them to cut it apart and continue reading and identifying context clues for the remaining portions of the article. For articles that have been precut, we continue passing out sections one at a time. In both situations, students continue to read the paragraphs and adjust and re-adjust their order based on new information. We move about the classroom while they work, offering support and guidance to struggling students.

The process of finding clues and placing the pieces in order is reminiscent of a puzzle, which can be engaging for students and also help them attain a state of "flow," popularized by Mihaly Csikszentmihalyi (Shernoff, 2013, p. 67). This state of flow is described as an "optimal state of cognitive and emotional engagement" and can be achieved when students feel enjoyment as they dig into tasks (Shernoff, 2013, p. 12). For example, they may feel a sense of satisfaction each time they identify a context clue that can help them sequence the text.

This process also encourages multiple readings of the text, which can benefit student comprehension. Each time a student rereads a passage they have an opportunity to glean new information or understanding.

When a student thinks they are done, we check the sequence of their text. Once we have confirmed a student's work, they can glue or staple the paragraphs in the correct order. We may also ask them to help us check the accuracy of their classmates' work.

Once the class has the text in the correct order, we assign one of the passages—in other words, one piece of a timeline – to a set of partners. The pair is asked to reread their passage and come up with a short summary. Table 8.1: Timeline Organizer may be used for this (see also Table 8.2: Timeline Organizer Example). Collaborating with a partner can further improve comprehension of the text as students work together to build a summary. The Common Core Standards emphasize collaboration as a critical skill (Common Core, 2010r). This skill has been shown to "foster reflective thinking," among other benefits (Storch, 2005, p. 154).

Table 8.1 Timeline Organizer

Student Name	
Date	
Time	
Main Event	

Table 8.2 Timeline Organizer Example

Student Name	
Date	*Monday, August 14, 2017*
Time	
Main Event	*The president re-addresses the first statement, but now saying "Neo-Nazis" and "KKK" by name.*

These partner-created summaries are then placed on a class timeline (see Figure 8.1: Timeline Example). The class timeline is a large sheet of butcher paper we put up on one wall of the classroom. This large visual serves as a reference point as students continue their study of the event. It can be left up for the duration of the study or removed daily as needed.

DEVELOPING QUESTIONS

The next phase of the current event case study is to develop questions. These student generated queries help direct research about the event. Offering students a choice of what question they would like to research can promote autonomy. This type of cognitive choice, in which students determine, develop, and select their own research question, may encourage lasting student motivation (Ferlazzo, 2015b, p. 5).

To help students develop strong research questions, we first model the process. We focus on one part of the timeline and generate multiple questions on a sheet of paper. For example, when focusing on the Charlottesville timeline, we selected the portion that discusses the murder of a young woman protestor named Heather Heyer. We developed the following questions:

- What was the criminal background of the driver?
- Why did the driver purposefully hit the woman?
- To what extent was the driver involved with white supremacists or other hate groups?
- What was Heather Heyer's background?
- What happened to the other people hit by the car?

In our experience, after coming up with a few questions, students then begin to share their own questions about the incident. We add these questions to our list.

We then give a set amount of time, usually five minutes or so, for students to choose a piece of the timeline (they may use the one they summarized or pick another section) and generate their own list of questions. If you are worried about too many students focusing on the same section of the timeline, you could assign parts to different groups. For example, we may allow one group to choose from the first three events, while another chooses from the next three events, and so on.

Once students have generated their lists, we instruct them to circle what they consider to be their top three most interesting questions. They share them with their partners, who are instructed to give their opinion on which question they think is the best and why.

Some students struggle to word questions properly or ask questions that may be too narrow or too vague. Sharing with a partner can help to avoid some of these issues, but you can never go wrong with teacher modeling. It can be helpful for the teacher to select a few student questions to rewrite with the class. For example, in our Charlottesville case study, many students asked, "Did the guy go to jail for killing the woman?" which we turned into "How was the driver punished?" We explain that this adaptation now opens up the research to look into what happened to the accused after the death of Heather Heyer, rather than leading students to the obvious answer of "Yes."

After giving and receiving feedback, and seeing the teacher model, each individual student chooses a research question. We then tell students to write this question near the event that inspired it – on both their personal copy of the timeline and the larger class version. We permit them to have the same or similar questions. If a teacher would prefer to not have duplicates, students may be asked to select one of the other questions from their previously developed top three.

Although this chapter describes the process of researching only one question, we often have students return to their lists or create new ones for further research. For example, a student may initially research why the city of Charlottesville decided to remove the Confederate statue. After learning more, students may begin to wonder what other Confederate statues exist or if other places have had similar conflicts about statue removal. These may become questions that guide a second round of research.

During the examination of any specific current event, it is easy to "not see the forest for the trees." In other words, we can get "caught-up" in the details of what happened during the event without spending substantial amounts of class time on bigger issues that might have given rise to that event, or on the more long-term consequences of the event. In the case of Charlottesville, for example, we created opportunities to discuss race and racism (both in the South and in our community) and who gets memorialized and why.

NOTE: The next phase describes a process to research student-generated questions about a current event through the lens of bias awareness. If teachers are pressed for time – as we are sometimes – another option is to just ask students to research their questions online without this more complicated process of examining media bias. If you choose that option, you can then skip directly to the "Written Analysis" phase.

BIAS AWARENESS AND RESEARCH

In the next phase of the current event case study, students are given guidance for researching their questions while also practicing how to identify bias in the news. Identifying bias is the first step in a longer process of helping students to become careful consumers of news.

Our teaching of bias begins by introducing the term *loaded language,* and defining it as words or phrases that are purposefully used to evoke certain emotional responses. Identifying loaded language within their research can help students become aware of the bias in an article. For example, we might read the following descriptions of the protests in Charlottesville: "a day of racial rage, hate, violence and death" or as a "mass of white nationalists" (Helm, 2017). We compare this to a different article where Unite the Right protestors describe themselves as, "advocating for white people" or as a "white civil rights organization" (Charlottesville, 2017).

We explain to students how both articles are talking about the same topic, but the use of *advocating* and the term *civil rights* by protest organizers is done to make it seem as though their motives are positive. By equating the white supremacy rally with the Civil Rights movement, the organizers are attempting to impact the reader's view of the groups involved in the Unite the Right rally. These are purposeful word choices that show their bias.

We also ask students to consider another form of bias – is the article leaving out relevant information? We explain that if someone's background is skipped over, it could be because the background of this individual may influence the reader's perception of them – positively or negatively. For example, one article about the Charlottesville events notes that a death was caused when "someone drove a car through a crowd" (Seelye & Bidgood 2017) with no further mention of the intent, background, or involvement of the driver with hate groups. This may give the impression that the incident was not intentional. The motive and background of the driver is relevant to understand the larger picture of the events in Charlottesville.

Obviously, teachers will need to find different examples of "loaded language" about other current events. Unfortunately, the hyperpolarized media and Internet will make it easy to find them.

To deepen our discussion and analysis of bias, we introduce a chart that ranks the text complexity of sources as well as the liberal or conservative bias. Though there are many charts available online, we use the Media Bias Chart 4.0 from Ad Fontes Media (www.adfontesmedia.com). We point out to students that none of these rankings are infallible and may change over time.

Instead of making copies of the chart for students, we have them create a more simplified version in their notebooks (Figure 8.2: Media Bias Chart Example). Their copy will include the sources they will use to research their questions. We have students follow along with the teacher as we select 10 or so news outlets, placing them on our own chart based on the complexity of the writing and political bias. We explain to students that the higher up on the chart a source is placed, the more prior knowledge of politics is required to understand the article. In addition, these complex sources may also require more advanced reading skills. The horizontal axis of the chart arranges sources according to their political leanings (left or right leaning). We make sure the sources students are given to copy on their chart show a wide range on the political spectrum.

To guide students through the next step of the process, we share Table 8.3: Current Event Research Guide. At the top of the page we instruct students to write their research question. Beneath that, students are asked to place "key words/phrases to look up." Inexperienced researchers often make the mistake of doing research by typing their entire question into an Internet search engine. Depending on the question, they may get little helpful information. The main suggestion we make is to be specific (adding dates or names of people and places).

Once students have had the opportunity to refine their search terms by completing the top portion of Table 8.3: Current Event Research Guide, we ask them to look at their media bias chart. We direct them to the websites of the sources listed on the chart to begin their search. For novice researchers, it's helpful to "narrow the road." In other words, instead of allowing students to search the entire Internet, which may be overwhelming and bring up other issues like validity, the chart directs them to specific sources.

They begin to read the articles that appear in the search results. We give students 10 or so minutes to explore the websites on their chart. Then, we ask students to select two articles that they feel answer their research question for further analysis.

Table 8.3 Current Event Research Guide

Research Question	
Key words/phrases to look up-	
News source and possible bias?	Evidence/answer/related information
Basically this tells me the answer to my question is . . .	

Table 8.4 Current Event Research Guide Example

Research Question	
What was the police involvement in the Charlottesville events?	
Key words/phrases to look up Police intervene + Charlottesville Police actions in Charlottesville August 2017	
News source and possible bias?	Evidence/answer/related information
Washington Post Left center bias	"Anger over how the police responded came from all directions and intensified after the death of a woman struck by a car that plowed into a group of counter protesters. Experts said police appeared outnumbered, ill-prepared and inexperienced." "At one point, police appeared to retreat and then watch the beatings before eventually moving in to end the free-for-all, make arrests and tend to the injured. Gov. Terry McAuliffe (D) declared a state of emergency about 11 a.m. and activated the Virginia National Guard."
Fox News Right bias	"The chaos boiled over at what is believed to be the largest group of white nationalists to come together in a decade: the governor declared a state of emergency, police dressed in riot gear ordered people out and helicopters circled overhead. The group had gathered to protest plans to remove a statue of the Confederate Gen. Robert E. Lee."
Written Analysis Basically this tells me the answer to my question is . . .	
The police didn't intervene at the beginning but then did later on when there was already too much chaos. Based on the *Washington Post* article it seemed the police were not prepared for that type of situation, while on the other hand, Fox News said they did intervene. I think the police did get involved, but they intervened later on when the situation was to the point it got out of control so they were not able to make a big difference and people felt like they didn't do anything.	

We instruct them to choose one that is left leaning and another that is right leaning according to their chart. Students begin noting down relevant information from the articles on Table 8.3: Current Event Research Guide (for a student completed example see Table 8.4: Current Event Research Guide Example). As you can see from the student example, we ask them to write down at least two quotes from the articles that can help them answer their research question.

Information Literacy

We just discussed a short activity that helps to bring awareness to media bias. This lesson covers a part of the larger competency students must build known as information literacy. The American Library Association defines this literacy as a set of abilities requiring individuals to "recognize when information is needed and have the ability to locate, evaluate, and use effectively the needed information" ("Evaluation Information," n.d.). In other words, our students need to be taught how to carefully consume information, checking for "fake news," bias, e-safety, and ethical issues, among other skills. We should help them develop the ability to "employ skills of data collection and analysis." Students need these abilities to become "active and engaged participants in public life" as promoted by the National Council for the Social Studies. Here are a few quick ideas to support building your students' information literacy:

- Give students a guide or criteria to help them check for the validity of a news story. Public Broadcasting System (PBS) has a good video on Identifying "Fake" News from Common Sense Media (Identifying "Fake" News, n.d.). There is also a printable guide from *On The Media* called the Breaking News Consumer's Handbook (n.d.). Both of these sources, and others available online, can help give students some idea of "red flags" to be aware of in news stories. After reviewing key criteria in small groups and as a class, students can identify one to three news stories of their choice and evaluate each one based on what they learned.

- Teach students to follow a claim upstream or identify a claim from a news source and search to see if it is corroborated, or previously corrected, by another source. Students can check a claim by putting it into a search engine to see if the same, or similar claim, is backed up by multiple, reputable news sources (Caulfield, 2017).

- Introduce students to a website like Politifact (www.politifact.com/truth-o-meter), which allows them to check the validity of stories they may have seen online. Students can search for stories by topic or by inputting key terms into a search engine.

- Have students analyze political campaign ads for accuracy and the use of common fallacies. This assignment can be a good way to help students learn how to identify tactics used in propaganda (Baker, 2016, February 21).

WRITTEN ANALYSIS

The final phase of our current event case study involves students doing a written analysis to sum up their research findings for their selected question. This provides both accountability, since students have to demonstrate that they have done the research, as well as an opportunity to further develop literacy skills.

Table 8.3: Current Event Research Guide includes a section at the end of the organizer for students to answer their questions. We direct students to write an evidence-based response using the Answer, Back it up, Commentary (ABC) writing structure described in Chapter 5: Writing in Social Studies. In this structure, students answer their research question using examples and ideas from the texts.

If this is the first time you have used this ABC structure, then you will want to use the modeling process and examples found in Chapter 5: Writing in Social Studies. A simple example of this written analysis can be found at the bottom of Table 8.4: Current Event Research Guide Example. Requiring students to synthesize their research into an evidence-based response helps to practice higher-order thinking skills (Marzano, 1991, p. 523).

A teacher can make these student answers public and have classmates comment on each other's responses by providing sentence starters or guidelines. We like to keep it simple by instructing students to share one thing their classmates did well and one question they have. We also ask students to put their names on their comments.

One strategy that has worked for us is to have students attach their answers to the class timeline near the event that inspired their question. Another idea is to post them online using a platform like Google Classroom or Edmodo. These sites allow you to restrict viewers to only members in your class. In either case, we encourage students to read the work of their peers and to make comments.

ADDITIONAL IDEAS FOR INCLUDING CURRENT EVENTS IN THE CLASSROOM

Although our case study has a large emphasis on research, there are many other ways to include current events in social studies. Here are a few ideas:

- Weekly Article – At the beginning of the week, present students with an article on a current event. Students are assigned the article as their weekly reading. Then, they are instructed to make a connection between the reading and the topics being studied in class. Students write a brief summary of the connection between the two and turn it in as an assignment.

- Article Blizzard – Students are given a current event topic and instructed to find articles from a variety of sources, thus generating a blizzard of information. Students analyze their article and place it on a media bias chart, highlighting details they believe show evidence of bias.

- Write the Headline – Students are given an article on a current event with the headline removed. After reading the article, students are instructed to create an eye-catching headline and lead that previews the main events of the story.

- Daily News – Show a brief news clip(s) of a current event. Some news outlets even have daily news segments like Cable News Network (CNN), which has a program called CNN 10 (www.cnn.com/cnn10). These 10-minute segments are followed by a weekly news quiz provided on Fridays. In addition to watching these daily clips, we always have students respond to a question afterward. Then, we call on a few students to share with the class.

- One-Minute Presentation – Students are given class time to identify a news article that attracts their interest. They then prepare a one-minute presentation with visuals (either a slide show or a poster) summarizing the event, explaining why it is interesting to them, and offering a question for their classmates to discuss (see Chapter 11: Questions for Learning).

- Making Connections – Students are challenged to find a current news article that they can connect to the topic they are studying in their history, government, geography, or economics class. They then have to summarize the event and explain its connection. As in all assignments, showing a teacher model first will result in greater student understanding.

- Explainer Videos – Many news outlets create short videos simply explaining current events. Students can be challenged to create their own versions on events of their choice. Many examples can be found in Larry Ferlazzo's blog post "The Best Online 'Explainer' Tools for Current Events" (http://larryferlazzo .edublogs.org/2012/01/07/the-best-online-explainer-tools-for-current-events).

- Predictions – Students can choose articles on current events and predict what they believe will happen next and, most important, *why* they believe their prediction could be accurate.

DIFFERENTIATION

The language used in newspaper articles can sometimes pose a challenge to English language learner (ELL) students. To support these students, it may be helpful to direct them to more accessible sources. In the article "Ideas for E.L.L.s: Finding Reliable Sources in a World of 'Fake News'" written for the *New York Times* by Larry Ferlazzo (2017, January 26), multiple sources are provided. Many of these sources give students the option to use news videos to collect evidence. Videos can help provide context as well as visuals to support the information being read in class. Many news outlets have short video reports on different aspects of a topic. Students can watch videos at a slower speed and also read the transcripts to find evidence for answering their research questions. By completing research in this way, students are still gaining access to a variety of news sources and evidence, while also having language support. We have found this type of scaffolding helpful to all students, including those who learn differently.

ADVANCED EXTENSIONS

One way to push students even further with this current event case study is to have them complete a second (or more!) round of research. After making their answers and evidence public, students can develop new questions based on their classmates' findings. A teacher could instruct students to use these as their "new" research questions. In this way, students can build off of each other's ideas to further develop an understanding of the current event.

Another idea might be to have students do independent research on a different, but related, event and write about how the two compare. For example, the events in Charlottesville involved racially motivated protests and rallies that took a violent turn. Students could apply the skills they learned from the previous case study to research and find a similar event from the past. Then, students can be asked to identify similarities as well as differences between the two events and write about them in an essay.

Student Handouts and Examples

Table 8.1: Timeline Organizer
Table 8.2: Timeline Organizer Example
Figure 8.1: Timeline Example
Figure 8.2: Media Bias Chart Example
Table 8.3: Current Event Research Guide
Table 8.4: Current Event Research Guide Example

What Could Go Wrong?

A current event case study, or any current event activity, can easily focus only on surface level details – who, what, when, why, and how. It requires less energy and is less "risky" to keep the discussion at that level. However, if we are serious about assisting our students to become informed and active citizens in society, we must also look for opportunities to use current event "incidents" to promote critical thinking about broader related issues. We would have considered our lesson on Charlottesville a failure if we hadn't created space for discussions on racism, social justice, the role of monuments in our society, and who gets memorialized and why. Those broader topics are unlikely to come up magically and require teacher preparation. See Chapter 16: Discussions for strategies to effectively facilitate these types of classroom conversations.

If you do not have access to computers and/or Internet at your site, there are various ways to approach the research portion of this activity. If students have technology access outside of school, modeling the research process and then asking students to complete it at home may be an option. Another possibility is to narrow the field of research questions, perhaps by placing students into small groups with the same question. After limiting the number of research questions to four or five, provide a few articles from different news sources that address the questions of each group. Although students are more limited with their research in this version, teachers are also able to have more control over what articles students are reading and using for research.

Technology Connections

There are many other strategies that can be used to teach current events beyond the ones described in this chapter. Larry Ferlazzo has a list of ideas in his blog post "The Best Resources and Ideas for Teaching About Current Events" (http://larryferlazzo.edublogs.org/2016/10/16/the-best-resources-ideas-for-teaching-about-current-events). Larry also has an extensive lesson plan on teaching ELLs about "fake news," which can easily be modified for proficient English speakers. You can find it at the New York Times Learning Network headlined "Ideas for E.L.L.s: Finding Reliable Sources in a World of 'Fake News'" (www.nytimes.com/2017/01/26/learning/lesson-plans/ideas-for-ells-finding-reliable-sources-in-a-world-of-fake-news.html).

Another idea is to have students make their own short news videos and post them for others to see on a site like Google Classroom or Edmodo. Students can use their written analysis as the basis for the news video and then use their phones to make short videos that can be posted online. Many options for helping students to make videos can be found at Larry Ferlazzo's "Guide to Making Videos on the Web" (http://larryferlazzo.edublogs.org/2010/05/03/guide-to-making-videos-on-the-web) and at "The Best Resources for Learning to Use Instagram" (http://larryferlazzo.edublogs.org/2013/02/18/the-best-resources-for-learning-to-use-the-video-app-twine).

Figures

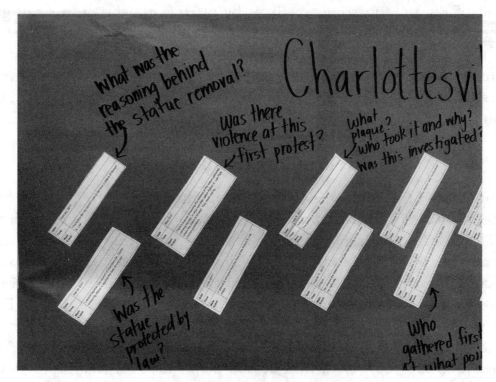

Figure 8.1 Timeline Example

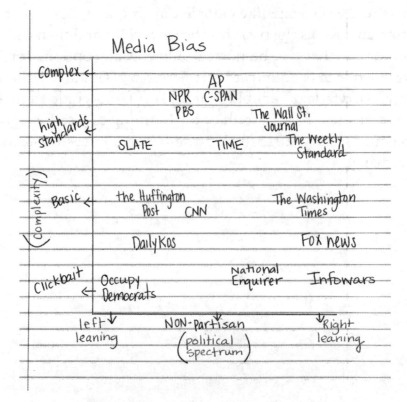

Figure 8.2 Media Bias Chart Example

CHAPTER 9

Genre Study

What Is It?

In this strategy, students study a genre, or type of writing, and then use that writing as a model for creating their own text. In response to a prompt, students can use evidence to create a graphic novel, movie poster, social media post, or other "real-world" texts. This fresh take on evidence-based writing is a more creative, and potentially more self-motivating, way to have students demonstrate their learning. When students use evidence to back up their writing, all genres of writing can become a "research paper."

This chapter provides two different ways to do a genre study. In the first variation, students write a scene in a Bollywood movie script to show knowledge of India. In the second, student writers respond to a prompt about China with an evidence-based paragraph and then *choose* a genre to further extend their response. There are many ways to apply these instructional strategies in different social studies classes and in different units. Suggestions for these modifications can be found later in this chapter.

Why We Like It

Exploring different genres of writing in a social studies classroom allows you to inject novelty into any assignment as students use information they've learned to demonstrate content knowledge. Students can be inspired by interesting types of writing and can practice critical thinking skills as they identify characteristics of these genres to use later in their own work. Choosing *how* to share information in a creative way promotes student autonomy, while also encouraging students to dig deeper into the content.

Teachers are able to differentiate instruction fairly easily using this strategy. They can provide scaffolding for less-experienced writers by narrowing the genre options or offering greater student choice for those who are more proficient.

Supporting Research

Genre study encourages students to revisit the content learned in class, or to conduct more research to find needed information to produce a selected genre of writing (Moulton, 1999, p. 537). In addition, genre study "connects reading and writing" and "develops writers as critical thinkers and users of language" (Dean, 2008, p. 7). In other words, when students are required to read carefully in order to mimic a writing genre, they tap into higher-level literacy skills.

Research also shows interactions with multiple genres can create a wealth of knowledge for students to access as they continue their studies in multiple content areas and encourages metacognitive reflection (Reiff & Bawarshi, 2011, p. 333). See Chapter 4: Thematic Data Sets for more on metacognition and its benefits.

Common Core Connections

Analyzing the structures of multiple types of text and how they work to make a point or give information is required by the Reading Standards of the Common Core (2010s). In addition, the Writing Standards also highlight having students consider the audience and purpose of the different genres of text while writing (Common Core, 2010t).

Social Studies Connections

The skills used to complete either of the genre writing tasks described in this chapter help students to address Evaluating Sources, Using Evidence, Communicating Conclusions, and Taking Informed Action. These goals come from the College, Career, and Civic Life (C3) Framework from the National Council for the Social Studies (2010). Depending on the topic of writing, this strategy can touch on multiple themes in the National Council of the Social Studies Curriculum Standards. For example, the two sample lessons in this chapter address "Culture" and "People, Places, and Environment," as well as exploring the theme of power and authority.

APPLICATION

Each genre study project described here takes one week to complete and usually occurs at the end of the unit. In the first example we focus on one genre, a movie script. In the second example, the teacher presents multiple genres and allows the students to choose one. Both of the examples come from a geography classroom. The movie script completes a unit on India and the student choice genre project concludes a unit on China.

Movie Script Project

This movie script example is specifically for a Bollywood film. To prepare students, we make sure to tell them during the study of India that they will be writing a Bollywood film script during the latter portion of the unit.

Students are required to use what we've learned in class to write two scenes to complete a partial movie script provided by the teacher. In their writing, we ask students to include concepts like societal organization, the divide between urban and rural life, and/or gender role expectations in India. We study India because of its rich culture and history as well as its growing importance internationally. For example, India has one of the fastest growing economies and a population that is set to overtake China as the largest in the world within the next decade ("World Population," 2017).

During our unit study of India, students read about Bollywood and, like people around the world, become interested in the stories and artistic elements of that film genre. We introduce this project by reminding students that Bollywood films sell more tickets worldwide than Hollywood and generate millions of dollars for the economy each year. Bollywood films have recently begun delving into social issues like widow remarriage and government corruption. This new focus aligns well with our project because we encourage students to include a key cultural concept from our study of India throughout their scripts. We also like this genre because many Bollywood films are G rated, though you could certainly choose a different movie genre to explore with similar success.

It is important to emphasize, however, that we do not teach about India through the lens of a Bollywood movie. Learning about these films and their cultural influence is one small part of a multiweek exploration of the geography, economics, culture, and history of the country.

We've broken this project down into the following three parts: Studying Examples, Assignment Directions, and Extensions.

Studying Examples

Video Clips

Students should view multiple clips of the targeted movie style prior to writing. Depending on the social studies topic, there might be several options for both the type of movie and its content. During our unit on India, we show our students video clips from Bollywood films because it helps students visualize concepts that we are learning in class, such as the social hierarchy, economic growth, and cultural practices like arranged marriages. Of course, we remind students that these film scenes are often exaggerated and may or may not always reflect reality.

In this lesson, viewing multiple video clips helps students understand the tone and style of Bollywood films. The clips should be short, usually around five minutes long. In our experience, showing an entire movie doesn't seem to make a difference in the final product students create – plus the films can be quite lengthy. There are a vast array of Bollywood movies on Netflix and Youtube. Students may also have suggestions.

There are two different activities we do with the video clips prior to students writing their own scripts. The tasks are designed to first help students develop a deeper understanding of the culture and society as portrayed in Bollywood films. They also provide students the opportunity to closely study a film script prior to writing their own.

In the first activity, students begin by watching one or more video clips and making a list of characteristics that stood out to them. To help students get started, the teacher can model an example or two. After giving students a few minutes to note their ideas, we ask two or three to share with the whole class. We then create a class list. Students often write words like *dramatic, colorful, action packed, musical,* and more. We leave the class list posted during the entire project as a student reminder.

The second activity is to choose one very short Bollywood film scene to study in-depth. Students watch the scene at least two times – this is a strategy we often use with film clips. The first time, they watch without writing anything down. During the second viewing, they take detailed notes. We use these notes to complete a graphic organizer, Table 9.1: Taking Apart a Scene, which asks students to note the character dialogue and actions, as well as information from the background or setting. Once students complete this graphic organizer on their own, we give them a chance to partner share before sharing with the whole class. In this way, we are giving students multiple opportunities to analyze a scene. You don't need to review the entire graphic organizer as a class – just enough to make the point that there is a lot of information being given in each scene. This activity helps students to get an idea of the details required in a script. In order for an audience to see or know something, the script writer must include it.

Both of these activities happen prior to the week of the script-writing project and can be limited to 30 minutes or less.

Table 9.1 Taking Apart a Scene

List as much as possible in each section		
Character Dialogue	**Character Actions**	**Setting/Background**

Movie Script

Next we give students the first three scenes of a teacher-created Bollywood movie script, Figure 9.1: Bollywood Script Starter. We pass out the script and assign a few students the different character parts to read out to the class. Depending on your students' comfort level, you could have them actually act it out. If your students are not ready to act, they can simply read the dialogue while the teacher reads camera directions, setting, and character actions.

After reading through the entire script once, the teacher goes back through the first scene and models how to annotate the different parts of the script while students follow along. In this case, the annotations are labels to direct students to the different parts of a film script (like camera directions, setting, character actions, and so on) as seen in Figure 9.2: Annotated Bollywood Movie Script Starter. While reviewing this scene, the teacher should point out character names, any dialogue, and words in parenthesis that describe the character's action or tone of voice. The teacher should also call attention to camera directions and any descriptions of the setting. Working through the script in this manner helps students note the structure of the text.

Students then work in pairs to read the second scene and label it (dialogue, setting, and so on) in the same way they annotated the first one. Then, the teacher can call on students to share the annotations with the whole class. Based on your students' level of understanding, you can decide if labeling the different parts of the third scene is necessary.

Assignment Directions

After students have annotated the Bollywood script, they receive Table 9.2: Bollywood Script Assessment Rubric. The rubric helps to clearly outline the requirements and expectations for the movie-script project. When we review the rubric, we tend to emphasize the column labeled 4 so students are clear on what they need to do in order to earn the highest grade.

While this script writing can be done as a partner activity, the process described here is for an individual assignment. Each student must write a minimum of two scenes to conclude the storyline of the Bollywood script they were given in class by the teacher (Figure 9.1: Bollywood Script Starter). Each scene must be two pages long and describe the setting at the beginning of each, have dialogue between characters, and include character actions. Students need to include content from our unit of study, such as referencing cultural concepts or norms. We also require students to use at least four vocabulary words from the unit in a way that seems natural and not just randomly dropped into the script. The final requirement is that the

Table 9.2 Bollywood Script Assessment Rubric

Criteria	1	2	3	4
Format	Script has many formatting errors, making it difficult to read and understand. Script does not meet length requirements.	Script has multiple errors with formatting which do not greatly impact the reader's ability to understand the script. Script does not meet length requirements.	Script is mostly formatted properly, but may include a couple of errors with formatting. Script meets, or comes within a half page of, length requirements.	Script is formatted properly including all features: setting description, character's speaking, tone, and actions, as well as camera directions. Script meets/exceeds length requirement of 2 scenes, each being 2 pages long.
Content	Cultural concepts from the unit and basic content knowledge are missing.	Cultural concepts from the unit are minimally included in storyline and/or lack of basic content knowledge included.	Cultural concepts from the unit are included, but embedded inconsistently in the storyline and/or show only very basic content knowledge.	Cultural concepts from the unit (social ranking system, arranged marriage, gender roles, etc.) are embedded throughout a clear storyline, proving content knowledge.
Vocabulary	Script uses 2 or less unit vocabulary words and shows a lack of understanding in its use.	Script uses at least 2 unit vocabulary words and shows a basic understanding of its use.	Script uses 2 unit vocabulary words accurately. Or, uses 4, but with only a basic understanding of their use.	Script includes 4 unit vocabulary words accurately to improve the story.
Bollywood Style	Script unsuccessful at capturing the style of Bollywood films lacking most/all the elements: appropriate conflict, resolution, over-the-top action, drama, coincidences, and happy ending.	Script attempts to capture the style of Bollywood films, but may be missing some elements: appropriate conflict, resolution, over-the-top action, drama, coincidences, and happy ending.	Script mostly captures the style of Bollywood films by including some: appropriate conflict, resolution, over-the-top action, drama, coincidences, and happy ending.	Script captures the style of Bollywood films including appropriate conflict, resolution, over-the-top action, drama, coincidences, and a happy ending.
Daily Work	Student struggled to stay on task most of the work time and needed constant redirection.	Student struggled to stay on task at times and needed occasional redirection.	Student mostly worked each day to improve script as evidenced by daily ticket out the door.	Student worked each day to improve script as evidenced by daily ticket out the door.

script stays true to the common Bollywood style. This means it should be "over the top," predictable, and have a happy ending.

After clarifying the assignment expectations, students begin to brainstorm ideas for their scenes. We often ask students to come into class the following day with three possible story ideas they have written down – each must be at least two sentences long. After students have a few story ideas, we have them choose one. We lead this decision-making process by telling students to choose which is easiest for them to visualize as a movie in their mind. After settling on a storyline, we have students write a one-sentence summary of the purpose for each of their scenes. Though we only require two scenes, many students choose to write more, and we allow this as long as there is a clear purpose for each one.

It is important to remind student writers that each scene needs a purpose. In the first year of doing this project we struggled through more than one student film script of endless character dialogue with no function. We have found that having students write out the purpose of each scene before they write helps avoid unproductive dialogue and action. For example, the purpose might be that "Aarav discovers that Saanvi has run away." Students then write out the scene with that purpose in mind. This makes it much easier to edit the scene and throw out unnecessary dialogue or actions that don't assist the reader in understanding the storyline.

Once students are settled on their storyline and have a purpose for each of their scenes, we give them time to write their script. We usually provide students two or three days of class time to complete the assignment. Having our classes set up in small groups makes it easy for us to encourage students to ask their peers for advice before asking the teacher. In our experience, many student questions can be answered by their classmates, by directing students to the rubric, or by suggesting they review the Bollywood script example (Figure 9.1: Bollywood Script Starter).

Though this example focuses on India and the specific Bollywood style of a movie script, the possibilities are endless. For example:

- Show the famous picture of George Washington crossing the Delaware and have students turn it into a scene from an action film.

- Have student partners write scenes for a crime show that requires them to include a specific constitutional amendment. This activity works well in a government class. We first place several different crimes on small strips of paper in a hat. We put amendments from the Bill of Rights in another hat. We then have students pick both a crime and an amendment. Next, we instruct them to write a script for a TV show that includes both the crime they were given and how it relates to their selected amendment. One example could be vehicle theft and the Fourth Amendment. The students might come up with a story where someone's Fourth Amendment rights were violated when they were wrongly searched after the crime was committed.

- Use the style of a Latin American telenovela, or soap opera, to dive into families and soldiers separated by the American Civil War and/or civil wars in other countries. The teacher could provide primary sources like letters between families separated by a war for students to use as research to write their script. These documents can be found by searching "family civil war letters" online.

Writing an accurate script requires students to have a deeper understanding of the content. They may be more motivated to revisit information learned in class or to seek out further knowledge in order to bring these historical moments to the "big screen."

To find model film scripts for any genre, just search "TV scripts" or "movie scripts" online.

Project Extensions

Students often love to share their work. Some extension ideas include having students share their scripts in small groups, or allowing some to be acted out in class. Animating a scene online, as referenced in the Technology Connections section, can also work and takes less time. Another option might be to contact your students' English or drama teacher to see if they would support using some of their class time to write or act out student scripts. Students could also film their scenes using their phones outside of class and upload their creations to Google Classroom, Edmodo, a class blog, or other online site.

STUDENT CHOICE GENRE PROJECT

In this project, student writers respond to a prompt using the ABC writing structure discussed in Chapter 5: Writing in Social Studies. Then, they choose and create a genre to elaborate and expand on their evidence-based paragraph. Students can choose from a variety of genres such as a poem, news article, comic strip, and so on. We typically ask students to create a visual element to go along with their paragraph and genre of choice (many genres incorporate a visual element already). For example, a student can be given a prompt asking, "What is a major challenge facing Mexico?" They can respond with an evidence-based paragraph citing class materials on the topic and then choose to write a poem about the immigration crisis. Their visual element might be an image of a family crossing a river.

This type of project is important for students because it allows student choice, which can increase engagement and autonomy. It also exposes students to different ways of communicating their ideas.

Here is a description of the process broken into three steps: Introducing the Prompt and Project, Exploring Genre Stations Activity, and Work Time. Student examples are included in the Figures.

Introducing the Prompt and Project

Teachers begin by introducing students to a prompt to assess their learning of a recently studied topic. For example, we posed a broad question for our concluding project on China: "Based on what we learned in class, what makes China unique?" In a US history class you might ask students, "What was a major consequence of World War II?" In world history, you could ask, "What is one factor that contributed to the revolution in France? How?" or you could use a prompt like "Choose one of the major philosophers from the Enlightenment and show how their ideas impacted change in Europe."

Students are then instructed to review unit materials to begin developing an answer to the prompt, "Based on what we learned in class, what makes China unique?" Students individually make a short list of possible answers and then share with the whole class, generating a class list of ideas on the board. Students contribute information they learned from the unit such as China's rapid economic growth, system of government, challenges with pollution, population size and the government's desire to control its growth.

We give students time to consider the class responses, select one idea from the list they would like to use as their answer to the prompt, and confirm that they have adequate supporting evidence. Then, we ask students to draft an evidence-based paragraph to respond to the prompt using the Answer, Back it up, Commentary (ABC) writing structure from Chapter 5: Writing in Social Studies. It may help to select an answer from the class list and write an example response like Table 9.3: China Response – Teacher Model.

In our experience, students often want to use the teacher's answer. To deal with this, we have two suggestions. One, the teacher can make their answer "off limits" for students. In other words, direct the students to choose a different answer on which to base their paragraph. The second option is to allow students to use the answer, but *not* allow them to use the same evidence and commentary as the teacher. In this case, students *would* be allowed to write about pollution as an issue in China *but* would need to find alternative evidence and supply their own commentary different from that used in Table 9.3: China Response – Teacher Model.

Once students have been introduced to the prompt and have written their response, the next step is to go over the genres that students might choose to go along with their paragraph. First, we show students some examples of completed projects like Figure 9.3: Student Example: China Poem and Figure 9.4: Student Example: Social Media. If this is the first time doing this project, it may be worth creating a

Table 9.3 China Response – Teacher Model

Prompt
What makes China unique?
Answer
One thing that makes China unique from most other countries around the world is the massive economic growth it has experienced in recent decades. According to the China Data Set, in recent years this economic growth has led to an increase of wealth for the people of China. This wealth allows many people to do things they weren't able to do in the past, such as traveling internationally. Over 150 million Chinese citizens traveled outside of China in 2018, which is half of the population of the entire United States.

teacher example to illustrate exactly what is expected of students (of course, you can also show students the examples in this book).

Next, we give out Table 9.4: Student Choice Genre Assessment Rubric, which serves as the directions and outlines the requirements for the assignment. As explained in the previous section, we find that giving the rubric to students early clarifies exactly what is expected in the project.

While reviewing the rubric with our students, we explain that their project should include the following: an answer to the prompt using the ABC format and a

Table 9.4 Student Choice Genre Assessment Rubric

Criteria	1	2	3	4
Prompt Response (ABC paragraph)	Paragraph missing evidence, very weak or no analysis.	Paragraph uses very weak or disconnected evidence, analysis portion minimal.	Paragraph uses some evidence, but alignment with genre could be improved, analysis is basic.	Paragraph uses cited evidence from the unit to clearly answer prompt through a thorough analysis.
Elements of Genre	Key elements do not match selected genre, very little effort put forth to utilize genre in response.	Some major issues with key elements and/or lack of effort to blend genre and response.	Most key elements present and definite effort made to blend genre and response.	All key elements present and done in such a way as to blend response and genre seamlessly.
Visual Element	Visual element not present.	Visual seems disconnected or very little effort put forth.	Visual coordinates with genre/response in a basic way.	Visual elaborates/extends genre to further response.
Daily Work	Student was unproductive most days in class, needed redirection, accountability tickets missing or lack of completed tasks.	Student turned in only some accountability tickets and/or needed redirection more than twice during the assignment.	Student turned in accountability ticket daily with most tasks completed each day.	Student turned in accountability ticket daily with appropriate tasks completed each day.

representation/expansion of that paragraph in their genre choice, as well as a visual. These three components must be displayed on a poster. We point out these features on the examples as we review them. Lastly, students must do a daily "ticket out the door" during the project. This is a brief description of what has been accomplished each workday of the project and helps to keep students on task during independent work time.

Exploring Genres Station Activity

Students have now seen an example of the project, which includes one genre they could choose for their assignment. The next step is to allow students to explore more genres they may choose for their project. We do this by rotating students through genre "stations." Each station contains three examples of a genre as well as a list of key elements for each one (see Figure 9.5: Genre Cheat Sheet for lists of key elements). These examples include, but aren't limited to, an obituary, poem, police report, comic strip, movie poster, social media profile, wanted poster, postcard, advertisement, movie script, movie poster, or magazine article. If you are in a one-to-one device school, the genres could be easily expanded to different kinds of multimedia presentations. The examples we use in our classrooms are real-life examples collected from printed text. We keep a folder for each genre and add examples as we come across them during the year. Many can be found in newspapers or magazines. It's also easy to do a quick online search and print a few examples of each one.

To explore the stations, we break students into small groups and give them a few minutes at each. We ask students to consider which genres pique their interest. Students rate the genre on a scale of 1–5 at each station – 1 being "not at all" and 5 being "very interested." We also ask students to include one sentence explaining their rating as shown in Table 9.5: Genre Rating.

After giving students time to explore each genre station, we ask them to select their top choice, return to that station, and copy down the key elements required for that genre. This helps to guide them as they work to create their own responses.

Note: We recognize that this station activity can be a lot of work and take up substantial time. One alternative to these stations is to limit the number of genres, quickly review each one as a class, and make copies of the key elements available for students.

Work Time

Once students have selected their genre and reviewed the key elements, it's time for them to create their project. Students attach all three parts of the project (ABC response, genre, visual) onto a poster. We structure our class so that they have between 30 and 45 minutes for two to three days to work on this project. You may need to modify the times and amount of days depending on your students.

Table 9.5 Genre Rating

Genre Type	Rating (1–5)	Explain Rating
(example) Poem	(example) 4	(example) I like poetry and I think I could write a poem about the gender imbalance in China.

We also make sure to remind students that they are required to turn in an update of what they completed at the end of each day. This daily work is one of the criteria on the grading rubric for this project (Table 9.4: Student Choice Genre Assessment Rubric).

Project Extensions

We often do a gallery walk for the Student Choice Genre Project. We turn our classroom into a museum by hanging student work throughout the room or, sometimes, in the hallway. In this case we might have our "museum" organized by genre. One area could be for movie posters, one for police reports, and so on. We like to keep the task simple and have students make a comment on a sticky note of one thing the creator did well and one thing to consider for improvement. We give students a set amount of time to review a poster from each genre area and then a signal to move to the next station.

Another activity we periodically do is a student work "paper pass" at the end so that students can see each other's projects. For a paper pass we have students sit in small groups and pass each other's work around for review. We have found this kind of authentic audience, especially if announced in advance, to be highly motivating. Again, it is helpful to have a specific task to complete during this activity, such as writing a one-sentence summary of each piece of work.

See the Technology Connections section for how to publish student work online.

DIFFERENTIATION

For the movie script project, students can draw out the scene prior to writing in order to scaffold important vocabulary. With help from the teacher, students can label actions taking place, character dialogue, and features of the setting as shown in Figure 9.6: Scene Diagram Example. This gives the extra support where English language learners (ELLs) need it most, while still allowing the students to capture their unique ideas. Partnering students is another way to support ELL students. They can take turns dictating and writing a scene together. We have had many successful scripts written in this way.

For the student choice project, one way to support ELLs and students with learning differences can be to guide them toward specific genres. We make this recommendation based on what we think may be more accessible to them based on our knowledge of their interests and skills. Partnering can also provide an opportunity for collaborative learning between English-proficient and ELL students, particularly if the teacher can identify a student who is willing to be a "buddy" to an ELL student.

ADVANCED EXTENSIONS

For the movie-script project, consider increasing the length requirement for more proficient writers and/or increasing the number of vocabulary words required to be woven into the script. Additionally, requiring students to incorporate current events into the script is another way to increase the difficulty level.

For the student choice project, one idea is to have them complete two projects with each expressing a different viewpoint. For example, two poems about pollution in China: one from a citizen's point of view versus a poem from a business owner's perspective. This kind of activity encourages students to focus on how the same issue or event can be seen differently depending on a person's experience.

Student Handouts and Examples

Table 9.1: Taking Apart a Scene

Figure 9.1: Bollywood Movie Script Starter

Figure 9.2: Annotated Bollywood Movie Script Starter

Table 9.2: Bollywood Script Assessment Rubric

Table 9.3: China Response – Teacher Model

Figure 9.3: Student Example: China Poem

Figure 9.4: Student Example: Social Media

Table 9.4: Student Choice Genre Assessment Rubric

Figure 9.5: Genre Cheat Sheet

Table 9.5: Genre Rating

Figure 9.6: Scene Diagram Example

What Could Go Wrong?

In the Bollywood film script assignment, some students may balk at the idea of having to finish the provided film script and want to create an original instead. However, we have found that allowing students to create their own completely original film script is more work than students realize. Most of our students haven't been able to successfully complete an original Bollywood film script from beginning to end in the given time for the project. We have found that helping students get started with the teacher-created scenes leads to greater success. Additionally, if you extend the project to act-out-and-record scripts, be mindful of students who may not have access to technology. Try pairing students up, or finding technology access at your school site to support them.

Technology Connections

Students can bring their movie scripts to life using Bombay TV as described in Larry Ferlazzo's blog post, "Send a Message from Bollywood" (http://larryferlazzo .edublogs.org/2007/10/09/send-a-message-from-bollywood). Bombay TV provides clips from Bollywood movies and allows users to write their own subtitles. Also, students can use *Dialogue,* an app that allows students to use their phone to type, easily format, and print a screenplay. Another option is to create an animation. See a list of them in Larry Ferlazzo's blog post, "The Best Ways for Students to Create Online Animations" (http://larryferlazzo.edublogs.org/2008/05/11/the-best-ways-for-students-to-create-online-animations). If students choose to produce comic strips, there are many options to create those online as well; take a look at "The Best Ways to Make Comic Strips Online" (http://larryferlazzo.edublogs .org/?s=comic+strips). Additionally, for examples of many different writing genres, as well as a place to publish student work, check out the article from the *New York Times,* "Out of the Classroom and into the World: 70-Plus Places to Publish Teenage Writing and Art" (www.nytimes.com/2018/11/15/learning/out-of-the-classroom-and-into-the-world-70-plus-places-to-publish-teenage-writing-and-art.html?rref=collection%2Fsectioncollection%2Flearning&action=click&con tentCollection=learning&region=stream&module=stream_unit&version=latest& contentPlacement=10&pgtype=sectionfront).

Attribution

Portions of this section are adapted from a presentation given by Bob Crongeyer, co-director of the Area 3 Writing Project and teacher in the Robla School District in Sacramento.

One activity also includes elements of a book review project created by Jeff Johnson, English teacher at Luther Burbank High School in Sacramento.

Figures

Main Characters

Aarav	15-year-old student, the hero
Sai Matthews	Aarav's father, successful businessman
Elissa	Aarav's mother
Saanvi	15-year-old student, the heroine
Muthu	Saanvi's mother

Scene 1

FADE IN ON JASMINE FLOWERS

(Jasmine flowers, Saanvi's hands twirling her hair, Aarav humming a sweet sounding song. Saanvi looks back and smiles. Suddenly, Aarav's mother is heard speaking on the sound track.)

OPEN INTO A KITCHEN, BOY SITTING AT TABLE, HEAD RESTING ON HAND ON HIS CHEEK, STARING INTO THE DISTANCE, BOOK OPEN IN FRONT OF HIM ON TABLE

Elissa: (with a smile and teasing voice) Oh, is this the way you do your homework? (startled, Aarav suddenly pretends to be reading)

Elissa: What are you thinking about so deeply?

Aarav: (sighs) Oh, nothing.

Elissa: What a big lie (with a smile). You are thinking about something, I am sure.

Aarav: (after a pause) Mother? Which is your favorite flower?

Elissa: (thinking) Hmmm. . . I think it has to be the rose.

Aarav: (after a pause) I love Jasmine flowers best, (pause for 2 seconds and then quickly speaking) Saanvi also loves them!

Elissa: Hey now, who is this girl? Saanvi?

(Aarav is silent)

Elissa: (big smile) Who is Saanvi?

Aarav: (blushing, shyly) She goes to my school.

Elissa: (smiling) Not just a classmate? A girlfriend? Can it be true?

(Aarav is so shy he can't respond)

CAMERA ZOOMS OUT TO SEE THE WHOLE KITCHEN

(Aarav's Mother begins to sing a sweet sounding song about young love)

Elissa: You just bring her to meet me one day, okay? (she gives Aarav a hug)

Scene 2

FADE IN, A ROAD, WE HEAR TWO VOICES LAUGHING AND TALKING

(Aarav and Saanvi walk down the road, coming up to Aarav's house. They wear their school uniforms and carry their school books in their arms. They seem happy and carefree.)

Aarav: Look! This is my house (pointing at his house)

Saanvi: (looks where Aarav is pointing)

Aarav: Don't be afraid, please come in for a bit.

Figure 9.1 Bollywood Movie Script Starter

Saanvi: (shy, and now with a sad look on her face) I can't, maybe on some other day.

Aarav: (walking towards Saanvi with his hand outstretched) No, No. Don't be afraid, Father is not home today and my Mother wants to meet you.

(Saanvi looks around and walks forward towards the large garden in the front yard. Seeing the flowers, she stops for a moment.)

Aarav: Do you like this garden?

Saanvi: Yes, except you have no jasmine, my favorite flowers.

Aarav: (looks at Saanvi and takes her hand) That is why I've brought my jasmine flower.

OPEN ON INSIDE OF HOUSE

(Aarav enters the living room)

Aarav: (excitedly) Mother! Mother!

(Aarav's Mother enters the living room from the kitchen, towel in her hand)

Elissa: Why are you so happy today my son?

Aarav: Mother, didn't you ask me to bring Saanvi one day? Well, I've brought her to meet you.

(Aarav's mother looks at Saanvi. Saanvi stands in the doorway, looking nervous. Aarav's Mother looks at her, Saanvi looks at the floor)

Elissa: Come in Saanvi, and meet me.

(Saanvi takes two slow steps forward and slowly bows to touch the feet of Aarav's mother. His mother lifts her from the floor in a huge hug as Saanvi begins to cry.)

Elissa: Why are you crying my dear? (Mother wipes her tears with the towel) Please smile, it's lovely to meet you. (slowly a smile appears on Saanvi's face)

Scene 3

FADE IN, SAANVI'S HOUSE – DAY

(Saanvi's house, she is watering the jasmine plants. a watering can in her hand. Suddenly the sound of a car is heard and Saanvi looks to the side. The car parks and door opens, a man gets out, he closes the door. We see the feet of a man walking, his new leather shoes shining in the daylight.)

SAANVI'S LIVING ROOM

(Saanvi comes running into the room. Her mother, who is sitting in a chair, looks up at her, startled)

Saanvi: (out of breath) Aarav's. . .

Muthu: Aarav's? What? (confused look)

Saanvi: Aarav's Father! He's here!

(Saanvi's Mother looks startled and wipes her face with her hands trying to smooth her hair and straighten her sari. She stands and moves towards the door. There is a knock on the door, Saanvi's mother opens the door, Aarav's father enters the room. He gazes around the room with a look of disgust.)

Muthu: Namaste! Please come in!

Sai: No, I will be here for only a moment. I know you may not know who I am, I am Sai Matthews, the managing director of Mumbai Chemical.

Muthu: I know who you are, my daughter Saanvi has told me.

Sai: The girl who was watering the plants a minute ago?

Muthu: Yes (pausing)

Figure 9.1 (Continued)

(Saanvi stands behind the kitchen door listening in, her face is excited)

Sai: Your husband? Where is he?

Muthu: He died, eight years ago (sadly)

Sai: I am sorry to hear that (after a pause) Elissa, my wife, told me that Aarav and your daughter are (pauses) studying together in the same class. It seems that there is some kind of (pausing) friendship between them. (suddenly adding) I am not totally against any such friendship and I don't have any objection even if it becomes a marriage

(We see Saanvi behind the door, her face in a huge smile)

Muthu: Marriage? They are too young to think of any marriage now. Maybe in a few years. . .

Sai: (interrupting) yes, yes, that's right! I have only just come to be introduced to you. (He moves towards the door) I am a little busy, there is a board meeting at five o'clock and I must be there. (He looks at his watch, takes two steps towards the door and then looks back and says seriously) One more thing. Being a director for one of the leading businesses of Mumbai today, I will have no difficulty to get 30 or 50 lakhs of Rupees as dowry for my son, and I will do what it takes to make sure that happens.

(silence fills the room for 3 seconds, Saanvi's mother looks to the floor considering what to say)

Muthu: Everything that belongs to me is Saanvi's also, but it won't equal the amount you require.

Sai: (seriously) If that is so, it is better for our children to end to this *friendship* today. (he opens the door and takes a step out, turning back) Tell your daughter, she should leave my son alone! (he slams the door closed)

CLOSE UP ON SAANVI'S FACE

(Tears begin to run down Saanvi's face and she sings a sad song about being broken hearted while she goes to her room and appears to pack some clothes into a bag)

FADE OUT

Figure 9.1   (Continued)

Main Characters

Aarav	15-year-old student, the hero
Sai Matthews	Aarav's father, successful businessman
Elissa	Aarav's mother
Saanvi	15-year-old student, the heroine
Muthu	Saanvi's mother

Who is in the film

Scene 1 ← *Scene #*

FADE IN ON JASMINE FLOWERS ← *setting, set the scene, open the scene* — *camera directions* —

(Jasmine flowers, Saanvi's hands twirling her hair, Aarav humming a sweet sounding song. Saanvi looks back and smiles. Suddenly, Aarav's mother is heard speaking on the sound track.) *images on screen*

OPEN INTO A KITCHEN, BOY SITTING AT TABLE, HEAD RESTING ON HAND ON HIS CHEEK, STARING INTO THE DISTANCE, BOOK OPEN IN FRONT OF HIM ON TABLE *camera directions*

Elissa: (with a smile and teasing voice) Oh, is this the way you do your homework? *character speaking, tone, how you say it*

(startled, Aarav suddenly pretends to be reading) ← *character actions*

Elissa: What are you thinking about so deeply? ← *dialogue*

Aarav: (sighs) Oh, nothing. *actions/tone of voice* *character*

Elissa: What a big lie (with a smile). You are thinking about something, I am sure.

Figure 9.2   Annotated Bollywood Movie Script Starter

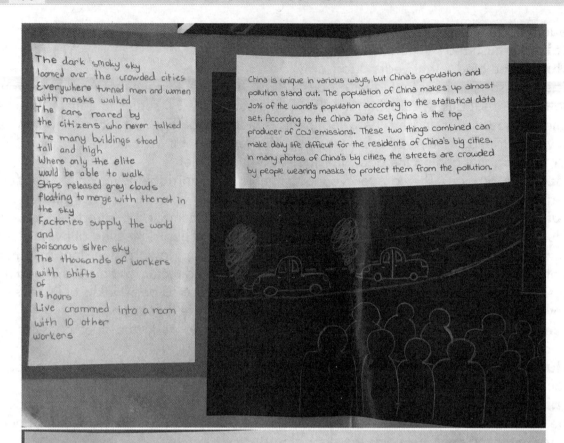

Figure 9.3   Student Example: China Poem

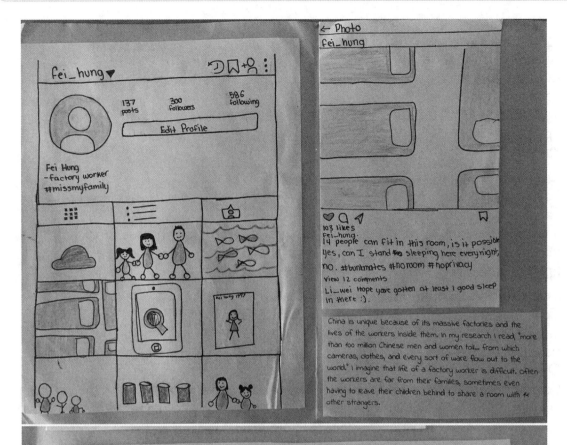

China is unique because of its massive factories and the lives of the workers inside them. In my research I read, "more than 100 million Chinese men and women toil... from which cameras, clothes, and every sort of ware flow out to the world." I imagine that life of a factory worker is difficult. Often the workers are far from their families, sometimes even having to leave their children behind to share a room with 14 other strangers.

Figure 9.4 Student Example: Social Media

Essential Elements of an Obituary
Announcement of death
Biographical sketch
Family
Service times
Special messages
Photos

Essential Elements of a Poem
Sound (alliteration, rhyme)
Form (how a poem looks, lines, stanzas)
Imagery (five senses) and figurative language (words or phrases to picture things in a new way)
Speaker's voice

Essential Elements of a Police Report
Case number, date of report, and reporting officer
Incident type
List of witnesses with information about them
One-sentence synopsis for the reader about the case
Detailed paragraph about the incident (interviews with the victims and the witnesses)
Paragraph about when the police officer went to the crime scene. What they found interesting, possible evidence, and possible arrests.

Essential Elements of Wanted/Found Poster
Picture of person
Description of person (age, gender, identifying marks, looks)
Description—last known location, circumstances around disappearance
Wanted for. . .
Warning/watch out for
Contact info
Reward

Essential Elements of Advertisements
Irresistible offer
Unique advantages of product
Compelling headline/slogan
Sell the benefits/results of product
Make it risk-free (30-day money back guarantee)
Graphics/visuals
Sense of urgency (hurry, quick, before it's gone)

Figure 9.5 Genre Cheat Sheet

<u>Essential Elements of a Social Media Post</u>
User name
Pictures
Comments
Followers
Likes
GIFS
Shares
Texts
Emojis
Captions
Personal profile
Settings
Location
Tagged photos
Bio

<u>Essential Elements of a Postcard/Letter</u>
Stamp
Address
Salutation/greeting/closing
Body of the letter
Front visual on postcard
Describes place of visit

<u>Essential Elements of a Comic Strip</u>
At least three "panels"
Dialogue
At least two characters
Background scenes

Figure 9.5   (Continued)

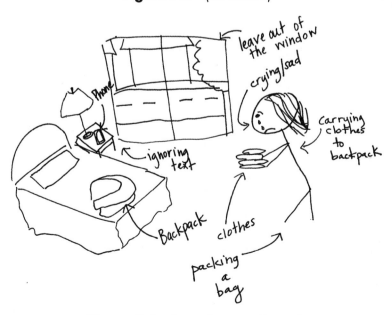

Figure 9.6   Scene Diagram Example

CHAPTER 10

Concept Attainment

What Is It?

Concept attainment is a strategy first created by psychologist Jerome Bruner (Bruner, Goodnow, & Austin, 1956). Educator Hilda Taba also contributed to its development (Taba, n.d.). This strategy helps guide learners toward a deeper understanding of a concept or rule (for example, when to use different verb tenses). Instead of the teacher explicitly explaining the concept to students, this strategy asks them to create their own interpretation through "yes" and "no" examples provided by the teacher. A "yes" example describes an important feature of a concept, whereas a "no" example describes something that does *not* align with the concept. Students compare and contrast these examples to determine the attributes or characteristics of a concept. This activity falls under the umbrella of inductive learning as students go from detailed examples to a "big idea" in a multistep process (Boulware & Crow, 2011, p. 491). Deductive learning, on the other hand, begins by introducing the broader concept or rule and then following with examples that reinforce it. See Chapter 4: Thematic Data Sets for more information.

In this chapter, we share a basic concept attainment protocol we use in our social studies classrooms to help students first understand and then extend their knowledge on a given concept. This protocol includes the following steps: choosing a topic, making a list of examples and nonexamples, studying the examples for commonalities, hypothesizing attributes, and testing hypotheses with student-created examples ("How the Strategic Teacher Plans for Concept Attainment," 2007).

Why We Like It

Concept attainment can be intriguing and motivating due to its novelty factor. In addition, it can be seen by many students as an engaging "puzzle." See Chapter 8: Current Event Case Study for more on the idea of how puzzles might motivate students.

We have found a high level of success when using concept attainment in the classroom. This strategy can be used to introduce a concept or to review one. In our experience, concept attainment leads to a deeper and longer-lasting understanding of the concepts.

Supporting Research

Concept attainment incorporates two different effective learning strategies—identifying similarities and differences and creating and testing hypotheses (which is what students are doing as they see the yes/no examples). Both strategies have been shown to increase student achievement (Marzano, Pickering, & Pollock, 2001).

Research also shows that there can be significant improvement in understanding for students who learn by using concept attainment versus those who learn using a textbook approach (Peters, 1974–1975). The same study showed similar results for readers of varying levels.

Common Core Connections

Pattern recognition, which is the key element of concept attainment, is highlighted in the Common Core, including identifying patterns in events and in word changes (Common Core, 2010i, 2010j). Thinking in this structured way helps students to identify patterns that they can apply in learning complex concepts.

Social Studies Connections

The National Council for the Social Studies promotes problem-solving and analytical skills as key to developing civic competence (National Council for the Social Studies, n.d.-b).

Application

The five-step process described in the following subsections includes choosing a topic, making a list of examples and nonexamples, studying the examples for commonalities, hypothesizing attributes, and testing hypotheses with student-created examples ("How the Strategic Teacher Plans," 2007).

We first describe in detail how we use this strategy to help students understand types of government, in this case democracy. We also provide several ideas about how to apply this instructional strategy with different social studies topics. We then explain how we use concept attainment to improve student writing.

Note: Concept Attainment is not a strategy we use every day or every week. We use it now and then to maximize its novelty effect when introducing or reviewing key concepts.

DEMOCRACY CONCEPT ATTAINMENT

We introduce the concept attainment protocol at the beginning of our US government course in order to review and reinforce the basic ideas of how democracy is supposed to work as a type of government (this lesson functions as an introduction, not as a detailed analysis of the concept).

Choosing a Topic

The first step in the process involves choosing the topic we want students to understand. In this case, it is the system of government we call democracy.

Making a List of Examples and Nonexamples

The next step is to create a list of "yes" and "no" examples of the concept. Table 10.1: Democracy Concept Attainment is the chart we created to illustrate attributes that are found – and not found – in an ideal democracy. For example, the "yes" column includes, "Power resides in the hands of citizens." On the other hand, the "no" section states, "Power given to a single person."

Table 10.1 Democracy Concept Attainment

Yes	No
	Power given to a single person
Power resides in the hands of all citizens	
	Small group of people, not chosen as representatives, make all decisions
Citizens vote to make decisions or vote for representatives to make decisions on their behalf	
	Only one political party allowed
Multiple political parties allowed and necessary	
All adult citizens are allowed to participate in making decisions through voting	
	Unfair or restricted elections
	Only people seen as the "best" or superior are allowed to rule
	Rulers are seen as chosen by a "higher power"

In our experience, it's a good idea to only use short examples. This length prevents the activity from becoming tedious.

Studying the Examples for Commonalities

Once we have created several examples for both sides of the chart, it's time to get started in the classroom. We begin by projecting the chart so that only the very top of the page (showing the words "yes" and "no") is visible. We withhold student copies at this time in order to ensure students are following along with the gradual revealing of examples instead of jumping ahead.

If this is the first time students have done concept attainment, it may help to give a brief overview of what they should expect. A teacher could say something like,

> *Today, we are practicing concept attainment. That means instead of just having to listen to me tell you a bunch of important information, I'm going to show you examples and have you figure out the big ideas. It's almost like you are a detective looking at clues to solve a case.*

Then, it's time to reveal the first "yes" example, "Power resides in the hands of citizens." Read the example aloud to students and instruct them to consider what is happening in this passage. Then, reveal the first "no" example, "Power given to a single person." Ask students to consider how the "no" example is different from the "yes."

Continue revealing the "yes" and "no" examples – one at a time – reminding students to "think about what these examples have in common or how they are different from one another." For example, after the first two "yes" examples and the first "no" example are revealed, the teacher can ask students to share with a partner their predictions about what topic is being described in the "yes" column. Students share their ideas with the class, and the teacher either affirms or clarifies that the answer is democracy, and that the "yes" examples demonstrate the attributes of a democracy (in other words, its characteristics).

Hypothesizing Attributes

The next step is to help students identify the attributes. The teacher can model this process. For example, we might say,

> *I notice that the first two examples include the words citizens and that those citizens "vote" or have "power." I'm going to underline those words because they are clues to figuring out an attribute of a democracy. A democracy is a type of government where the people in the country, the citizens, are involved in the decisions. I'm going to write down "citizens make decisions" in the margin of the "yes" column.*

We then pass out copies of Table 10.1: Democracy Concept Attainment to students. We further explain that an "attribute" is a quality or characteristic of something or someone. For example, "Ms. Johnson says good morning to all her students. Her attributes could be pleasant, professional, friendly, etc." We then ask them to review the passages and note the attributes represented in the "yes" items. We typically give students a few minutes to note these attributes in the margins and then have them compare what they wrote with a neighbor. We then repeat the process with the items from the "no" side of the chart.

For the "yes" category, students may write things like: *People are part of the government,* "*It's talking about The United States,*" or *There's more than one person in charge.* For the "no" category, they might write "King or Queen," "Dictator," or "one party." Students then share with the whole class while the teacher lists the attributes on the board or under the document camera.

If students need more support with identifying attributes, it may help to create a word bank. Giving some options helps to "narrow the path" for students while still encouraging them to carefully consider which attributes are being exemplified in Table 10.1: Democracy Concept Attainment.

Once we have shared all examples, we review the student-created list of attributes to check for agreement and/or suggestions for final modifications. We ask students to create a title for this chart, which up to this point has been nameless. The title should represent the larger concept the chart exemplifies. Students may generate titles like Democracy, A Type of Government, or Government in the United States, which are all acceptable. We often choose just one to use for clarity.

Testing Hypotheses with Student-Created Examples

Though students typically do well at understanding the larger picture of the concept of a democracy, they may not walk away from this activity with a sense of ownership without being able to contribute their own ideas. To meet this need, we provide an opportunity for student partners to add their own examples to the concept attainment chart or change some of the ones listed under "yes" to "no," or vice versa. For example, students might offer a new "yes" item that "People can join whatever political party they want or not join one at all." Or, they may change the "yes" item that states, "All adult citizens are allowed to participate in making decisions through voting" to a "no" item by saying "Only a small number of people can vote in elections."

After students have completed their own examples, we have them share with the class. Afterward, we reinforce the concept of democracy by asking students to write a paragraph summarizing the key ideas of this topic using the class list of attributes. These paragraphs can then be turned in for accountability purposes. See Figure 10.1: Dictatorship Paragraph Example for a summary paragraph developed after a concept attainment lesson on dictatorships.

This strategy can be used to teach other social studies concepts:

- The differences between primary and secondary sources
- Other types of government (dictatorship, monarchy)
- Different economic systems (capitalism, communism)
- Different world religions

CONCEPT ATTAINMENT TO IMPROVE WRITING

Concept attainment is a good strategy for writing instruction because it efficiently and effectively gives students feedback to edit their own writing. This lesson follows a similar process of choosing a topic, making a list of examples and nonexamples, studying the examples for commonalities, hypothesizing attributes, and testing hypotheses with new examples.

A teacher can begin by pinpointing a concept that students seem to be struggling with in their writing. The example in Table 10.2: Concept Attainment for Citing Sources could be used to help students accurately cite sources. We make our examples based on the most common errors in student work. Please keep in mind that while student work is an excellent source of models for both "yes" and "no" examples, we don't want to put students on the spot. We recommend adjusting the wording slightly or typing up the examples to help to keep the writers anonymous. Or,

Table 10.2 Concept Attainment for Citing Sources

Yes	No
According to the CIA Factbook, Brazil's population is . . .	
	Brazil's population is . . .
In the article "Running for Freedom" the writer claims . . .	
	The writer says . . .
	He says, ". . ."
In his book Larry Ferlazzo states, ". . ."	
	Larry says . . .
The Declaration of Independence states, ". . ."	
	"All men are created equal."

another option is to request student permission. In a classroom culture that views mistakes as opportunities to grow, often students *want* to publicly contribute their work. It's not unusual for our students to shout out during the lesson highlighting errors, "I wrote that!"

After creating the list of student examples, we show and read aloud each one on Table 10.2: Concept Attainment for Citing Sources. We ask students to write down and then share with their partner what the list is trying to illustrate. We might direct students to "Make a list of what you *should do* when citing sources" or ask "What should we *not do* when citing sources?"

Students can then apply the concept by writing an evidence-based paragraph that cites text. This will show whether they understand it or need further modeling. For more on evidence-based writing structures see Chapter 5: Writing in Social Studies.

Concept Attainment can be used to teach numerous writing skills including:

- Writing Resumés – In an economics course a teacher can help students see the style of writing that is appropriate for a resumé. Students will note, for example, that the "Yes" examples are absent of "me," "my," or "I." See Table 10.3: Resumé Concept Attainment.

Table 10.3 Resumé Concept Attainment

YES	NO
Communication – Translated English to Spanish for newly arrived immigrant students to assist them in developing mathematical knowledge.	
	Communication – Bilingual
	Good Communication Skills
Collaboration – Worked in small groups to develop highly regarded academic presentations.	
	Collaboration – Worked with others to complete projects.
	Problem Solving, Strong Work Ethic, Leadership, Handling Pressure
	Conflict Resolution – friends always come to me to help them with their problems
Conflict Resolution – Employed strategies learned in leadership course to assist peers in dealing with challenges in school.	
	Conflict Resolution – I used strategies I learned in my leadership class to help students at my school

YES	NO
Strong Work Ethic – Volunteered to assist teachers when opportunity arose, offering to pass out papers, carry items, and organize the classroom.	
Cashier at Wendy's – Expertly handled financial transactions to ensure efficient customer service was provided.	
	Cashier at Wendy's – tried to be on time most days and worked to control temper and not get fired.

- Evidence Analysis – Show students examples of effective analysis in an argument and poorly executed versions. Students can study what makes the difference between strong and weak analysis of evidence.

- Writing a Good Introduction – Show students how to start an essay with a strong opening. Display for students elements of an effective introduction (which, in general, could include a "hook," thesis statement, providing readers with context, giving a road map of what you are going to say) using a concept-attainment chart. Table 10.4: "Hooks" Concept Attainment is an example of how to teach students effective openers, also known as "hooks" (these can include an interesting fact, quotation, anecdote, engaging question, along with others).

Table 10.4 "Hooks" Concept Attainment

YES	NO
Imagine waking up many mornings to the smell of explosives or chemical weapons like napalm. That was the life of many Vietnamese for 30 years.	
	My essay is about the Vietnam War.
It's estimated that over three million unexploded mines remain in Vietnam from the war that took place there and ended in 1975.	
	Did you ever hear about the Vietnam War?
Is there ever really a winner in a war?	
	The Vietnam War happened a long time ago and it was bad.
What does winning a war look like?	
	Have you been to Vietnam?
Ho Chi Minh, the leader of North Vietnam, once said, "You can kill 10 of my men for every one I kill of yours. But even at those odds, you will lose and I will win."	
	The United States won the war.

- Writing a Good Conclusion – Help students understand the attributes of an effective conclusion in a concept-attainment chart (which, in general, could include rephrasing the thesis statement, summarizing main points, explaining why the topic is important, a call to action).

- Addressing Common Grammar Issues – Use concept attainment to highlight common student errors such as incorrect verb tense and writing in a passive – instead of active – voice.

DIFFERENTIATION

Concept attainment can be modified for ELL students by incorporating images into the lists. Placing images next to the text can provide instructional support for ELL students to access the language. For example, a teacher could modify Table 10.1: Democracy Concept Attainment by adding pictures to the columns. A picture of a King wearing a crown could be added to "Power given to a single person." A picture of people headed to clearly labeled voting booths could be placed next to "Citizens vote to make decisions or vote for representatives to make decisions on their behalf."

Another way to support ELLs and students with learning differences is to have students create the images. By quickly sketching a visual for each of the examples in a concept-attainment list, students can process and improve their memory for the item. Research has shown that drawing pictures can be especially helpful to remember meanings (University of Waterloo, 2016).

ADVANCED EXTENSIONS

Once students have become familiar with the concept-attainment strategy, they can create their own examples. Students can show their understanding of a given topic by coming up with a list of "yes" and "no" examples. For instance, in a world history course, students may be divided into small groups and assigned an empire from history (The Kingdom of Kush, Roman Empire, Mongol Empire, Aztec, etc.). Students then use their class materials or do further research to create lists of examples and nonexamples that illustrate the attributes of their assigned empire.

After creating their lists, students can "teach" their concept to a different group following the same protocol described in the application section of this chapter. Students can then write summary paragraphs or create illustrations that incorporate the attributes of each empire.

Student Handouts and Examples

Table 10.1: Democracy Concept Attainment

Figure 10.1: Dictatorship Paragraph Example

Table 10.2: Concept Attainment for Citing Sources

Table 10.3: Resumé Concept Attainment

Table 10.4: "Hooks" Concept Attainment

What Could Go Wrong?

Students may not always get the concept. If you find students struggling to understand the concept even after modeling, try shortening or simplifying the examples or adding visuals.

Another idea is to start with a concept students already know. For example, list a series of even numbers under the "yes" side and odd numbers under the "no" side. Work up to larger, more complex concepts. Remember, concept attainment may be very different from how most students have learned before, so it may take them a while to get the hang of it.

Technology Connections

For more information, including lesson examples, on concept attainment and other forms of inductive learning, see "The Best Resources About Inductive Learning & Teaching" (http://larryferlazzo.edublogs.org/2015/01/16/the-best-resources-about-inductive-learning-teaching).

Figures

A dictatorship is a type of government where the leadership has total power. Usually there is one leader or a small group of leaders. The people who live under this type of government don't have much power even though the government may try to make it seem like they do. Often a dictatorship happens when there is a conflict or other disruption in the country and someone steps in to take power. Nazi Germany was an example of a dictatorship.

Figure 10.1 Dictatorship Paragraph Example

SECTION II

Analysis Tools

CHAPTER 11

Questions for Learning

What Is It?

Obviously, questions – and their answers – are critical for the success of any class-room. In this chapter, we offer a systematic approach to both teacher-generated and student-generated questions. We begin by sharing four types of teacher-generated questions: essential, guiding, text-dependent, and hook. Jay McTighe and Grant Wiggins popularized these types of questions in their book *Essential Questions: Opening Doors to Student Understanding* (2013). Then we discuss how to assist students in developing higher-level questions.

Why We Like It

We like how essential questions provide an opportunity to connect the past to the present by linking together overarching themes of power, ethics, and the human condition. When asking students questions like, "Why do humans sometimes oppress each other when one group gains power?" while studying colonialism, learners can connect to modern day examples of oppression. Students can use a question like this one to tap into possible struggles with power that they, their families, or their communities have faced and are facing.

In addition, using hook and guiding questions can increase the accessibility of essential questions. These questions act like stepping-stones to help students achieve higher-level thinking. Hook questions help capture student interest. Once interest has been generated, guiding questions help direct students toward specific information (McTighe & Wiggins, 2013, Chapter 1). Students can then use this information to respond to an essential question. In this way, these three questions work together to scaffold critical thinking as students are asked to predict, infer, analyze, and make connections.

Using a variety of questioning techniques can boost relevance in the classroom (Obenchain, Orr, & Davis, 2011, p. 191). Student-generated questions in particular can help to increase curiosity. In our experience, when students create their own questions, they develop a sense of ownership and seem more willing to delve into research to find answers.

Supporting Research

One of the best ways to make social studies content more meaningful to students is through historical inquiry: using evidence to investigate historical questions (Foster & Padgett a 1999, p. 357). In other words, students need to study "big" questions, as well as to ask their own. Students who participate in a process of inquiry can develop critical thinking skills, a greater understanding of their own identity, and an increased ability to connect the past to the present (Foster & Padgett, 1999, pp. 357–358).

Other research has shown that providing opportunities for students to generate questions for a topic of study can lead to increased ownership and engagement ("Educators Want Students to Ask," 2012).

Common Core Connections

The Common Core encourages the use of questions to increase engagement by asking teachers to "construct questions and tasks that motivate students to read inquisitively and carefully" (Coleman & Pimentel, 2012, p. 20).

In addition, both teacher and student-generated questions help students analyze informational text, which in turn can support evidence-based writing (Coleman & Pimentel, 2012, p. 8).

Social Studies Connections

The College, Career, and Civic Life (C3) Framework from the National Council for the Social Studies notes the importance of questions, both teacher and student-generated, with the inclusion of the "Inquiry Arc." This arc outlines the steps of inquiry needed to guide students in their pursuit of knowledge to become active and successful civic participants (National Council for the Social Studies, 2010, p. 12). The framework states that "central to a rich social studies experience is the capability for developing questions that can frame and advance an inquiry" (National Council for the Social Studies, 2010, p. 23).

Application

In the sections that follow, we explain four types of teacher-generated questions: essential, guiding, text-dependent, and hook.

Essential questions are "big" questions. They can relate to many social studies contexts and be revisited multiple times while eliciting higher-order thinking (McTighe & Wiggins, 2013, Chapter 1). An example might be "Does labeling and stereotyping influence how we look at and understand the world?" This question could easily fit into many social studies classrooms linking together social justice issues throughout history.

Guiding questions are queries that can help guide the learner toward key information needed in order to address components of an essential question (McTighe & Wiggins, 2013, Chapter 1). For example, "What effect did stereotypes have on Japanese Americans during WWII?" This kind of question helps point students to key content without being overly directive. We also explore using text-dependent questions, as a version of guiding questions to help direct student to specific content within a text.

The fourth type of question explored in this chapter is called a hook question, which helps engage learners in the topic in order to connect to both guiding and essential questions (McTighe & Wiggins, 2013, Chapter 1). An example might be "If the police forced you to leave your home and possessions because of your ethnicity, how do you think you would feel and why?" Students are likely to have a strong response to this type of question without much assistance from the teacher.

Examples for each type of teacher-generated question are included in Table 11.1 Types of Questions Examples.

Essential questions are the ones we would introduce when opening a unit to give students an idea of what they should be able to answer by the end. In fact, we often close out a unit by having students revisit these questions. Guiding questions are used at various times during a topic of study when we are examining a group of texts or materials focused on one aspect of the essential question. We use hook questions whenever possible to stimulate higher levels of student engagement prior to intense work on one or multiple texts.

The latter section of this chapter will discuss student-developed questions. This practice is key to the process of inquiry, a major focus of both the Common Core and the National Council for the Social Studies (Common Core State Standards Initiative, 2010u; National Council for the Social Studies, 2010, p. 17, dimension 1).

Questions obviously require answers, and there are multiple ways students can respond to them. These responses include various types of writing (short answer and extended), sharing with a partner, sharing with a small group or a class, and so on. Students may also use technology to respond to questions. Applications like Google Classroom or Edmodo make it fairly easy for students to share responses online.

Table 11.1 Types of Questions Examples

Essential Question	Guiding Question	Hook Question
How does the area you live in affect your life?	What are the major land features of our local area?	What natural disaster could have the biggest impact on our area and why?
What factors make places around the world unique?	How is the landscape related to the culture of a people in a given area?	How is the place you live special?
How might it feel to live through a conflict that disrupts your way of life?	What was the experience of soldiers during World War I?	Which was worse, mustard gas or trench foot?
What is the relationship between choices and consequences?	What led to the decision to drop the atomic bomb on Japan during World War II?	What would it be like if suddenly 90% of your city was gone?
What is the root cause of prejudice and social bias and how can they be overcome?	What were two major elements of the Civil Rights movement?	How have you been treated unfairly?
Is there a price to obtaining freedom from oppression? If so, what is it?	What risks did the colonies take when declaring independence from Great Britain?	Is war worth it?
Whose story is told in history?	What, if any, attributes were shared by writers of foundational documents for the United States?	Does history tell your story?
How can you balance rights and responsibilities?	Why isn't yelling "fire" in a crowded movie theater protected by the First Amendment?	Should you be held responsible for everything you say?
Why do people have to work?	What are some protections workers have in the United States?	What is your ideal job?

Source: Essential Questions from or modified from the following sources: https://wabisabistore.com/blogs/essential-questions/a-list-of-over-100-awesome-essential-questions?_pos=5&_sid=bbee66510&_ss=r, www.wallingford.k12.ct.us/uploaded/Curriculum/SOCIAL_STUDIES_K-12/SS_K-12_EUs_&_EQs.pdf, www.teachthought.com/pedagogy/examples-of-essential-questions, www.ascd.org/publications/books/109004/chapters/What-Makes-a-Question-Essential%A2.aspx

TEACHER-GENERATED QUESTIONS

General Advice

We suggest taking the time to brainstorm questions prior to teaching a lesson. Generating questions to guide instruction is a key element of "backward design." Planning a unit by beginning with what students are expected to know and be able to do at the end (along with the questions to assist them in getting there) is a strategy popularized in the education world by Grant Wiggins and Jay McTighe (Bowen, 2017). This doesn't mean that a question that pops into mind during a lesson should be discarded because it's not in the "plan." It does mean, however, that planning in advance can benefit both teachers and students.

Teachers should also carefully consider how they respond to student answers. For example, asking "Can you elaborate on that?" or a similar comment can encourage students to provide a more complete and well thought-out response. This doesn't mean that *every* student response needs follow-up. However, answers that are vague, incorrect, or, on the other hand, particularly insightful, can provide opportunities for fruitful follow-up discussions. When a student answer is clearly incorrect, the point is not humiliation but encouragement of a class environment where mistakes are acknowledged and viewed as learning opportunities. So, our response to a wrong answer might be "I can see how you might think that, but . . ."

Additionally, a teacher needs to consider that well thought-out responses take time. Much research has been done on the concept of "wait time" – the pause between when a teacher asks a question and a student answers it. Increasing wait time to just three seconds can result in improved student answers, including increased length of response and decrease in failure to respond (Rowe, 1986, p. 3). Another option is to ask students to write down their responses and share them with a partner prior to a larger class discussion.

Essential Questions

Essential questions get to the heart of the big ideas in social studies. These open-ended questions encourage students to think about major issues present throughout history and ones that challenge our world today. Instead of requiring students to memorize names, dates, and facts, essential questions bring up themes that can help students make connections between past and current events, along with their own life experiences. For example, an essential question like "How might conflict be avoided?" may cross through many social studies courses during investigations of wars (past or present) and connect to students' personal experiences of conflict. Another question like "What story does a map tell?" may touch on themes common in geography, such as migration or landscapes. It might also relate to topics from world history, including power or political change (Who made the boundaries on the map? What perspectives does the design of the map represent?). It could also lead to students creating a map of their own neighborhood and exploring the community story it tells.

These questions can be used in multiple ways. We often open a unit of study with an essential question. A teacher may also have students respond to the question to assess prior knowledge before deciding what to include in a unit. We often utilize an essential question on a synthesis chart that students keep in their folders (described in Chapter 14: Synthesis Charts). Students can add information to their synthesis chart to help them respond to the question as they move through a unit.

In our classrooms, we often use these questions to anchor a series of readings. In other words, they can be used as an encompassing prompt on a given topic. For example, after reading selections that describe combat from the Vietnam War, students can use this information to answer an essential question on the effects of war.

A question such as "What might be the worst long-term impact of a near-death experience?" could help students consider the effects of war long after the battles are over. It may benefit students to stop at the end of each reading to add new textual evidence to a response.

Essential questions have no predetermined correct answer but, instead, can encourage responses that evolve and change over time. Students may modify their answers as they learn different perspectives. They may revisit a question multiple times throughout a single unit or even across several units. These questions can frame key learning goals for the entire year. For example, the question "What causes change?" may fall under a larger theme of cause and effect in social studies and could apply to multiple units throughout the year.

Another example of how essential questions can encourage student thinking might be when addressing a standard about World War I. A teacher may ask "What was the human impact of World War I?" This question asks students to consider how all people, not just soldiers, may have been affected by this war – civilians in the war zones, US families of soldiers who fought in the war, and so on. This question could be revisited many times during the unit as new information is uncovered. A teacher may connect this question to a larger theme in history by modifying it into a question like "How might it feel to live through a conflict that disrupts your life?" Though the essence of the question is the same, this modified version encourages students to consider the effects of conflict in general – beyond WWI.

Guiding Questions

In some ways, guiding questions are open-ended, but they are far more directive than essential questions. They can help bridge the gap between information presented in class and the essential questions provided to students. We generally use guiding questions during reading to lead students toward information that they may need to answer an essential question. We may use a guiding question like "What was the experience of the soldier during WWI?" when reading a series of letters home from soldiers or looking at a series of photos of trench warfare.

Students may note that the experience of soldiers could help them respond to the unit's essential question, "What was the human impact of World War I?" The key with this type of question is using it as a stepping-stone to access the higher-level thinking that tends to come along with an essential question. For example, we take an essential question like "How might it feel to live through a conflict that disrupts your life?" or a more content-specific question like "What was the human impact of World War I?" and develop smaller guiding questions to go with it (see Table 11.2: Essential and Guiding Question Example). These guiding questions support students to develop a more sophisticated, evidence-based answer to the essential question.

Table 11.2 Essential and Guiding Question Example

EQ: What was the human impact of World War I?		
GQ: What was the experience of the soldier during World War I?	GQ: What challenges did civilians confront due to World War I?	GQ: Which political leaders lost power due to World War I?

These types of questions can also serve as a way to check for comprehension after learning new information.

For more examples, please see Table 11.1: Types of Questions Examples.

Guiding questions can be a useful planning tool for teachers. Developing guiding questions can help teachers focus their instruction and select texts which cover specific content. There is an overwhelming amount of information for many topics in history. Sifting through historical data can be difficult, and guiding questions can help narrow the focus for both students and teachers.

Text-Dependent Questions

Guiding questions can also be text-dependent questions used to help direct students to specific content within a text. These questions require the reader to respond using evidence from the text. Sometimes, teachers ask questions that don't require reading of the text but, instead, focus only on the students' feelings or opinions about it. Text-dependent questions, on the other hand, can promote engagement *and* connections by requiring a deeper reading of the text. These types of questions can push students to think critically about the text as they look for evidence to support their answers (Bekel, n.d.).

For example, after reading the Treaty of Versailles, students might be asked "What would you have been thinking if you were present at the signing of this treaty?" This question doesn't *explicitly* require a response incorporating information from the text. Instead, a text-dependent question could be, "Which punishment given to Germany was the most severe and why?" This question requires students to use information from the text to respond *and* allows students to share their opinion as well. These questions are teacher-created and can be given to students throughout the reading of a text.

Based on the work of Douglas Fisher and Nancy Frey (Bekel, n.d.), we create text-dependent questions that fall into three categories:

- Initial questions may probe the reader's *general understanding of key ideas* from the text. For example, "What was the main goal of the Treaty of Versailles?" or "What are three ways the Treaty of Versailles affected Germany?"

- Next, questions might analyze the *structure of the text, word choice, and author's purpose*. For example, "Why did the authors choose to use the word _____?"

or "Why do you think the authors of the treaty included restrictions on military size?"

- Finally, the highest level of questions can ask readers *to make inferences or arguments as well as intertextual connections*. For example, "In what ways might the Treaty of Versailles have gone against the spirit of President Woodrow Wilson's 14 points?" Or "How might the treaty have been different if Germany had been allowed to contribute?"

Hook Questions

A hook question is a stimulating question that can immediately elicit a strong response. These questions can be thought provoking and can help build student motivation. Once students are "hooked" by a question, they may be more interested in searching for information to respond to guiding questions. These guiding questions, in turn, help students in developing answers to the larger essential questions. In this way, all three types of questions work together to promote critical thinking in social studies.

For example, during the study of World War I we use the hook question, "Which is worse, mustard gas or trench foot?" to engage students prior to reading soldiers' personal accounts of trench warfare. The scrolling cursive handwriting and colloquial way of speaking from early 20th-century documents can be intimidating. The hook question can create a higher level of interest to "dig in" to this type of difficult text.

We can also use a hook question to prompt students to make personal connections. These questions can draw students' attention to a key piece of information and provide an important opportunity to practice empathy. For example, when discussing the use of mustard gas during World War I, we could ask "Imagine constantly being on the edge of death. What might it be like to think the air you are breathing may become deadly at any time?" To truly learn from history, we need to put ourselves in other people's shoes. Hook questions can help students consider multiple perspectives.

Hook questions are typically used at the beginning of an activity, but can also be asked at other times. For example, when there is a lull in energy, a stimulating question may be just what is needed to bring it back up.

STUDENT-GENERATED QUESTIONS

Student-generated questions are as important as teacher-generated questions. Shanna Peeples, the 2015 National Teacher of the Year, notes in *Education Week* that allowing students to create their own questions changes them from being bystanders to "active participants" in their own learning (Ferlazzo, 2017, November 28).

Student-generated questions can be developed to pique interest at the start of a unit or to dive deeper into a topic. They can also provide a window into the mind of the student, helping the teacher to target instruction.

Students creating questions is an important process in itself. Extensive research shows that developing "question-asking" skills can lead to greater personal, academic, and professional success (Brooks & John, 2018). In addition, as students generate their own questions, they can become more motivated to find the answers – in class readings and through their own research.

Here is a list of ways to support students in developing their own questions:

- When beginning a unit, write the topic on the board. Instruct students to generate a list of questions they have about the unit on sticky notes and place them on the board near the topic. Give students a set amount of time in order to create a sense of urgency – we typically do two or three minutes. Use the student-generated examples to create a class list of key questions to guide learning.

- Teach students the difference between right-there and think-about questions. Right-there questions are those where the answer is easily located within the text – something that can be pointed to because it's "right there." Think-about questions extend beyond the text and may ask readers to make connections or inferences in order to respond to them. A teacher can direct students to practice creating both types of questions for a selection of text. (See Chapter 2: Reading Strategies and Chapter 3: Read-Aloud Protocol for more about these types of questions.) They can then answer the questions themselves or have their classmates respond to them.

- Another way to begin a unit of study with student-generated questions is to use a Know-Want-Learned (KWL) graphic organizer. These charts ask students to begin by writing down what they think they already know about a topic. Next, students are asked to generate questions, or what they want to know about a topic. Later, and throughout the unit, students add new information to the last column (the learned section) of the chart as they find answers to their questions. They can also then generate more questions based on these new "learnings."

- Prior to reading an article or other primary source document, direct students to give the article a quick scan and generate questions based on the title, any subheadings, or pictures. Then, during reading, instruct students to note any answers to their questions that may arise. Pause throughout the reading to allow for further questioning as students learn more. These additional rounds of questioning can encourage students to ask deeper and/or more specific questions. For example, students may ask about how many soldiers died on the battlefront in an initial reading about the American Civil War. Later, they may develop that topic further by generating a question that investigates the weapons used during the war and if it was ethical to use them.

- After reading a text, ask students to create their own writing prompt. Then, direct students (or have them ask a classmate) to answer their question using an evidence-based argument. The creation of their own prompts can allow students to feel ownership while, at the same time, gauging their comprehension of the material. For example, after reading a letter home from a soldier during WWI, we might expect a student to form a question about the experience of war. If not, this may be a clue that they don't understand the content and that we may need to provide further information on the topic.

- After brainstorming questions using one of the aforementioned methods, have students categorize the questions. Students can categorize by topic, type of question, or by level of difficulty. For example, if students are categorizing by level of difficulty they may see "What was one cause of World War I?" as an easier question than "To what extent was money a cause of World War I?" The first question can be addressed with well-known, concrete answers. The second question requires their opinions backed by an analysis of evidence from unit materials. The teacher could then instruct students to find the answers for two questions from each category.

- Give students academic starters or frames to help them create a variety of questions. Students can be encouraged to develop higher level and more creative questions for any of the previously mentioned activities by providing these scaffolds. For examples of question stems that students can use, check out the blog post "28 Critical Thinking Question Stems for Any Content Area" from TeachThought (2017). Many question-starters for Bloom's Taxonomy or Revised Bloom's Taxonomy are also available online.

- After any activity for which students are asked to develop questions, a follow-up assignment (even for extra credit) can be to find the answers and share them in writing, in a poster, or in an oral presentation.

- Have students do a "What If?" history project. In these projects, students take an important event from history and ask the question "What if it had happened differently?" Students are encouraged to wonder and explore alternative historical timelines. For more about alternative timelines, see Chapter 7: Timelines Revisited. Larry Ferlazzo also has a blog post "What If? History Projects" (2019), which includes student examples and assessment rubrics.

DIFFERENTIATION

Questions that are less focused on content about the United States may work better for English language learners (ELL) students. For example, while newcomer ELL students may have limited knowledge of US history, they can likely relate to more general questions like "What is power?" or "Who should be a leader?" Of course, question starters can be helpful scaffolds for all students, including ELLs and those who learn differently.

Another tip is to make sure that the text aligns with the questions. It may be difficult for students who learn differently to have to sift through extra, unrelated material in order to find the information to answer a question. Teachers may want to create edited versions of texts that only contain key information. For more on "engineering the text" see Chapter 3: Read-Aloud Protocol and Chapter 13: Analysis of Primary Sources.

ADVANCED EXTENSIONS

One advanced extension activity might be dividing students into small groups and instructing them to develop essential questions for each unit of study. Students can generate several questions and then select one to answer. They can also compete with each other for the most thought-provoking hook question for a particular text. After each student generates hook questions, they can vote in their small groups for which question they think is best. Then, the class can review those questions and they can select a "winning" question. Students can then respond to the winning question in writing or in a small-group discussion.

Another idea is for students to create thought-provoking questions for each level of the Revised Bloom's Taxonomy (n.d.). The revised taxonomy ranks levels of thinking in the following way: remember, understand, apply, analyze, evaluate, and create. By first providing key words and examples from each of the types of questions, students can then create their own. For example, the remember-level questions might use words like *define, describe,* or *quote*. When considering World War II, students may ask a question like, "How would you describe the event that officially entered the United States into World War II?" Then, students can create a question for the next level of thinking, understanding. Considering the same topic, students might create a question like, "Why was the attack on Pearl Harbor during World War II a pivotal moment?" They can continue to move through the thinking levels, crafting questions for each. Students can respond to these questions using materials from the unit or from additional online research.

Student Handouts and Examples

Table 11.1: Types of Questions Examples

Table 11.2: Essential and Guiding Question Example

What Could Go Wrong?

Questions *we* think are engaging don't always engage *students* in the same way. Even the most carefully thought-out questions may not create magic in your classroom. It's important to keep trying a variety of questions to get a feel for what types of queries or topics will pique student interest. Continuing to ask questions, and even better, encouraging your students to ask questions is the best way to move toward deep learning in social studies.

Another issue that may arise is that not all questions will be answered – and that's okay. Sometimes it just isn't possible to provide an answer to every question asked in class. In our experience, the *process* of developing and considering questions is what creates engagement, interest, and relevance.

Technology Connections

For additional ideas on how to use questions in the classroom, see Larry Ferlazzo's blog post "The Best Posts & Articles About Asking Good Questions — Help Me Find More" (http://larryferlazzo.edublogs.org/2012/05/23/the-best-posts-articles-about-asking-good-questions-help-me-find-more).

CHAPTER 12

Image Analysis

What Is It?

This chapter explains how we use a protocol to facilitate the analysis of images such as photos, paintings, political cartoons, and videos. We view these analysis activities as a form of "close reading." "Close reading," according to the late Grant Wiggins (2013), is a structured way to reread complex texts to determine meaning. The skills required to closely read written texts can be applied to different forms of media (Lehman & Roberts, 2013, p. 6). Our image-rich culture suggests that it's important for students to practice close reading of images to help them develop visual literacy: "the ability to interpret, recognize, appreciate, and understand information presented through visible actions, objects, and symbols" ("Museums, Libraries," n.d.).

Why We Like It

In our experience, this visual strategy reaches students who might struggle with reading and writing but "light up" when working with visuals. Research suggests that visuals are easier than words to recognize and process (Dewan, 2015, p. 2). In other words, the use of images can increase engagement for a diverse set of learners. The benefits of using images are especially evident for English language learners (ELLs) who may not yet have the language skills to build context from only reading text.

We also like the way this strategy helps our students practice "close reading" of images. In the modern era, where students are constantly bombarded by visuals, we may incorrectly assume that students are proficient in visual literacy (being able to understand information presented visually) ("Museums, Libraries," n.d.).

Though students spend a large part of their day viewing images through social media, many lack the skills to analyze and understand images in an academic setting. Employing a thoughtful protocol – a way to guide students through viewing a series of images – can help them develop this important skill.

Additionally, this strategy gives students the opportunity to practice higher-order thinking and reach deeper content comprehension. For example, students may read a text about Japanese American Internment camps and learn basic information. However, applying a protocol to related images can help students bring this information "to life" by helping them note important details, make evidence-based inferences, and evaluate relevance.

Supporting Research

Various studies support the notion that helping students develop media literacy fosters critical thinking (Stein & Prewitt, 2009, p. 136). Further, studies on cognition have found that the use of media can support deeper learning (Dewan, 2015, p. 2).

In addition, research has shown that reading images is much like reading text: "as a reader, we don't simply see an image – we take in a range of data . . . across a series of sequential images" (Apkon, 2014, p. 77). Yet, just as students need guidance with reading to reach comprehension, students need help to analyze and interpret images as well (Finson, Olson, & Emig, 2015, p. 56). The graphic organizers in this chapter provide our students with this needed support.

Educators and researchers Douglas Fisher and Nancy Frey, as well as others, suggest that close reading is the investigation of a text done by noting details and patterns (2014b, p. 368). We, and many others like media literacy expert Frank Baker (2014), have applied a modified version of close reading to images.

Common Core Connections

The *Common Core for History/Social Studies* asks students to "Integrate and evaluate multiple sources of information presented in diverse formats and media (e.g., visually, quantitatively, as well as in words) in order to address a question or solve a problem" (Common Core, 2010s). This chapter provides a detailed process to support students in this kind of analysis.

Social Studies Connections

Primary sources are a major focus of the College Career and Civic Life (C3) Framework from the National Council for the Social Studies (NCSS, 2010, p. 48). These sources include images such as photos, paintings, and political cartoons.

Students need to know how to analyze them in order to use them as evidence in the inquiry process, the foundation of the C3 Framework (NCSS, 2010, p. 6).

Application

We will explain a protocol used to help students analyze four types of images – photographs, paintings, political cartoons, and videos. We explain the unique purpose of each kind of image and then provide guidance about how to analyze them using a four-phase protocol: prewriting to set the stage, noting what we see, making evidence-based inferences, and evaluating relevance. These phases are a modified version of Todd Finley's application of "deep viewing" (2014), which itself is modified from concepts developed by Ann Watts Pailliotet (1993).

The first phase of the protocol, prewriting to set the stage, helps students activate prior knowledge by helping them make connections to the images (Alber, 2011). Students are encouraged to slow down and notice details in the second phase, noting what they see. We provide graphic organizers to help guide this process.

Students are asked to reach a conclusion based on what they noticed in the picture for the third phase of the protocol, making evidence-based inferences. To help students reach higher levels of thinking, we model and provide sentence frames to support these written responses.

We use written prompts in the last phase of our protocol, evaluating relevance. Students explain how the image is both relevant to their personal lives and to the greater topic that the image represents.

Although we use these four phases of analysis for all of the different images in this chapter, we will also explain the modifications we make for each medium. Content examples from our social studies classrooms are used as models for each analysis activity. We conclude every section with additional strategies to facilitate analysis of images. All the activities listed in this chapter can be applied to a variety of social studies topics.

PHOTOGRAPHS

A photograph is a familiar medium that can serve as a primary source in all social studies classrooms. These types of images can work as a time machine to see and understand real people, places, and events.

Photographs of events or people can inject authenticity into the classroom. Like real historians, students can analyze and interpret the historical or social value of a picture (with teacher guidance). In addition, close reading of photos can encourage meaningful conversations and develop background about a topic (Ferlazzo & Sypnieski, 2018a, March).

Protocol

In the following section, we model how we facilitate the analysis of a photograph with an example from our US history courses. To introduce the study of Japanese American internment camps during World War II, we guide students through the four phases of analysis: prewriting to set the stage, noting what we see, making evidence-based inferences, and evaluating relevance. We provide a graphic organizer, Figure 12.1: Image Analysis Chart, to help scaffold this process.

Using a picture is a novel way to introduce a new unit. Since images are easier to recall than words, starting a new topic with a photograph can provide historical context that students can use to understand the upcoming content (Dewan, 2015, p. 2). For example, our picture about Japanese American internment can introduce students to concepts like forced relocation, a major idea of the unit.

Prewriting to Set the Stage

Prior to viewing any photos, we begin by presenting a writing prompt to students in order to activate prior knowledge and prepare them to make connections. For example, *before* projecting our picture about Japanese American internment, we pose the following question: "How do you think it feels to be forced to move? Have you, or anyone you know, ever experienced anything like this?" We tell students they can share similar experiences they have read about or seen in a movie if they can't think of a personal response.

After five minutes of writing time, students share their responses with a partner. We often hear stories of being evicted, deported, parents/guardians moving families when kids wanted to stay, and students sent out of class or expelled from schools. We thank students for sharing such personal information. Then, we make it a point to mention that it takes a lot of bravery, and emotional strength, to share such difficult experiences. Yet, doing so can help us connect to each other, and the topic we are studying, in a more meaningful way.

We need to always remember that, yes, we must cover content, but must also make sure we do no harm. We must be "trauma-informed." Trauma is "a reaction to a shocking or painful event or series of negative events" (Responding to Trauma, 2016). We must be ready to support our students when a classroom activity can trigger personal pain. We may need to follow up this activity in ways ranging from a quick personal conversation to an immediate call to Child Protective Services, or connect students with a counselor.

Using prompts to help set the stage for personal connections can happen in any social studies unit. For example, when studying Brazil in geography class and prior to showing a photo of Carnival, we might ask students to write about community-wide parades or celebrations that they have experienced. While studying the First

Amendment, and before showing an image of the march to Selma led by Martin Luther King Jr., we ask students if they have ever had to take a risk to stand up for a personal belief (we give our own examples, which might include a political act or supporting a student who was being treated unfairly by an administrator or another teacher).

Noting What We See

After prewriting to set the stage, we pass out Figure 12.1: Image Analysis Chart. We walk students through the first three questions, which ask them to focus on what they *see* in the photo on a basic level. We explain that it's difficult to do a careful analysis of an image before identifying the main elements.

We project Figure 12.2: Japanese American Evacuation – Photo (making sure the image's title cannot be seen) and read the task from the first box in Figure 12.1: Image Analysis Chart, "After viewing the picture silently for one minute, please write one or two things that **stand out** to you." Next, we say something like:

> *Now that time is up, for the first box, I am going to write "a young child with a worried look" because that is the first thing that caught my attention.*

We ask the class to raise their hands if they noticed the same thing, and if so, to write it down – if they haven't already done so. We invite others to share if they noticed something different, and provide positive feedback. This way, students see there are no "correct" answers and all insights are valuable.

Next, we move on to the second question, which says, "Now, please **list** everything **you see** in the photo. Don't worry about the order of the items, just include as many details as you can." Students are given three minutes to write. Then they compare papers with a partner for about 30 seconds. This sharing process reinforces that not everyone notices the same things.

In the third question, students are asked to list what action(s) seem to be taking place in the picture. We think aloud and note that people just seem to be standing in Figure 12.2: Japanese American Evacuation – Photo. We write this observation in the third box for students to copy down. They are invited to list any other activities they see in the photo.

We then ask students to think like a professional photographer for question four: "What seems to be the main focal point, or central subject, of the picture? What is in the background? What could you see if you extended the boundaries of the picture?" We explain that a *focal point* is what the photographer is trying to draw attention to in the picture, whereas *background* might be people or items in the scenery or surroundings. This may help students begin thinking about the intentions of the photographer. For example, we list the young child as the focal point in the image. For background, we list the adults that surround him. If students need more support, we share an example from Figure 12.3: Teacher Model – Photo Analysis Chart.

The last step for the fourth question on Figure 12.1: Image Analysis Chart asks students to make an educated guess about what is *not* in the picture (What could you see if you extended the boundaries of the picture?).

To scaffold their response, we sometimes rephrase this question: "What do you think the photographer cut or left out?" Students typically mention the faces of the adults and a large crowd of people including more young children.

In the fifth question, students are asked to further describe the focal point of the picture they identified previously. This prompt can help them analyze the main subject of the image.

Evidence-Based Inferences

The sixth question asks students to determine the topic or purpose of the picture, as well as its possible time period. To scaffold making evidence-based inferences, the analysis chart provides sentence frames. We model how to use these frames by saying something like:

> ***I think this picture might be about*** *a group of people waiting around to be taken somewhere they don't really want to go* ***because the image shows*** *a young child who seems to be unsure about where he is, along with a bag and people waiting around.* ***I believe the time period is around*** *the early 1900s* ***because*** *the picture is in black and white and I have seen similar clothes in movies from that time period.*

We purposely write a sample conclusion that does not include *all* of the clues available, leaving some for students to craft their own inferences. For example, we did not mention what appears to be military boots, the hanging paper tag on the child, or the portion of a train in the background. After the model, partners work together to complete the sentence frames in the sixth question. Then, we call on a few students to share their completed responses.

With some dramatic flair, we unveil the title of the picture (if a title is not available, we just provide information about it). We do this so students can compare their conclusions. For this picture about Japanese American internment, we show the official title from the Library of Congress: "Los Angeles, California. Japanese

American evacuation from West Coast areas under U.S. Army war emergency order. Japanese American child who will go with his parents to Owens Valley."

Although some students may celebrate being "right" about their evidence-based conclusions, we end this phase of the photo analysis by emphasizing the effort and critical thinking that all students invested into the "detective work."

It is important to remember that students have yet to study the topic of the photo: in this case, Japanese American internment during World War II. The last section of the graphic organizer invites them to list questions that they now have about this topic. They can connect these questions to future unit work.

Evaluating Relevance

Now that students have noted details about the image and determined its subject matter, we help them assess the relevance of the picture. We start with personal relevance by having students reflect back to the opening prompt of this activity, "How do you think it feels to be forced to move? Have you, or anyone you know, ever experienced anything like this?" We might say something like,

> *Reread your response to the opening prompt about being forced to move. Is there anything in your response, or in the responses of other students in class, that might connect to this picture? Explain.*

Students then share their comments with a partner and we call on a few to share with the whole class. We often hear students saying that the picture reminds them of feeling confused or even lost in the middle of a sudden move. Sometimes, students share that *they* remember having their things sitting on the pavement as they rushed out of their home.

Then, we help students reach higher levels of critical thinking by assessing the historical relevance of the photo. We often provide a series of reflective, evidence-based prompts like the following:

1. What do you think was the purpose of this photograph when it was taken? What makes you think this?

2. For a historian studying Japanese American internment during World War II, what do you think is the historical significance of this photo? In other words, why might it be important? Explain your reasoning.

We typically use strategies from Chapter 5: Writing in Social Studies to support students when responding to these prompts.

Although we use Figure 12.1: Image Analysis Chart and Figure 12.2: Japanese American Evacuation – Photo to introduce a unit on Japanese American internment during World War II, they can be used for other purposes. For example, the image of the little boy could be used to bring attention to the *process* that Japanese Americans had to endure while being relocated. This picture can also provide a good historical comparison when studying current issues of immigrant detention centers or refugee camps.

Additional Strategies

Here are some additional methods and examples to facilitate analysis of photographs in social studies.

- Creating a Word Cloud for an Image: We have students write everything that they notice about a picture on a Google Doc. Then, we upload these words to an application like WordCloud.com (www.wordclouds.com). Word clouds are a visual representation of the key ideas from a text (the more frequently a word is used, the larger it appears in the "cloud" of words). Students can then use the prominent terms in the word cloud to make inferences about crucial information in the photograph. For example, we show the portraits of Booker T. Washington and W.E.B. DuBois when studying their views during our unit on the Jim Crow South in the United States. After uploading student notes describing the portraits, we project the word cloud (see Figure 12.4: DuBois and Washington Images – WordCloud). Enlarged terms such as *professional* and *official* (because of their formal clothing) help students infer that these men held positions of authority and were likely respected.

- Creating a Slideshow for a Series of Photos: Instead of having students analyze one image, students can analyze several to identify patterns or themes and potentially reach higher levels of critical thinking. For example, when we are beginning the study of a country in geography, we like to show groups of pictures that represent certain categories, such as land and climate, culture, and social challenges. We organize sets of images in a slideshow: four to five images of land and climate, then four to five images representing culture, and so on. Students use Table 12.1: Image Slideshow – Graphic Organizer to note what

Table 12.1 Image Slideshow – Graphic Organizer

Category	What I notice . . .	Questions or Reactions

they see in the pictures. Then, they work with partners and use their notes to infer the theme or category for each set of pictures. If this activity is being used in the middle of a unit, students can also write a connection between the image and something they have previously learned about this topic. Developing these connections can serve as a reason to reread the information.

- Building on the Observations of Others: Using an application like Padlet (https://padlet.com) can help students see, and build upon, what their peers have noticed in a photo. Students do this on a web-based "bulletin board" created by the teacher. For example, when studying the 14th Amendment, students can analyze a picture of a march for voting rights in the segregated South. After viewing the image, we can invite students to share what they see in the picture on the class Padlet. Then, they respond to the comments of other students. We provide sentence frames to help structure their responses: "I agree with this comment because . . ." "I don't agree with this comment because . . ." "This comment makes me wonder . . . ." This real-time collaboration exposes students to multiple perspectives while helping them expand their evaluation of the picture. Other tools similar to Padlet can be found in the Technology Connections section.

- Creating a Photo Essay: The next step in higher-order thinking after analyzing and evaluating is *creating* images. Most of our students have cell phones that include a camera, which makes this type of activity even more doable. For example, in our government class, we have students explore the theme "the personal is political" in their lives. We review a list of major political issues in the news (immigration, freedom of speech, the environment, healthcare, and so forth). Then, students are asked to find items, places, scenes, or people in their lives that represent a few of the issues and photograph them. To scaffold this activity, we have students brainstorm what they could possibly capture with their cameras to fit their selected themes. Students can write about why they chose their themes and how each image connects to it. They can also present their photos and explanations to the class.

PAINTINGS

Paintings have existed for thousands of years and can be windows to different historical eras. While photos are often candid, paintings tend to be more staged.

Similar to photos, paintings can be used to evoke an emotional response about a topic. For example, when studying labor unrest in Latin America, we like to show Diego Rivera's "The Uprising" (1931). In the painting, a mother is holding a crying baby while fighting off military soldiers. Next to – and around her – are other civilians (all in worker's clothing) confronting uniformed soldiers. This painting can help our students empathize with the human cost of revolution. In addition, the figures of "everyday" people – just like them – standing up to oppression can be inspirational to students.

Also, paintings can be used to counter negative narratives about specific cultures or countries. For example, to counteract narratives depicting the African continent as being "underdeveloped," we show paintings from Kenyan artists like Patrick Kinuthia (www.patrickkinuthiaart.com). Dispersing these paintings throughout a unit about Kenya and other nearby countries communicates not only depictions of Africans *by* Africans but also showcases the continent's thriving cultures.

With a few minor changes, the protocol for photographs can also be used for paintings.

Protocol

When introducing a unit on the Great Migration of African Americans from the South to the North, we like to use paintings by Jacob Lawrence. This African American painter was a member of the Harlem Renaissance. His "Migration Series" (1940–1941) depicts this mass movement that took place between World War I and the 1970s (https://lawrencemigration.phillipscollection.org/the-migration-series). The paintings depict Black Americans escaping the violence in the South in order to build new lives in the North.

We walk students through the same process we apply to photographs using Figure 12.1: Image Analysis Chart. We provide model answers and teacher think-alouds to guide them through the first three phases: prewriting to set the stage, noting what we see in the painting, and making evidence-based inferences. After students have attempted to determine what the painting represents (sixth question), we unveil its title along with a short biography of the painter. In this case, we like to use short video clips and articles about Jacob Lawrence from The Phillips Collection Museum of Modern Art (https://lawrencemigration.phillipscollection.org/artist/about-jacob-lawrence).

For the fourth and final phase of image analysis, evaluating relevance, the same prompts used for photographs are easily applied to this medium. We also like to include one of the following when students are evaluating a painting:

1. What do you think this artist wanted us to feel or understand through this piece? Please provide evidence from the painting to support your answer.

2. Now that you know who the painter is, how does it change the way you view the painting?

These questions help direct students' attention to the artists' perspectives that may have influenced the image.

Additional Strategies

The additional strategies listed for the analysis of photographs are also applicable to paintings. In addition to those, here are even more ideas for analyzing paintings in social studies:

- Paintings to Study Economics: Thanks to the *Economics and Art Webpage* by the Purdue Center for Economic Education (https://intra.krannert.purdue. edu/sites/econandart/Pages/Menu.aspx), teachers can use paintings to teach about topics like banking, markets, and capital resources. After analyzing a painting using the four-phase protocol discussed in this chapter, students can assess *how* the image displays or represents a specific economic concept from class.

- Paintings to Practice Critical Analysis: Especially when teaching about race in American History, works by artists like Titus Kaphar (https://kapharstu-dio.com/category/painting) can serve as a source for critical analysis. Kaphar plays with the styles of traditional western art to expose issues of racism. For example, his *Behind the Myth of Benevolence* painting ". . . is inspired by an iconic portrait of Thomas Jefferson that has been 'peeled' away from the canvas to reveal a portrait of an enslaved black woman" (https://kapharstudio.com/behind-the-myth-of-benevolence). This type of work exposes our students to different viewpoints and challenges dominant narratives in history – the perspectives of those in power who often dictate whose version of history is presented in textbooks and the media and how it is presented.

- Paintings as Activism: After studying a variety of social justice issues in ethnic studies, we explore historical and current activist paintings. In addition, we utilize artist interviews, written, audio, or on video, to learn about the motivations behind their work. By joining forces with an art teacher (or some YouTube tutorials!), students can learn some basic painting techniques. After picking a social justice issue, they create a painting about their cause and display it at school. At our school, we often have teams of students work together to complete culturally relevant murals around campus. Students then use the same four phases of analysis described in this chapter to analyze and review each other's work.

POLITICAL CARTOONS

Political cartoons are drawings that use caricatures and text to express the political views of the artist on a certain topic. Research in visual communication has shown that "interpreting cartoons is a complex process that requires people to draw on a whole range of different literacies" (El Rafaie, 2009, p. 181).

Furthermore, political cartoons are designed to be provocative and elicit an emotional response. Although political cartoons can be humorous, they should also be regarded as a serious and important social commentary designed by skilled artists (Dougherty, 2003, p. 258). They stand apart from other images in that they have historically served as a direct challenge to those in power (Lange, 2019).

Protocol

Our analysis of a political cartoon follows the same four phases as photographs and paintings, and uses a graphic organizer, Figure 12.5: Political Cartoon – Analysis Chart. The modified questions for this medium can help students build both visual and textual literacy.

We'll use an early 1900s cartoon about the women's suffrage movement to show how we guide students through the four phases of the protocol. Prior to this image analysis, students have already done some reading on voting rights for women in the late 1800s and early 1900s.

Prewriting to Set the Stage

As with photos and paintings, when we are preparing students to analyze a political cartoon, we provide a prompt that builds context for the topic and elicits student connections. For the political cartoon about women's suffrage, we ask the following:

> Think about the roles women have in your home, family, or even in your circle of friends. What is expected of them? Is it the same as the men? Please provide examples.

Students discuss their responses in partners, and we call on a few students to share with the class.

Noting What We See

To encourage collaborative work during the analysis, we put students in pairs and have them move their desks close to each other. We then distribute Figure 12.5: Political Cartoon – Analysis Chart and Figure 12.6: "Election Day!" – Political

Cartoon. When practicing in-depth analysis of these types of images, we find it beneficial to pass out a hard copy of the image for students to annotate. Providing *one* copy of the political cartoon to each pair can encourage dialogue and cooperative analysis.

The first three questions in the graphic organizer (Figure 12.5: Political Cartoon – Analysis Chart) are all similar to the *photograph* analysis chart in the previous section – with the exception of the second question. This question asks students to note any text used in the political cartoon.

Depending on how much experience students have with image analysis, it may be helpful for a teacher to scaffold the process. For the first question, "In bulleted form, list everything that you **see** in the picture," we say something like the following about Figure 12.6: "Election Day!" – Political Cartoon:

> *In this image, I see a woman who is wearing a coat, hat, and carrying an umbrella dressed to leave the house. I am going to write that down. In addition, I am going to add that I see a man sitting on a chair holding two babies. Now, you keep listing what else you see in the picture.*

We continue modeling answers for questions two and three. We also provide time for students to work with partners, and for some to share with the entire class. Please refer to Figure 12.7: Teacher Model – Political Cartoon for sample answers.

Evidence-Based Inferences

Questions four through six guide students to draw conclusions based on the details of the image. Students must analyze the symbolism in the cartoon in order to answer these questions. In addition, they have to use the details in the image to make an inference about its time period.

Modeling is key to helping students move from just listing what they see to critically thinking about the meaning(s), or message, of the image. For example, with the image about women's suffrage, we help our students to identify symbols by saying the following:

> *For the fourth question about symbols, I am going to list* apron *for what the man in the chair is wearing. A person who is cooking and cleaning in the home usually wears an apron. During this time period, this role typically belonged to women. So, next to* apron *I am going to write "shows he has become the 'woman of the home' and has taken over housekeeping responsibilities."*

We support student evidence-based conclusions for question 6 (What do you think the artist wanted the audience to believe? What is the overall message?) by providing a sentence frame:

The overall message of this political cartoon is _____

_____.

The cartoon illustrates this message by showing _____

_____.

See Figure 12.7: Teacher Model – Political Cartoon for a completed example.

Evaluating Relevance

We use the same style of prompts listed in the photo analysis activity to analyze personal and historical relevance. We first ask students to connect the image back to their prewriting response about typical roles of women. Then, we ask questions to help students evaluate the perspective or value of the image for our unit of study. Some additional prompts for political cartoons are:

1. *(After providing the date to the class)* Consider the date the political cartoon was created. Do you think more people agreed or disagreed with the message of the political cartoon when it was first published? Explain.

2. Who have we read about so far that would support the message of this image? Who would disagree? Explain.

Additional Strategies

Here are some additional activities to help students analyze political cartoons in social studies.

- Engaging with Memes: Memes, or Internet images with captions that are intended to be funny, are the modern cousins of political cartoons. In order to hook students and practice image analysis with a medium familiar to them, a teacher could perform an online search for memes related to a social studies topic and show appropriate ones to the class. Then, students can follow the analysis process by noting what they see, making inferences, and evaluating the relevance of the meme. Students could also make memes using historical images. Please refer to Larry Ferlazzo's blog post "The Best Tools for Making Internet Memes" (2013).

- Identifying Additional Literary Devices: Students can take their analysis skills to the next level by identifying hyperbole, irony, symbolism, metaphor, and so on in political cartoons. Teachers can do mini-lessons on the different types of devices and model how to find them. Then, in small groups, students can work together to identify them in a cartoon. This focused critical analysis can help students reach clearer conclusions about the artists' intent.

- Creating Cartoons: Students can create political cartoons about topics they are studying in class. This task can be done as a final unit project. Having students display their political cartoons and inviting their peers to analyze and discern their message can help to assess the design and quality of the image. The *New York Times Learning Network* has a good lesson plan titled "Drawing for Change: Analyzing and Making Political Cartoons" (Gonchar, 2015).

VIDEO

Unlike our first three examples, videos are recordings of *moving* images. They typically include ongoing dialogue, human interactions, music, and scenery. These characteristics make video a dynamic and engaging visual medium.

Although videos can be effective learning tools, it is important that students are actively involved while viewing them and not just staring at a screen (Ferlazzo & Sypnieski, 2012).

By modeling how to closely read or analyze video, students can watch a clip or longer movie "critically and not passively" (Baker, 2016, November).

Protocol

The protocol we use to analyze videos and the graphic organizer we created, Table 12.2: Video Analysis Chart, serve to actively engage students. This analysis follows the same four phases as the other activities, although the chart has been modified.

Table 12.2 Video Analysis Chart

Driving Question(s):

What did you notice?	Comments or Questions About It

We will explain the protocol we use to guide students through video analysis using an example from an economics class. We use a short film to help students understand supply and demand: the relationship between the quantity and price of a resource or product that suppliers wish to sell and consumers wish to buy. Prior to this video analysis, students have already read the definition and a few examples of this concept.

Although there are limitless online video choices, choosing one for classroom instruction should be done carefully. Here are some criteria to keep in mind:

- Avoid dry and monotonous clips (even if they are informative). Aim for creative and engaging.

- Make sure the footage you show clearly meets your learning goal and is not overshadowed by unrelated content.

- Keep length in mind: do students need to watch an entire movie, or just a specific portion? We lean heavily toward showing very short clips – as with text, quality over quantity is key. In addition, choosing a short clip has the benefit of allowing multiple viewings to help deepen student comprehension.

- Be careful with video footage that you think might trigger emotional distress in students. A warning ahead of time or a class protocol to allow students to skip the video can be helpful.

In this case, we selected a video from YouTube Channel, *We the Economy* (Chu, 2014), which has a series of videos that explain economics topics in an accessible and highly creative way. To help our students gain a deeper understanding of supply and demand, we show the video "Supply and Dance, Man!"

Prewriting to Set the Stage

Before analyzing a video, we like to provide an opportunity to help students think about the main idea or concept that they are about to watch. This activity can help students build their background knowledge and can prepare them to learn new information.

For example, prior to watching the clip about supply and demand, we ask students to review their class materials about the topic. Then, we provide a prompt like one of the following:

- With a partner, make a bulleted list of what you understand about supply and demand.

- What is an item that a lot of students at our school have or want? Do people pay a lot of money for this item? Is it difficult to get?

In this case, the goal of the video analysis is to help students deepen their understanding of a concept that has been previously introduced. These questions help them identify what they know about the topic and can provide a framework for their viewing.

When studying supply and demand, we explain to students that we will watch a short video to help gain a deeper understanding of the concept. Providing some background on the video prior to viewing can help students focus on the most pertinent aspects and not be distracted by details – like choreography. For example, we explain that the video *Supply and Dance, Man!* (Chu, 2014) illustrates, in a musical style, supply and demand by showing dancers buying canes from two different vendors. This brief summary can prepare our students to pay attention to the dynamics of buying and selling canes and *not* just the dance moves.

Noting What We See

We distribute and review Table 12.2: Video Analysis Chart. This figure is left blank for readers to use. Table 12.3: Video – Teacher Model shows a completed example using the supply and demand video.

We first read aloud the "driving questions" at the top of Table 12.2: Video Analysis Chart. Presenting them to students at the beginning can help them focus their

Table 12.3 Video – Teacher Model

Driving Question(s):
What are the important aspects of supply and demand? Why might this concept be relevant to our everyday lives?

What did you notice?	Comments or Questions About It
Time-Stop: 2:15 *I noticed that the stores were not selling anything until one dancer bought a cane, and others wanted one, too.*	*This reminds me of how shoes become popular at school, and everybody wants to buy the same pair.*
Time-Stop: 3:40 *I noticed that as the canes became more popular they ran out. Once they ran out, they ordered more and raised the price.*	*They knew the canes were popular, so they raised the price to make more money.*
Time-Stop: 5:25 *I noticed that once the price got to $20, people did not want the canes anymore. They soon had too many canes and had to drop the price to sell more.*	*The storekeepers got greedy!*
Time-Stop: 6:30 *I noticed that the lowered price of $8 is what made everybody happy. People got their canes at a good price, and shop owners got money.*	*I wonder if the storeowners are actually happy about this, or if they would rather sell fewer canes for a higher price?*

notes while providing purpose for the video. After watching, students can answer these questions to evaluate the relevance of the topic. For this video on supply and demand, we ask, "What are the important aspects of supply and demand? Why might this concept be relevant to our everyday lives?"

Then, we explain how the handout helps students note information about the video. In the left-hand column, they write what they notice. The right-hand column is where students comment on or ask a question about the video. We identify "stop times" in advance to give students opportunities to take notes on important parts of the clip. Students have about a minute or two at each pause to add notes to their charts and discuss what they noticed with a partner.

To help students get started, we provide a model response that students can copy for the first stop time. For the *Supply and Dance, Man!* video, we write on the left column "I noticed that the stores were not selling anything until one dancer bought a cane, and others wanted one, too." For the right side, we comment "This reminds me of how shoes become popular at school, and everybody wants to buy the same pair."

We instruct students to continue taking notes and discussing the video using the same process. In addition, we clarify that the open-ended style of the graphic organizer allows for a variety of responses. For a completed example, please see Table 12.3: Video – Teacher Model for examples of notes (and appropriate stop-times) for the entire video.

We continue the cycle of stopping to take notes and engage in peer discussion until students have watched the entire video. This analysis process is easily adaptable for videos on any social studies content.

Evidence-Based Inferences

After watching and writing what they noticed in the video, it is time to address the first driving question at the top of Table 12.2: Video Analysis Chart: "What are the important aspects of supply and demand?" We do this by developing and writing conclusions based on their notes. We provide the following sentence starter to facilitate this process:

Based on the video, I can say that supply and demand has to do with . . .

We ask students to write down two to three evidence-based conclusions using this sentence starter (or their own).

For further support, we provide a think-aloud to show students how to use their notes in making evidence-based conclusions. For the video about supply and demand, we say something like:

In my chart, I wrote, "I noticed that the canes increased in popularity as they became less available. Once they ran out, they ordered more and increased the price." This makes me think that supply and demand has a lot to do with people's desires and how sometimes that leads us to spend more money. So, to complete my sentence-starter, I am going to write "Based on the video, I can say that supply and demand has to do with the desires of people and their willingness to spend more money to fulfill their wants and needs."

Evaluating Relevance

We have students evaluate the relevance of the main message of the video to conclude the activity. To help students with this task, we have them revisit the second driving question at the top of their organizer, "Why is this concept relevant to our everyday life?" Another way to phrase this question for students is "Where, in our lives, do we see supply and demand in action?"

We advise students to keep their video notes out to help them answer the prompt. Here is where a series of guiding questions can help students "see" supply and demand in their lives. We might post and use the following:

- How do you think business owners in our area decide what prices to set for their products?
- How do the decisions of business owners affect us?
- What happens when prices go up for a common item or product?
- How do increased prices affect our everyday lives?
- When we buy products or services, how do we decide what is worth the money?
- Do you think businesses spend a lot of time thinking about us, the consumer?

Students are directed to pick three questions from our list to answer. We invite them to add any other opinions they may have to their response.

Additional Strategies

Here are some additional ways that students can analyze video.

- Pausing to Summarize and Predict: This task can be done throughout the viewing. For example, the teacher can pause the video every three to six minutes and have students summarize what has happened so far with a partner. Then, after calling on two or three students to share their summaries, they can discuss what might happen next. Predictions are shared with the class, and the teacher continues showing the video and pausing it for additional student summaries and predictions. This strategy can help to engage our young viewers by creating a sense of anticipation. In addition, it can aid in deeper comprehension by encouraging students to discuss the video content.

- Content Focused Guiding Questions: Although we like how our video analysis chart is open-ended and hard to do incorrectly, there are other ways to note information from video. Teachers can create a specific list of student questions targeting particular content. In fact, for many longer movies, a simple online search for premade viewing guides can save a lot of time. We recommend placing students in viewing pairs so they can help each other catch the answers. In addition, making sure that the questions are carefully dispersed throughout the viewing, and not back-to-back, helps to prevent student confusion.

- Passing Notes: This can be okay in class! Before students watch a video, we have them set up a blank piece of paper in the following way: fold the paper in half "hamburger" style and label the top half "What I notice" and the bottom half "What I am wondering." We start the video and direct students to add notes to the top and bottom sections of their paper. Then, after five minutes of viewing, we pause the video and have students pass their paper down to another student. After giving them a minute or two to scan each other's notes, we direct students to respond, in writing, to at least one item on the paper. They can attempt to answer questions written by others, or explain why they agree or disagree with other comments. This task can help students consider new perspectives about the video. We continue this cycle for the duration of the video, with each paper going to a new person each time.

- Student-Created Videos: Students can create their own videos to teach any concept they have learned in class. See the Technology Connections section for related resources.

DIFFERENTIATION

Although using images in social studies is an effective way to make content accessible, the cultural context required to discern meaning can be challenging. To help students analyze images, front-loading certain cultural or political symbols can be helpful. For example, explaining the image of Uncle Sam prior to studying certain political cartoons can help students understand how the image is used as a commentary on the United States.

In addition, the speed of dialogue and narration in videos can be a challenge for some of our students (and for us, too!). Slowing the speed, providing closed captioning, and/or multiple viewings can help students take notes more successfully.

ADVANCED EXTENSIONS

To encompass all the visual mediums in this chapter, students can work in groups of three to four and curate a "museum corner" as a way to respond to an essential question. For example, if students are studying segregation in the southern United States, they can explore the question "Should laws always be followed?" Students review their classwork for examples that illustrate segregation laws being challenged or followed, and the consequences of both.

Once each member of the group has identified a specific historical example, they each choose to create a photo, painting, political cartoon, or video. Their artwork should not only portray their historical event but also their response to the essential question. After all the art pieces are complete, students can make a multimedia presentation about their work where they analyze each piece for the class and explain how it answers the essential question.

This activity allows students to choose both their historical example and their medium, which can increase engagement. In addition, creating art to apply historical knowledge helps students practice critical thinking.

Student Handouts and Examples

Figure 12.1: Image Analysis Chart

Figure 12.2: Japanese American Evacuation – Photo

Figure 12.3: Teacher Model - Photo Analysis Chart

Figure 12.4: DuBois and Washington Images – WordCloud

Table 12.1: Image Slideshow – Graphic Organizer

Figure 12.5: Political Cartoon – Analysis Chart

Figure 12.6: "Election Day!" – Political Cartoon

Figure 12.7: Teacher Model – Political Cartoon

Table 12.2: Video Analysis Chart

Table 12.3: Video – Teacher Model

What Could Go Wrong?

When analyzing images, students can get frustrated if there is an overemphasis on getting the "right answer." Instead, we want to place the emphasis on teaching students *how* to analyze. For this reason, it is important to model the process for students by sharing our thinking aloud and providing examples. It makes critical thinking an activity everyone can practice, improve, and – eventually – do independently.

Be mindful of not spending multiple whole-class periods analyzing one image. Balance time, content, and student engagement – it's always better to leave students wanting more than to leave them wondering when it's ever going to end.

Technology Connections

The Library of Congress (www.loc.gov/pictures) is a helpful resource to find photographs about specific topics in social studies. For additional strategies to analyze visuals in your classroom, Larry Ferlazzo's blog post "The Best Resources on Close Reading Paintings, Photos & Videos" (https://larryferlazzo.edublogs.org/2015/08/05/the-best-resources-on-close-reading-paintings-photos-videos) may be helpful.

A list of tools similar to Padlet, where students can collectively view and annotate images, can be found at "The Best Online Virtual 'Corkboards' (or 'Bulletin Boards')" (http://larryferlazzo.edublogs.org/2011/03/30/the-best-online-virtual-corkboards-or-bulletin-boards).

Videos specifically for the social studies classroom can be found at the "7 Excellent YouTube Channels for Social Studies Teachers" post from *Educational Technology and Mobile Learning* (www.educatorstechnology.com/2016/04/7-excellent-youtube-channels-for-social.html). In addition, the *New York Times* has a valuable post titled "8 Compelling Mini-Documentaries to Teach Close Reading and Critical Thinking Skills" (https://learning.blogs.nytimes.com/2016/03/10/8-compelling-mini-documentaries-to-teach-close-reading-and-critical-thinking-skills). In the post, they explain different strategies to help students move from noting details to making evidence-based inferences.

Ideas for how students can create their own videos can be found at *The Tech Advocate*'s post, "5 Movie Making Apps for Student Projects" (www.thetechedvocate.org/5-movie-making-apps-student-projects) and at Larry Ferlazzo's website "A Potpourri of the Best & Most Useful Video Sites" (http://larryferlazzo.edublogs.org/2012/11/06/a-potpourri-of-the-best-most-useful-video-sites).

Figures

Name_____Date_____Period_____

1. After viewing the picture silently for one minute, please write one or two things that **stand out** to you.

2. Now, please **list** everything **you see** in the picture. Don't worry about the order of the items – just include as many details as you can.

3. What **action(s)** seem to be taking place in this picture?

4. What seems to be the main **focal point**, or **central subject**, of the picture? What is in the **background**? What could you see if you extended the boundaries of the picture?

5. **Describe** the **main subject**: Can we see the entire subject? How is the subject positioned (looking at camera? looking away?)

6. After discussing with your partner, what do you think this is a picture of? What kind of **situation** could this be? What might be the **time period**? Justify your response with evidence from the picture.

I think this picture might be about _____

_____ because the image shows _____

_____. I believe the time period is around _____

_____because_____.

7. What **question(s)** do you and your partner have about this picture? What does it make you **wonder** about?

Figure 12.1 Image Analysis Chart *Sources:* www.edutopia.org/blog/ccia-10-visual-literacy-strategies-todd-finley, www.archives.gov/education/lessons/worksheets/photo.html, https://understandmedia.com/topics/media-theory/111-how-to-analyze-a-photograph.

Figure 12.2 Japanese American Evacuation Photo *Source:* www.loc.gov/pictures/resource/fsa.8a31170.

1. After viewing the picture silently for one minute, please write one or two things that **stand out** to you.
   - *the little boy with a worried look*
   - *The strange boots the person next to the little boy is wearing*

2. Now, please **list** everything **you see** in the picture. Don't worry about the order of the items - just include as many details as you can.
   - *The little boy and everyone else are wearing coats*
   - *They are outside*
   - *There are a lot of people and seem to be facing away from the young child*
   - *The person behind the boy is carrying a baby*
   - *I think there is a train in the background*
   - *The strange boots person make me think that person is from the military*
   - *The ground seems like cement*
   - *A bag with some fabric on the ground*
   - *A tag hanging from the coat of the child*

3. What **action(s)** seem to be taking place in this picture?
   They seem to be still and just standing. The young child does seem like they might take a step.

4. What seems to be the main **focal point**, or **central subject**, of the picture? What is in the **background**? What could you see if you extended the boundaries of the picture? In other words, what is not included in it now? *The young child is the focal point. There seem to be adults and maybe a train in the background. You would probably be able to see the faces, and expressions of the adults along with a lot more people and children. The place looks like it is crowded.*

5. **Describe** the **main subject**: Can we see the entire subject? How is the subject positioned (looking at camera? looking away?)
   We can see all of the young child, but he (I think) seems to be looking at something else other than the camera. The child looks a little worried. Not scared, but concerned.

6. After discussing with your partner, what do you both think this is a picture of? What kind of **situation** could this be? What might be the **time period**? Justify your response with evidence from the picture.
   I think this picture might be about *a group of people waiting around to be taken somewhere they don't really want to go* **because the image shows** *a young child who seems to be unsure about where he is at along with a bag and people waiting around.* **I believe the time period is around** *the early 1900s* **because** *the picture is in black and white and I have seen similar clothes in movies from that time period.*

7. What **question(s)** do you and your partner have about this picture? What does it make you **wonder** about?
   I wonder where they are going and why?
   Is this child an orphan?

Figure 12.3 Teacher Model – Photo Analysis Chart

Figure 12.4 DuBois and Washington Images – WordCloud *Source:* left: www.loc.gov/pictures/item/2003681451/resource/cph.3a53178/?sid=3e650091222fc676bd991edf0936a04b; right: www.loc.gov/pictures/resource/hec.16114.

Title of Political Cartoon:

1. In bulleted form, list out everything that you **see** in the cartoon:

2. Is there any **text** in the cartoon? Please copy it down here and explain how the text is used. (What is it labeling?)	3. What **action** do you see in the cartoon? Please make sure to mention both who or what is moving and in what direction (or towards what).
4. Please list items that you think are **symbols** (something that represents or stands for something else) in the cartoon. List the symbols and then explain what you think they stand for.	5. **When, or what time period,** do you think this cartoon was made? What in the picture makes you think so?

6. What do you think the artist wanted the audience to believe? What is the **overall message**?

The overall message of this political cartoon is that

_____.

The cartoon illustrates this message by showing

_____.

Figure 12.5 Political Cartoon – Analysis Chart *Sources:* (www.archives.gov/files/education/lessons/worksheets/cartoon_analysis_worksheet_former.pdf, www.loc.gov/teachers/professionaldevelopment/tpsdirect/pdf/Analyzing-Political-Cartoons.pdf, pp. 1.10–1.11).

Figure 12.6   "Election Day!" – Political Cartoon *Source:* www.loc.gov/pictures/item/97500226.

Title of Political Cartoon:
_____*"Election Day!"*_____

1. In bulleted form, list out everything that you **see** in the cartoon:
   - *Man, woman, and two babies; woman is about to leave and man is seated holding two babies who are crying, there is a scared cat underneath him*
   - *The woman is holding an umbrella, wearing a coat, is holding papers and is giving an unhappy look to the man*
   - *The man looks scared and is looking at the woman; he is wearing an apron*
   - *Their room (house?) looks messy: table is covered with random dishes, one looks broken on the floor*
   - *Something is steaming from the stove, but nobody seems to be noticing it*
   - *There is a sign in the upper right hand side of the wall that says "Votes For Women"*
   - *At the bottom, there is a title that says "Election Day!" and a bowl with little pieces of paper and paper that looks like a newspaper page*

2. Is there any **text** in the cartoon? Please copy it down here and explain how the text was used. (What was it labeling?) • *"Votes For Women": a framed sign in the house* • *"Election Day!"- the bottom title of the cartoon*	3. What **action** do you see in the cartoon? Please make sure to mention both who or what is moving and in what direction (or towards what). *The woman, I think the mom/wife, seems to be on her way out based on the umbrella she is carrying, her gloves, and coat she has on. Plus, she seems to be facing away. The babies seem to be squirming, like they are really upset. Dad is seated holding the upset babies.*
4. Please list items that you think are **symbols** (something that represents or stands for something else) in the cartoon. List the symbols and then explain what you think they stand for. • *Apron: shows he has become the woman of the home* • *Crying babies: shows that they are not happy mom is leaving* • *Broken dish: is a symbol of a home that is falling apart* • *Steam from stove: is a symbol that no one is looking after the cooking* • *The tie the woman is wearing: symbolizes that SHE is the man of the house*	5. **When, or what time period,** do you think this cartoon was made? What in the picture makes you think so? *The man, the woman, and the babies in the picture all have clothing from an older time: her skirt is really long and both of their shoes are pointy and at the ankle (don't see that style anymore). The room they are in has no modern appliances.*

6. What do you think the artist wanted the audience to believe? What is the **overall message**?

The overall message of this political cartoon is that <u>*women's suffrage is bad for families, men, and America.*</u> The cartoon illustrates this message by showing <u>*a household that supports voting for women but now is falling apart because the mom feels like she has the power to leave. The cartoon makes it look like the man is being abandoned and left with all the housekeeping responsibilities*</u>.

Figure 12.7 Teacher Model – Political Cartoon

CHAPTER 13

Analysis of Primary Sources

What Is It?

Primary sources are text documents, images, videos, or audio recordings created during the time period being studied. These historical artifacts must be analyzed through a critical lens in order to tell their story accurately. They can also give voice to the people who lived during that era.

This chapter explains how we introduce primary sources to our students and teach strategies to analyze them. The steps in these activities not only facilitate critical thinking but also increase comprehension (Patterson, Lucas, & Kithinji, 2012, p. 69). In addition, the strategies can be applied to primary sources for any topic in social studies.

Why We Like It

We like how these strategies make primary sources accessible to our students. The "step by step" process embedded in these analysis tools help students methodically approach all kinds of texts or images. Reading a formal government source or the diary of an explorer is less overwhelming when students have a structure to guide them. We don't just hand them the Declaration of Independence and say, "read it."

In addition, we appreciate how these activities support inquiry-based learning in our classrooms. Instead of students being *given* the answers to essential social studies questions, they are practicing higher-order thinking to find their *own* answers.

We also like the way these structures engage students in the process of analyzing sources so they can experience history coming alive. For example, by analyzing a letter to the king of Spain, they can sense the awe Hernán Cortés felt when he first saw the Aztec city of Tenochtitlan. By working effectively with our analysis strategies, authentic material, like this letter, can make learning more relevant.

Supporting Research

The use of primary sources in social studies can enhance critical thinking skills (Patterson et al., 2012, p. 69). To help students reach these higher levels of analysis, research indicates that "an intentional, carefully scaffolded, and transparent approach is needed" (Patterson et al., 2012, p. 81). The strategies utilized in this chapter can provide important scaffolding to support our students when analyzing primary sources.

Common Core Connections

The use of primary sources is a fundamental aspect of the *Common Core for History/Social Studies*. For example, the Key Ideas and Details strand states that students need to "Cite specific textual evidence to support analysis of primary and secondary sources" (Common Core, 2010v). Additionally, the same strand notes that students need to be able to read a primary source and identify the key ideas (Common Core, 2010w).

Social Studies Connections

An essential part of the College, Career, and Civic Life (C3) Framework created by the National Council for the Social Studies is inquiry-based learning, or a structured investigation of a question. Activities in this chapter incorporate the analysis of "the origin, authority, structure, context, and corroborative value of the sources" to practice critical thinking and gain a deeper understanding of historical phenomena (NCSS, 2010, p. 54).

Application

This section explains three strategies we use with our students to teach analysis of primary sources. The first activity is designed to introduce primary sources to our students in an engaging way. Our second strategy incorporates a set of sentence starters to help students perform a brief evaluation of a source. We like the way this structure teaches our students an accessible and do-now process that students can learn to use independently. The third activity uses a graphic organizer to support a more thorough evaluation of text-based primary sources. These tools can be applied across all social studies courses.

We conclude the application section by briefly sharing additional strategies to practice primary source analysis with students.

PRIMARY SOURCE ENGAGEMENT ACTIVITY

The following engagement activity can help students see that primary sources can be a fountain of information, instead of irrelevant relics from the past. We guide students through a hands-on activity where they assess the advantages and disadvantages of yearbooks as primary sources.

Most students are familiar with yearbooks and tend to be interested in a primary source from *their* school. However, we refrain from formally referring to yearbooks as "primary sources" until the end of the activity when students are asked to determine if (and why) it is a primary source.

After first borrowing a collection of older yearbooks from our school's librarian, we begin our lesson by asking students to provide the definition of one to a partner. After calling on a few students, we establish that this item is typically a book that reviews a school year from the past by including pictures and brief text describing students, staff, and major events.

We tell them that we will be looking at old yearbooks from our school to assess their value as historical items. Students are assigned partners and asked to have paper and a pen or pencil. They are given a few minutes to look through the books and note on their papers what stands out to them. We call on a few students to share with the class. Hairstyles, clothing, the difference in racial representation, and writing style are just a few of the observations shared by students.

For the next step, we have students discuss with their partner, using their observations: What could historians learn by studying yearbooks? To model the task, we "think aloud" the following:

> *Many of you listed that hairstyles and clothing stood out to you. These observations make me think that studying yearbooks could teach historians a lot about popular trends.*

We provide students a few minutes to list ideas on their paper. If we see they are struggling to determine what could be learned, we provide more examples. For instance, the ethnic and racial background of students can tell historians about the demographics in the area. Additionally, certain words in the writing might also reflect common terminology of that era.

Then, in a similar fashion, we ask them what a historian might *not* be able to learn about the past from yearbooks. In other words, what do they *not* tell us about the year they were created? We usually provide another example like,

> *I only see pictures of students and staff. I don't see any images or information about who were the major political leaders in the area, or country, at the time. This makes me think that if a historian wanted to learn about the political leaders in the region, they could not rely on a yearbook.*

Students are asked to make a short list of how yearbooks may *not* be helpful to historians. Then, we call on a few students to share their ideas.

Next, using the board or the screen, we provide the following definitions and examples of primary and secondary sources:

> A primary source is generally defined as a record created by a direct participant in an event or activity in the past. Primary sources differ from secondary sources in that secondary sources are interpretations of the past – usually written by historians – that are created after the fact. ("Understanding DBQ's & Primary Resources," n.d., p. 1)
>
> For example, a letter written by a soldier from World War I is from someone who was a direct participant in the event he is writing about. A section about soldiers in World War I from our textbook is a secondary source. ("Understanding DBQ's & Primary Resources," n.d., p. 1)

It may be helpful to provide other examples of primary and secondary sources to make sure students understand the differences between them. Then, we ask the class, "Are yearbooks primary or secondary sources? Why?" We direct students to discuss the answer with a partner. After a couple minutes, students respond to the prompt in writing. Many of them write that it is a primary source because it is created by people of that time and place – the school's students and staff.

To help students reflect on what they learned in the activity we conclude with a simple prompt: "What new information have you learned about primary sources today?"

We like that we can refer to this activity when using primary and secondary sources throughout the year to remind students of the advantages and disadvantages of each one.

AT A GLANCE PRIMARY SOURCE ANALYSIS

After our students understand the definition of a primary source and how it can be used to learn about the past, we project and distribute copies of Figure 13.1: At a Glance Analysis of Source. This handout contains sentence starters that we use for source analysis all year long.

We begin by distributing Figure 13.2: Hernán Cortés' Account of Tenochtitlan. Instead of *beginning* with models, we instruct students to try it on their own first. We point out that this process is an opportunity for students to practice a growth mindset: a belief that intelligence can be developed with effort. In other words, students can practice staying motivated by embracing this moderate challenge of completing these sentence starters independently. We encourage them to persist even if it gets difficult. In addition, by having students reflect on their individual strategies with the class *after* they try it on their own, we create an opportunity for students to practice metacognition – awareness of one's thought process.

To be clear, modeling is an essential tool in any teacher's toolbox. Most of the time, we do it prior to student practice. However, we sometimes try to mix things up by first having students make initial attempts at writing and then showing our examples, as in this case.

After we explain our reasoning to the class, we set a timer and announce students have five minutes to complete the sentence starters from Figure 13.1: At a Glance Analysis of Source to analyze Figure 13.2: Hernán Cortés' Account of Tenochtitlan.

When the time concludes, we have students pair-share what they wrote for each one and explain how they reached that answer. Figure 13.3: At a Glance – Student Example shows one student's initial response.

After students share with each other how they finished each sentence starter, we unveil how *we* finished them for the Cortés letter. In addition, we share what *exactly* the sentence starter is asking them to do. For example, for the first sentence starter "This is a . . ." we clarify that an explanation of the type of source is required here. Then, on Figure 13.4: At a Glance – Teacher Copy, we complete this sentence starter: "This is a <u>letter</u>."

Then, we ask a crucial question: "*How* did I determine this was a letter?" Students may share that the first few lines from the source sound like Cortés is talking *to* someone, and therefore it must be a letter. We list the strategies students share on our teacher version. Students copy them down on their copy of Figure 13.1: At a Glance Analysis of Source. We comment that a variety of strategies can work and are worth remembering for future document analysis. In addition, asking students how they reached their answers helps students improve their problem solving – metacognition (Blake, 2016).

We continue this unveiling of our answers and the sharing of thinking strategies for each sentence starter. We provide the date for the third, "Date of creation is . . .," because it is not mentioned in the document. We point out to students that they may have to do additional research to figure out the details of a primary source. Students update their responses as well as adding other strategies used by classmates and by the teacher on their copy of Figure 13.1: At a Glance Analysis of Source.

By storing the sentence starters in a classroom folder or notebook, or displaying them on a poster, they remain easily accessible for continual use. The open-endedness of the sentence starters makes them applicable to any kind of primary source, whether image or text.

Students can perform this short analysis every time they receive a primary source in class. The goal is for them to eventually internalize this structure and perform this basic analysis without guidance from the teacher.

IN-DEPTH ANALYSIS OF SOURCE

While the previous strategy provided a cursory overview of the document, students have yet to analyze the content in any depth. We continue the study of Hernán Cortés' letter describing the Aztec city of Tenochtitlan as soon as we complete Figure 13.1: At a Glance Analysis of Source.

It is helpful to provide students with historical context prior to analyzing a source. In this case, before the analysis of this letter, students have already learned about the general motives of European explorers and conquerors between the 1400s and 1600s. Specifically, they read about Cortés and his role in colonizing what is now Mexico.

We introduce Figure 13.5: In-Depth Analysis of a Written Source by providing copies to students and projecting one on a screen or whiteboard. We explain that we will continue where we left off in the last activity by addressing three themes: identification, message, and motive. These three themes (presented as separate sections on the handout) are inspired by different strategies of primary-source analysis that we have used in the past.

We review the three sections of the handout with students, specifically the guiding questions in the left-hand column, to help students understand what the three themes mean. We explain that *Identification* is responding to the questions "What is it?" "Who created it?" and "When was it created?" We go on to say that *Message* means literally "What does it say?" and "What does it tell us about the writer and the historical moment?" Finally, we tell students that *Motive* means "Why is the person doing this or why is this event happening?"

Before continuing with the reading of the letter, we ask students to consider what they can already answer in the handout. For example, if students have completed Figure 13.1: At a Glance Analysis of Source, it may be helpful to direct them to review it. In this case, we model how to use the notes from this handout to answer most of the first section, Identification, on Figure 13.5: In-Depth Analysis of a Written Source. We write: "This source is a letter. It was created (written) by Hernán Cortés in 1520."

Students finish noting any other helpful information from Figure 13.1: At a Glance Analysis of Source. Next, we introduce the following annotation strategies (verbally and in writing) to continue our in-depth analysis:

> *First, highlight any text that stands out to you in the primary source document and write, in the left margin, why it stood out. Second, label the same text you highlighted, in the right margin, with one of the following section headers that you think the text might connect to: identification, message, or motive.*

We begin by modeling for students how we would apply the annotation strategies as shown in Figure 13.6: Cortés' Letter – Teacher Copy. We read the source aloud while the class follows along. We stop about halfway through the first paragraph and say:

> *One thing that stood out to me that I will highlight is the phrase "of the many rare and wonderful objects it contains." Next to the highlighting, on the left, I am going to write "tells me city was amazing, Cortés saw that." Now, I am going to refer to my In-Depth Analysis Chart to see what section this fits best. I think this phrase is part of what Cortés is trying to convey, so I am going to write "Message" in the right-hand margin of this quote.*

We challenge students to make connections with the other themes of the chart. To model this for students, we point out text that represents other themes from the handout. For example, in Figure 13.6 Cortés' Letter – Teacher Copy, we highlight the phrase "account will appear so wonderful as to be deemed scarcely worthy of credit." We explain that we think this quote connects to "Motive" because perhaps Cortés was motivated to impress someone with this letter.

After reading and annotating with students for the first two paragraphs, we turn the task over to them. We assign students a partner when we get to the third paragraph. They are instructed to take turns reading the passage aloud and continue implementing the same reading strategies. We urge students to not get bogged down by unfamiliar terminology. Multiple reads and the analysis process will help provide additional understanding.

Once students complete the reading in partners, we gather everyone together to start completing Figure 13.5: In-Depth Analysis of a Written Source. Since we have already completed the first section "Identification," we move on to the second section, "Message." Here we point to key details in the source that represent this theme. For example, for the Cortés letter, we might say:

> *The letter seems to be describing, in detail, why the city of Tenochtitlan is an amazing place. For example, in the text, it says, "to convey to your Majesty a just conception of the great extent of this noble city of Tenochtitlan, and of the many rare and wonderful objects it contains." This tells me that they are trying to "convey," or express, how "great" this city is by describing its "rare and wonderful objects."*

A teacher can also point to key details to help students determine the recipient of the message, one of the subquestions for this theme. This type of guidance models for students the need to use multiple aspects of the text *and* extend thinking beyond the text to think like a historian. For example, a teacher might point out the word *Sire* or that Cortés' name is Spanish. These key details can help students conclude that it must have been written to a ruler, and some students may even figure out that the letter is directed to the king of Spain.

We use guiding questions in order to scaffold the "Motive" section. These directive questions help to narrow the path and can lead students to consider the intentions of the author. In other words, we want students to consider *why* this primary source was created in the first place. For example, they know from the "Message" section that Cortés wanted to show that Tenochtitlan was magnificent. To help students determine the motive, we might ask the following:

> *Why would Cortés want to show how magnificent this Aztec city was? Consider the unit we are studying and the roles of European explorers during this era. What were they after, according to our classwork? Why would people like Cortés write such detailed letters to the royalty of his country?*

Although some students might already ask themselves these questions, it is important to model this type of thinking. It shows our students that source analysis is much like detective work and that the bigger picture must be considered to understand the motivation of a source. Please refer to Chapter 11: Questions for Learning for more information on guiding questions.

After sharing our guiding questions, we allow a minute or so for discussion in partners and then ask a few students to share with the entire class. Students eventually see that perhaps Cortés wanted to impress his "boss." Please refer to Table 13.1: In-Depth Analysis – Teacher Copy to read other possible motivations.

Table 13.1   In-Depth Analysis – Teacher Copy

Identification • What is it? Genre? Is it written? An item? Visual? • Who created it? • When was it created?	*This source is a letter. It was created (written) by Hernan Cortés in 1520.*
Message • What does it say? • What does it tell us about the writer and the historical moment? • Who is the message for? • Please provide a summary.	*This letter is describing the Aztec city of Tenochtitlan in great detail. Addressed to the King of Spain, it clearly conveys amazement at the size, location, and layout of the city. In addition, their market is described in great detail.*
Motive • Why was this created? • What do you think were the intentions of the authors/creators? • Do not confuse the message with the motivation, although they are connected.	*This letter wanted to describe the Aztec city and impress the King of Spain. By commenting on the magnificence, he wanted to impress his boss. In addition, Cortés was making sure his reputation, or legacy, was preserved.*

Sources: www.commackschools.org/Downloads/OPCVL%20Reference%20Sheet2.pdf, https://historyproject.uci.edu/files/2016/11/6Cs_PSAnalysis.pdf.

Of course, any of the scaffolding strategies (highlighting and annotations, key details, guiding questions) can be applied to all of the analysis sections in Figure 13.5: In-Depth Analysis of a Written Source. Table 13.2: Scaffolding Strategies for Analyzing Primary Sources breaks down these moves for primary source analysis:

Table 13.2 Scaffolding Strategies for Analyzing Primary Sources

Strategy	It looks like . . .	We use it because . . .	We use it when . . .
Highlighting and Annotations	. . . the teacher modeling how to highlight text that stands out to them once or twice per paragraph. They label their highlighting in the left margin explaining why it stood out. In the right margin, they write which part of their analysis chart they think their highlighting connects to (identification, message, and motivation).	. . . it is an open-ended way to *begin* processing a primary source. . . . students can make connections to text . . . it scaffolds further analysis by helping students understand the source as a whole.	. . . students are analyzing a specific primary source for the first time
Key Details	. . . the teacher "thinking aloud," or pointing out, key details from the text that might offer important information.	. . . this type of guidance models for students the need to use multiple aspects of the text *and* extend thinking beyond the text to think like a historian.	. . . we want to lead students to specific text that can help them determine any section of Figure 13.5: In-Depth Analysis of a Written Source.
Guiding Questions	. . . the teacher thinking aloud specific questions about the text to help students consider different perspectives.	. . . it helps facilitate critical thinking about the text . . . it shows our students that source analysis is much like detective work.	. . . we want to lead students to specific text that can help them determine any section of Figure 13.5: In-Depth Analysis of a Written Source.

Post-Analysis Reflection

After students complete their first in-depth analysis, we have students answer the following reflection prompts:

1. Why do you think the analysis sections in the handout were listed in that order?

2. Which aspect of the handout was the most challenging for you? Easiest? Please explain.

3. How can this activity help us connect to or understand history?

Students share their responses with partners. Then, some are selected by the teacher to read their reflection to the whole class. We like how this exercise helps students see that they are not alone in their struggle with in-depth analysis. In addition, we appreciate how these questions help them identify and understand the underlying purposes of the activity.

Note: Primary sources can also be photographs, political cartoons, paintings, video, and other images. Although strategies from this chapter can be applied to images, determining the "message" of an image is best done with the activities from Chapter 12: Image Analysis.

ADDITIONAL KEY STRATEGIES

Here are some additional ideas to help your students analyze and use primary sources in social studies.

- Primary Source Data Set: Although we introduce primary source analysis to our students with *one* source, we eventually have them move on to *sets* of primary sources. Working with sets of sources is an opportunity to practice inductive reasoning (making generalizations based on examples – see Chapter 4: Thematic Data Sets) while exposing students to different perspectives. We start by determining a question we want our students to investigate. Then, we compile a mix of primary source images and texts (and a few secondary ones to provide context to the topic) addressing the question. For example, when studying the roots of slavery in the world, we ask students "How prevalent has slavery been in world societies and how were enslaved people viewed by those in power?" To address this question, we provide Figure 13.7: Roots of Slavery: Primary Source Data Set. We make sure the sources we include in the primary source data set fall into at least three categories. The three categories we use in our source data set are: treatment of enslaved people, views on slavery, and descriptions or types of enslaved people. Students begin working with this data set by first analyzing each source using Table 13.3: Data Set Analysis Chart, to determine the identification and message for each source – the first two steps in the in-depth analysis section of this chapter. Once students have analyzed the sources, we provide Table 13.4: Categorization Chart to help categorize them. For each source listed, they justify their placement by writing what text or ideas in the source represent the category. Using this evidence, students write an essay answering the investigation question. We also like students to use evidence from this activity in a structured class discussion about Reparations (refer to Chapter 16: Discussions for related ideas).

Table 13.3 Data Set Analysis Chart

Identification • What is it? Genre? Is it written? An item? Visual? • Who created it? • When was it created?	Message • What does it say? What does it tell us? • Who is the message for? • Please provide a summary.
1.	
2.	
3.	
4.	
5.	

(Continued)

Table 13.3 (Continued)

6.	
7.	
8.	

- Document-Based Questions (DBQ): This well-known primary source strategy is a different version of the source data set activity described previously. The questions in Table 13.3: Data Set Analysis Chart are general and applicable to almost any source. Instead of using the same questions to analyze sources, teachers can provide *specific, content*-focused questions – custom-made for each source. These two to five DBQs help guide students to certain information in each source to help them answer the essential question of the entire primary source set. For example, instead of answering a general question like "What does it say?" for the Cortés letter, students can be asked, "How does Cortés describe the layout of Tenochtitlan?" Answering these questions can lead to specific content and scaffold a student's response to an essential question like "Which civilization was more 'advanced' – the Aztecs or the Spanish?" The DBQ Project (www.dbqproject.com/about-us) has more information and resources about this strategy. For example, students can use writing tools such as graphic organizers or structured academic discussions to form arguments. In addition, The Stanford History Education Group's "Reading Like a Historian" website (https://sheg.stanford.edu/history-lessons) has free lesson plans on a variety of topics that use DBQ.

Table 13.4   Categorization Chart

Name _____ Date _____		
Category #1:	**Category #2:**	**Category #3:**
Source #_____ **Why I think it goes under** **this category:**	**Source #_____** **Why I think it goes under** **this category:**	**Source #_____** **Why I think it goes under** **this category:**
Source #_____ **Why I think it goes under** **this category:**	**Source #_____** **Why I think it goes under** **this category:**	**Source #_____** **Why I think it goes under** **this category:**
Source #_____ **Why I think it goes under** **this category:**	**Source #_____** **Why I think it goes under** **this category:**	**Source #_____** **Why I think it goes under** **this category:**

- To Introduce a New Unit or Topic: After determining the main components of a unit, a variety of primary sources can be collected that represent different aspects of the content. After compiling and numbering a mix of 10–15 images and texts, we like to have our students analyze them in partners as an engaging and introductory activity for the unit. For example, when we are introducing a unit on Apartheid in South Africa, we compile pictures of protests, anti-apartheid leaders like Nelson Mandela speaking to the public, and excerpts of pro-apartheid legislation. We partner students up and start by randomly distributing one primary source to each pair. Students have two minutes to review their source together and discuss what stands out to them. Then, on a piece of paper, they write the number of their source and their observations about it. Next, the whole class rotates the sources so everyone gets a new one. This process continues until students have seen all, or most, of the sources. Afterward, students can predict what they think the upcoming unit will be about and/or predict what some of the sources are saying or showing. Everyone stores their notes for easy access throughout the unit. Then, as the unit unravels and the primary sources from this activity are used to teach the content, the teacher can direct students back to their notes. They can periodically check to see how accurate their predictions were. This revisiting of educated guesses can help students access and build prior knowledge while helping students anticipate or engage with the content (Digital Public Library, 2016).

- Fact Checking Secondary Sources: This next activity comes from Joe Sangillo at Discovery Education (n.d.). To encourage critical thinking around source credibility, students can fact-check a current news article, online social media post, a section of a textbook, or a movie, with primary sources. After first identifying the exact information they want to corroborate, students can search online for primary sources. For example, a source may describe Native Americans during the westward movement of the United States in an incomplete manner. Students can then research primary sources to confirm, deny, or provide more context. In the search engine box when researching online, students can type the topic plus the terms *background, primary sources, multiple perspectives*, or *conflicting accounts*. To evaluate the accuracy of how a historical event is portrayed, students can go to Gilder Lehrman's website (www.gilder-lehrman.org) or the Library of Congress Databases (www.loc.gov/collections). Additionally, they can use Figure 13.5: In-Depth Analysis of a Written Source to analyze the sources. After locating enough evidence to prove the historical account accurate or inaccurate, students can explain their findings in writing.

- Transcribing Primary Sources: This strategy can inject authentic, historical work into social studies classes while helping our students balance civic duty with empathy. Thanks to websites like *Last Seen: Finding Family After Slavery* (http://informationwanted.org), students can actually volunteer to transcribe real, heartbreaking ads of former slaves looking for their family members. These transcriptions are then made searchable online and can be used by the public for academic or family research. See the Technology Connections section for more resources on primary source transcription.

DIFFERENTIATION

The language and format of primary sources can prove intimidating for any student, but especially for students with learning differences and for English language learners (ELLs) (though it's important to remember that the *reasons* for those challenges are very different). Various steps might need to be taken to make these sources accessible. First, engineering the text by creating headings and white space, along with adding vocabulary definitions and images, can be helpful – this process is described in more detail in Chapter 3: Read-Aloud Protocol. We might also just pick one or two paragraphs from the original passage that we feel most clearly communicate the thesis of each author and have them just read those portions. For these ideas or more about "engineering the text," please refer to Elsa Billings and Aída Walqui's WestEd article "Topic Brief 3: De-Mystifying Complex Texts: What Are 'Complex' Texts and How Can We Ensure ELLs/MLLs Can Access Them?" (n.d.).

Audio versions of some primary sources can be found online, like the "Digital Collections" page of the *Library of Congress* website (www.loc.gov/collections/?fa= original-format:sound+recording). Students can replay these recordings as needed.

We always try to remember what our students *can do* versus what they *can't do*. This activity can both challenge them and give them the opportunity to practice intellectual thought about complex ideas. Primary source analysis does not have to consist of "watered down" versions of rich texts.

ADVANCED EXTENSIONS

Although the second analysis strategy is titled "In-Depth Analysis," it can be made *even more* complex. One way to challenge students is by adding the following themes and accompanying guiding questions to their source analysis:

Confirmation

- What other facts or ideas does this source confirm? Refer to class work or outside research.
- Who might agree with what this source says? Why?

Disagreement

- What other facts or ideas might contradict this source? Refer to class work or outside research.
- Who might disagree with the message of this source? Why?

These two elements further the practice of considering historical context when analyzing primary sources.

Student Handouts and Examples

Figure 13.1: At a Glance Analysis of Source

Figure 13.2: Hernán Cortés' Account of Tenochtitlan

Figure 13.3: At a Glance – Student Example

Figure 13.4: At a Glance – Teacher Copy

Figure 13.5: In-Depth Analysis of a Written Source

Figure 13.6: Cortés' Letter – Teacher Copy

Table 13.1: In-Depth Analysis – Teacher Copy

Table 13.2: Scaffolding Strategies for Analyzing Primary Sources

Figure 13.7: Roots of Slavery: Primary Source Data Set

Table 13.3: Data Set Analysis Chart

Table 13.4: Categorization Chart

What Could Go Wrong?

Not previewing primary sources and identifying challenges students might face when analyzing them can lead to unnecessary confusion. Becoming familiar with a source allows us to plan specific supports. In addition, we can also identify which sections of text can help students with Figure 13.5: In-Depth Analysis of a Written Source.

Another challenge that can arise is when students become frustrated and unmotivated when confronting arcane language in primary sources. "Why *not* use a version that is easier to read?" is a comment we have heard often from students. It's important to acknowledge the very real frustration that certain words can pose. We share that we get frustrated, too! To this end, it is crucial to use ideas from Table 13.2: Scaffolding Strategies so students feel supported. We explain that we use primary sources to exercise critical thinking, a skill applicable to multiple areas of life. In addition, to be informed citizens, we all need the ability to decide for ourselves what is meaningful in history.

Technology Connections

Larry Ferlazzo's post titled "Jackpot! Great Interactives to Support Teaching & Learning with Primary Sources" (http://larryferlazzo.edublogs.org/2018/07/12/jackpot-great-interactives-to-support-teaching-learning-with-primary-sources) shares a list of interactive platforms students can use when analyzing primary sources. For example, Eagle Eye Citizen (www.eagleeyecitizen.org) encourages analysis of sources to solve challenges interactively in history, civics, or government. These tools can encourage the detective aspect of working with primary sources.

For even more resources or innovative ideas for using primary sources, please refer to Larry Ferlazzo's post, titled "The Best Resources for Using Primary Sources" (http://larryferlazzo.edublogs.org/2017/06/29/the-best-sites-where-students-can-transcribe-historical-texts).

For additional places where students can transcribe historical written documents or audio recordings, go to "The Best Sites Where Students Can Transcribe Historical Texts" (http://larryferlazzo.edublogs.org/2017/06/29/the-best-sites-where-students-can-transcribe-historical-texts).

Attribution

Our Primary Source Data Set activity is modeled on a similar strategy practiced by Victoria Stolinski, a social studies teacher at Luther Burbank High School in Sacramento, California. The Fact Checking Secondary Sources activity was based on Joe Sangillo's article "5 Strategies for Using Primary Source Documents in Social Studies Classrooms" from the Discovery Education website *Front and Central* (n.d.).

Figures

1. This is a . . .
I know this because:

2. It was created by . . .
I know this because:

3. Date of creation is . . .
I know this because:

4. What stands out to me is . . . because . . .

5. I wonder . . .

Figure 13.1 At a Glance Analysis of Source

In order, most potent Sire, to convey to your Majesty a just conception of the great extent of this noble city of Tenochtitlan, and of the many rare and wonderful objects it contains, of the government and dominions of Moctezuma, the sovereign; of the religious rites and customs that prevail, and the order that exists in this as well as other cities appertaining to his realm: it would require the labor of many accomplished writers, and much time for the completion of the task. I shall not be able to relate an hundredth part of what could be told respecting these matters but I will endeavor to describe, in the best manner in my power, what I have myself seen; and imperfectly as I may succeed in the attempt, I am fully aware that the account will appear so wonderful as to be deemed scarcely worthy of credit; since even when we who have seen these things with our own eyes, are yet so amazed as to be unable to comprehend their reality. . . .

This great city of Tenochtitlan [Mexico] is situated in this salt lake, and from the main land to the denser parts of it, by whichever route one chooses to enter, the distance is two leagues. There are four avenues or entrances to the city, all of which are formed by artificial causeways, two spears' length in width. The city is as large as Seville or Cordova; its streets, I speak of the principal ones, are very wide and straight; some of these, and all the inferior ones, are half land and half water, and are navigated by canoes. All the streets at intervals have openings, through which the water flows, crossing from one street to another; and at these openings, some of which are very wide, there are also very wide bridges, composed of large pieces of timber, of great strength and well put together; on many of these bridges ten horses can go abreast.

This city has many public squares, in which are situated the markets and other places for buying and selling. There is one square twice as large as that of the city of Salamanca, surrounded by porticoes, where are daily assembled more than sixty thousand souls, engaged in buying, and selling; and where are found all kinds of merchandise that the world affords, embracing the necessaries of life, as for instance articles of food, as well as jewels of gold and silver, lead, brass, copper, tin, precious stones, bones, shells, snails, and feathers. There are also exposed for sale wrought and unwrought stone, bricks burnt and unburnt, timber hewn and unhewn, of different sorts.

Finally, every thing that can be found throughout the whole country is sold in the markets, comprising articles so numerous that to avoid prolixity and because their names are not retained in my memory, or are unknown to me, I shall not attempt to enumerate them. Every kind of merchandise is sold in a particular street or quarter assigned to it exclusively, and this is the best order is preserved. They sell every thing by number or measure; at least so far we have not observed them to sell any thing by weight. There is a building in the great square that is used as an audience house, where ten or twelve persons, who are magistrates, sit and decide all controversies that arise in the market, and order delinquents to be punished. In the same square there are other persons who go constantly about among the people observing what is sold, and the measures used in selling; and they have been seen to break measures that were not true.

Figure 13.2 Hernán Cortés' Account of Tenochtitlan

1. This is a . . . *letter.*
I know this because:
It sounds like the author of this piece is talking to someone.

2. It was created by . . . *Hernán Cortés.*
I know this because:
That's what the citation at the bottom of the document says.

3. Date of creation is . . . *at least over a hundred years ago.*
I know this because:
The style of writing does not seem modern and writing is being used to describe the place they are in, not other technology.

4. What stands out to me is . . . *how he explains everything.*
because . . . *everything, even bridges, are described in extraordinary detail.*

5. I wonder . . . *where Salamanca, the city he refers to, is?*

Figure 13.3 At a Glance – Student Example

1. This is a . . . *letter.*
→ *In other words, what type of source is this?*
→ *How to do: read citation, read text to see who it is directed to or for.*
I know this because:
It is addressing someone and the citation at the bottom says, in Spanish, that it is a letter.

2. It was created by . . . *Hernán Cortés*
→ *In other words, who made this? Author? Artist?*
→ *How to do: read citation, read text: does the creator refer to themselves or their role?*
I know this because:
that's what the citation at the bottom of the document says.

3. Date of creation is . . . *1520*
→ *In other words, when was this made?*
→ *How to do: usually the citation, or the topic of the item can be a clue*
I know this because:
I did additional research once I figured out it was Hernan Cortés. This is the year he published his letters.

4. What stands out to me is . . . *the word "Tenochtitlan"*
because . . . *it makes we wonder what language it comes from.*
→ *In other words, what caught your attention?*

5. I wonder . . . *if this place (Tenochtitlan) still exists today.*
→ *In other words, what would you like to know more about?*

Figure 13.4　At a Glance – Teacher Copy

Identification • What is it? Genre? Is it written? An item? Visual? • Who created it? • When was it created?	
Message • What does it say? • What does it tell us about the writer and the historical moment? • Who is the message for? • Please provide a summary.	
Motive • Why was this created? • What do you think were the intentions of the authors/creators? • Do not confuse the message with the motivation, although they are connected.	

Figure 13.5   In-Depth Analysis of a Written Source

In order, most potent Sire, to convey to your Majesty a just conception of the great extent of this noble city of Tenochtitlan, and of the many rare and wonderful objects it contains *[Message]* of the government and dominions of Moctezuma, the sovereign; of the religious rites and customs that prevail, and the order that exists in this as well as other cities appertaining to his realm: it would require the labor of many accomplished writers, and much time for the completion of the task. I shall not be able to relate an hundredth part of what could be told respecting these matters but I will endeavor to describe, in the best manner in my power, what I have myself seen; and imperfectly as I may succeed in the attempt, I am **fully aware that the** account will appear so wonderful as to be deemed scarcely worthy of *[Motive (wants to impress)]* credit; since even when we who have seen these things with our own eyes, are yet so amazed as to be unable to comprehend their reality....

[tells me city was amazing, Cortés saw that.]

This great city of Tenochtitlan [Mexico] is situated in this salt lake, and from the main land to the denser parts of it, by whichever route one chooses to enter, the distance is two leagues. There are four avenues or entrances to the city, all of which are formed by *[Motive (again, impress)]* artificial causeways, two spears' length in width. The city is as large as Seville or Cordova; its streets, I speak of the principal ones, are very wide and straight; some of these, and all the inferior ones, are half land and half water, and are navigated by canoes. All the streets at intervals have openings, through which the water flows, crossing from *[Message (informs of details)]* one street to another; and at these openings, some of which are very wide, there are also very wide bridges, composed of large pieces of timber, of great strength and well put

[Wow, the city is in a lake?]

[Makes it sound like Venice.]

Figure 13.6 Cortés' Letter – Teacher Copy

Investigation Question: How prevalent has slavery been in world societies and how were enslaved people viewed by those in power?

"The slave trade is the ruling principle of my people. It is the source and the glory of their wealth . . . the mother lulls the child to sleep with notes of triumph over an enemy reduced to slavery . . ."

–King Gezo of Dahomey (now the African country of Benin) explaining he would cooperate with the British except end his slave trade.
Source: http://www.bbc.co.uk/worldservice/africa/features/storyofafrica/9chapter1.shtml

". . . here there is a certain place where slaves are sold, especially on those days when the merchants are assembled. And a young slave of fifteen years of age is sold for six ducats, and children are also sold. The king of this region has a certain private palace where he maintains a great number of concubines and slaves."

–Leo Africanus, who visited Gao, the capital of Songhay (a major African Kingdom) in 1510 and 1513.
Source: http://www.bbc.co.uk/worldservice/specials/1624_story_of_africa/page83.shtml

"The demand for slaves was not large enough to call for specialization in this field of commercial activity (King). Prisoners of war, foreign slaves, and their descendants made up a huge part of the slave population in Mesopotamia (King). The bulk of the Sumerian and Akkadian slaves originally came from the ranks of the native population, which is the case for every city-states at some point in time . . ."

"As we follow evidence through history, we see that slavery was a huge advantage for any new empire to become a success and thrive. Evidence has shown us that this was a way of life for nearly every country in existence. Slaves were needed for labor, whether it be for farmers or building walls to the empire. Slaves were therefore very important to their success."

–description of slavery in the Sumerian and Akkadian civilization (3100 BC) in the Mesopotamian region
Source: http://sites.psu.edu/ancientmesopotamianwarfare/slavery/

Figure 13.7   Roots of Slavery: Primary Source Data Set

"Let us first speak of master and slave, looking to the needs of practical life and also seeking to attain some better theory of their relation than exists at present. . . . Property is a part of the household, and the art of acquiring property is a part of the art of managing the household; for no man can live well, or indeed live at all, unless he be provided with necessaries. And so, in the arrangement of the family, a slave is a living possession, and property a number of such instruments; and the slave is himself an instrument which takes precedence of all other instruments. . . . The master is only the master of the slave; he does not belong to him, whereas the slave is not only the slave of his master, but wholly belongs to him."

–Aristotle, Greek philosopher on the politics of slavery, 330 BCE
Source: http://www.wright.edu/~christopher.oldstone-moore/Aristotleslavery.htm

–*Aztec Slave market (Sahagún, Historia . . . de Nueva España)*
Source: http://tarlton.law.utexas.edu/aztec-and-maya-law/aztec-social-structure

Figure 13.7 (Continued)

—Slaves pouring wine. A Roman mosaic from the second century A.D. in Tunisia. Image *Source:* https://www.romanports.org/en/articles/human-interest/334-the-mosaics-depicting-roman-ports-and-maritime-trade.html

The Maya had a system of serfdom and slavery. Serfs typically worked lands that belonged to the ruler or local town leader. There was an active slave trade in the Maya region, and commoners and elites were both permitted to own slaves. Individuals were enslaved as a form of punishment for certain crimes and for failing to pay back their debts. Prisoners of war who were not sacrificed would become slaves, and impoverished individuals sometimes sold themselves or family members into slavery. Slavery status was not passed on to the children of slaves. However, unwanted orphan children became slaves and were sometimes sacrificed during religious rituals. Slaves were usually sacrificed when their owners died so that they could continue in their service after death. If a man married a slave woman, he became a slave of the woman's owner. This was also the case for women who married male slaves.

—"Maya Social Structure," Tarlton Law Library, The University of Texas at Austin. *Source:* https://tarlton.law.utexas.edu/aztec-and-maya-law/maya-social-structure

Figure 13.7 (Continued)

–Captives being brought on board a slave ship on the West Coast of Africa (Slave Coast), c1880.

Source: https://www.gettyimages.com/detail/news-photo/captives-being-brought-on-board-a-slave-ship-on-the-west-news-photo/463911399

Figure 13.7   (Continued)

CHAPTER 14

Synthesis Charts

What Is It?

Synthesis is the act of combining information to create new ideas ("Synthesis," n.d.) In this chapter, we share how we facilitate synthesis, supported by a graphic organizer, in order to help students practice higher-order thinking. Students identify key information from multiple sources about a topic being studied in class. Then, we help students synthesize, or create new ideas, by guiding them to notice patterns or connections that exist within the information listed on their chart. Students then pull this varied content together and combine it with their own thinking to develop a position supported by evidence. This completed chart can serve as a pre-writing tool. It can help bridge the gap between initial exposure to information and analyzing it to develop a personal thesis. Scaffolding can be adjusted depending on the needs and experience level of students. This graphic organizer can be applied to any social studies content.

Why We Like It

Synthesis charts can help students engage in higher-order thinking tasks. Synthesis is usually placed as one of the more difficult levels of cognitive learning on the revised Bloom's Taxonomy (n.d.). While many classroom activities seem to center around the lower levels of remembering and understanding, we like how the use of a synthesis chart provides a clear pathway to higher levels of thinking. Additionally, this process is similar to one a historian might use: gathering evidence to make interpretations ("Historians Defined," n.d.).

Using a synthesis chart gives students a reason to go back to their class materials in response to a given prompt. In other words, this strategy pushes students to make multiple "touches" on previously covered material, which can result in deeper understanding.

Supporting Research

A report from the National Science Foundation states, "Our ability to generate and collect digital information continues to grow faster than our means to organize, manage, and effectively use it" ("Knowledge Lost," 2003, p. iv). This report validates what many classroom teachers already know – there is more information available than ever before. Yet, students often lack the skills needed to accurately interpret this material in order to draw conclusions.

Research also shows that *explicitly* teaching synthesis can help students improve their ability to create new ideas based on evidence (Lundstrom, Diekema, Leary, Haderlie, & Holliday, 2015, p. 72).

Additionally, the pattern-seeking skills required for synthesis have been shown to make learning more transferable to new situations (Sparks, 2015).

Common Core Connections

The *Common Core for History/Social Studies* requires that students "Integrate and evaluate multiple sources of information presented in diverse formats and media...in order to address a question or solve a problem" (Common Core, 2010s). Students can meet this standard by using synthesis charts to integrate multiple sources in order to respond to a prompt. The standards also challenge students to synthesize as they "connect insights" and "determine central ideas" (Common Core, 2010x).

Additionally, rereading class materials and completing a synthesis chart can help students identify patterns they can apply in learning complex concepts or topics. The Common Core highlights the importance of finding patterns in events, words, and sentences (Common Core 2010i, 2010j, 2010k).

Social Studies Connections

The College, Career, and Civic Life (C3) Framework created by the National Council for the Social Studies presses students to identify and evaluate multiple sources and then use them as evidence in constructing an argument (NCSS, 2010, p. 54). The inclusion of a synthesis chart can help students organize evidence and cite sources as they develop a claim.

Application

In this section, we share how to create and implement synthesis charts in the classroom.

A good time to use synthesis charts is after students have completed a larger reading task or a series of activities on a topic and need to extend their thinking to make new meaning, create a judgment, or develop an argument. For example:

- Students in a US history course may use a synthesis chart to collect evidence from their unit materials in order to write an essay on the lasting impact of the American Civil War.

- Geography students may use a synthesis chart after reading a Thematic Data Set (see Chapter 4: Thematic Data Sets) about Brazil. This activity can prepare students to write an argument about the role of government in reducing the deforestation of the Amazon rainforest.

- US government students might use a synthesis chart to collect information from court cases related to freedom of speech to help them prepare for a debate on student consequences for inappropriate social media posts.

CREATING A SYNTHESIS CHART

Because synthesis can be a challenging activity, we break the process into multiple parts. Together, these smaller steps help support our students to reach synthesis. Scaffolding can be removed as students become more familiar with the process.

Our synthesis chart is divided into two parts. Part One has three sections: Prompt, Topics, and Resources. Part Two has two sections: Summary and Synthesis. See Table 14.1: Synthesis Chart Template for a blank example.

Prompt

We engage students in this process by asking a question that requires synthesis in order to develop an appropriate response. We often use an essential question from our current unit of study as the prompt for our synthesis chart. Whether they are essential questions or not, the prompts we use for synthesis charts must be open-ended, thought provoking, and require students to "take a stand" in responding to them. For more about questions, including essential questions, please see Chapter 11: Questions for Learning.

It is important to make sure the selected prompt requires student research in order to answer it. In other words, the question should be complex enough that students *need* to dive back into the class materials in order to respond. For example, Part One in Table 14.2: Brazil Synthesis Chart asks, "Based on what you have learned, what are Brazil's two most valuable assets?" This question calls for students to consider many different elements of Brazil in order to synthesize or make a judgment about its assets and formulate an argument.

Topics

The next element in Part One of the synthesis chart is a space for topics, which runs horizontally across the top. This section calls student attention to broader areas,

Table 14.1 Synthesis Chart Template

Prompt				
Part One				
Topics → _____ **Resources ↓**				
Part Two **Topics →**				
Summary: What are the patterns you see here?				
Synthesis (judgment/argument): Teacher may add a scaffolding question here				

Table 14.2 Brazil Synthesis Chart

Prompt	Based on what you have learned, what are Brazil's two most valuable assets? (Consider the land and climate, people, economy, and culture)			
Part One				
Topic → **Resource ↓**	Land and Climate (teacher example)	People/Population	Economy	Culture
CIA Factbook	— 8,515,770 sq. km — mostly tropical climate — "deforestation in Amazon Basin destroys the habitat and endangers a multitude of plant species indigenous to the area."			
Brazil Data Set	"The Amazon rainforest has the greatest variety of plant life per square kilometer on earth." Many of these plants have health benefits. People travel to Brazil to visit the forest. It is the largest Rainforest in the world.			
Amazon video clip notes	Rare trees (nut trees, mahogany) illegally being cut down for lumber or forest clearing for ranchers.			
Favela Readings (magazine article)				
Pele Movie				
Part Two				
Topics →	Land and Climate	People	Economy	Culture
Summary What are the patterns you see here?	Brazil is very big and the Amazon Rainforest is valuable for many reasons, including natural resources and tourism.			
Synthesis (judgment/ argument) What is most valuable about this asset/ topic and why?	Considering many plants are only found in the Amazon Rainforest, Brazil's land and climate is one of its most valuable assets. Additionally, it brings tourism.			

which can help them organize key information in order to write a response. The content of the "topic" section may change depending on the demands of the prompt.

In some graphic organizers, like Table 14.2: Brazil Synthesis Chart, the topics correspond to *categories* studied during a unit (Land and Climate or Economy in our unit on Brazil). The categories can guide students to needed information as they research their answer to the prompt, "Based on what you have learned, what are Brazil's two most valuable assets?" See Table 14.3: Brazil Synthesis Chart Example for a completed version.

In other cases, the topics may be *guiding questions* that direct students' attention toward key information in order to answer a prompt. For example, Table 14.4: Identity Synthesis Chart is from a unit on Identity in an ethnic studies class. The topics are questions like "Who are my ancestors?" and "What is my culture?" These questions and their responses help guide students in answering the central prompt "Am I the best version of myself? Why or why not?"

Another example of using *guiding questions* as topics comes from a unit we do on immigration. The central prompt is "What is the role of immigration in society?" Guiding questions include "What is the economic impact of immigration?" and "What are noneconomic impacts of immigration?"

In all three of these examples (Brazil, Identity, and Immigration), the teacher chooses the topics. Once students are familiar with the process, however, they can be given the prompt and challenged to identify the appropriate topics needed to develop a response.

Remember, these topics are ones that students should have already studied prior to developing their synthesis chart. For example, if the question is "What do you think were the two most important reasons why the American Revolution generated popular support?" students would likely be able to identify topics like taxation, lack of political representation, mandatory housing of British soldiers, and shutting down trade in Boston.

Resources

The Resources column in Part One of the chart contains the titles of sources that may contain information to help students respond to the prompt. For example, in Table 14.2: Brazil Synthesis Chart, we suggest that students refer to "CIA Factbook," "Brazil Data Set," and "Amazon video clip notes." Students collect these items from their folders and review them for information to add to their charts. We often leave blank boxes in this column so that students are able to select additional sources.

Table 14.3 Brazil Synthesis Chart Example

Prompt	Based on what you have learned, what are Brazil's two most valuable assets? (Consider the land and climate, people, economy, and culture)		
Topic → **Resource ↓**	Land and Climate (teacher example)	People/Population	Economy	Culture
CIA Factbook	– 8,515,770 sq. km – mostly tropical climate – "deforestation in Amazon Basin destroys the habitat & endangers a multitude of plant species indigenous to the area"	There are 208,846,892 people. 47.7% of people are "white" and 43.1% are "mulatto" which is mixed white and black.	The 8th largest economy in the world, but the economy has been struggling lately because of some issues with corruption Per Capita income is $15 600.	64.4% of people are Roman Catholic. Portuguese is the official language.
Brazil Data Set	The Amazon rainforest has the greatest variety of plant life per square kilometer on earth. Many of these plants have health benefits. People travel to Brazil to visit the forest. It is the largest Rainforest in the world.	The people in Brazil are mostly a mixture of Portuguese, African, and Indigenous. Sao Paulo has the largest population of Brazil's cities.	Historically Brazil has been known for its agriculture. They produce a lot of oranges and coffee. Today they also produce oil.	Brazil is a melting pot of cultures. Their most famous holiday is Carnival a Catholic holiday with African influences. Neighborhood samba schools compete.
Amazon video clip notes	Rare trees (nut trees, mahogany) illegally being cut down for lumber or forest clearing for ranchers.	Some people have been killed trying to protect trees in the Amazon.	People wanting to grow crops or raise livestock is a reason why they are clearing the land and cutting down the rainforest.	Indigenous people still live deep in the Amazon, but their culture and future is at risk because of deforestation.
Favela Readings (magazine article)		Mostly the people in the favelas are poor.	Economic opportunity is limited in the favelas. Kids drop out of school at a young age to work low skilled jobs. Some have to commute really far for work.	The biggest parade competition was created by the people in the favelas. They spend a lot of time and money building floats and costumes each year.

(Continued)

Table 14.3   (Continued)

Pele Movie		The people in the favela seemed to mostly be darker skinned Afro-Brazilian.	Pele worked with his dad as a janitor when he was younger.	Soccer is Brazil's favorite sport. The fans go crazy for soccer.

Part Two

Topics →	Land and Climate	People	Economy	Culture
Summary: What are the patterns you see here?	Brazil is very big and the Amazon Rainforest is valuable for many reasons, including natural resources and tourism.	In Brazil it seems like many people are mixed ethnicity.	It's large economy is mainly based on agriculture and livestock. Even though the economy is large, it has many poor people.	Celebration seems to be a big part of Brazil's culture.
Synthesis: (judgment/argument) What is most valuable about this asset/topic and why?	Considering many plants are only found in the Amazon Rainforest, Brazil's land and climate is one of its most valuable assets. Additionally, it brings tourism.	Brazil's people/population is valuable because it helps to build the nation's culture. The mixture of Portuguese, Indigenous, and African cultures is different from anywhere in the world.	The fact that it has a large economy creates opportunities to do something creative to help ALL its people.	Brazil's most valuable cultural asset might be their view of life. Brazilians view life as something to be celebrated. This is why millions visit Brazil each year for Carnival.

Table 14.4 Identity Synthesis Chart

Prompt	Am I the best version of myself? Why or why not?		
Part One			
Topics → **Resources ↓**	Who are my ancestors?	What is my culture?	What are my hopes, dreams, and goals?	What is my place/ purpose in this world?
Partner Interview				
"I am" poem				
Family questionnaire				
Identity Timeline				
Part Two			
Topics →	Who are my ancestors?	What is my culture?	What are my hopes, dreams, and goals?	What is my place/ purpose in this world?
Summary: What are the patterns you see here? (Who am I?)				
Synthesis (judgment/ argument): How close am I to who I want to be and what should I be doing to improve?				

Summary and Synthesis

After students have completed reviewing their resources and filling in the information under each topic in Part One of the chart (not all resources talk about all topics, so there may be some blank boxes), it's then time for Part Two of the synthesis chart.

Part Two of the chart is where the synthesis occurs. We divide this process into two steps.

In the first step, we ask students to summarize any patterns or big ideas they notice for each topic in Part One of their chart. In other words, they review each column for patterns or key ideas. Then, in Part Two of the chart, they put their key idea in the row titled "Summary: What are the patterns you see here?"

For example, in Table 14.3: Brazil Synthesis Chart Example after reading about the people of Brazil, it becomes clear that many people are mixed ethnicity. This idea is added to the Summary row. After reading about the culture of Brazil, students conclude that celebration is a key aspect and add it to the Summary row as well. This process, the first step of synthesis, is repeated for each topic on the synthesis chart. Multiple examples of this summary step are included in the Implementing Synthesis Chart with Students section further on.

For the second step, students are directed to synthesize, in this case make a judgment, based on the summaries they developed for each topic. They put this judgment in the row titled Synthesis. To further support students with this step, we often add a question to the Synthesis section that acts as a scaffold to help students make a judgment in order to answer the prompt. For example, in the Brazil Synthesis Chart, the main prompt is, "Based on what you have learned, what are Brazil's two most valuable assets?" To support students with the Synthesis row for this chart, we added the question "What is most valuable about this asset/topic and why?" Answering this support question for each topic (each column), based on their previously developed summary, prepares students to respond to the prompt. Once they have determined the value of each of the topics/assets (the purpose of the prompt), they can more easily identify which two they feel are most important and why. Then, they can use – and elaborate on – the most valuable assets of Brazil in their written response to the prompt.

IMPLEMENTING SYNTHESIS CHARTS WITH STUDENTS

To get the biggest bang for your buck with a synthesis chart, modeling is key. Many students will struggle with synthesis even with support. Without scaffolding, they may do it incorrectly or not even attempt it. What follows is a description of how we support the synthesis process for two different prompts. The first example helps students synthesize so they can respond to a prompt about Brazil, while the second facilitates reflection on their identity.

Brazil Synthesis Chart

After selecting a prompt that requires synthesis in order to respond, it may be helpful to break down the prompt. Sometimes, doing this kind of analysis may be as simple as offering synonyms. For example, Table 14.2: Brazil Synthesis Chart asks "Based on what you have learned, what are Brazil's most valuable assets?" We can help students by clarifying the words *valuable* and *asset*. In this case, we may explain *valuable* as most important or most beneficial. We could explain *asset* as something that benefits the country, like something that brings in tourism. In other words, the prompt is asking students to evaluate *which* resources are most important and/or beneficial for Brazil.

Once students understand the prompt, the teacher may need to review the topics. For example, in Part One of Table 14.2: Brazil Synthesis Chart, it may help to clarify what type of content might fall under the topic of Culture. We remind students that religion and sports are parts of culture and that clarification might help them identify content about Brazil for their chart.

Now that students have reviewed the prompt and the topics, we point out the list of resources students should use to gather information for Table 14.2: Brazil Synthesis Chart ("CIA Factbook," "Brazil Data Set," and "Amazon video clip notes," and so on). We model physically taking out the materials and reviewing them. Then, we share aloud the thinking process for selecting information. For example, when reviewing notes from a video about the Amazon for our Table 14.2: Brazil Synthesis Chart, we might say:

> *I see on my video notes I wrote that ". . . rare trees (nut trees, mahogany) are illegally being cut down for lumber or forest clearing for ranchers." That seems like something important to know about the land and climate of Brazil, so I'm going to add it to my chart.*

We then write that key idea onto the chart as seen in the completed column of Table 14.2: Brazil Synthesis Chart. Students continue this process on their own or with a partner. A teacher may require a certain number of items for each topic or resource for accountability purposes.

Next comes what is often the most difficult portion to complete – Part Two: Summary and Synthesis (see Table 14.2: Brazil Synthesis Chart and Table 14.3: Brazil Synthesis Chart Example). These rows are where the synthesis process happens. The first step is Summary. This step directs students to summarize key information for each topic by answering the question, "What are the key patterns you see here?"

We model completing this task by reviewing the items listed in each box under the first topic Land and Climate. We share aloud how to look for repeated ideas and patterns among the information. We might say,

> *Under the land and climate topic, I noticed that in more than one place the resources mention the size of the country and the Amazon rainforest, as well as its natural resources. In the box labeled "What are the patterns you see here?" I'm going to write "Brazil is very big and the Amazon rainforest is valuable for many reasons, including natural resources and tourism.*

Then, we give students time to repeat this process for each of the topics.

Once students have completed the Summary section, we move on to Synthesis where students start to form a judgment or argument based on the summaries for each topic. This is where we might include a scaffolding question to help students synthesize in order to answer the prompt. For example, in Part Two of Table 14.2: Brazil Synthesis Chart we added the following scaffolding question: "What is most valuable about this asset/topic and why?" This kind of addition can highlight the thinking required to complete the section.

We model the process of using the summary information to start forming judgments. For example, we might say:

> *Now, I need to decide how important this asset might be. I think it is very important. Considering many plants are only found in the Amazon rainforest, Brazil's land and climate is one of its most valuable assets. Additionally, it brings many tourists to the area.*

Students then apply the same synthesis process for all of the topics. We circulate around the room to provide assistance.

Once students have been successful in creating judgments based on evidence, they are ready to use the synthesis chart to respond to the prompt. They could do an extended response using the ABC writing structure discussed in Chapter 5: Writing in Social Studies. They could also develop a full-fledged essay or a digital presentation.

If students are going to use the ABC writing structure – (A) answer the question, (B) back it up with evidence, and (C) provide commentary – we recommend that they use a judgment from one of their topics to serve as an *answer* (the "A" in ABC writing structure). The evidence collected in the chart, along with citing where it came from, can serve to back up the answer (the "B" in ABC writing structure). Then, students can wrap up the paragraph by providing commentary (the "C" in ABC writing structure), in this case, a further explanation of why a selected asset is or is not the most valuable.

We model applying this writing structure by using the completed example column from Table 14.2: Brazil Synthesis Chart. For example, we might write:

> The unique plants in the Amazon rainforest are one of the two most valuable assets found in Brazil. According to the Brazil Data Set, this rainforest "has the greatest variety of plant life per square kilometer on earth and many of its plants offer health benefits." Many countries and pharmaceutical companies have been exploring and experimenting with what they have found there.

In our experience, modeling how to use a synthesis chart, as a tool to support our thinking and writing processes, is critical to student success. If students need additional support, teachers can create sentence frames or additional writing structures (see Chapter 5: Writing in Social Studies).

Identity Synthesis Chart

There are a variety of ways to modify a synthesis chart to meet the content demands and ability level of students. In this variation, we share how to use a synthesis chart to help students answer the prompt "Am I the best version of myself? Why or why not?" This prompt concludes a unit on identity in an ethnic studies class.

We begin this activity by first distributing Table 14.4: Identity Synthesis Chart. Then, we direct students' attention to the prompt, "Am I the best version of myself? Why or why not?" We acknowledge that this is a big question people might spend their whole life trying to figure out. However, for the purposes of this class we want to focus on specific information that aligns with the course content. With this goal in mind, we provide guiding questions along the top row to lead students toward the topics we want them to reflect on and incorporate in their response. These topics, selected for their prevalence in our content, include ancestors, culture, goals, and purpose.

After reviewing these topics, we provide an opportunity for students to generate an additional one they would like to include in their chart. An extra box has been left intentionally blank to allow for this in Table 14.4: Identity Synthesis Chart. The question they create may direct attention toward an additional attribute of their identity they think is important to consider in order to respond to the prompt, "Am I the best version of myself? Why or why not?" For example, in Table 14.5: Identity Synthesis Chart Teacher Model the additional box has been filled in with "How do I think other people see my identity?" Another question might be "What aspects of my identity do I struggle with most?" or "How has my identity changed over time?"

After reviewing the topics, we point students' attention to the column titled Resources. This column lists class materials that may have information about the required topics. Next, we model for students how to review their class materials from the Resources column and input information into the chart. For example,

Table 14.5 Identity Synthesis Chart Teacher Model

Prompt	Am I the best version of myself? Why or why not?				
Part One					
Topics → **Resources ↓**	Who are my ancestors?	What is my culture?	What are my hopes, dreams, and goals?	What is my place/ purpose in this world?	*How do I think other people see my identity?*
Partner Interview	*My grandparents on my dad's side are from Europe. On my mom's side, I'm not sure, they have all been in the United States for a long time. They came from the midwest to California in the 1800s.*	*We grew up celebrating Christmas, Easter, the 4th of July, Halloween. Everyone in my family speaks English. My Dad's dad spoke another language. Most family members would identify as Christian.*	*I want to be a good teacher and a good life long learner too. I want to write a book for other teachers. I want to be a good mom.*	*To help others. Be a good listener and practice empathy in all areas of my life.*	*Organized and disciplined – very happy and always smiling.*
"I am" poem	*A country that doesn't exist anymore (Czechoslovakia) and one my grandfather's family fled (Hungary). Working class – middle class families.*	*Multiple Christmases, one at Dad's and one at Mom's. Home cooked meals, jam, and cookies. Work hard and be successful, be the best.*	*I dream of finding a balance between work, home, and me. I will help others to be more accepting of differences.*	*Be a leader, be a guide, show "them" a way, not "the" way because there is more than one.*	*Anxious and worried about everything - a perfectionist.*
Family questionnaire	*My family tree has roots in Czechoslovakia, Hungary, Great Britain, Ireland, and France. All European countries. I think all of my ancestors are caucasian.*	*My family wishes I would go to church more. My family and I disagree on politics. My family has "American" culture.*	*My family wishes I would go to the park and watch my children play more often.*	*In my family I am an equal partner to my spouse - we make decisions together, especially ones that will impact our children.*	*My family sees me as "Mom" and that I have a lot of shoes.*

Table 14.5 (Continued)

Identity Timeline	My family moved to Sacramento in the 1980s, most of my family lives in California and has for a few generations.	When I was younger, my brother, cousins, and I would sing religious songs and perform for our family.	I have a mixture of professional and personal goals like getting my Masters and becoming a Mom.	Something important was when I was in high school I was captain of my cheer team. That was one of my first leadership positions.	From this chart people would see the different jobs I've had like working at a pizza place and a restaurant as well as teaching.
Part Two					
Topics →	Who are my ancestors?	What is my culture?	What are my hopes, dreams, and goals?	What is my place/purpose in this world?	How do I think other people see my identity?
Summary: What are the patterns you see here? (Who am I?)	European and Caucasian ancestors. No recent immigrant experiences.	My family's culture tends to be more "Christian" and "traditional" in the eyes of white culture.	I want to do a lot of things and it's a challenge to fit in everything.	I like to be in charge and see myself as a helper.	My outside doesn't always match my insides.
Synthesis (judgment/argument): How close am I to who I want to be and what should I be doing to improve?	I can do a better job meeting and developing relationships with people of different cultures.	I am living my life on my terms. I choose the religion, music, and food I bring into my home.	I am confident in what I want to do. However, lots of responsibilities sometimes interfere with my being able to do everything.	In terms of my purpose, I should spend more time enjoying the small moments of being a mom.	There is a big difference in how I think people see me and how I want them to see me. I need to respond without fear of how I am perceived.

from the Family Questionnaire resource, the European background of the teacher is added to the chart under the "Who are my ancestors?" topic (see Table 14.5: Identity Synthesis Chart Teacher Model). We give students time to look through their materials and add information to Part One of their charts.

Once students have added information to Part One of their charts, it's time to start Part Two. The first step of Part Two, Summary, directs students to look for patterns within each topic. To scaffold this process, we add the question "What are the patterns you see here?" to the Summary section of the chart. This question can help guide students toward the main ideas for each topic.

Again, modeling this process for students is key. We model reviewing and looking for patterns in the column titled "Who are my ancestors?" We think aloud the following for students:

> *When I read this, I notice I wrote about different countries in Europe or mentioned Europe multiple times. I also notice there hasn't been any* **recent** *immigration in my family. I am going to write that down as a pattern. "European and Caucasian ancestors. No recent immigrant experiences."*

Another way to help students is to provide sentence starters that summarize key ideas and assist students in identifying patterns. These general "starters" can be used for synthesis charts focused on any subject:

- This topic is mainly about . . .
- For this topic, the sources talk about _____ multiple times. Based on this I think . . .
- The most important ideas in this topic were . . .
- When I look at all these items together, it seems like . . .

To help students with the second step, Synthesis, often the most difficult part, we provide the following question: "How close am I to who I want to be and what should I be doing to improve?" For this box, we review the information in the column titled "Who are my ancestors?," then we think aloud the following:

> *When I think about who I want to be, it isn't just "Caucasian" or "European." I can make sure that I expose myself and my children to different groups of people, which I don't do often enough. I am going to write "I can do better to get to know and develop relationships with people outside of my ethnic culture."*

A teacher may want to scaffold this step further by providing sentence frames. For example, to support students on the identity synthesis chart, we could use sentence frames like:

- I am . . . and to get closer to the best version of myself I should . . .

- I am close to the best version of myself regarding . . . . . because . . .

- I have a long way to go with . . . to be the best version of myself because . . .

- There is/is not a big difference between who I am and who I want to be because . . .

After completing the Synthesis portion of the chart, we guide students to use the information to respond to the prompt "Am I the best version of myself? Why or why not?" using the different writing strategies we reviewed earlier in this chapter.

Another idea is to turn the prompt response into a visual response by creating a flipbook or foldable, a type of three-dimensional graphic organizer. See the Technology Connections section for online resources for these kinds of "foldables."

Students could post these foldables around the classroom to make them public or do a "paper pass," a structured sharing of student work, as described in Chapter 9: Genre Study. Seeing each other's responses to the prompt "Am I the best version of myself? Why or why not?" can help students to get to know their classmates better and strengthen the sense of community in the classroom.

DIFFERENTIATION

Our synthesis chart is already a very well-scaffolded activity. The key differentiation occurs previously when students are exposed to classroom content for the first time. *That* is when videos need to be played at slower speeds, when text needs to be "engineered" (see Chapter 3: Read-Aloud Protocol) and when background materials may need to be provided in English language learners' (ELLs') home languages.

ADVANCED EXTENSIONS

More experienced students may prefer to develop their own topics for a synthesis chart as well as select their own resources. In addition, these students may not need the step-by-step modeling offered to the rest of the class. They can be encouraged to get started on the chart individually and also be challenged to create a more extensive response to the prompt.

Student Handouts and Examples

Table 14.1: Synthesis Chart Template
Table 14.2: Brazil Synthesis Chart
Table 14.3: Brazil Synthesis Chart Example
Table 14.4: Identity Synthesis Chart
Table 14.5: Identity Synthesis Chart Teacher Model

What Could Go Wrong?

Giving the synthesis chart to students before they have had a chance to thoroughly read and learn about a topic can lead to frustration. A teacher should make sure that students have spent enough time with resources from the unit prior to working on a synthesis chart. Students may also have difficulty completing the chart if they can't find their resources. For this reason, we recommend a folder for each student to keep all unit materials in one place. In our classrooms we often provide an area for students to store them.

Additionally, the judgment/argument section of the synthesis chart, where students actually *synthesize* the information, may be difficult for students. It is important that the teacher model this process. Don't give up if students are struggling. Instead, break the synthesis down into smaller steps. Rather than analyzing a whole column of information and noticing a pattern, have students compare two items to see what they may have in common before introducing more examples.

Technology Connections

Students could use a site like Padlet (https://padlet.com) or NoteApp (https://noteapp.com) to collect and organize information for Part One of a synthesis chart. Both sites are online tools that function like a corkboard. Students can collaborate or work independently using one of the applications to create a collection of images and notes about each of the topics. These collections can then be analyzed for patterns and key ideas from multiple sources.

To get more ideas for foldables, and alternative ways to respond to the synthesis chart prompt, see Larry Ferlazzo's blog post "The Best Teacher Resources for Foldables" (http://larryferlazzo.edublogs.org/2009/06/07/the-best-teacher-resources-for-foldables).

Attribution

Many different versions of synthesis charts can be found online. Our synthesis charts were adapted from the ones given to us by our Writing Project colleagues Lara Hoekstra and Brooke Nicolls.

SECTION III

Speaking and Listening

CHAPTER 15

Listening and Speaking Activities

What Is It?

In this chapter, we provide structures to help students engage in active listening. Neuroscientist and education researcher Judy Willis describes active listening as a structured way of listening in which judgment is suspended until the speaker has finished (Willis, 2018). Additionally, active listeners *show* they're listening through body language and giving the speaker their undivided attention.

This chapter provides short activities to help students practice active listening. Then, we share guidelines to follow when preparing students to listen to a guest speaker, a podcast, and classmates. These guidelines explain what students and teachers should do prior, during, and after listening to help students achieve the most effective learning experiences.

Providing time for students to give presentations in class promotes critical public-speaking skills while creating opportunities for their classmates to actively listen to them. To this end, the last section in this chapter briefly shares examples of how to "set students up to succeed" in making these public presentations.

Why We Like It

We like how these activities and guidelines help students improve their active listening. This type of listening is not only a key component of good communication but also helps students to learn and build relationships ("Build Better," n.d.).

We also appreciate these strategies because student engagement is often heightened by the novelty of using a podcast or guest speaker (Adams, 2013). Students often welcome listening to a voice *other than* the teacher's, including their classmates.

Supporting Research

Active listening activities can promote being open-minded and prepare students for productive dialogue (Rogers & Farson, 1987, p. 1). These listening skills can help to build positive connections between students, which – in turn – can create a more supportive learning environment.

To be most effective, active listening needs to be multidimensional and incorporate different cognitive tasks (Canpolat, Kuzu, Yıldırım, & Canpolat, 2015, p. 176). We include these elements by structuring a variety of tasks prior, during, and after listening.

Common Core Connections

The Common Core notes the importance of listening skills by including an entire section devoted to the Speaking and Listening standards. They require that students be able to respond to questions and make connections to larger ideas during discussions (Common Core, 2010y). Additionally, the standards list the need for students to analyze different types of information sources, including oral presentations (Common Core, 2010y).

SOCIAL STUDIES CONNECTIONS

Listening is recognized as an important skill in social studies. The College, Career, and Civic Life (C3) Framework from the National Council for the Social Studies (NCSS) states that civil and democratic discourse is both a "purpose and outcome of a strong, meaningful, and substantive social studies education" (NCSS, 2010, p. 21).

Application

We will begin by sharing a mini-lesson as well as a few other ideas to help students develop good listening skills. These activities also emphasize the *importance* of listening skills. Then, we will share guidelines for successfully using guest speakers, podcasts, and student presentations in the classroom.

ACTIVE LISTENING MINI-LESSON

We begin this lesson on active listening by asking students to respond to a prompt: "Write about a time you felt you weren't being listened to. How did you know the other person wasn't listening? What did that feel like?" We ask this question to get students started from a place of empathy – seeing and feeling from another person's perspective.

After giving students time to write, usually no more than five minutes, we do a pair-share. We ask students to talk with a neighbor and then call on a few students to share with the class. Then, we ask students why they think it's important to listen to others. We give them a minute to think and then call on students to share and make a class list.

Typically students share things like "to get the right information," "so people will listen to you," and "to be respectful." Starting with these two questions helps set the stage for a lesson on active listening by accessing students' prior knowledge on the topic.

Next, we show students a video about active listening. The specific one we show is Active Listening: Katie Owens at TEDxYouth@Conejo ("Active Listening," n.d.). There are many other videos online about active listening, but we like this one because it is given by a teenager and is concise. During the video, we ask students to write down three things done by good listeners. To ensure its accessibility to all students, we often show it twice, at a slower speed, and with subtitles. You may also want to have students "pair-share" as an additional check after the clip. We then call on a few students to share and make a class list of "what good listeners do" on the board or projector.

We review the three actions of good listeners: eliminate distractions, appropriate body language, and provide feedback. Next, we divide students into pairs for a quick activity that reinforces the elements of "good listening." We ask students to complete Table 15.1: Active Listening Graphic Organizer. This organizer asks students to give examples and nonexamples of what good listening sounds, looks, and feels like. We like this activity because students work together and the student-created examples make explicit what they should be doing, or not doing, while listening. We typically put these up on the wall and refer to them when students need a reminder of the "do's and don'ts" of good listening. In our experience, having these examples in the students' own words can work well to promote desirable behavior.

Table 15.1 Active Listening Graphic Organizer

What good listening sounds like . . .	What good listening looks like . . .	What good listening feels like . . .
What good listening *does not* sound like . . .	What good listening *does not* look like . . .	What good listening *does not* feel like . . .

The following activities can be fun ways to periodically practice listening skills:

- Play "Telephone" – line students up in two lines and whisper a short phrase to the person at the end of each line. The first team to whisper the message down the line and then correctly write it on the board wins the game.

- Animal noise line up – Write down the names of animals on small slips of paper and pass them out to students. Students must line up from smallest to largest animal, but can only make their assigned animal's noise to assist in figuring out the size order.

- Student Interview – Give students a list of questions to ask their partners. Then, students must introduce their partners to the rest of the class by presenting information they learned from their interview.

- Two truths and a lie – Organize students into a large circle, or a few smaller circles, to share three things: two truths and one lie. Other students in the circle must guess which is the lie.

- Blind Drawing – Pair students up and have them sit back to back. Give one student a drawing that they must describe to their partner. One student attempts to draw the image without seeing it, based only on the verbal instructions from the other.

GUEST SPEAKERS

In our experience, guest speakers can be a great source of knowledge, but often struggle to convey that knowledge in an engaging way. After all, they aren't teachers. It is *our* job to help prepare our guests and students so that the event is a success and our speaker will return.

Additionally, guest presentations will have a more positive impact on students' educational experience when they are thoughtfully planned. To make our speaking events successful for both students and the speaker, we carefully plan what happens prior, during, and after an active listening opportunity.

Prior to Speaker

Before you invite a guest speaker, it's important to have clarity about why you want this person to come to your classroom. Ideally, your guest speaker is there to answer a focused question that has arisen during the study of your course content. Instead of inviting a local city council member to talk about politics or voting, ask them to talk about a local measure or specific issue that directly impacts your students. For example, we invited a council person to discuss the need for – and process of – getting a crosswalk between a bus stop and the school. Other guest speakers have included people working in careers that our students were interested in; parents who have first-hand knowledge of topics being studied (like the plight of refugees); and college students (who have graduated from our high school) to provide suggestions to our classes on how to best prepare for higher education.

Next, it may help to give your guest speaker an outline for what students should know or understand by the end of the presentation. In addition, suggest that they include a visual element for their presentation. It could be a few simple slides that are projected to help direct the presenter and students. Also, work with the speaker to come up with questions to ask students during the event. For example, we might encourage speakers to ask open-ended questions, avoiding rhetorical or single response ("yes" and "no"). This type of questioning helps students avoid feeling like they are being quizzed. Teachers can explain "how" to ask a question (for example, discussing the benefits of "wait time" – see Chapter 11: Questions for Learning), and provide guidance on facilitating partner and whole-group sharing. If your presenter doesn't feel comfortable with this format, you may want to take the lead and ask students questions. We have compiled these suggestions into a handout to give to presenters, Figure 15.1: Suggestions for a Guest Speaker.

Though a teacher may hesitate to guide so much of the guest speaker's presentation, a successful event is going to be better for everyone involved. We have found that many guest speakers appreciate support from the classroom teacher. Resistance to preplanning the event may be a good indicator of a presenter that you want to skip.

It's also important to prepare your students for your guest speaker. It may be helpful to remind students what a good listener does and looks like (see Table 15.1: Active Listening Graphic Organizer). Explain to students that the guest isn't a teacher and there may be times when they struggle – students should be polite and professional. It may be a good idea to prep your students with a little background on your speaker, as well as his/her purpose in your classroom. Be specific in telling students what they will do during the event and how they will be held accountable afterwards.

Students can generate questions as an assignment prior to presentations. For example, if students know they need to draft an action plan to create a crosswalk connecting a popular bus stop and the school, they can develop related questions for the councilperson. They might ask, "What is the first step in getting a crosswalk built?" or "Do we need to get signatures from community members to build a crosswalk?" Listening for answers to their questions during the presentation can motivate students to practice active listening. For more on student-generated questions see Chapter 11: Questions for Learning.

During Listening

Aim for making the guest speaker's presentation as interactive as possible. Create opportunities throughout for students to complete tasks. The event is less likely to feel like a lecture and more like a collaborative learning experience by pausing every 5–10 minutes and having students *do* something.

Encouraging peer sharing and allowing opportunities for students to get out of their seats helps keep the energy level high. For example, the guest speaker (with the help of the teacher) may pose a question and ask that students respond by standing on a continuum of "strongly disagree" to "strongly agree" (refer to Chapter 16: Discussions). The presenter can then select students to explain their rationale for where they chose to stand on the continuum.

Another variation on this might be to give students four choices to respond to a question and label the choices "A," "B," "C," and "D." You can prelabel the corners of the room with the same letters and have students select a corner to represent their response to a given question and then share their rationale. For example, after asking students, "How should we get feedback from the community about building a crosswalk?," students can select their choice by standing in the prelabeled corner: "A" send out groups of students to knock on doors in the local area, "B" send out a flyer in the mail with a link to an online survey, "C" hold a community meeting, or "D" stand in front of local businesses and ask people to sign a petition. Then, students can be asked to share the pros and cons of their choice.

In addition, we have found it helpful to have an assignment to complete during the presentation for student accountability. The task can be as simple as having students respond to questions about the presentation topic on a graphic organizer.

After Listening

It's important to have post-listening tasks. These assignments provide further incentive for listening during a presentation and help to hold students accountable. In addition, they can help students process the information shared by the speaker. A simple post-listening task can include turning in a graphic organizer with written responses to the questions asked during the presentation. Students may also use the information gained from the guest speaker to respond to a larger ongoing inquiry. For example, students could write a problem-solution essay about a local issue. They can cite the guest speaker as a source of evidence to provide support for one or more possible solutions.

In addition to a content-focused assignment, we have found that it's a good idea to provide an opportunity for students to reflect after the speaker's visit. We usually ask them to write about what the speaker did well, what students learned and what they are still wondering, as well as suggestions for improvement. Portions of the student responses may be used in a thank-you letter to the presenter. Use your best professional judgment when deciding what student responses you share with your guest speaker.

Note: One thing you want to make sure you do after having a guest speaker is to thank them. Believe it or not, many guest speakers are very intimidated by speaking to a classroom full of students. We want to show them we honor and appreciate their time and knowledge, so sending a thank-you note is always appreciated. In your thank-you note, include specific comments from your students about what they enjoyed or learned from the speaker. If students completed an assignment or task as a result of the presentation, include a description. A speaker will be more likely to return to the classroom if they feel appreciated and able to contribute to students' learning. Please see Figure 15.2: Guest Speaker Thank-You Template and Figure 15.3: Guest Speaker Thank-You Example.

PODCASTS

A podcast is a radio show that can be listened to on a smartphone or computer. The NCSS appreciates the powerful impact podcasts can make. Their partnership with the StoryCorps podcast (https://storycorps.org) encourages students to listen to – and create their own – episodes (NCSS, n.d.-d).

We frame our podcast protocol in the same way as our guest speaker protocol – what to do prior, during, and after listening to a podcast.

Before Listening

Carefully select a podcast that fits with the topic your students are studying in the classroom.

After selecting a podcast, prelisten to it carefully to plan how to make it most accessible to students. For example, depending on what you want students to gain, a teacher may or may not want to use all portions of a show. Additionally, prelistening to the podcast will help to determine where to pause – and check for comprehension or have students discuss their ideas with a partner.

It may be a good idea to prepare some visuals to go along with the podcast. Though we are mostly focusing on listening skills, incorporating visual elements can encourage further student engagement. Photos from the geographical areas included in the show or of concepts covered (for example, if it's a history podcast, showing images of specific battles or figures) might be helpful to students. Additionally, having explanations of potentially confusing terms available ahead of time, including visuals or clarifying examples, can help with comprehension.

Providing students copies of a podcast transcript can enhance student engagement and comprehension as they follow along with the audio recording.

During Listening

We have found it useful to have a graphic organizer that students fill out as they listen. All students can benefit from graphic organizers that point them toward the key ideas presented in the podcast.

The type of graphic organizer you create depends on the podcast itself and what specific knowledge you want students to acquire from it. For example, a US government class may be listening to an episode from season one of the podcast *Serial*. This show investigates a case of a teenager convicted of murder. Students may use this podcast to study the criminal justice system. A teacher can direct students to note specific evidence collected or errors they note in the prosecution's case. Students can use a handout like Table 15.2: *Serial* Podcast Listening Graphic Organizer to analyze the collection of evidence and process of a murder trial.

Table 15.2 *Serial* Podcast Listening Graphic Organizer

Episode _____		
Who is being interviewed and **what** evidence is provided	Points to "guilty," why?	Points to "not guilty," why?

Here are a few other tips to consider when creating a graphic organizer:

- List the questions chronologically so they are answered in the order they are asked.

- Choose a mix of questions. By using comprehension and analysis questions, a teacher can check for understanding and facilitate critical thinking. Pausing the episode to answer analysis questions can be a good way to encourage students to stop and think in order to respond to these more challenging questions.

- Place time stamps for where in the podcast the questions are answered. You may only need to do this for a few – not all – of the questions. This also may help the teacher remember where to pause the listening.

We also recommend that students listen to stretches of no more than 10–15 minutes without pausing for comprehension checks. Depending on the age and level of your students, you may need to reduce this listening time further. These time spans allow the teacher to control the flow and energy of the class. Teachers can use similar strategies to those described in the guest speaker section of this chapter to break up the listening. Get students talking and moving to maintain energy and focus (for example, "Share what you wrote with a student who has different colored socks").

After Listening

Expectations for what students should be able to do or know at the end of the podcast should be made clear before beginning. After listening, students should use their graphic organizers and any other notes or materials from the podcast to respond to a written prompt or to participate in a discussion. For example, after having students listen to the *Serial* podcast, we may ask them "What piece of evidence do you think was most convincing to the jury?" or "What critical errors do you think may have been made in the prosecution's case?" We have also had success using the small-group discussion protocol described in Chapter 16: Discussions following our podcasts.

STUDENT PRESENTATIONS

Peer-to-peer presentations are important for both listeners and presenters, but often speaking and listening opportunities are few and far between in the classroom (Zwiers, n.d.). Through public speaking, speakers can learn how to effectively present information in an engaging way. At the same time, the audience can practice active listening skills in order to learn something new and be able to pose clarifying or follow-up questions. The abilities developed through these presentations can be helpful for students both inside and outside the classroom. They are the foundation of good communication, which is a key skill that employers desire (McCarthy, 2017).

Student presentations can be as simple as a student quickly explaining their definition of a vocabulary term (see Chapter 1: A Fresh Look at Vocabulary) or a more extensive version using digital slides and taking several minutes. These presentations can happen in small groups or with the whole class.

Here are three student presentation methods that we use successfully in our classrooms:

- Jigsaw – Students are placed in small groups where they become experts on a topic through reading and discussion. Then, students are placed in new groups with an expert from each of the previous groups. In other words, the new groups have an expert from each topic. These experts present their knowledge to their new group members who may take notes, complete a graphic organizer, or respond to questions. For example, students might be learning about the American Civil War. Each group is assigned to become experts of a topic by reading an article provided by the teacher. These topics could include: weapons, major battles, roles of women, experience of African Americans. After reading the article, the expert groups prepare a short presentation that each member will give to their new group – each member makes a small poster to help guide their presentations. Once students have become experts, they are placed into new groups. Each of the new groups should have one expert from each topic: weapons, major battles, roles of women, experience of African Americans. In the new groups, each member gets a set amount of time to present their information while the group members take notes. Students may use a graphic organizer like Table 15.3: Jigsaw Presentations.
- Digital Slide Presentation—Students can create, and then present, a series of slides on a given topic. It may be a good idea to scaffold the slide making by having students watch a few video clips about "good" digital presentations. We have used *How to Create an Awesome PowerPoint Presentation* (https://youtu.be/gNG0etmnwuk) with good results, though there are countless others available online. For example, students may be assigned an important person from the Civil Rights Movement and create a digital slideshow documenting their contributions. We encourage presentations to generally last no more than three minutes.

Table 15.3 Jigsaw Presentations

Topic _____	Questions	Image to Represent Topic
Three Important Things 1. 2. 3.	1. 2.	
Topic _____ Three Important Things 1. 2. 3.	Questions 1. 2.	Image to Represent Topic
Topic _____ Three Important Things 1. 2. 3.	Questions 1. 2.	Image to Represent Topic
Topic _____ Three Important Things 1. 2. 3.	Questions 1. 2.	Image to Represent Topic

- Pechakucha Presentation – In this special style of digital presentation origi-nated by Astrid Klein and Mark Dytham, the presenter has 20 slides and 20 seconds per slide to give the audience the desired information (www.klein-dytham.com/pechakucha). It can be used for any kind of topic and is a strat-egy that can make both presentations and listening to them a little more interesting. For more resources on supporting student presentations, please refer to the Technology Connections section.

With each activity, we recommend facilitating before, during, and after listening tasks. These tasks may be simple, like the class making predictions before a stu-dent shares a definition of a vocabulary word. They may also be more complex, like responding to open-ended questions or using information from the presentation to complete an essay or prepare for a discussion.

One simple audience task could be to have them write anonymously on a piece of paper one thing they liked about the presentation and one thing they thought could be improved (offering models for these comments could be helpful). Plan-ning tasks for each of the three phases (before, during, after) helps to hold everyone accountable and ensures everyone is getting the most out of each presentation.

DIFFERENTIATION

Active listening is a challenge for many native English speakers, so the task may be doubly challenging for English learners or students who learn differently. As with many activities, creating graphic organizers that include sentence starters ("The first important thing the speaker said was _____.") can be helpful to students when listening to guest speakers.

Many podcasts have transcripts available online. Copies where the text has been "engineered" with definitions, subheadings, and images can be helpful differentiation tools. (For more on engineering the text see Chapter 3: Read-Aloud Protocol.)

ADVANCED EXTENSIONS

One advanced extension is for students to create their own podcast episode. We begin by assigning a topic that corresponds to the current unit of study to pairs or small groups of students. Next, students work together to write a script for their episode. This script should be checked and edited prior to recording. Writing the script beforehand helps hold students accountable for carefully planning both the content and organization of their episode. Then, students record their podcast and post it on a digital platform. A teacher may want to have students create listening questions for their peers to answer while they listen to the student-created episodes.

There are many resources to help students to create their own podcasts, and they aren't overly complicated, especially if you have easy access to a smartphone or computer. Carefully listening to a podcast in the classroom will help prepare students to create their own. Some specific websites that give instructions for student-created podcasts are listed in the Technology Connections.

Another option might be to help students organize a guest speaker visit. With guidance, students can brainstorm a topic or question and find a speaker. By utilizing students' families and neighbors, you might be surprised at all the "experts" you have in your local community. Sourcing knowledgeable people from your local area may mean people with degrees and titles or not – one doesn't need a graduate degree to be well informed. Choosing speakers that reflect your students and community is a good practice for cultural responsiveness.

Note: It is important to speak with your school administrators about security clearance for any guests you bring to your school site.

Student Handouts and Examples

Table 15.1: Active Listening Graphic Organizer

Figure 15.1: Suggestions for a Guest Speaker

Figure 15.2: Guest Speaker Thank-You Template

Figure 15.3: Guest Speaker Thank-You Example

Table 15.2: *Serial* Podcast Listening Graphic Organizer

Table 15.3: Jigsaw Presentations

What Could Go Wrong?

Even with the best-laid plans there is still the possibility that a guest speaker event go could awry. If this happens in your classroom, don't be afraid to pause the event and insert an activity to liven it up or give reminders of what a good listener does. Then, reflect afterwards to figure out what you can learn from this event to prevent a recurrence. Sometimes, that means choosing a different speaker. While we may find the speaker's experience and knowledge vast, that doesn't always mean their presentation skills will be strong.

Podcasts may present a similar issue – although the podcast may be engaging to most, sometimes students just don't want to listen to them. Instead of trying to force the issue, be prepared with an alternative way for students to learn about the topic. For example, maybe they would prefer to listen on their phone with headphones or read the transcript instead.

It's important to preview podcasts before classroom use because they are not regulated by the Federal Communications Commission (FCC) and may have language or content not appropriate for some listeners. Many popular podcasts have censored versions available online.

Technology Connections

There are many ways to listen to podcasts. Many of the more well known programs have episodes that you can access online. If they aren't available online, or if it's easier for you to play them from your smartphone, you can use an application like Stitcher (www.stitcher.com) or Spotify (www.spotify.com/us) to find and play episodes.

Some of our most used podcasts for social studies include *Serial* (https://serialpodcast.org/about), *Presidential* (www.washingtonpost.com/graphics/business/podcasts/presidential/?noredirect=on&utm_term=.4a6e2807c6e6), *This American Life* (www.thisamericanlife.org), *Hidden Brain* (www.npr.org/series/423302056/hidden-brain), and *StoryCorps* (https://storycorps.org). The last three podcasts in this list also have information on their websites for educators including guiding questions for listening.

For help with student created podcasts check out KQED's "Podcasting with Youth Radio" (https://teach.kqed.org/course/podcasting-with-youth-radio) or podomatic (www.podomatic.com). Another good resource for creating podcasts is Larry Ferlazzo's blog post "The Best Resources for Student Podcasting" (http://larryferlazzo.edublogs.org/2018/06/24/the-best-resources-for-teacher-student-podcasting).

Additional ideas to support student presentations can be found in Larry Ferlazzo's blog post "The Best Sources of Advice for Making Good Presentations" (http://larryferlazzo.edublogs.org/2009/05/25/the-best-sources-of-advice-for-making-good-presentations).

Attribution

Portions of the active listening mini-lesson were adapted from a lesson created by our colleague Nichole Scrivner, a fantastic English teacher from Luther Burbank High School in Sacramento, California.

Figures

The list below contains suggestions to consider when planning to speak to a class. It may be helpful to plan with the classroom teacher.

- Determine the topic of the presentation

- What should students know or be able to do at the end of the presentation? *Or* What is the big question students should be able to answer by the end of the presentation?

- Plan to share a few key ideas that students should write down.

- Consider visuals that could be included to help support the presentation.

- To help break up the presentation, consider some questions to ask along the way. Open-ended questions tend to be more successful than rhetorical or simple "yes" and "no" types.

Figure 15.1 Suggestions for a Guest Speaker

Your Name
Street Address
City, State, Zip
Date

Recipient Name
Title
Company
Street Address
City, State, Zip

Dear (Recipient Name),

Thank you for speaking at (name of class and school) about (the topic). We know you have a busy schedule and we appreciate the time you took to help us learn about this important topic.

I really appreciate how you (one thing the guest speaker did well). I also really enjoyed learning (one thing you learned from the presentation). This information will be useful as I (how you will use the information from the presentation to complete the assignment/project).

Thank you again for your time.

Most Sincerely,

(Student Name)

Figure 15.2 Guest Speaker Thank-You Template

Abigail Smith
456 7th Street
Sacramento, CA, 56789
April 4, 2019

Marcos Johnson
Funding and Project Development
City of Sacramento
915 I Street
Sacramento, CA 95814

Dear Mr. Johnson,

Thank you for speaking in Ms. Ramos' Government class about building crosswalks in our city. We know you have a busy schedule and we appreciate the time you took to help us learn about this important topic.

I really appreciate how you used a lot of examples to help explain the big ideas. I also really enjoyed learning that there is an entire department devoted to transportation in our city. This information will be useful as I construct and present an action plan to our school site council on the crosswalk needed in our area.

Thank you again for your time.

Most Sincerely,

Abigail Smith

Figure 15.3 Guest Speaker Thank-You Example

CHAPTER 16

Discussions

What Is It?

Discussions in the social studies classroom can help build the capacity of our students to engage in intellectually rigorous conversations that include multiple tiers of vocabulary. In addition, students can learn listening skills and how to think on their feet. However, these kinds of discussions do not happen magically. In this chapter, we describe how and when we facilitate informal (minimal prep) and formal discussions (more prep required). We also provide ideas for how to use academic conversations to scaffold writing.

Why We Like It

We like that the scaffolding in our discussion activities explicitly teaches our students *how* to have an academic conversation. Open-ended discussion questions and easy-to-use sentence starters make peer dialogue accessible for a variety of learners.

Our open-ended discussion strategies encourage students to share their opinions and personal experiences while eliciting empathy – the ability to share and relate to another person's experience. When students make personal connections with the topic or the responses of other students, the content and the discussion process become more relevant.

We appreciate how the strategies in this chapter energize our classrooms. Many students welcome the novelty of classroom dialogue to break up longer reading and writing assignments. Furthermore, these interactions help foster relationships that otherwise might not develop with independent assignments.

Supporting Research

Research has found that classroom discussions can increase students' enjoyment of a class, as well as enhance retention and understanding of content knowledge. They can also assist in the development of better problem-solving skills (Corcoran, n.d.).

Discussion-based approaches that utilize authentic and open-ended questions (like the ones in this chapter) may help students deepen their critical thinking skills by encouraging more student talk and further elaboration of ideas (Soter et al., 2008, p. 373).

Research has also shown that group discussions can help students build their argumentative writing skills (Reznitskaya, Anderson, & Kuo, 2007, p. 464).

Common Core Connections

The Common Core emphasizes the importance of developing communication skills within the Speaking and Listening strand (Common Core, 2010z). Many goals of the Comprehension and Collaboration section can be met with the activities in this chapter. For example, our strategies help students "initiate and participate effectively in a range of collaborative discussions" (Common Core, 2010aa). In addition, students "respond thoughtfully to diverse perspectives" (Common Core, 2010bb).

Social Studies Connections

The College, Career, and Civic Life (C3) Framework created by the National Council for Social Studies states that in order to "determine credibility toward building claims with evidence, they (students) should have multiple opportunities to practice civil, democratic discourse with diverse partners" (NCSS, 2010, p. 57). To ensure democratic and civil conversations in our social studies classrooms, teachers can utilize the structures in this chapter to promote respect and equal participation.

Application

This section is divided into informal and formal discussions. By informal, we are referring to short discussion activities that are low-prep for both teachers and students. Our formal discussions, on the other hand, require more prep and tend to take more time – sometimes a whole class period. We consider both types of discussions integral to building effective communication skills and deeper comprehension of content.

In the first section, we provide a list of strategies for facilitating informal discussions: Think–Pair-Share, Sharing Rotations, Designated Sharing Partner, Commenting on the Comment, and "No Hands" Policy for Whole Class Sharing.

In the second section, we explain two formal discussion activities we use in our classroom: a Small-Group Discussion Protocol and our version of a Fishbowl Discussion. We conclude with additional strategies for formal discussions in social studies.

We usually model the strategies – with the help of one or two students – to show exactly what we are looking for when they are doing a Think–Pair–Share, or any other discussion strategy. After modeling, we then debrief with students what body language is indicative of effective communication skills – leaning in, turning toward the person you are talking with, eye contact, and so forth.

We also demonstrate what not to do – not listening, getting distracted by other students, and so forth. Setting a clear standard for respectful and academic discourse helps students get the most out of their conversations while creating an inclusive classroom. See Chapter 15: Listening and Speaking Activities for active listening strategies.

INFORMAL DISCUSSION STRATEGIES

Novelty helps prevent boredom and develops our students' conversation skills, which is why we employ a variety of methods to facilitate discussion. Here is a list of our "go-to" informal discussion strategies:

- *Think–Pair–Share* refers to a strategy in which students think independently, and then pair or partner with another student to develop a response to share. We like to use this *collaborative* learning strategy to scaffold the development of thoughtful responses. In these kinds of activities, students do their own thinking first, connect with others for conversation and feedback, and then apply what they learned to improve their initial response. *Collaboration* is different from *cooperation,* where students may start and finish a task together but often do not apply peer feedback to improve individual work (Ferlazzo, 2016). Think–Pair–Share can be useful when answering an open-ended question, interpreting a quote, reacting to a projected image, and so forth. For example, if we are reading a text as a class and find an important quote, we might say: "Take 30 seconds to think about why this quote might be important." After 30 seconds, we would then say, "Now share your thoughts with your elbow partner." An elbow partner refers to the closest person on the left or right of a student. While students are discussing, the teacher has the opportunity to listen and informally assess students' comprehension or note key ideas that arise. After students have had an opportunity for discussion, we often call on students to share with the class. Additionally, after receiving feedback from a partner, students can write a response.

- *Sharing Rotations* (also known as "Speed Dating") is a strategy where students meet with multiple people for short discussion. This activity gets students up and moving, which can freshen the energy of a classroom. In addition, it is an organized way to expose students to multiple perspectives. First, students are given time to think about a response to a question and often are asked to write it down. Next, the teacher numbers off students and assigns the odd numbered to be the "movers". When the teacher gives the cue, the movers all get up and move to the right, into the next empty seat, to discuss their responses. All students remain seated until the teacher cues them to move again.

   We also like to use this activity after students have written answers to a series of questions. After counting students off, students are directed to meet and discuss their answer to the first question with their first partner. Then, after the teacher's cue, the movers get up and move to a second partner to share their answers to the next question, and so forth, until all answers are shared. For accountability purposes, in between rotations, we sometimes call on students to share what their partner said with the whole class. Another idea is to instruct students to take notes on any unique insights gained from each of their partners.

- *Designated Sharing Partner* is when we assign students a designated partner to discuss class work, clarify directions, or even help each other get caught up if they were absent. Students should know that when we ask an open-ended question and direct students to "Discuss with your designated partner" they always go to the same person. For example, we like to use this strategy to ask students to meet with their designated partners to discuss their progress on a writing assignment like an essay about the role of hippie culture in the 1960s. Depending on what they are sharing, we like to call on students to give reports on what they discussed. Or, after the designated partners are done discussing, students can write a quick reflection about their conversation mentioning what went well or what was challenging – which they can turn in to the teacher. This strategy is especially helpful for strategically pairing certain students together – like an English proficient student with an ELL student. These "designated partners" can be changed every week or every few weeks.

- *Commenting on the Comment* is a strategy where the teacher asks students to comment on other students' answers. In other words, after the teacher calls on one student to respond to a question, the teacher then selects another student to comment on the first student's response. This strategy helps students expand ideas while holding them accountable for listening. We provide a sentence starter like "What I hear you saying is. . ." or any of the other sentence starters from Table 16.1: Response Frames. In addition, we make sure to provide wait time (a pause after we have called on a student to respond) to increase the chances of a successful response. For example, when discussing American involvement in the Korean War, we like to ask a question like "To what extent was American involvement justified in the Korean War?" A student might respond with "Based on what we have learned in class, if Americans were worried about the spread of Communism, then it was a good idea to protect South Korea, and the rest of Asia." The next student could comment something like "What I hear you saying is American involvement was justified, but I also wonder at what point should the United States have pulled out of the conflict?"

Table 16.1 Response Frames

What to say when you *agree*:	What to say when you want *clarification*:
1. I really liked _____'s idea about. . .	1. Do you mean that. . .
2. You made a great point about. . .	2. In other words, are you saying. . .
3. I'd like to add on to_____'s idea about. . .	3. Can you elaborate on that?
4. I hadn't thought about what_____ said about. . .	4. I have a question about. . .
5. My idea builds on _____'s idea. . .	5. Can you clarify the point about _____ for me?
What to say when you *disagree*:	**To help keep the group on track:**
1. That's a valid point, but I feel. . .	"I'd like to redirect the discussion and get back to _____'s turn, please."
2. On the other hand. . .	
3. I see it differently based on. . .	OR
4. True, but what about. . .	
5. I understand _____'s idea, but I feel that. . .	"I'd like to remind everyone of our group norms, especially _____." (e.g., "one person speaks at a time")

Sources: Used with permissions. www.amazon.com/gp/product/0787987611/ref=dbs_a_def_rwt_bibl_vppi_i3, Gail Bruce from http://crlpstatewideoffice.ucsd.edu/index.html.

- *No-Hands Policy for Whole Class Sharing* means that students don't raise their hands to volunteer responses. Instead, we encourage whole-class processing (Ferlazzo, 2014). This refers to strategies that place thinking tasks on all members of the class instead of the few who might *normally* volunteer responses. We want to avoid students "hiding in plain sight" by only calling on a select few. Though there are many different ways to encourage "whole class processing," we try to keep it simple by writing student names on index cards and drawing a name from the stack. This raises the level of urgency because all students are aware they may be called on at any time. However, we are also strategic in who and when we call on certain people. There may be times when a student needs a jolt of self-confidence, and we know they have an answer to a question, so we will call on that person. We may let a shy student or an English language learner (ELL) know ahead of time that we will ask them to share with the class. Another way to encourage whole-class processing is to provide students with whiteboards that they can write their responses on and hold up to show their answer. This way, all students are held accountable to respond.

FORMAL DISCUSSION STRATEGIES

We primarily use two strategies for in-depth academic discussions: a small-group discussion protocol and our version of a fishbowl discussion.

We like to use small-group discussions as a precursor to extended writing. In our experience, this process helps students think critically and prepare ideas. In addition, we like to use this activity to help teach students academic discourse. Our students are full of great ideas, but may struggle with articulating their opinions to their classmates. The use of this strategy over time helps them develop these skills while becoming more comfortable discussing complex social studies topics with their peers.

The second strategy, fishbowl discussion, helps students process content by having them share their answers to questions about a text. This structure can expose students to multiple viewpoints while helping them achieve deeper comprehension. The fishbowl discussion strategy can also help students prepare for writing, but can also serve as a formal assessment of content knowledge.

Unlike informal discussion strategies that we use on the spot to help students process smaller chunks of information, we use formal discussion activities to tackle multiple texts or longer and more-complex articles.

Small-Group Discussion Protocol

This highly structured activity provides students with response cards that help scaffold academic conversation between students on any given topic. Students answer open-ended questions in order to develop a deeper understanding of complex ideas. The goal of this activity is not to quiz the kids on quick facts, but to help them process social studies content through peer dialogue.

The original activity, which we have since modified, came to us from Gail Bruce at the California Reading and Literature Project (CRLP) ("Teachers as Learners," n.d.). The response frames used for this activity incorporate sentence starters from Jeff Zwiers, Stanford researcher and author of several books and articles about academic conversations (www.jeffzwiers.org). We like to use this specific activity to not only deepen content comprehension, but also promote critical thinking and relevancy.

Preparation is required to ensure a productive and smooth roll out of this activity. First, the teacher needs to determine heterogeneous student groups (mixed abilities, ethnic background, personalities) prior to starting the activity. This type of group arrangement promotes peer-to-peer support and limits the stigmatization of students with different learning abilities (Glass, 2002). In our experience, this type of grouping also exposes our students to diverse viewpoints, which can enrich the discussion. Secondly, we recruit three students the day before implementing the protocol to help us model the strategy. We usually practice for a few minutes so they are comfortable.

The first two phases of the protocol, Modeling Protocol and Deconstructing Protocol and Reviewing Norms, take about 30 minutes. The last two phases, Students Attempt Protocol and Post-Writing Prompt, take another 30 minutes (20 and 10 minutes each, respectively). Obviously, a detailed modeling process doesn't have to happen *every* time students do a discussion. Once they have practiced the modeling and deconstructing parts of the protocol, future discussions can begin with a quick five-minute review of the norms.

Modeling Protocol

We begin this activity by telling students that they will be participating in a structured small-group discussion about a recent topic from class. For example, we used this strategy after spending about a week studying the terrorist attacks in Paris, France in 2015 and the growth of anti-Islamic sentiment in Europe.

Instead of talking them through the structure, we model the protocol with the three students we practiced with the day before. The teacher is the fourth member of the group.

All members of the model group push their desks closely together facing one another and are positioned in front of the class. In the middle, we place a large cup that includes the following:

- 10–15 typed-out questions, cut into strips about an inch wide: Please refer to Figure 16.1: Question Strips – Terrorism in Paris for an example of these questions in their precut form. For example, when studying terrorism in Paris and anti-Muslim sentiment in France, we ask open-ended questions like "What are the lasting effects of terrorist attacks on society?" The strips are held together with a binder clip labeled "new." We use a binder clip because they are easier to label.

- An extra binder clip: to hold question strips that students have answered to keep them separate from the remaining strips. We typically label this binder clip "completed."

- Four popsicle sticks numbered 1, 2, 3, 4: The purpose of these numbered sticks is to ensure everyone has the opportunity to participate in the discussion. Each student is assigned a number and the facilitator rotates through each of the numbers as the discussion occurs. It may be a good idea to have a few extra popsicle sticks labeled number five that can be used to accommodate a larger group. In our experience, small-group discussions are ideally four to five students.

- A facilitator card: This card is for the student in the group who is in charge of reading the questions, selecting students to respond (by using the popsicle sticks), supporting them when they are answering, and prompting the group to take notes on key insights every three rounds. The first two times we do this activity we choose the student facilitators in advance. We talk with them the previous day to discuss their role. Figure 16.2: Facilitator Card reminds the facilitator of their duties.

The last items provided for the group are four copies (one for each group member) of Table 16.1: Response Frames. The handout includes sentence starters that students can use to agree, disagree, ask questions for clarification, and help keep each other on track – the skills required for academic conversations (Zwiers & Crawford, 2009). Please refer to Figure 16.3: Small-Group Discussion Materials for a picture of all of the items we use for this strategy.

In addition, we ask members of the group to bring a pen/pencil and a sheet of paper to take notes.

To begin modeling the discussion protocol, we sit down and the teacher acts as the facilitator to model the duties exactly. We read Figure 16.2: Facilitator Card so everyone is clear about the role of the facilitator: they are in charge of selecting popsicle sticks to determine who answers the question and providing support to the group when needed.

After explaining the role of the facilitator, the teacher selects and reads one of the questions held together with the binder clip labeled "new" for the entire group. For our topic about terrorism in Paris, we could ask the question we mentioned earlier, "What is the lasting effect of terrorist attacks on society?" After placing the question in the "completed" binder clip, the facilitator then shakes the cup with the four popsicle sticks and selects one. The facilitator *does not* return this stick to the cup. The student assigned with the selected number initiates the discussion.

After the first student has responded, other members are now allowed to contribute. Once the discussion of the initial question winds down, the facilitator draws a number from the remaining sticks for the next question. This continues until all four group members (including the facilitator) have been selected to *initiate* the discussion. Once all four sticks have been drawn, they are placed back in the cup to start the rotation over again.

What follows is a sample dialogue for the modeling of the protocol in response to the question, "What is the lasting effect of terrorist attacks on society?" from Figure 16.1: Question Strips – Terrorism in Paris.

After the facilitator has selected the popsicle stick labeled "3" from the cup:

FACILITATOR (TEACHER):	*"Okay, person number three, your turn to answer the question."*
STUDENT 3:	*"Ummm, okay, I think one of the lasting effects of terrorist attacks on society is that people get and stay very scared. Like, they are always going to be wondering when will the next attack be."*
FACILITATOR:	*"Okay, now the rest of us need to comment on her answer. Remember to use the sentence starters in Table 16.1: Response Frames."*
ONE OF THE STUDENTS IN THE GROUP (USING THEIR RESPONSE SHEET):	*"Umm, hmmm, well **you made a great point** about people staying scared. People will probably be the most scared that day, but I mean, if I was there, I would be traumatized and stay scared. You can't just forget that, you know?"*
ANOTHER STUDENT (USING THEIR RESPONSE SHEET):	*"**On the other hand**, I also feel like everybody would get really paranoid. Like, they would always be trippin' and thinking: 'Does that guy have a gun? Should we even go out anymore?' I mean, my cousin was shot at once and he is just not the same. He is always watching his back."*

At this point, the other students are allowed to continue discussing the question with the use of the sentence starters. Once we are all done commenting, we pick another question and start the cycle again. We do this for about three rounds when we are modeling for an entire class. After the third round, we announce (as the facilitator) that it is time to write down one idea or comment that has stood out to us in the last three rounds of discussion. We state that there will be a prompt we all have to respond to afterward, and these notes can be helpful. Everyone takes a couple of minutes to list one or two comments from the dialogue on their paper.

Deconstructing Protocol and Reviewing Norms

After the model discussion is done, we ask the rest of the class to check-in with a partner about what stood out to them about the protocol. After they pair-share, we call on a few students to share with the entire class. Student answers vary greatly, but many times they say that nobody interrupted or that all students seemed to be using guides from the paper (Table 16.1: Response Frames) to help them answer the question.

Asking what stood out to students is a good way to *begin* deconstructing the discussion, but they might not get to every part of the protocol. To get more specific, we like to hold up each item (the large cup, numbered popsicle sticks, question strips, binder clips, and so forth) and ask, "What did we use this for?" Usually we let students call out the answers. "The cup is to hold all the items in!" and "The popsicle sticks are to decide who answers the question" are some typical responses. We also like to hold up the paper and pencil that one of the model group members used to take notes on the discussion – to remind students they will be taking notes during their discussion.

Each time we hold up an item, we also clarify for students any other details. For example, we clarify that Table 16.1: Response Frames provides a variety of easy-to-use sentence starters that we want students to use when they make a comment. We explain that using these phrases can help students feel more comfortable and skilled at participating in productive academic conversations. In addition, we tell students that we will be listening for the use of the sentence starters since they are key to keeping academic conversation flowing. We acknowledge that this type of dialogue might not feel natural, but point out that it will get easier with more practice.

Next, we project (or make a big poster) of Figure 16.4: Group Discussion Norms. We call on students to read them aloud to the class. We share that it is important for each member to put forth their best effort to make this discussion not only productive, but meaningful, by adhering to the group norms.

Please refer to Figure 16.5: Discussion "Cheat Sheet" for Teachers for a concise outline of this protocol.

Students Attempt Protocol

After discussing norms, we distribute Table 16.1: Response Frames and quickly review their choices for agreeing, disagreeing, and asking for clarification. We ask students to circle two from each response section that they would feel comfortable using in a discussion.

To make the transition into groups as seamless as possible, we announce that each student will be assigned a group number (we identify the location for each group at this time). We project a prepared chart with everyone's name under a certain number and direct everyone to go to their groups and immediately get started. We remind students to bring their copy of Table 16.1: Response Frames, a writing utensil, and paper.

It is important for the teacher to circulate around the classroom during this activity (and, in fact, during every lesson!). In our experience, there is always a group or two that struggle; some students act out or shut down in fear of sounding "dumb" or the facilitators are slow to get started. We never hesitate to step-in and assist with either an example answer or walking the facilitator through their steps. In addition, we remind facilitators to allow note-taking time after every third question. Please refer to our "What Can Go Wrong" section for more advice on how to make this protocol successful.

While walking around, we like to comment on students who are doing a good job and make sure to note this to recognize publicly, later. We also jot down the names of students who are struggling so we can conference with them and brainstorm future supports. We pause the activity when students are about halfway through their questions and provide positive reinforcement. Using our notes, we give shout-outs to students who are helping each other, trying their best to comment with the response frames, and so forth. We try to be as specific as we can with our praise so that other students can emulate the praised behavior. In addition, as we have discussed earlier, praising specific actions can be effective to encourage the development of a growth mindset.

Typically, we give students a one-minute warning when it is time to wrap-up their discussions. We tend to end the activity after one group finishes so that others don't sit idle for too long. We don't worry if groups have not completely answered all of them. We direct students to store their Table 16.1: Response Frames in a safe place (and we make lots of extra copies!) for easy access throughout the year.

Post-Writing Prompt

After students end their discussion, we tell them that they will now be answering a prompt about the topic. They can use their notes from the small-group discussion to help them respond to the prompt.

For example, when discussing terrorism in France, we usually ask: "What implications, or long-term consequences, do you think the Paris terror attacks will have for the United States and the world? Use examples from your group discussion to support your response."

We often like students to use one of our scaffolding structures like PEE (Point, Example, Explain) from Chapter 5: Writing in Social Studies to help them organize their thoughts.

Fishbowl

This strategy is a version of a Socratic seminar: a student-driven discussion about a complex text. A fishbowl is an approachable, yet effective, way to facilitate a *classwide* discussion. The name *fishbowl* comes from the two concentric circles students are placed in: the inner circle is made of about five to six students facing each other (the inside of a fishbowl) and the rest of the class is seated to form the outer circle (looking into the fishbowl). The smaller, inner circle discusses a question while the outer circle listens and takes notes.

This seating arrangement helps structure the discussion and ensures that everyone is exposed to multiple viewpoints. This strategy is especially useful for helping students deconstruct and build deeper understanding of a longer, complex text. As an example, we will explain how we facilitate a fishbowl discussion about prison reform in our ethnic studies class.

Preparing for the Fishbowl

The fishbowl preparation begins when students are first reading the article they are going to discuss. Ensuring that students attain a basic understanding of the text sets students up to effectively participate during the fishbowl activity.

We do two phases of reading. For the first phase, students read and annotate the article. We typically ask them to highlight what stands out and write questions or comments in the margin. It may be helpful to model this for the first couple of paragraphs of the text. For more reading strategies, please reference Chapter 2: Reading Strategies.

For the second phase of reading, we usually provide about four to five questions about the article that students need to answer. These questions will also serve as the discussion questions during the fishbowl. Each one is text dependent, but open-ended enough to make room for a variety of answers. For the article about prison reform in the United States we ask, "How has the War on Drugs campaign from the 1980s affected the United States?" and "How does having an incarcerated parent affect a child and/or society?" Here are some topics and questions that could be used for other social studies classes:

- Geography: After reading different examples about how climate change is affecting economically impoverished areas around the world, we ask:
  - How is climate change causing human migration in some parts of the world?
  - Why aren't governments doing more to confront the effects of climate change in their countries?
- World History: Students can read two articles offering different perspectives on Napoleon Bonaparte. One says he should be considered a hero and the other, a villain. Then, they can respond to the following:
  - Why is Napoleon considered a hero by some historians?
  - Why are Napoleon's actions viewed by some historians as morally problematic?
- Economics: After reading two articles debating whether gross domestic product (GDP) is a fair measure of a "successful" country, students can answer questions like:
  - How, according to some experts, is GDP a fair measure of a "successful" country?
  - What, according to some experts, might be a better way of measuring the "success" of a country?
- Government: After analyzing pictures (using strategies from Chapter 12: Image Analysis) depicting protests from around the world and studying the First Amendment from the US Constitution, we like to ask the following:
  - Using clues in the picture, why do you think the people in the pictures are protesting?
  - Why did the Founding Fathers insist on having this First Amendment in the Constitution?

After we introduce the questions, students use and *list* textual evidence from the article for each question on Table 16.2: Evidence for Fishbowl. We encourage students to write this evidence in bullet-point form so it is easy to refer to them during the discussion. Answering the questions in advance helps to scaffold student participation. For an example, see Table 16.3: Evidence for Fishbowl Example (Prison Reform).

Table 16.2 Evidence for Fishbowl

Directions: Use this handout to list any evidence from the reading (quotes, facts, paraphrased information) that may help you answer the questions. You will be able to use these notes to help you during the discussion.

Question 1:_____

_____

_____

_____

_____

_____

_____

_____

_____

_____

_____

_____

_____

_____

Question 2:_____

_____

_____

_____

_____

_____

_____

_____

_____

_____

_____

_____

_____

_____

Question 3:_____

_____

_____

_____

_____

_____

_____

_____

_____

_____

_____

_____

_____

_____

Question 4:_____

_____

_____

_____

_____

_____

_____

_____

_____

_____

_____

_____

_____

_____

Table 16.3 Evidence for Fishbowl Example (Prison Reform)

Directions: Use this handout to list any evidence from the reading (quotes, facts, paraphrased information) that may help you answer the questions. You will be able to use these notes to help you during the discussion.	

Question 1: How has the "War on Drugs" from the 1980's affected the United States?	Question 2: How does having an incarcerated parent affect a child and/or society?
• Used to be **500,000** in prison in the **1980s**, now it is past **2** million. • "Tough on Crime" laws for drug dealers made prison numbers go up. • African Americans have especially been hit by these laws: five times more African Americans in prison than whites • -mandatory minimums" made sentencing for drug dealers uniform	• -child may feel void of missing parent on all major holidays and birthdays • difficult for child to turn to incarcerated parent for advice or other emotional needs • financial strain on the family, down to a one-income household • stigma: - some people judge you and your family for having a parent in jail
Question 3: Why do some experts consider crime sentencing in the United States unfair?	**Question 4:** Why do you think prison reform is so controversial?
• we have the highest prison population rate in the world • the way we punish drug offenders is actually different, and more harsh, than many other countries • drug punishments are not consistent: "crack" offenses associated with poor people of color, result in harsher sentences than cocaine offenses by whites • drug crimes are being treated as violent crimes	• some people worry that being too easy on drug offenders sends the wrong message (makes drugs okay) • some believe it could make the drug problem worse • certain political careers rely on "tough on crime" stances • but recently, there has been more of a mixed political support for prison reform

Fishbowl Discussion

We begin by arranging six to eight desks in the middle of the room and place the rest of the desks in a bigger, outer circle. The desks in the outer ring are close enough to hear the discussion. We like to sit in the outer ring so we can easily see and hear students.

The classic fishbowl has one group of students stay in the small circle and discuss the entire time. However, we adopted a rotating groups variation from the education website *Teaching Tolerance* (Stereotypes and Tonto, n.d.) so all students can actively participate.

For the rotating variation of this strategy, we begin numbering students off one through four. After giving numbers to all students, we explain that if students were numbered one, they will be in the *first* group of students to sit in the inside circle and respond to the *first* question about the article. Groups two, three, and four will begin on the outside circle. Once time is up (about five minutes), students numbered two get up and sit inside the fishbowl and comment on the *second* question, while the ones go to the outside circle. This rotation continues until every group has had an opportunity to sit inside of the fishbowl and discuss their assigned question.

Here is a helpful list of teacher do's and don'ts during a fishbowl:

- *Do* actively monitor student participation throughout the activity. Make sure one group does not take too long to share, give clear cues for transitions, and make sure students speak up so they can be heard. We also like to keep a roster handy and make quick notes about students with meaningful, or unique, responses to provide positive shout-outs.

- *Don't* dominate, or even lead, the conversation with your opinions or insights. This activity is about students creating meaning for themselves (with our support, of course). Some clarifying or guiding comments can be helpful, but the teacher's contributions should be kept at a minimum.

- *Do* address students who are struggling. Although our scaffolds try to ensure that everyone has something to share, there are still students who are nervous, or perhaps still not clear on what they might want to say. If you see a student struggling in the circle, you could try to unobtrusively provide support – perhaps by kneeling down and whispering a quick question to help them warm up. Something like "What are your thoughts on what the previous person said?" or "Does that remind you of anything?" can help them engage in conversation. Giving all students Table 16.1: Response Frames can also be a useful scaffold.

- *Don't* be too rigid about time. Ideally, students will move beyond sharing only the prewritten responses on their paper to make the experience more relevant and in-depth. If students are having a good conversation, but time is up, adding an extra minute or two could be worth it.

Especially with topics like prison reform (since students might have relatives directly affected by the issue), it is important that we practice trauma-informed teaching, or use strategies that are responsive to the needs of students that have experienced trauma (The Room 241 Team, 2018). By first building strong relationships and getting to know our students, we can give a heads-up to members of our classroom who might have personal reactions to the topic. In addition, if students choose to share personal or emotional connections with the class about this or any topic, a trauma-informed teacher will follow-up with the students or with a counselor.

Table 16.4 New Insights Chart

Directions: Use this handout to take notes on the discussion. Note two or three comments or responses that are **new to you or that you have not thought of before.**	
Round 1:	Round 2:
Round 3:	Round 4:

While students in the inner circle discuss the questions and share insights, the outer circle notes two to three responses from other students on Table 16.4: New Insights Chart. We have found that requiring and structuring the note taking can help students stay engaged and can be a helpful resource for writing after the fishbowl.

After five minutes of the inner circle discussing, or if the conversation is starting to slow down, we open up the floor to the outer circle. They are invited to comment or add any other pertinent information to the discussion. The inner circle is allowed to respond back, if they choose.

Once the discussion has been opened up to the rest of the class, and students have made a few comments, we continue rotating.

Post-Fishbowl Writing

To help students apply their new understandings from the discussion, we like to provide writing prompts about the subject. In addition, we want students to practice critical thinking about the topic using their discussion experience and notes.

For example, after a fishbowl about the article on prison reform, we ask:

- What has our conversation helped you realize about the criminal justice system in the United States?

- Considering our discussion today, what are the two most important aspects about prison reform that you think all Americans should know about? Why these two?

Here are some additional questions students can address after participating in fishbowl activities from other social studies content areas:

- Geography: What has our conversation helped you realize about the role of climate change in economically impoverished areas?

- World History: Considering our discussion today, what makes someone worthy of the title "hero" in world history? Does Napoleon meet this criteria? Why or why not?

- Economics: After discussing with your peers, should the term *GDP* be viewed as the main form of success for a country? Please explain why or why not, using examples from the discussion.

- Government: After discussing the protest pictures and the First Amendment to the Constitution, why do you think the ability to protest peacefully is a legal right in some countries but illegal in others?

We use strategies from Chapter 5: Writing in Social Studies to help students write responses to these prompts.

ADDITIONAL KEY STRATEGIES

Here are two additional ideas to facilitate discussions in social studies:

- Values Continuum: For this strategy, one side of the classroom is designated as the "I agree" side and the other designated as "I disagree." Students are asked to stand and show their opinion on statements or questions provided by the teacher. These statements are short, simple to understand, but yet multilayered – typically prompting students to reflect on their personal or cultural values. For example, if a teacher wanted students to explore why everyday Germans supported the Nazi Party, they could present statements like "It is okay to support politicians who do some bad things as long as they help the country overall" or "Being patriotic means agreeing with the government of your country." To show their opinions on these statements, students can stand on either side (agree or disagree) of the class or anywhere in between to show mixed feelings. Students are called on to justify where they stand on the statement. This activity can also be used to review a previously read text by asking students to use evidence from the article to justify where they stand on the continuum.

- Volleyball Debate: This strategy structures a class debate to encourage collaboration or a "volleyball" response: each side of the debate provides three student responses like the three hits allowed in volleyball before sending it to the other side. For example, if students are studying a local proposition in their government class, the teacher can provide sources explaining the possible benefits or drawbacks of such a law. After choosing which side they agree with, students start identifying evidence and listing it on Table 16.5: Evidence for Debate. Then, they meet as a team and share the evidence they can use to defend their position. Each student is responsible for getting three pieces of evidence from other team members.

  For the debate, the classroom is split down the middle: each team turns their desks to face each other. After flipping a coin to see who goes first, a student on one side shares evidence to support their position. Then, two other students *on the same side* are allowed to chime in and back up their team member with further evidence or insight. Repeating information already mentioned or having one student share multiple points is not allowed: teams have to coordinate and communicate who says what evidence and when. This strategizing is done right after one side has finished their three comments and the teacher allows the other side one minute to plan their responses. Students go back and forth until both sides feel like they have shared their main points. To wrap up the activity, each side has to write a summary of the debate including what stood out to them most.

Table 16.5 Evidence for Debate

Which side of the debate did you choose:
Please list three pieces of evidence that you think you could use to defend your position on this issue:
1.
2.
3.
Please list three pieces of information from your debate team members that supports your position:
1.
2.
3.

DIFFERENTIATION

To help scaffold the small-group discussion for students who learn differently, we allow them to write down responses in advance by providing them the questions prior to the activity. Then, students can read their responses when it is their turn. This support can help to ensure everyone in the group has something to say and can prevent students from being put on the spot. Modifying in this way can also be helpful with ELLs because it gives them an opportunity to get clarification or help with their responses. This scaffold can also lead to lower anxiety levels around speaking a new language.

Especially for ELL students, providing appropriately leveled texts for any kind of discussion is paramount. See the Technology Connections section for online resources. Reading strategies should be modeled and guided throughout the reading to ensure content comprehension.

If a discussion group is struggling with a question, allowing the facilitator to skip it and come back to that prompt later can relieve some pressure on students. It can also help preserve the momentum in the discussion.

To further help students become comfortable and familiar with the strategies in this chapter, they can be invited to participate in a mock discussion. Instead of covering social studies content, students can practice any of the structures in the application section to talk about food, school, or pop culture. A friendly topic of discussion can help make the activities more approachable while providing the practice needed for future academic discussions.

ADVANCED EXTENSIONS

Students can be challenged to move past their role as a participant in academic discussions to the role of a creator. This process requires students to carefully analyze an article in order to develop questions about the content. After providing an article about a current topic in class, student groups of two to three choose one, and create questions. Then, other students respond in either a small-group discussion or fishbowl. They are also asked to prepare the materials for the discussion such as typing up the questions and cutting them into strips for the small-group discussion or modifying Table 16.2: Evidence for Fishbowl with four questions for their article. Then, each group can design a concluding prompt for other students to answer at the end of the discussion.

Student Handouts and Examples

Table 16.1: Response Frames

Figure 16.1: Question Strips – Terrorism in Paris

Figure 16.2: Facilitator Card

Figure 16.3: Small-Group Discussion Materials

Figure 16.4: Group Discussion Norms

Figure 16.5: Discussion "Cheat Sheet" for Teachers

Table 16.2: Evidence for Fishbowl

Table 16.3: Evidence for Fishbowl Example (Prison Reform)

Table 16.4: New Insights Chart

Table 16.5: Evidence for Debate

What Could Go Wrong?

Not setting up groups carefully, especially for the small-group discussion protocol, can lead to disruption, weak discussion, or worse, student conflict. It is important for the teacher to have strong relationships with students to be able to determine the best group context for them. For example, a student who is extremely shy and anxious can sit next to a student they feel comfortable asking for help. Also, making sure to place students who tend to distract each other in separate groups can be helpful.

Lack of monitoring during group discussions can make small problems fester or make some students feel that the teacher does not care about their success. It is important to walk around and carefully listen and observe students – especially the first few times when using any of the structures in the chapter. Diligent monitoring can lead to opportunities for positive reinforcement of specific behaviors, especially social and emotional ones like active listening or empathy.

Technology Connections

For more resources and ideas for facilitating classroom discussions, please refer to Larry Ferlazzo's blog post "The Best Resources Sharing the Best Practices for Fruitful Classroom Discussion" (http://larryferlazzo.edublogs.org/2014/09/21/the-best-resources-sharing-the-best-practices-for-fruitful-classroom-discussions).

To help facilitate student discussions beyond the classroom, Voxer (www.voxer.com) can be helpful. This easy-to-use application lets students use push-to-talk (PTT) functions for communicating with peers for group project facilitation or helping each other with homework.

"The Best Places to Get the 'Same' Text Written for Different 'Levels'" (http://larryferlazzo.edublogs.org/2014/11/16/the-best-places-to-get-the-same-text-written-for-different-levels) can be a useful source for "fishbowl" articles.

Attribution

The basic framework for our small-group discussion protocol was designed by Gail Bruce and the CRLP. In the framework, the CRLP uses sentence starters that come from Jeff Zwiers, Stanford researcher and author of several articles and books about academic conversations.

Figures

1. In your opinion, how is a terrorist act different from a criminal act?
2. According to the article, most of the suspects from the Paris attack were French citizens or had grown up in France. What does this possibly imply?
3. Why do you think ISIS has had some success recruiting in the "ghetto-like suburbs of Paris"?
4. Is it fair to think of Muslim immigrants differently because of these terrorist attacks? Explain.
5. Do you believe ISIS terrorist attacks will keep happening? Explain.
6. Do you think attacking ISIS with military force will help stop the attacks? Explain.
7. To what extent did discrimination towards Muslim immigrants lead to terrorist attacks versus terrorist attacks leading to discrimination towards Muslim immigrants?
8. What is the lasting effect of terrorist attacks on society?
9. Why might someone choose to become a suicide bomber? Can a suicide bomber be a rational person?
10. At what point will it be "enough" for ISIS? (Amount of land to control? Certain amount of deaths? Never enough?)
11. How might the rise of ISIS and discrimination towards Muslim immigrants compare/relate to the rise of Hitler and the Nazi party?
12. Is ISIS a global threat? Explain.
13. At what point should intelligence agencies act on a potential terrorist threat?

Figure 16.1 Question Strips – Terrorism in Paris

Facilitator's Responsibilities:

1. Pull a numbered stick to determine whose turn is next.

2. Read the questions to the group. Remember that:
   - Group members may need the question read twice or need to see the question themselves.
   - Provide wait-time: let people think for a while, uninterrupted.

3. Prompt the rest of the students to comment after the question has been answered (people can take turns to the left, then switch the other way next time).

4. After every three questions or so, instruct group members to write information from the discussion that has stood out to them.

Figure 16.2 Facilitator Card *Source:* Gail Bruce from http://crlpstatewideoffice.ucsd.edu/index.html.

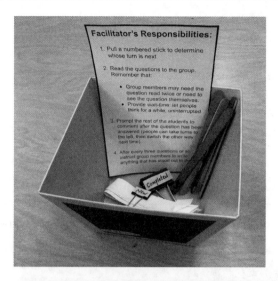

Figure 16.3 Small-Group Discussion Materials

Everyone participates

One person speaks at a time

Use professional language (see sentence starters)

No put-downs

Listen with your eyes and your ears

Figure 16.4   Group Discussion Norms *Source:* Gail Bruce from http://crlpstatewideoffice.ucsd.edu/index.html.

Materials for discussion activity:

1. Craft sticks, index cards, plastic spoons, pieces of paper numbered 1, 2, 3, 4, 5
2. Cup, jar, envelope from which to draw numbers
3. Five copies of **Figure 16.1 Response Frames**
4. Binder clips, paper clips, or clothespins for keeping prompts organized, clips labeled:

   a. "New" category

   b. "Completed" category

The Protocol:

1. Assign groups and appoint/prepare the facilitator for each group.
2. Number off 1–4 (or 1–5) within groups.
3. First prompt is drawn.
4. Facilitator draws a numbered stick to determine who addresses the first prompt and gives student time to respond.
5. Group members comment on the first response using the discussion sentence starters.
6. Start the cycle over again.
7. After the third question, students need to take notes and write one thing that has stood out to them about the conversation so far.

Figure 16.5   Discussion "Cheat Sheet" for Teachers

SECTION IV

Additional Key Strategies

CHAPTER 17

Project-Based Learning

What Is It?

Project-based learning (PBL) is an inquiry-based process of developing content knowledge and skills through a project. These projects address *real-world* problems like the impact of gun violence, improving their school, or responding to inequities in the immigration system. This type of learning positions students to be active participants in the construction of knowledge. The level of engagement is high when students are working in small groups to solve "real" issues.

In this chapter we share an approachable outline for PBL that can be applied to any social studies class. We walk through the key steps of PBL: planning a project, introducing the problem or project to students, structured work time, and presentation. Tips for assessment and reflection are also included in this chapter. We provide a sample project following these key steps. In this example, students create a textbook insert providing information about an underrepresented perspective of the Vietnam War. This section concludes with a list of other ideas for PBL in social studies classes.

Why We Like It

In our experience, students are more engaged when they feel like what they are doing matters in the real world. Students can see themselves as agents of change when they apply the skills they learn in social studies classes toward creating solutions for real-world challenges – like problems in the community (excessive use of force by the police, the need for additional mass transit, lack of affordable housing, etc.) or issues at school (curriculum that is missing diverse representation, concerns about school discipline policies and the lack of restorative practices, the availability of appropriate cafeteria meals for students of all religious faiths, etc.).

This type of learning can help students develop collaboration and communication skills needed for their academic and professional future. These projects reflect what happens in many jobs – a problem or question leads to the development of a potential solution. In this way, project-based learning is a good way to help our students experience the real world.

Supporting Research

Research shows that authentic learning opportunities, like those that come from project-based learning, can help students learn more deeply and perform better on academic achievement tests (Baron & Darling-Hammond, 2008, p. 3). In addition, PBL can be helpful in erasing the achievement gap (also known as the opportunity gap) (Ferlazzo, 2011, April 27) between low socioeconomic students and their peers (Halvorsen et al., 2012, abstract).

Furthermore, in this chapter, we incorporate components researchers say are critical to successful PBL: carefully selecting authentic projects, structuring collaboration between peers, and utilizing multidimensional assessments (Vega, 2012).

Common Core Connections

The Common Core emphasizes problem solving, collaboration, communication, and critical-thinking skills across the standards (2010cc). These skills are integral to a well-crafted project like the one we outline in this chapter.

Social Studies Connections

One of the guiding principles of the College, Career, and Civic Life (C3) Framework from the National Council for the Social Studies states that "Inquiry is at the heart of social studies" (NCSS, 2010). This type of learning activity is well aligned to the framework since PBL *is* a form of inquiry.

Application

The following sections describe six key steps in PBL: Planning the PBL, Introducing the Problem and Project, Structured Work Time, Presentation, Assessment, and Reflection.

We also provide an example project from a US history class, which follows the key steps of PBL. In this project, students create a textbook insert representing perspectives of groups that are often overlooked when learning about the Vietnam

War. Students then present this insert to a panel of social studies teachers from the school site in order to convince them to adopt this supplemental text as part of their instructional unit on the war.

We conclude this section with a list of ideas for other projects that may work well for various social studies classes.

KEY STEPS IN PBL

One of the biggest challenges regarding project-based learning is planning and structuring the project so that students can achieve the intended outcomes without being overwhelmed by the process. Here are the basic steps that can help social studies teachers implement PBL in their classrooms.

Planning the PBL

Beginning with the "end in mind" is a key way to ensure that any project is successful. Keeping in mind the knowledge and skills students should have at the end of the project can help guide the planning process. This type of planning is called backward design and was popularized by Grant Wiggins and Jay McTighe (Bowen, 2017).

Asking students what concerns they have about their school or community, and inviting them to survey their family and friends, can provide a rich list of potential projects. Teachers, too, can reflect on potential school and community issues in addition to talking with their colleagues about ideas.

The teacher can select the topic (statues/art in the community, perspectives not covered in textbooks, ways the school can become more environmentally conscious) and decide what the culminating project looks like (a presentation to city council about a new statue, a textbook insert, a proposal to the school administration). After students – and teachers – have developed more experience with PBL, more options can be provided to the class. For example, the class can choose the topic and each student group can decide on its culminating project. This chapter, however, only discusses the first more teacher-led example.

Using a tool like Table 17.1: PBL Teacher Planning Form and Checklist may be helpful for planning. This checklist can help a teacher determine if they have considered the key elements of a good project, including content standards, essential questions, clear benchmarks, what the presentation looks like, and so forth.

The planning stage is also a good time to create a rubric for the project. Creating this grading tool at the beginning can help a teacher think through and plan for the content and skills that students are expected to gain from the activity. The Assessment section of this chapter discusses rubrics in more detail.

Table 17.1 PBL Teacher Planning Form and Checklist

Project Name:_____ Dates_____		
Checklist	*Done?*	*What Does This Look Like in Your Project?*
1. **Key content** (specific standards, key terms) and **skills** (Common Core: evidence-based writing, speaking, and listening, etc.) are identified and addressed in the project.		
2. An **essential question** is provided that is challenging, open-ended, clearly connected to the content, and **relevant** to students' lives.		
3. An **authentic product** is created that is **presented** or provided for an audience beyond the classroom.		
4. **Student choice is embedded** throughout the project (topic, research focus, product style) that can lead to a sense of student ownership.		
5. **Reflection opportunities** are not only provided throughout the project, but are presented and utilized as an integral part of the PBL process (sufficient time is allotted, reflections are structured, and there is a focus on constructive critique, troubleshooting, and revision).		
6. **Benchmarks** are clearly communicated. Benchmarks are used as formative assessment opportunities.		
7. **Instructional activities and scaffolding** are created and prepped throughout the project in response to student's needs.		
8. **Inquiry is supported throughout** the project: opportunities for students to generate their own questions are provided, research is modeled and scaffolded, and student responses to the inquiry are supported.		

Sources: https://my.pblworks.org/system/files/documents/PBLworks-Essential-Project-Design-Elements.pdf (registration required), www.edutopia.org/sites/default/files/resources/edutopia-stw-manor-pbl-bestpractices-mobley-projectform-blankform.pdf, https://my.pblworks.org/system/files/documents/Project_Planner_v2019.pdf (registration required).

Introducing the Problem and Project

After the planning process is complete, we do an activity to hook students into the topic. We try to do something dramatic (like showing a provocative series of photos or a video clip explaining the problem) or create a special experience for students (going on a field trip or inviting a guest speaker to the classroom) in order to promote immediate interest. At the end of the activity, we introduce the question or problem to be addressed by student projects. This essential question helps to frame our project by allowing students to make connections between content, the real world, and themselves (see Chapter 11: Questions for Learning). Responding to this question serves as the goal for a project. Essential questions to jump-start PBL in social studies could include:

- What can our school do to be more environmentally conscious?

- What perspectives are missing or are less represented in our textbook?

- Who has been overlooked in the naming of schools, streets, or parks (ways that important historical figures are recognized), and what can be done to address these omissions?

- What is being done to combat gun violence in our community now, and what more should be done?

- How welcome do immigrants feel in our school and in our community, and what could be done to make them feel more welcome and supported?

After introducing one of these larger essential questions, we ask students to generate more specific subquestions. For an essential question like "Who has been overlooked in the naming of schools, streets, or parks (ways that important historical figures are recognized), and what can be done to address these omissions?" subquestions might be "Who are some of our most influential local leaders?" or "Who decides which historical figures are recognized in the community?"

The project will be a student response to the essential question. The subquestions are ones they will research to help them develop that response.

The teacher may have students generate questions on sticky notes and then post them on the wall to be reviewed by the class. Then, they can be converted into a class list, and these subquestions can be used during the research phase of the project.

Next, we explain the important components of the project to students. The elements of each project will vary, but we generally include reviewing and briefly explaining each benchmark, a description (or even better, an example) of the final product they are expected to create (for example, a presentation to a school board member about naming a school after an overlooked historical figure), an outline of the presentation requirements, and a timeline for the project.

While it is important to give an overall picture of the project, we must balance that with the reality that our students may become overwhelmed if we cover each requirement in detail. For this reason, we avoid an initial deep explanation of the project and, instead, assure students that we will tackle this challenge together, one step at a time.

Structured Work Time

After sharing the project requirements with students, we put them in groups (four to five students). Depending on the students, it may be a good idea for the teacher to choose the members of each group. This way the teacher can ensure that the groups are heterogenous (mixed abilities, ethnic backgrounds, personalities) prior to starting the activity. This type of group arrangement promotes peer-to-peer support and can limit the stigmatization of students with different learning abilities (Glass, 2002). Of course, if PBL is used more than once during the school year, students might be invited to periodically choose their own partners.

Once students are in groups, we share their first benchmark. For example, in the sample project discussed later in this chapter, the first benchmark is choosing a topic for a textbook insert they will be creating. We use benchmarks throughout the project to help hold students accountable for the progress we expect from them. A teacher can fill-in-the-blanks in Table 17.2: Planning and Progress Form – General for any project. This kind of form can also be provided using a project website or application like Google Classroom.

Table 17.2 Planning and Progress Form – General

Project Name:		
Students Being Evaluated:		
Evaluator(s):		
Essential Question		
Description of Product	We need to create …	
	Minimum Score on Product to Be Approved for Presentation: _____	
Description of the Presentation	Our presentation needs to include …	
Progress on Benchmarks:		
Benchmarks	**Completed**	**Comments**
Benchmark #1:		**Subquestion:**
Benchmark #2:		
Benchmark #3:		
Benchmark #4:		

After introducing the essential question, allowing time for the development of subquestions, and reviewing benchmarks with students, it's time to begin the research phase. Depending on the students, a teacher may need to provide a list of trusted resources to guide student research. For example, we may refer students to sites like the local newspaper or historical societies to begin their work. It may also be a good idea to arrange a visit to your school library. Arranging this in advance may allow the librarian to curate a selection of books or websites on the topic.

After helping students get organized prior to research, we provide structured work time. This scaffolding helps to ensure that groups have the guidance and support needed in order to successfully complete the project. Many of the supports also help to hold students accountable for their use of time. A teacher may use all or just a few structures depending on the students and the project.

- Graphic organizers for research – Creating a graphic organizer, either on paper or an online document, can help to focus students on key information during their research. This type of organizer can also remind students to note the sources of information for citation purposes. For an example, see Table 17.3: Research Chart.

Table 17.3 Research Chart

Source: Title, Author	Page #s or URL	Information that relates to or answers my question:

- Weekly discussions – Use the small-group discussion protocol from Chapter 16: Discussions to plan and debrief each week. In this type of conversation, small groups use a structure that provides opportunities for each member to contribute to the discussion. After being assigned numbers, the facilitator (a preselected leader) draws numbers from a cup giving each student a chance to respond to a prompt. After an initial answer is given by one student, others are encouraged to agree, disagree, or clarify using academic discussion starters. The discussion starters can be customized to address specific benchmarks, content, or other project-related concerns that arise. These conversations are also a good opportunity to debrief and reflect on the groups' progress on the project. Please refer to Figure 17.1: Group Discussion Starters.

- Genre study of project – This support guides students to study an example of what they are expected to produce – proposal for a solution regarding a local issue, documentary, action plan for implementing a solution, children's book, and so forth. Regardless of the project, it is helpful for students to review examples and identify key elements of the genre. For more about facilitating a genre study, refer to Chapter 9: Genre Study.

- Contact an expert – This person may be someone who has knowledge of either the social studies content or the type of product students are creating. For example, when creating a presentation to address the essential question "Who has been overlooked in the naming of schools, streets, or parks (ways that important historical figures are recognized) and what can be done to address these omissions?" a local historian may be helpful. Working with an expert provides students the opportunity to practice formal communication through business emails or phone conversations. A teacher may provide a template or frame like the one in Figure 17.2: Email Template to help students plan communication.

- Online surveys to track collaboration – Teachers can create weekly surveys to track group work using Google Forms or SurveyMonkey (www.surveymonkey.com). A teacher may ask students to rate different elements of their collaboration. For example, "On a scale of 1 to 5, 5 being the highest, rate how well you feel your team listens to your ideas" or "What did you accomplish this week?" These surveys can serve as formative assessments: The results can even be tabulated at the end to show the teacher trends or patterns within the different groups. The teacher can also use this information to plan more immediate interventions, if necessary.

Presentation

Making the project public is key to the authenticity of PBL. Presenting to an audience can motivate students to work harder. This goal of PBL may mean presenting their project to a panel of judges: other teachers, experts in the field (history professors, members of a city council or school board), community members (parents, business owners, local nonprofits), or other stakeholders (other students, public service personnel).

The presentation should have clear guidelines. Students should practice so that it falls within a given time range (e.g., four to seven minutes). Also, students will need clear expectations for the digital aspect of their presentation, if there is one. For example, if a slideshow is used, teaching students how to build a clear, informative set of slides is important. For more on student presentations, see Chapter 15: Listening and Speaking Activities.

Additionally, if students have a physical project to share with the audience, they need to consider how it will be displayed or shared. For example, they may need to determine at what point in the presentation the judging panel or audience gets a chance to see the project "up close."

We want to avoid setting our students up for failure by allowing them to present a partial or incomplete project to a panel. We also want to respect the time of the members of the panel as well. For this reason, it may be a good idea to make presentation readiness a benchmark. In other words, the project needs to meet a basic level of completion before it is deemed ready for a public presentation.

A teacher can make "presentation approval" a benchmark prior to the actual event. Making sure the slideshows are professional and free of errors will help ensure a successful presentation. To this end, groups can be partnered up to practice and give each other feedback on their presentations (perhaps with a checklist or rubric). This way, the teacher isn't solely responsible for evaluating each project for presentation readiness.

Assessment

Assessment should be embedded throughout the project, beginning with providing clear guidelines and expectations for students. Incorporating benchmarks can be a good way to embed formal assessment throughout PBL.

In addition to benchmarks, it's also worthwhile to include formative assessments throughout the project. These informal, low-risk assessments give the teacher information about the students' progress in order to target instruction. Some examples of formative assessments during PBL might include journals, self-assessments, class, or group discussions, and weekly reports. For more about formative assessment, please see Chapter 20: Assessments.

To assess the entire project, we have had success using a multidomain rubric like Table 17.4: General PBL Rubric. In other words, we use a rubric that evaluates both student skill development and content knowledge.

Table 17.4 General PBL Rubric

Area of Evaluation:
Standard(s):

Grading Scales	Unsatisfactory	Satisfactory	Proficient
Criteria			
Points			

Area of Evaluation:
Standard(s):

Grading Scales	Unsatisfactory	Satisfactory	Proficient
Criteria			
Points			

Area of Evaluation:
Standard(s):

Grading Scales	Unsatisfactory	Satisfactory	Proficient
Criteria			
Points			

Area of Evaluation: Standard(s):			
Grading Scales	**Unsatisfactory**	**Satisfactory**	**Proficient**
Criteria			
Points			

Source: www.edutopia.org/sites/default/files/pdfs/stw/edutopia-stw-manor-pbl-bestpractices-rubrics-controllingfactor-blankform.pdf.

Additionally, it may be helpful for students to have more than one opportunity to review and revise their work to achieve the highest level of success. For example, students may have more than one opportunity to turn in a draft of their project prior to final submission.

In our rubrics, we tend to stick to the following items for assessment: content or necessary knowledge (this may also include skills like writing a professional letter), use of evidence, conceptual integration of knowledge, collaboration, and speaking and listening. These items are adapted from lists created by researchers Brigid Barron, Linda Darling-Hammond, and Woai Hung (Vega, 2012).

Reflection

In our experience, a key factor of successful inquiry assignments is giving students time for reflection. Providing frequent opportunities to reflect allows students to more fully process content by discussing it with others, making connections to the content, tracking their progress, and identifying challenges.

Some ideas for reflection opportunities include:

- Students can respond to reflection prompts in their class journal or on a sheet of paper. These prompts may ask students to review content they are learning to determine if they are meeting the demands of the overarching questions, or to simply reflect on their group's progress.

- After completing a benchmark, ask students to reflect on that portion of the project. Students could be asked about what went well, what they would do differently, or questions they may still have about that specific benchmark assignment. This reflection could be done as a warm-up or closure activity.

- Students can be asked to reflect on the project overall, the content learned, and collaboration. A teacher could have them score an assessment rubric for themselves and write a rationale for each mark.

TEXTBOOK INSERT PROJECT

To more fully illustrate how to apply the key steps of PBL, we'll now explain a project we do that has students work together to create an insert that shares perspectives related to the Vietnam War that are not present in our textbook. Then, students present their creation to a panel of social studies teachers to persuade them to use it in their teaching of the Vietnam War. The timeline for this project is approximately three weeks.

Planning the PBL

Prior to rolling out the project with students, we carefully plan the key components using Table 17.5: PBL Teacher Planning Form and Checklist – Textbook Insert. In this checklist, we include the content standards that this project will address:

Table 17.5   PBL Teacher Planning Form and Checklist - Textbook Insert

Checklist	Done	Notes
1. Key content (specific standards, key terms) and skills (Common Core: evidence-based writing, speaking, and listening, etc.) skills are identified and addressed in the project		• **11.9 Students analyze US foreign policy since World War II.** • **NCSS Thematic Strands: "Time, Continuity, and Change"** • **Common Core Standard(s): Key Ideas and Details** CCSS.ELA-LITERACY.RH.11–12.1 • CCSS.ELA-LITERACY.WHST.11–12.2 • CCSS.ELA-LITERACY.WHST.11–12.1.D CCSS.ELA-LITERACY.WHST.11–12.1 **Common Core – Comprehension and Collaboration:** • CCSS.ELA-LITERACY.CCRA.SL.1
2. An essential question is provided that is challenging, authentic, open-ended, clearly connected to the content, and relevant to students' lives.		Students develop response to the overarching question "Whose perspective is missing from our textbook for the Vietnam War?"
3. Inquiry is supported throughout the project: opportunities for students to generate their own questions are provided, research is modeled and scaffolded, and student responses to inquiry are supported.		Students generate subquestions to respond to larger essential question. Research is scaffolded with modeling and the use of a research guide.
4. Student choice is embedded through-out the project (topic, research focus, product style) that can lead to a sense of student ownership.		Students generate perspectives. Students determine individual tasks within the project. Students select images and vocabulary to incorporate into textbook insert.

5. Reflection opportunities are not only provided throughout the project, but are presented and utilized as an integral part of the PBL process (sufficient time is allotted, reflections are structured, and there is a focus on troubleshooting)	Students reflect at the end of each benchmark through responding to reflection questions. Students reflect at the end of the project, by scoring their own rubric and providing rationale for each score.
6. Benchmarks for important steps in the project are clearly communicated. Benchmarks can be utilized as formative assessment opportunities.	Benchmark #1: choosing a perspective for the textbook insert Benchmark #2: research chart with six to eight sources on the group the textbook insert is representing Benchmark #3: completed graphic organizer that lays out draft of textbook insert Benchmark #4: completed typed draft of textbook insert Benchmark #5: completed outline for presentation

Sources: https://my.pblworks.org/system/files/documents/PBLworks-Essential-Project-Design-Elements.pdf (registration required), www.edutopia.org/sites/default/files/resources/edutopia-stw-manor-pbl-bestpractices-mobley-projectform-blankform.pdf, https://my.pblworks.org/system/files/documents/Project_Planner_v2019.pdf (registration required).

our state's content standards, Common Core, and curriculum standards from the National Council for the Social Studies. The organizer also guides us to consider other key information such as our essential question, how we will support student inquiry, benchmarks, and so on.

Introducing the Problem and Project

To help engage students for our textbook insert project, we use an image-based entry event. We like to present students with a slideshow of different perspectives of famous historical images. In this activity we want to emphasize the dangers of a single narrative. In other words, we want students to see the importance of including multiple viewpoints in telling a story in order to get a more complete picture of an event. For example, we first show students the well-known version of the famous image of Tank Man coming face to face with military tanks during the 1989 protests in Tiananmen Square. Then, we show a lesser-known image of the same event taken from a different angle. This less famous perspective illustrates that the confrontation was truly an act of bravery and resistance. Three other people seem to be in a rush to leave this already seemingly deserted area, a row of abandoned bikes in the foreground, as Tank Man heads toward the approaching military tanks.

We direct students to note initial reactions from the first famous image and then new ideas or questions that arise after showing a different perspective. Then, they share out their questions and reactions with a partner. The point is to get students engaged in the idea that a different view can change an entire story. Many other perspectives of famous photos can be found by searching online. For example, we used a few images from the website Guff (Denton, 2014).

Another way to introduce this idea is by showing the TED Talk by Chimamanda Ngozi Adichie called "The Danger of a Single Story" (Adichie, 2009). In this video, Chimamanda talks about the impact of reading single-narrative books as a child. She discusses how harmful it was for her to never see her story reflected in the books she read. For more resources on the dangers of a single story, see the Technology Connections.

Next, we present our essential question to students by saying the following:

> *I have noticed that if we only rely on our textbook, we may not get the entire story for a historical event. In fact, when studying the Vietnam War recently I found myself wondering* **"Whose perspective is missing from our textbook for the Vietnam War?**

We project the question for everyone to see. Then, we share that responding to this question is the purpose of our project: students telling the story of an overlooked perspective for a specific event in history – the Vietnam War.

After introducing this larger essential question, we ask students to generate more specific subquestions. These more specific questions help to narrow the path for student inquiry. For our project, we do this by asking students something like "In order to answer the essential question, what do we need to know?" or rewording the essential question, "After reading about the Vietnam War in our textbook, what perspectives are missing?"

To help students get started, we model our thinking process of generating subquestions that break down the larger essential question. We say something like,

> *When I think about the question "Whose perspective is missing from our textbook for the Vietnam War?" I think about my Hmong students. For those of you who don't know, the Hmong lived in Laos and fought with the United States during the Vietnam War. As a result, many Hmong families were forced to flee their homeland and came to the United States as refugees. I noticed that our textbook doesn't tell me anything about this group of people. I wonder, what happened to the Hmong people during the Vietnam War?*

On a sheet of paper, we list this question. Then, we direct students to generate their own and list them on a sheet of paper. After giving students a few minutes to create questions, we ask them to pick their top one and write it on a sticky note, which is then posted on the board. These sticky notes serve to identify perspectives students will be assigned as the focus of their project in the next step. For example, students may come up with questions like:

- How did the Vietnam War impact teenagers in the United States?

- What was life like for children and teenagers in Vietnam?

- What was the experience of African American, Latino, and other US soldiers of color during the Vietnam War?

- What was the experience of the Hmong during the Vietnam War?

- What was the experience for students (grade school, high school, and college) who were in the United States during the war?

- Was the Vietnam War different for men and women in the US military?

- How did the Vietnam War impact North and South Vietnamese civilians?

- How might the countries surrounding Vietnam have been impacted by the conflict?

- How were the US allies affected by the war?

- What was the experience of those who were drafted versus those that volunteered?

We have found that students often ask about groups with whom they share attributes (age, race, ethnicity, and so on). We also add questions that we feel students overlook.

We then explain that students will be creating a textbook "insert" to incorporate a missing perspective into the chapter about the Vietnam War. We add that each group will present their insert to a panel of social studies teachers from the school in order to persuade them to use it in their classes.

We make sure that students understand any other requirements, such as benchmarks (deadlines for portions of the project), weekly group meetings (to facilitate communication), frequent reflections (to help track productivity and address challenges), and the insert itself and presentation (the student product that responds to the question or problem).

Students complete the top portion of Table 17.6: Planning and Progress Form – Textbook, which asks them to write the essential question, description of product, and description of the presentation. This handout also lays out the benchmarks students will be expected to complete. At this point we typically show students Table 17.7: Textbook Insert Project Rubric to guide students through the specific project criteria.

Table 17.6 Planning and Progress Form - Textbook

Project Name: **Textbook Insert Project** Students Being Evaluated: Evaluator(s):	
Essential Question	**"Whose perspective is missing from our textbook for the Vietnam War?"**
Description of Product	We need to create ... **an insert, or section, for our textbook chapter about the Vietnam War. This chapter section needs to look and read like an official section in a textbook chapter. Most importantly, it needs to represent the experience and views of a group that was affected by the Vietnam War, but not included in the textbook.** Minimum Score on Product to Be Approved for Presentation: _____80_____
Description of the Presentation	Our presentation needs to include ... **professional presentation of our insert to a panel of social studies teachers at our school. The goal of this presentation is to convince the teachers to incorporate our insert into their teaching of the Vietnam War.**

Progress on Benchmarks:

Benchmarks	Completed	Comments:
Benchmark #1: choosing a perspective for the textbook insert		**Please write perspective here –**
Benchmark #2: research chart with **six-eight sources** on the group the textbook insert is representing		
Benchmark #3: completed graphic organizer that lays out draft for textbook insert		
Benchmark #4: completed typed draft of textbook insert		
Benchmark #5: completed outline for presentation		

Structured Work Time

After explaining the project, it's time to divide students into groups.

It's then time to complete the first benchmark – choosing a perspective for their textbook insert. We allow the groups to meet and discuss the different questions and list their top two choices. Students may choose a guiding question from the sticky notes that the class generated earlier like "What happened to the Hmong people during the Vietnam War?" If students are choosing their perspective, we often limit each perspective to being selected by only two groups.

This guideline helps to make sure that a variety of viewpoints are chosen, and presentations aren't redundant. The teacher may also assign these perspectives to each group.

After making a choice for their insert, it's time to prepare students for successful research. In order to support them with this task, we provide additional scaffolds. Instead of directing students to the Internet and saying "Go!" we ask students to develop a few specific questions that will help them focus their research on their chosen perspective. For example, if students have chosen to write about the Hmong perspective during the Vietnam War, they may come up with questions like "Who are the Hmong?" "Where did the Hmong live during the Vietnam War?" "What was the relationship like between the Hmong and the United States during the Vietnam War?" and so on. Then, each member of the group may tackle one of these questions. It may be helpful for the teacher to model this question generation with one perspective that is not assigned to a particular group.

Next, to support students during the research process, we hand out – or make available digitally – Table 17.3: Research Chart. This chart helps students to collect helpful information that connects to their subquestion and research questions, as well as cite their findings. A teacher could require each member of the group to research and complete the chart for three different resources for their textbook insert. Then, the completed charts are turned in as a benchmark.

After collecting research, it's time for students to determine how to take the information they found and portray it in the style of a textbook. In order to do this effectively, students need to study an example to determine and outline the key elements of a textbook section. For example, students may notice that a textbook generally includes multiple subsections, vocabulary words, images, and graphs. It is a good idea to outline the writing style as well: informational, no personal pronouns, and so forth. A graphic organizer like Figure 17.3: Textbook Insert Structure can help to format this type of writing.

Once students have completed a draft of their insert, the teacher reviews it and provides feedback on writing and content. Afterwards, an *optional* next step is to have it reviewed for content accuracy by an expert. For this project, a helpful expert may be a professor from a local college or university, social studies student teachers from a credential program, or teachers at the school. We provide students with Figure 17.2: Email Template to help them craft a professional email. If you are going to incorporate this activity, it would be important to contact a few professionals in advance.

Throughout the project, we give students time for weekly group discussions. These discussions can help students to plan their agenda for the week, reflect on their progress, and help improve group communication. We provide students with sentence starters to guide the discussion like those in Figure 17.1: Group Discussion Starters. For example, discussion starters may be: "Something I have been struggling with is …" "My goal for this week is to complete …" or "In order to complete (the next benchmark), I need to …" The starters can be changed out to frame the discussion toward a specific goal like reflection, planning, communication, and so on. During the discussion we might hear students say things like, "Something I've been struggling with is figuring out what my resource is saying – it's hard to read. I'm going to ask Ms. Johnson for help" or "In order to complete the graphic organizer that lays out the draft of the textbook insert, I need to create a visual."

Presentation

An authentic presentation opportunity is important to create relevancy for students. For our project addressing the question "Whose perspective is missing from our textbook for the Vietnam War?" it means students present their textbook inserts to a panel of social studies teachers at our school. The goal of their presentation is persuading the teachers to incorporate the insert into their instruction about the Vietnam War. Students can be motivated by the opportunity to impact what teachers do in their classrooms.

We provide guidelines to students for their presentations such as duration, content, and a digital element. The presentation should be between four and seven minutes long and have a slideshow outlining the key components of their textbook insert. Additionally, students need to provide reasons that including their insert would benefit teachers and their classes. We also have students print out copies of their insert for each panel member, as well as extras for curious audience members (community and family members, other teachers, and students invited by the presenters). Groups may also include excerpts from their insert in their slideshow.

All these requirements must meet a basic level of completion in order to meet benchmark 5 on Table 17.6: Planning and Progress Form – Textbook. Students must have this benchmark checked off in order to actually participate in the presentations.

Assessment

The benchmarks incorporated in this textbook insert project (choosing a topic, completing a research chart with six to eight sources, finishing a graphic organizer that functions as a textbook insert draft, and so on) are good ways to embed formal assessment throughout PBL. We also include formative assessment throughout the project with low-risk activities like journals, small-group discussions, and self-assessments. For more about assessment, please see Chapter 20: Assessments.

When it comes time to assess the entire project, we use Table 17.7: Textbook Project Rubric. This multidomain rubric evaluates many different areas of the project including content and skills students are expected to develop, integration of knowledge, collaboration, as well as speaking and listening. For each item being graded, we include criteria in a way that clarifies the expectations for both student and teacher. We allow students to review and resubmit work for any portions of the rubric where they score "unsatisfactory."

Table 17.7 Textbook Insert Project Rubric

Area of Evaluation: _Social Studies Content Comprehension and Use of Evidence_
Standard(s):
• **11.9 Students analyze US foreign policy since World War II.**
Trace the origins and geopolitical consequences (foreign and domestic) of the Cold War and containment policy, including the following: the Vietnam War
4. List the effects of foreign policy on domestic policies and vice versa (e.g., protests during the war in Vietnam, the "nuclear freeze" movement).
(Source: www.cde.ca.gov/be/st/ss/documents/histsocscistnd.pdf, pg. 52).
• **NCSS Thematic Strands: "Time, Continuity, and Change"**
"Through a more formal study of history, students in the middle grades continue to expand their understanding of the past and are increasingly able to apply the research methods associated with historical inquiry." (Source: www.socialstudies.org/standards/strands)
• **Common Core Standard(s): Key Ideas and Details**
CCSS.ELA-LITERACY.RH.11–12.1
Cite specific textual evidence to support analysis of primary and secondary sources, connecting insights gained from specific details to an understanding of the text as a whole.

Grading Scales	Unsatisfactory	Satisfactory	Proficient
Criteria	*Content about the Vietnam War and the perspective your group chose:* • Is not explained • Explained incorrectly • Too general, vague • Has no context • Is not analyzed	*Content about the Vietnam War and the perspective your group chose:* • Is accurate • Is explained with examples • Is easy to understand • Analysis is provided • Is supported with researched evidence: both primary and secondary sources	*Content about the Vietnam War and the perspective your group chose:* • Is accurate • Is explained in depth with examples • Is easy to understand • In-depth analysis is provided • Is clearly supported with researched evidence: multiple primary and secondary sources
Points	**0–69**	**70–89**	**90–100**
Comments			

(Continued)

Table 17.7 *(Continued)*

Area of Evaluation: *Integration of Knowledge Into Textbook Genre*
- **Common Core Standards – Text Types and Purposes:**
  CCSS.ELA-LITERACY.WHST.11–12.1
  Write arguments focused on discipline-specific content.
- CCSS.ELA-LITERACY.WHST.11–12.1.D
  Establish and maintain a formal style and objective tone while attending to the norms and conventions of the discipline in which they are writing.
- CCSS.ELA-LITERACY.WHST.11–12.2
  Write informative/explanatory texts, including the narration of historical events, scientific procedures/experiments, or technical processes.

Grading Scales	Unsatisfactory	Satisfactory	Proficient
Criteria	*The writing in the textbook insert:* • Is unfocused or off-topic (not clearly about the Vietnam War and the perspective chosen) • Is informal or unprofessional • Does not follow the sections of the graphic organizer which modeled a typical textbook section • Personal opinions are present without enough narration of actual historical events • Does not include images • Many grammatical or spelling errors	*The writing in the textbook insert:* • Is focused on the Vietnam War and the perspective chosen • Reads as a mostly formal and professional sample of writing • Generally follows the sections of the graphic organizer and therefore is organized like a textbook chapter • No personal opinions, just narration of historical events • Includes some creative details in the layout including images • Minimal grammatical or spelling errors	*The writing in the textbook insert:* • Is focused clearly on the Vietnam War and the perspective chosen • Reads as a formal and professional sample of writing • Accurately follows the sections of the graphic organizer and therefore is organized like a textbook chapter • No personal opinions, just detailed narration of historical events • Includes creative details in the layout, production, or writing (like supplemental use of digital media, high quality images, etc.) • No grammatical or spelling errors
Points	0–69	70–89	90–100
Comments			

Area of Evaluation: *Collaboration*
Standard(s): **Common Core – Comprehension and Collaboration:**
- CCSS.ELA-LITERACY.CCRA.SL.1
  Prepare for and participate effectively in a range of conversations and collaborations with diverse partners, building on others' ideas and expressing their own clearly and persuasively.
- 21st-century Skills

Grading Scales	Unsatisfactory	Satisfactory	Proficient
Criteria	*As a group:* • Insufficient focus on task • Only certain members of the group do most of the work • Issues with attendance and reliability • Disrespectful exchanges or refusal to work as a group	*As a group:* • Sufficient focus on task • Members of the group typically have equal workloads • Minimal issues with attendance and reliability • Conflict is dealt with respectfully, but may require teacher intervention	*As a group:* • Exceptional focus on task • Members of the group consistently have equal workloads • No issues with attendance and reliability • Conflict is dealt with respectfully and proactively
Points	0–69	70–89	90–100
Comments			

Table 17.7 *(Continued)*

Area of Evaluation: <u>*Presentation: Speaking and Listening*</u>
Standard(s):
Presentation of Knowledge and Ideas:
CCSS.ELA-LITERACY.SL.11–12.4
Present information, findings, and supporting evidence, conveying a clear and distinct perspective, such that listeners can follow the line of reasoning, alternative, or opposing perspectives are addressed, and the organization, development, substance, and style are appropriate to purpose, audience, and a range of formal and informal tasks.
CCSS.ELA-LITERACY.SL.11–12.5
Make strategic use of digital media (e.g., textual, graphical, audio, visual, and interactive elements) in presentations to enhance understanding of findings, reasoning, and evidence and to add interest.

Grading Scales	Unsatisfactory	Satisfactory	Proficient
Criteria	• Ideas not organized and hard to follow • Lack of preparation and communication among group members is evident in most aspects of presentation • Tone inappropriate for a professional setting, student presenters do not seem invested in their own presentation • No attempt to creatively engage the audience	• Ideas are organized and easy to follow • Clear preparation and communication among group members is evident in most aspects of presentation • A formal tone, or a tone appropriate for the setting and audience, is mostly used while student interest evident • Attempt to creatively engage the audience	• Ideas are organized in an easy to follow and creative manner • Clear preparation and communication among group members is evident in all aspects of presentation -presentation delivered with passion and emotional investment • Audience engaged
Points	0–69	70–89	90–100
Comments			

Reflection

We provide multiple opportunities for students to reflect throughout the project. For example, after completing Benchmark 2 on Table 17.6: Planning and Progress Form – Textbook, we give students a few questions. We ask students to respond to "What went well during this portion of the project?" and "What would you do differently next time (for this section) and why?" These types of questions are open-ended, but simple, ensuring all students can answer them regardless of their project success.

Another key reflection opportunity we provide is allowing students to score their work using a grading rubric (Table 17.7: Textbook Project Rubric). In other words, we ask students to give themselves a score for each of the criteria *and* provide rationale. This process helps us to see, from the students' perspective, how they felt they did in each area of the project. We have a clarifying conversation if we notice a large discrepancy between the teacher-given and student-given scores.

OTHER IDEAS FOR PROJECT-BASED LEARNING

In addition to the textbook-insert project in this chapter, there are many opportunities for PBL in social studies. Here are a few ideas:

- Census Education Campaign – In this project, students learn the history and purpose of the census and create materials to advocate for community members to complete their census forms. These materials may debunk myths that dissuade people from completing the census, sharing the importance of the data collection, and/or directions for completing the census in a variety of languages. This might be a good project for a government or US history class. Read more about this type of project at Larry Ferlazzo's blog post "The Best Resources to Learn About the U.S. Census" (Ferlazzo, 2010).

- Student-Created Unit – Students plan, organize, and create the activities for a unit on a given topic. In a geography class, groups could be assigned to make a unit on a country of their choice. This unit might include a data set (see Chapter 4: Thematic Data Set), a series of read-alouds (see Chapter 3: Read-Aloud Protocol), and so on. Figures and information on student-created data sets and read-alouds are provided in these chapters. The units could be taught to other students or presented in an exhibition.

- Community Problem/Solution – In terms of relevancy, suggesting solutions for an issue in the local community is another potential project. In a US government class, students could first gather information about challenges in the local community. Then, students could plan and organize a speaking event where they invite community members and/or political leaders. During this event, students could explain the issues such as homelessness, drugs, and gang violence, as well as present solutions like building a homeless shelter, walk-in counseling clinics, or job-training programs. These solutions should include the process of implementing the solution as well as the cost and the effect on the community.

- Get out the vote campaign – Students in a US government class could research and then target a population of voters that was underrepresented in recent local elections. For example, after analyzing recent election polling data, students may note that people between the ages of 18–25 had low voter turnout. They could then create a plan to encourage voting – targeting the previously identified group – and put it into action.

- Teaching younger students – After learning about an event in history, students could prepare and then teach an age-appropriate lesson to students at a local elementary school. There can be substantial value to having students teach others. Research shows that expecting to teach others actually enhances students' *own* learning of a topic (Everding, 2014). This finding means that putting our students into the role of teachers may actually help them learn social studies content in *our* classrooms. For example, in a US history class students could teach about their state's adoption into the United States. Other topics that students might teach about are the local indigenous groups that lived in the area or the history of one or two of the major immigrant groups in the school.

- Minidocumentaries (or podcasts) – Students could create a minidocumentary on a given topic, time period, issue, or influential person. In a world history class, students might research, script, and film documentaries that investigate past and present examples of imperialism in different areas of the world. For more on student-created films, please refer to Chapter 12: Image Analysis.

- Choose your own adventure – After learning about an important event in history, students create alternative timelines for how the story might have ended differently. They write, or film, these multiple options to create a choose-your-own-adventure project. This project is a play on alternative timelines (see Chapter 7: Timelines Revisited). Students in a world history course might make alternative storylines for famous explorers, imagining what might have happened if the new world had been untouched by Europeans. There are many resources for choose-your-own-adventure stories in Larry Ferlazzo's blog post "The Best Places to Read and Write Choose Your Own Adventure Stories" (Ferlazzo, 2009, May 2); see also "The Best Resources for Teaching 'What If?' History Lessons" at Larry Ferlazzo's blog for examples and lesson plans (Ferlazzo, 2012).

DIFFERENTIATION

When undertaking a project with students who may need extra support, thoughtful grouping is key. Making sure that English language learners (ELLs) and those who learn differently are placed in teams with helpful peers can make a world of difference. This thoughtful grouping might also extend to finding a special mentor for this group or for a particular student who needs more help with a given project.

Additionally, the research and writing portion of this project is often the most difficult for many students. Providing more support for ELLs and students who learn differently can be helpful. For example, during the research process, direct ELL students to specific websites that are more accessible. Students may also be provided writing frames in addition to the insert outline provided in Figure 17.3: Textbook Insert Structure.

It is also important to determine what strengths students have and find ways to incorporate those into the project. If a student struggles with extended writing, but does well at creating visuals or coming up with creative ideas, find a way to put those skills to use as well. Remember, we want to look at our students through the lens of assets, not deficits.

ADVANCED EXTENSIONS

Directing students to present their ideas to a wider audience is a good way to take a student project to the next level. For example, students could write a letter to textbook publishers explaining why they think their insert would be important to include in the next edition.

Additional tasks can also be added to a given project to increase the level of difficulty. For example, the textbook-insert project could be made more rigorous by increasing the task from one section to multiple sections or an entire chapter. Students could also create an assessment activity to go along with their insert.

Student Handouts and Examples

Table 17.1: PBL Teacher Planning Form and Checklist

Table 17.2: Planning and Progress Form – General

Table 17.3: Research Chart

Figure 17.1: Group Discussion Starters

Figure 17.2: Email Template

Table 17.4: General PBL Rubric

Table 17.5: PBL Teacher Planning Form and Checklist – Textbook Insert

Table 17.6: Planning and Progress Form – Textbook

Table 17.7: Textbook Project Rubric

Figure 17.3: Textbook Insert Structure

What Could Go Wrong?

It's easy to "bite off more than you can chew" when venturing into PBL, and that can lead to both the teacher and students feeling overwhelmed. Instead, start with small projects to get used to this type of student-centered learning. A teacher might also want to limit the number of standards addressed, learning outcomes, as well as carefully consider the duration of the project.

Handing out project directions and walking away can end a project before it's even begun. Expecting students to independently figure out how to execute a project and assuming that they already have all the skills necessary to make the project happen is not a realistic perspective. Even if project-based learning is a great example of student-centered learning, all students benefit from modeling and teacher guidance.

Technology Connections

Encouraging students to see multiple perspectives and consider what story is *not* being told is important. For more resources on the dangers of a single narrative, see Larry Ferlazzo's blog post "The Best Resources on the Danger of a Single Story" (http://larryferlazzo.edublogs.org/2016/12/20/the-best-resources-on-the-danger-of-a-single-story).

There is an incredible amount of information and resources available online for project-based learning. The Buck Institute for Education website (www.pblworks.org) is a useful place to visit for more about this type of learning. Another idea is to check out some completed projects from the High Tech High website (www.hightechhigh.org/student-work/student-projects).

To learn more about sharing student projects read, Larry Ferlazzo's blog post "Dreamdo Schools Is a Platform to Share Project-Based Learning Projects Internationally" (http://larryferlazzo.edublogs.org/2015/10/07/dreamdo-schools-is-a-platform-to-share-project-based-learning-projects-internationally). In addition to creating a project, this site lets students extend their learning beyond their own classroom to others around the world.

Figures

- "Something I have been struggling with is..."

- "My goal this week is to complete. . ."

- "In order to complete (the next benchmark) , I need to. . ."

- "Something that I think our group could really work on is. . .because. . ."

- "Something I think our group is really good at is. . . I feel like this is important because. . ."

- "Something I think we may need clarification with is. . ."

- "For the _____ benchmark, I rate my progress a _____ on a scale of 1-5. I gave myself this number because. . ."

- "Something that I think I/we have been getting better at is. . ."

- "In order to support our group, something specific that I am willing to commit to is. . ."

- "I think a possible strategy we can try is _____ because _____."

Figure 17.1   Group Discussion Starters

Email Template:

Dear <u>(address person by their formal title and last name)</u> ,

My name is _____ and I attend _____
_____. Currently I am working on a project called _____. The project entails _____
_____.
I am emailing you in the hopes that you could help me with _____
_____. Considering your expertise in _____
_____, it would be a great honor to have you involved.

I look forward to hearing from you. I am sure you are very busy and I intend to respect your time by _____.
If you are able to help, we can make arrangements that work best for you such as
_____.

Thank you for your time,

Student Name
Contact Number
Professional Email

Figure 17.2 Email Template

Title of section (needs to blend with the greater chapter that it would be in):

4-5 key terms for this subject:

Quick timeline of this group's experience with the Vietnam War: only add four or five major events and mention them briefly (the article should provide all the information for them):

Subheading 1:
Begin Writing Narrative

Continue Subheading 1:

Insert Image, wrap text around:

Figure 17.3 Textbook Insert Structure

Subheading 2: **Continue Narrative**	**Subheading 3:** **Continue Narrative**
Insert Image: Wrap text around	
Continue Subheading 2	**Close with Image: Wrap text around**

Figure 17.3 (Continued)

CHAPTER 18

Culturally Responsive Teaching

What Is It?

Culturally responsive teaching (CRT) is more than a strategy. According to Gloria Ladson-Billings, who helped pioneer this concept, CRT is "a pedagogy that recognizes the importance of including students' cultural references in all aspects of learning" ("Culturally Responsive Teaching," n.d.). Culturally responsive teaching aims to strengthen the learning capacity of diverse students through developing "learning partnerships" between students and teachers (Ferlazzo, 2015c). The importance of addressing the needs of diverse students is immediate: in the United States, students of color are now the majority population in K–12 public schools (National Center for Educational Statistics, 2019), while most teachers are white (Rich, 2015). Teaching with a culturally responsive mindset helps to address the needs of students who have often been marginalized by schools and society – and can also be beneficial for *all* students (Krasnoff, 2016, p. 8).

In this chapter, we will provide ideas for practicing cultural responsiveness in the social studies classroom.

Why We like It

Culturally responsive teaching can help create an inclusive community in our classrooms. Building authentic relationships and honoring the background of our students can benefit *everyone* in our classroom (Krasnoff, 2016, p. 8). We have found that these types of "safe" learning environments can encourage healthy risk-taking and build a more cooperative atmosphere.

We like the way a CRT mindset encourages us to view all students as contributors to the learning environment. Instead of reinforcing stereotypes of diverse student populations, CRT reminds us to incorporate strategies that honor and sustain the richness of our students' cultures. This approach can encourage students and teachers to use what is readily available *and* powerful: the stories and experiences of every person in the room.

Supporting Research

Research has shown that CRT can help students feel more personally connected and engaged – two factors that can lead to improved learning (Byrd, 2016, p. 6).

Additionally, CRT has several benefits: it can enhance students' sense of identity, increase academic engagement and achievement, and promote the growth of a critical consciousness – the ability to recognize and challenge systems of inequality (Byrd, 2016; Sleeter, 2011, p. 9).

Common Core Connections

Although there is no standard for culturally responsive teaching, we can build students' learning capacities by leveraging the cultural and linguistic tools that they bring to the classroom. These assets can help students meet the goals of the Common Core. Under the Craft and Structure strand, the Common Core mentions the importance of evaluating "differing points of view on the same historical event or issue . . ." (Common Core, 2010dd). Culturally responsive teaching brings this diversity of perspectives into the social studies classroom.

Social Studies Connections

Multiple thematic strands of the Curriculum Standards of The National Council for the Social Studies (NCSS) can be addressed in a culturally responsive classroom (NCSS, n.d.). Themes like culture, individuals, groups, and institutions can be present in culturally responsive social studies content. For example, students can study culture and explore individual identities, along with researching the historical role of institutions in creating and sustaining social or racial hierarchies. We provide ideas for such activities in the application section of this chapter.

Application

This portion of the chapter is organized into six subsections. Each one addresses a question that social studies teachers can consider in order to make their classrooms more culturally responsive:

- How aware, and reflective, am I of my own cultural lens in the classroom?
- Do my words with students, colleagues, and the community reflect a culturally responsive mindset?

- How am I building authentic relationships and classroom community with my students?

- How are my social studies content choices reflective of my students' everyday lives?

- How are my teaching *strategies* culturally responsive?

These reflective questions are inspired by Larry Ferlazzo's and Katie Hull Sypnieski's book *The ELL Teacher's Toolbox* (Ferlazzo & Sypnieski, 2018b).

For each section, we explain the purpose of the question by citing supporting research. Additionally, we provide related classroom experiences to illustrate the themes of each question. We also share resources, strategies, and activities that can help teachers practice CRT in any social studies classroom.

Asking ourselves these questions has helped us identify and seek out CRT practices and resources. We are the first to recognize that CRT is never done and we still identify moments in our classrooms when we have not been culturally responsive. To effectively respond to the needs of our diverse students, we must *continuously* ask these questions of ourselves, and each other.

Although the sequence of questions in the Application do not imply order of importance, we do feel like the first question – which is about basic self-awareness – is fundamental to CRT.

REFLECTIVE QUESTIONS

How Aware, and Reflective, Am I of My Own Cultural Lens in the Classroom?

What we do in the classroom, whether we realize it or not, emanates from our cultural "lens." In other words, our personal cultural experience leads to certain viewpoints about the world, especially cultures different from our own (Williams, 2013, p. 148). A culture clash in classrooms can result due to the fact that the majority of teachers in the United States are white, whereas student diversity continues to grow. This clash is often accompanied by implicit bias or by the subconscious attitudes and stereotypes that affect our understanding and decisions (Staats, 2015–2016).

Implicit bias of teachers can lead to a deficit view of students from diverse backgrounds. From our experience, this perception of students – like English language learners (ELLs), students of color, students with learning differences, or students that live in low socioeconomic neighborhoods – can be confused with sympathy. For example we might say, "Poor Claudia just arrived here from El Salvador, she is going to have such a hard time with school" or "You know, Damion is so smart. He just doesn't seem to care or want to work." These statements are an example of low expectations for our diverse students that are derived from implicit bias (Lombardi, 2016).

In addition, this deficit model can lead to seeing behaviors of culturally diverse students as problematic (Ferlazzo, 2015c). For example, we have noticed some teachers become very confrontational with students from some ethnic groups when they are talking loudly during a collaborative activity. What could be a simple request for reducing the level of noise often becomes a negative and punitive situation. In this scenario, and so many others, our cultural lens may get in the way of effectively reaching and teaching our students.

You can't interrupt a problem if you don't recognize it first. To best support our diverse student populations, it is critical that teachers acknowledge, explore, and inform themselves about their cultural lens and the effects of implicit bias in the classroom. When we have had the topic of implicit bias arise in teacher meetings or professional development, we have heard, or perhaps even participated in, thoughts like "But I am not racist!" or "You know, we can't ignore that these kids come from negative situations and are hard to teach." Simply put, many of us become defensive instead of taking a step back and reflecting about what biases we may bring to any given situation and what we can do about them.

Here are some ideas for exploring our own cultural lens in the classroom:

- Educate Yourself About Implicit Bias: Developing an awareness of our cultural lens can help us interrupt implicit bias. We have found the following elements of implicit bias to be important for teachers in developing their awareness of their cultural lens:

  - Implicit bias comes from our unconscious mind and does not necessarily align with our intentions or practices (Staats, 2015–2016).

  - The rigor of our work as teachers may make us more susceptible to rely on implicit bias. For example, the fact that teachers make multiple quick judgments in the classroom in any given minute – such as when to provide more support versus punitive consequences for a student not completing an assignment – means that our implicit bias is likely to come into play (www.aft.org/ae/winter2015-2016/staats, https://hechingerreport .org/20-judgments-a-teacher-makes-in-1-minute-and-28-seconds).

  - According to *many* studies, our implicit bias plays a major role in disciplinary action, grading, and meeting the needs of students of color who learn differently (Balonon-Rosen, 2016; Scialabba, 2017).

  - Teachers, being some of the most committed people to children's success, should be the most invested in learning about implicit bias: the pervasiveness of our subconscious bias can directly limit our biggest goal as educators for the most vulnerable students – learning. For example, when facilitating a more complex interactive activity in class, our unchecked implicit bias can affect the way we handle group participation: a student's loud interactions can be interpreted as disorderly when perhaps they were fully engaged. In our experience, quiet behaviors do not always equate to engagement (Balonon-Rosen, 2016).

For more resources about this topic (including how to test your implicit bias online!) please refer to the Technology Connections section.

- Observe Teachers Who Are Culturally Responsive: From our experience, observing culturally responsive teachers can be one of the most effective strategies to interrupt implicit bias in our classrooms. We all know them (and if you don't, look for them!) – the teachers that reach the kids many others don't and help them make meaningful progress in their academic skills. Taking the time to observe teachers who have been successful in tackling the opportunity gap (unequal access to education, resources, or opportunities) can provide helpful ideas.

  A few years ago, our administrative team placed teacher observations (not critiques) as a top priority. In teams of three or four, we rotated through a few different classrooms. During one round, we were focusing on how teachers utilized writing assignments in social studies. We *saw* how one teacher utilized writing prompts to help students make a personal connection to social studies. Students were asked to critically think about "upstanders" and "bystanders" when learning about the Holocaust. Not only were students asked to identify these figures in the content, but they were also directed to apply this to their own lives: "Please share a time in your life where you feel like you stood up for what is right. Then, share a time in your life when you wish you would have done so, but did not. Explain why for both." Next, as a model, the teacher provided personal examples from her life. For more about the benefits of observing colleagues, please refer to Shane Safir's (2016) article "5 Keys to Challenging Implicit Bias."

- Utilize Teacher Reflection Structures: In her book *Culturally Responsive Teaching and The Brain: Promoting Authentic Engagement and Rigor Among Culturally and Linguistically Diverse Students,* Zaretta Hammond (2014) – former teacher, consultant, and leader of educational equity for over 20 years—discusses the benefits of "Mindful Reflection." This strategy, designed by Barbara J. Dray and Debora Basler Wisneski, can help teachers identify and counter implicit bias in daily interactions with students (Ferlazzo, 2015c). When an incident has occurred in class like a student outburst or other negative interaction, the teacher can use this structure to evaluate it through three lenses: description, interpretation, and evaluation. While withholding judgment, the teacher writes a description of the event, in literal terms, without judgment. Then, the teacher needs to interpret: what does it mean to them when this type of behavior occurs? After these two steps, teachers reflect on the initial judgment they placed on the behavior, and consider the clarity or insight that might be gained from their interpretation.

Hammond also recommends reflecting on how the same incident might be interpreted or judged differently if it was a student from a different background. We have been surprised with the realizations we have had through this type of reflection – especially when comparing our reactions to similar behaviors from different students. For example, after "patting ourselves on the back" for our positive and affirming handling of a specific student's misbehavior, we soon had similar issues with another student – which we did not handle positively. This second student was sent out of class. After using the Mindful Reflection, we immediately realized, with dread, how the behaviors were not only identical, but the students were from different ethnicities.

This reflective practice helped us to consider the possible role of our implicit bias and has prompted us to be more thoughtful when handling behavioral issues in the classroom. In our experience, writing *portions* of this reflection can be especially powerful. Yet, considering time constraints, thoughtful reflection and a quick discussion with a colleague can be an option, as well.

Do My Words with Students, Colleagues, and the Community Reflect a Culturally Responsive Mindset?

The language choices we make can play a big role in reaching – or alienating – students of diverse backgrounds. We have found that our word choices in areas like student names, conversations with colleagues, and how we speak about our school site are a reflection of our CRT mindset – or lack of one.

Making a sincere and concerted effort to learn students' names, as well as their correct pronunciations, is a simple and powerful way to help students feel validated in class. Furthermore, teachers are often perceived as caring when they know their students' names (Cooper, Haney, Krieg, & Brownell, 2017, p. 1).

Keeping *our* cultural lens in mind (as addressed in the first question of the Application) is important when confronted with names we find unfamiliar. Comments like "Well, that's different!" when trying to pronounce the name of a student can make him/her feel like an outsider. Instead, in the first few days of the school year, we make sure to prioritize the learning of student names.

By introducing and using the language of a culturally responsive teacher, we can provide a much-needed contrast to dialogue or narratives that perpetuate stereotypes or deficit-based thinking. For example, at a meeting where we were discussing scaffolding strategies for longer writing assignments in world history, one teacher commented, "Look, *these* kids are just not going to do everything. We need to be practical with our goals." We calmly highlighted that statement's deficit mindset by saying "What exactly do you mean by 'these' kids?" This exchange led to a productive conversation of *how* we talk about our students and the implications of our language choices.

The language we use when speaking about our students with friends, family, and other educators is another opportunity to dispel myths and stereotypes about urban schools. Family members or friends have asked us why would we ever teach *there*, or talk about our student population like they were a lost cause. The opposite perspective isn't much better. We have been given the "You're a hero!" speech for trying to save *those* kids and being commended for teaching in *that* neighborhood. We like to think of our responses as an opportunity to refute the negative hype and dispel ignorance. We share how fortunate we are for working here, brag about our students' academic prowess, and give examples of how our diversity is one of the biggest assets of our school. Additionally, we share these feelings with our students.

Here are some ideas to reflect a culturally responsive mindset with our words:

- Practicing Names Before School Starts: Our colleague Nichole Scrivner gave us this helpful tip – a day or two before school starts, a teacher could look up class rosters and identify names that may be challenging to pronounce. She practices them out loud, prior to meeting the student. A teacher could also ask colleagues about the pronunciation or look up how to pronounce it online. Another idea that can help a teacher *remember* how to say a name correctly is to write that student's name phonetically on a personal copy of a roster, seating chart, or on a sticky-note.

- Name Tents: In the first few days of school, we provide students with construction paper, which they fold in half and stand on their desks to make "name tents." We give students a chance to write their name on one side of the tent in large letters. On the other side of the tent we ask them to respond to a simple get-to-know-you question that also introduces them to the class subject. In this way, one side of the tent serves as a helpful reminder of that student's name while the other can be shared to learn more about the student. For example, we ask our geography students, "What is your favorite place in the world and why?" Each day, for the first week or so, students are not only directed to place their name tent on their desk, but we also ask a handful of students to introduce themselves to the class and share their response to the question. We do this every day until everyone has had a chance to share. The visibility of the name tents and the short student presentations help everyone remember names.

- How We Refer to People in Challenging Situations: When studying social issues in social studies like homelessness, addiction, and ICE raids and deportations, we need to remember that there is a high chance students in our class have been affected by at least one of these issues – if not all three. The words we commonly use for people affected by these situations have the potential to be dehumanizing. For example, when discussing local initiatives to address homelessness in government, one of our students shared, comically, that he once saw a "hobo" talking to himself and acting "crazy." We responded by thanking the student for making connections to what we were studying, but shared that words like "hobo" and "crazy" can be insulting. In fact, we explain, there are students at our school who have family members that are homeless or who have been homeless themselves. Almost immediately, one of our students quietly shared: "My uncle has been homeless for years. We try to go look for him to take him food, but sometimes we just can't find him. It is really hard for my family. My mom and grandma are always worried." We thanked that young man for sharing something so difficult and asked the rest of the class to be careful with their words because they might be describing someone in our classroom or someone we love. It is important to remember, as always, to follow up with students who share these kinds of difficult situations.

How Am I Building Authentic Relationships and Classroom Community with My Students?

A major thread in CRT is building genuine relationships with our students and creating a classroom environment in which they develop these kinds of relationships with each other. A welcoming classroom environment is especially important for our students who already deal with discrimination or a sense of "otherness" in their daily lives. In addition, research has shown the important role a strong classroom community can play in the academic success of student groups who are often marginalized by schools (Krasnoff, 2016, p. 9).

A key is to create *authentic* relationships and community from the beginning (the first day of school) and in a variety of structured ways in class throughout the year. In our early years of teaching, we thought that randomly facilitating icebreaker activities would automatically translate into deep respect between all members of the classroom. We quickly learned that a 30-minute activity did inject energy, but did not address more serious issues in our classroom: students giggling when a student's summary of a historical event isn't accurate, students feeling emotionally "unsafe" and refusing to participate in a debate in a government class, or even hesitating to share personal or cultural connections to subjects like immigration, or xenophobia in a unit on industrialism in a world history class.

For this reason, from the first day of school, we make community building a priority. We push back against colleagues who worry about not being able to "cover all the content" or complain that they are "not good at that touchy-feely stuff." We ask "Have you had challenging students that have derailed your well-prepared lessons?" and "Do students frequently give up or not even attempt challenging work in your classroom?" A "yes" to either of these questions means community building and investing in authentic relationships is not an "extra," but a necessity.

In addition to the questions above, we also ask ourselves the following ones when assessing our efforts to build authentic relationships with our students:

- *What do I do and say in the classroom that shows students I really believe in them?*
- *Do my students respect me or do they just like or fear me?*
- *What am I doing to earn not only their respect, but also their trust?*
- *What am I doing that is supportive (or detrimental) to my most insecure students?*

Here are a variety of relatively simple ideas that we employ in our social studies classes in response to these questions. Nothing is a "magic bullet." What is true for all strategies is true here: some ideas are more effective with some students and not so effective with others. The key is novelty, intention, and constant reflection.

- Beginning of the Year Questionnaire: We like to have students complete Figure 18.1: Beginning of Year Questionnaire in the first few days of school. This modified version of Larry Ferlazzo's (2019, August 26) student survey gives students an opportunity to guide us to better serve them as individuals. Questions like "What name would you like to be called in class?" and "What are three things you would like me to know about you?" can help open a line of communication between teacher and students. In addition, it can help them feel acknowledged and valued. Especially as social studies teachers, this form can also be an opportunity to explore student perceptions of the subject with questions like "What has your experience in social studies classes been like? Please be honest and explain your response with an example." *The key is to make sure you read the questionnaires!*

- Being a Warm Demander: This term refers to a teaching style that Zarretta Hammond (2014), author of *Culturally Responsive Teaching and the Brain,* identifies as effective with students who have been marginalized in schools. Holding high standards and encouraging "productive struggle" (giving students opportunities to work through difficulties before teachers jump in to offer assistance) are key elements of being a "warm demander" and building authentic relationships with students (Blackburn, 2018). This teaching approach includes "building rapport and trust" (following through with positive phone calls home), expressing warmth "through nonverbal ways" (leaning down by their desk to meet at eye level when talking), and asking about important people in their lives (https://crtandthebrain.com/wp-content/uploads/Figure-6.2_Warm-Demander-T-Chart.jpg). Especially when we are guiding students through a difficult task like an extended evidence-based essay, these "teacher moves" build the relationships that encourage students to step up when challenged academically.

- Community Circles (also known as Restorative Circles) – Using this strategy to build classroom community through discussing real issues in and outside the classroom has been a game changer in our practice. Community Circles are structured activities in which students take turns discussing a specific issue or topic. We begin by moving chairs or desks into a large circle. Then, we introduce a talking piece (a small item students can easily hold). We explain to a student that whoever is holding the talking piece has the floor while everybody else has the opportunity to listen. Guidelines are introduced to create a space of respect and inclusion like "Show respect by listening" and "Help build our community by sharing your thoughts." Then, the facilitator (usually the teacher, but eventually may be a student) poses open-ended questions to help students explore feelings around a certain topic (classroom issues such as cheating or community issues like immigration raids). After a question is asked, the talking piece is passed around and students take turns answering. Passing is allowed but participation is always encouraged. We have used this process to address social and emotional topics like empathy and goal setting, as well as content. Figure 18.2: Senior Year History Community Circle shows examples of the types of questions we use to acknowledge the mixed feelings 12th graders may have about their future, while also helping them connect to the class content. The nonaccusatory tone and structure of this strategy is especially powerful when we have used it to explore more difficult topics: poor behaviors with subs, more serious issues like local police shootings, or provocative subjects in the curriculum like voting rights, the effects of nationalism, and the cost/benefit of war. We have also provided Figure 18.3: Community

Circle Template that can be used as a planning tool for any community circle. We like how Marieke van Woerkom's article "Building Community with Restorative Circles" (van Woerkom, 2018) provides an additional breakdown of this strategy.

How Are My Social Studies Content Choices Reflective of My Students' Everyday Lives?

Although some states are adopting ethnic studies curriculum that specifically teaches about people of color and systems of oppression, there is no doubt that fundamental curriculum change can be slow. Many of our students, including young women and students belonging to the LGBTQ+ community, rarely learn about people like themselves in our often Eurocentric social studies textbooks.

By intentionally incorporating content examples that represent our students' backgrounds, struggles, and daily lives, we can make social studies classrooms a place where students see themselves. In other words, students can come to understand the relevance of history, government, economics, and geography. These types of connections with the content can lead to deeper engagement in social studies while also encouraging civic involvement (Korbey, 2018).

Here are some ideas and resources we use to challenge the traditional narrative conveyed in many social studies textbooks and make room for perspectives that represent our diverse student population:

- Thematically Teaching About Marginalized Groups: Instead of teaching social studies topics chronologically, we like to organize content thematically – when possible. For example, we don't use a chronological approach when teaching about colonization because it tends to glorify European conquest. Instead, we present our students with case studies that emphasize how indigenous people resisted colonizers and preserved their cultural identity. We try to represent populations from different regions of the world – Natives in both North and South America, African tribes, Polynesian kingdoms, and kingdoms in India.

- Inclusion of Diverse Primary Sources: Thanks to dynamic and rich primary source databases like Gilder-Lehrman (www.gilderlehrman.org) and the Library of Congress (www.loc.gov/collections), social studies teachers can find a variety of documents or media that represent diverse groups throughout history. Better yet, a few short mini-lessons on how to navigate the sites can empower students to find primary sources of diverse historical figures for themselves. For example, when studying philosophers in government or economics, students can research documents or artifacts that reflect the thoughts of influential leaders from a variety of different ethnic groups. For example, we expose students to Chanakya, an Indian philosopher who is credited with contributing to classic economic thought, and Xun Kuang, a Confucian philosopher known for his ideas on social hierarchy and power.

- Not Shying Away from Social Justice Issues: When it comes to the development of societies, the story is rarely rosy. Yet, history is often told in a simplistic, and many times, "one viewpoint" manner. For example, when students are studying The Declaration of Independence, which uses key phrases like "unalienable rights" and "all men are created equal," we should not shy away from teaching that Thomas Jefferson and other Founding Fathers enslaved people. Sharing this information can enlighten our students about the complexity of famous figures and fundamental social justice issues. Or, in another unit in which students study the cycles of of xenophobic policies in the United States (Chinese Exclusion Act or deportations of Mexican Americans during the Great Depression), students can identify connections to current immigration issues like ICE raids or deportations in neighborhoods. These social justice issues should not be skipped when teaching about the history of the United States. The history of marginalized groups *is* American history. Although our more traditional training teaches us to "get through the content" and "stick to the pacing chart," we need to be critical and ask, "Who decided the content? Are the backgrounds of my students being represented?" These questions can lead us to presenting history in a more contextualized manner and also help our students further engage and understand the roots of many of the issues we have today.

- Moving Away from Victimization: Although the injustices against many groups in history must be taught, it is our responsibility to move beyond the pain inflicted and shine light on the resistance and accomplishments of these groups. For example, so many of our African American students have told us that they are tired of slavery being the only perspective on their ethnic group. They ask, "Why can't we learn about what we accomplished despite all these challenges? Weren't there black people that were not slaves?" The second question is especially disturbing – due to the lack of representation of empowered and accomplished people of color, many of our students wonder if they even existed in history! Not only is this potentially damaging to our students' self-view, it is *inaccurate*. Instead, we need to be intentional about exposing our students to historical figures or groups of people who have been "upstanders": people who have challenged injustice.

We like to ask ourselves the following questions when we are preparing to teach any topic in social studies: How will we highlight the resistance of oppressed groups? What historical examples are we going to provide to show how, despite obstacles, persistence and accomplishments were demonstrated by these groups of people? For example, when we do teach about slavery in the southern United States, we make sure to teach about the resiliency and perspectives of African American families who were enslaved. We also provide examples of how they actively fought to retain their culture and their dignity despite inhumane treatment.

- Incorporating Everyday Community Challenges: Issues like encouraging neighborhood participation in responding to the US Census, providing information about the rights of immigrants, and participating in nation-wide demonstrations about school violence have all been opportunities for our students to connect social studies content to their lives outside the four walls of our classroom. It is important for teachers to actively seek these connections and incorporate them into their curriculum. Teachers can easily learn a lot by asking students to periodically write about their worries and concerns outside of school. It can be as simple as a regular warm-up activity where students write and then share. These quick writes can then be mined for future lessons.

How Are My Teaching Strategies Culturally Responsive?

Culturally responsive teaching strategies focus on helping diverse students develop their learning capacities. Culturally responsive teaching is not a feel-good pedagogy that only focuses on cultural celebrations, music, and holidays from different ethnic groups. Yes, we should honor our students' home heritages, but only within a broader strategy of highlighting many assets throughout the curriculum.

Zarretta Hammond (2014) states what she considers to be the main goal of CRT: helping students improve "their brainpower and information processing skills" (Ferlazzo, 2015c). In an interview with Jim Knight from Instructional Coaching Group, Hammond states that teachers "look to culturally responsive teaching as a tool for engagement; yet, they continue to teach in the same way where they are doing most of the processing. Engagement comes when we are doing complex cognitive work that is fun" (Knight, 2018). In other words, we need to focus on strategies that put students in the position to actively and critically process information. Like an influential administrator of ours used to ask us (while using his hand to turn imaginary gears on the side of his head as a metaphor for processing) "Who in the room is doing the thinking? You, the students, or both?"

We hope it is evident in every chapter of this book that our activities encourage *students* to critically think about social studies while helping them develop a variety of skills – no chapters on how to lecture! Here are a few more ideas to help our diverse students build their learning capacity:

- Information Processing: In her "Ready for Rigor" framework, Zaretta Hammond (2013) identifies key characteristics of strategies that help students process information: identifying and providing appropriate challenges to stimulate brain growth, giving students opportunities to use oral strategies to process information, connecting new content to culturally relevant examples, and teaching students moves or cognitive routines that emulate "the brain's natural learning systems." For example, we utilize five phases of inductive reasoning in Chapter 4: Thematic Data Sets (considering questions, reading, and annotating for understanding, classifying/categorizing, analyzing, and applying and extending knowledge) to teach students moves to help them process text deeply.

  Prior to reading a data set about the 1920s, we introduce or provide some questions for students to consider reviewing the text. We might ask, "How were traditions challenged during this era? Who could be considered the 'winners' and 'losers' in American society during this era?" When our students read the passages in our data set about 1920s culture, we teach them how to utilize reading strategies to help them identify key facts such as the increased availability of birth control, dance crazes like the Charleston, and the rise of prohibition.

  Then, we have them look for patterns in the text and group the information into categories like "growth of the income gap," "urbanization," and "changes for women." This categorization strategy draws on the brain's innate desire to seek patterns and facilitates higher-order thinking. Students critically analyze examples for each category and create generalizations of the era – for the category of urbanization, students may note that this phenomena was driven by immigration and migration from other parts of the United States. To facilitate the application of knowledge, students can use facts from the 1920s data set to answer the following question: To what extent were the 1920s a time of opportunity for Americans?

- Culturally Relevant Writing Prompts: These types of prompts help students process social studies content by asking them to identify and explain a personal connection. For example, when studying the favelas of Brazil, we use culturally relevant prompts to help students explore the important role of music in the lives of those who live there. To help students process orally and identify a personal connection, we ask them to discuss the role of music in their own lives. We then provide the following prompt "Consider what we have read about life in the favelas. Why do you think that music plays such a powerful role in these neighborhoods? What does it provide? Use examples from the text that support your reasoning." We find that this kind of activity helps students process content more effectively because they can access prior knowledge.

In US history, we use the following series of prompts when studying the Disabilities Rights Movement in the United States in the 1960s. First we ask students, "Think of a time where you felt someone was judging you for something you had no control over – your looks, your last name, your family, your skills, and so forth. How did you respond to this unfair criticism?" After students discuss their responses, we then ask students to write about the following: "How can someone maintain their sense of dignity and identity despite constant exclusion?"

When studying different religions in world history, we provide students with a list of different values like honesty, loyalty, and so forth. Then, we provide students time to respond to the following prompt: "Review this list of values and circle the five that mean the most to you. Explain each choice." Then, after students share their choices, we ask them to write a response to the following: "Compare your list of values to those of the major religions we have been studying. Which religions are most similar to your list of values? Are you surprised? Why or why not?"

- Feedback That Promotes a Growth Mindset: When students have a growth mindset, they have an understanding that their intelligence and abilities can improve with effort. Much research has demonstrated that this type of thinking can lead to higher levels of achievement (Dr. Dweck, n.d.). A teacher can help students learn this concept by using the lesson in Chapter 19: Social and Emotional Learning. Then, social studies content can be utilized to provide real examples of growth mindset being applied by historical figures. Nelson Mandela and his fight to end Apartheid in South Africa or relentless female suffragists like Alice Paul are examples of people who achieved much by implementing a growth mindset combined with gaining the support of others. Lessons like these give us language we can use in providing feedback that encourages students to develop and maintain a growth mindset. For example, if students are starting to complain about "not getting it" despite strong effort, we can say "You don't get it *yet*. You might be having a hard time, but believe it or not, you are making progress." For more phrases that encourage effort and intellectual struggle, please refer to the free "Growth

Mindset Feedback" tool created by MindsetWorks (Growth mindset feedback, n.d.). We like to keep a copy taped up by our desk to encourage us to try different types of feedback for any kind of situation.

- Stylistic Imitations: In this activity, students stylistically imitate a text to learn about social studies content, think critically, and make deep personal connections. For example, when studying the Harlem Renaissance, we study poems by Langston Hughes to not only expose students to black culture, but to also learn about issues of black identity during the 1920s, 1930s, and 1940s. We pay special attention to Hughes' poem "Theme for English B": a poem directed to Hughes's English professor. In it, issues of race, identity, and personal struggles are interwoven into a reflection on a homework assignment. Once we have carefully analyzed the poem with reading strategies from Chapter 2: Reading Strategies, we guide students to write their own stylistic imitation of the poem and share about their race, identity, and personal preferences and struggles. We tackle the poem section-by-section as a class, and offer sentence starters from the poem that students can use. We share our own stylistic imitation of the poem as a model. Sentence frames can also be provided. When done, we have a poetry reading where students share their creation with a group of five people. Afterwards, we have students reflect on not only what they learned about themselves and others, but also what they learned about African Americans and the Harlem Renaissance.

  We have had similar success having students write stylistic imitations of portions of the Declaration of Independence where students declare freedom from something they no longer want in their life. In addition, students can write their own version of the United Nations' Universal Declaration of Human Rights where they can list specific rights that they feel young people should have in the modern world. Or, students can stylistically imitate Dr. Martin Luther King Jr.'s "I Have a Dream" speech and write about their dreams and visions for the future and society.

- Practicing Caution with Simulations: Although helping students *experience* social studies is a noble goal, it is important that teachers practice caution when considering simulations. This strategy asks students to take on a role in a certain historical period in order to develop a deeper understanding of history. According to Hasan Kwame Jeffries, history professor and host of the Teaching Hard History podcast, more harm than good can often result from this teaching strategy (Gonzalez, 2019). For example, in a simulation about the American Civil War, many students, especially students of color, would feel highly uncomfortable taking on the role of a Confederate soldier protecting the institution of slavery. In other words, we run the risk of trivializing the role of race and slavery itself in this horrific conflict. Additional simulations like pretending to be part of the Nazi Party and faithful to Hitler, or treating real-life combat zones as a choose-your-own adventure story similarly encourage students to "have fun" in situations that were and are emotionally traumatic (Onion, 2019).

On the other hand, living-history activities that include the following characteristics can be effective: not categorizing students into oppressed groups or trivializing historically traumatic events that may trigger trauma in students, and prioritizing analysis and reflection of the decisions people in history had to make by considering their circumstances (Gonzalez, 2019; Onion, 2019). Simulations about farming during the gilded age, as featured on the Teaching Channel website ("Farming in the Gilded Age," n.d.) or simulations that have students build multiple chairs (using paper cut-outs), to learn about the benefits and drawbacks of the assembly line in manufacturing ("The Industrial Revolution," n.d.), can all meet this criteria. Yet, safe simulations are few and far between: proceed with caution.

DIFFERENTIATION

Although English language learners (ELLs) easily fall into the category of students from diverse backgrounds, a culturally responsive teacher can use more explicit strategies to help students value their primary language and home country. The rush to teach immigrant students English can make them feel like their home language (L1) and experiences in their native country are a burden and not an asset. Instead, we can make space in the classroom where students can be proud of their home language and feel encouraged to "bring" their culture to school. We can promote a culturally responsive classroom by:

- Asking students to share how to say certain words in their L1.
- Encouraging the unique perspectives of students to help teach social studies content (like encouraging students to feel free to share or even help teach a unit that they may have unique background knowledge about – but *never* placing an expectation on them or putting them on the spot). For example, students who are Muslim could be invited to share details about their faith, or be a fact checker, during a unit on Islam. Or, if a teacher is planning a unit about a student's home country, asking him/her for advice, pictures, key terms, music samples, or even food ideas can enrich the study for everyone.

- Connecting students with culturally responsive literature in their language: We like to provide excerpts of literature that connect to social studies topics, but are also available in other languages. A book like *Antes De Ser Libre*, available in Spanish and English, by Julia Alvarez, shares heartbreaking stories about life under the oppressive Trujillo regime in the Dominican Republic and the difficulty of having to move to the United States. We like to use excerpts from this book when teaching about oppressive military regimes. When studying modern-day terrorism, we have used excerpts from *I Am Malala*, the autobiography of Malala Yousafzai, a young champion for educational rights who was shot by the Taliban.

Be careful not to confuse "productive struggle" with unfair hardship when working with students who learn differently. On the other hand, we should not automatically assume that students who learn differently can't benefit from a healthy challenge. We have found that quick, quiet, or even private conversations with our students can create a safe avenue of communication throughout a possibly challenging activity. For example, if we realize a task might be challenging, we first like to ask them what they think: "Do you want to try this first and then see how you feel? What part do you think you might need help with? What if I help with _____ then you can do _____?"

ADVANCED MODIFICATIONS

A project-based learning activity (PBL) can be an effective culturally responsive strategy to help students address concerns in their daily lives, connect with social studies content, and challenge them to apply academic rigor to developing solutions. See Chapter 17: Project-Based Learning for ideas.

Student Handouts and Examples

Figure 18.1: Beginning of Year Questionnaire
Figure 18.2: Senior Year History Community Circle
Figure 18.3: Community Circle Template

What Could Go Wrong?

Many people confuse culturally responsive teaching with multicultural education (celebrating diversity) and social justice education (helping students identify and study injuices). Although they do overlap and all aim to improve student outcomes, it is important to be clear on their distinctions. Culturally responsive teaching is a teaching mindset that leverages the backgrounds of our students to help them build their ability to learn (Ferlazzo, 2015c).

Teachers may believe a few engaging strategies or tricks are all that are needed to make class engaging and emotionally safe for students who have been marginalized by schools. Not only does this line of thinking dilute CRT, but also many times, this perception leads teachers to view CRT as separate from regular teaching (https://crtandthebrain.com/five-teacher-mindsets-that-undermine-crt). To maximize the benefits of CRT, it should be viewed as a holistic and continual teaching mindset. We utilize the questions in this chapter as part of our daily practice.

Technology Connections

To explore your implicit bias, test it! Thanks to the word and visual association tests created by Project Implicit (https://implicit.harvard.edu/implicit/education.html) anyone can test their implicit bias in areas such as race, skin tone, disability, and others.

For more articles and resources about implicit bias, Larry Ferlazzo's blog post "We Should Be Obsessed with Racial Inequity" (http://larryferlazzo.edublogs.org/2017/02/18/we-should-be-obsessed-with-racial-equity) is a good place to start.

Attribution

Figure 18.1: Beginning of Year Questionnaire was created by Larry Ferlazzo, an editor of this book. Our stylistic imitation activity comes from Dr. Janet Hecsh, professor at California State University, Sacramento.

Figures

What is your name? _____

Preferred pronouns? _____

What would you like to be called in class (if different from above)? _____

What are two things you would like me to know about you?

1. _____

2. _____

How would your best friend describe you? _____
_____

How would your parents/guardians describe you? _____
_____

What are at least two goals you have for yourself over the next 12 months (can include academic and nonacademic goals)?

_____

_____

I make a lot of phone calls home to make positive comments about students. I will not call home to say something not-so-positive without talking with you first. Please write here the best phone number to reach your parent or guardian:

_____

What do you feel you are good at? What are things you would like to get better at?

_____

_____

What has your experience in social studies classes been like? Please be honest and explain your response with an example.

_____

_____

_____

Figure 18.1 Beginning of Year Questionnaire *Sources:* Modified from: http://larryferlazzo.edublogs .org/2019/08/26/heres-the-questionnaire-my-students-complete-on-the-first-day-of-school.

Purpose of the Circle:
To check in on each other and reflect on the summer. We will also reflect on what we need to accomplish this year, senior year, to make our dreams and goals a reality.

Getting Our Hearts and Minds Focused (poem, quote, song to help people emotionally engage with the topic for today):
"Planning is bringing the future into the present so that you can do something about it now." – *Alan Lakein, author*

Ground Rules and Purpose of "One Mic":

1. Show respect by listening.
2. Help build our community by sharing your thoughts.
3. Agreement can be found despite different viewpoints: always remain open-minded.
4. Respect and utilize our "one mic":

Holding it gives each of us the chance to speak and be heard, and not holding it gives you the opportunity to listen to your community members. You also have the right to pass, and we can return to you once the rest of the circle has had a chance to speak. Keep in mind that to build our community, we need everyone to have a voice . . . like a democracy!

Questions to Explore Topic of the Circle:

1. What was the highlight of your summer?
2. On a scale of 1 to 5, how are you feeling about senior year? Why?
3. Let's close our eyes for a minute. Visualize the **best** version of yourself on the morning of September 1, 2020 (no longer in high school). What are you getting up to do that day? What are you working towards?
4. Let's think about our own, personal history. What is something you have been good at in the past year that can help you reach the best version of yourself this year?
5. There is a saying that we need to learn from our history to not repeat it. What is something you have struggled with in the past and would like to improve on so that you can get to the best version of yourself?

Concluding Statement and Question:
Let's not look at senior year as a list of things that need to get done. More so, let's look at senior year as the perfect opportunity to get to the best version of ourselves. Isn't that what school is all about?

Please provide one word about how you feel after today's circle.

Figure 18.2 Senior Year History Community Circle *Sources:* https://restorativeschoolstoolkit.org/sites/default/files/Community%20Building%20and%20Respect%20Agreements.pdf, www.healthiersf.org/RestorativePractices/Resources/documents/RP%20Curriculum%20and%20Scripts%20and%20PowePoints/Classroom%20Curriculum/Teaching%20Restorative%20Practices%20in%20the%20Classroom%207%20lesson%20Curriculum.pdf.

Purpose of the Circle:

Getting Our Hearts and Minds Focused (poem, quote, song to help people emotionally engage with the topic for today):

Ground Rules and Purpose of the Talking Piece:

1. Show respect by listening.
2. Help build our community by sharing your thoughts.
3. Agreement can be found despite different viewpoints: always remain open-minded.
4. Respect and utilize our "one mic":

Holding it gives each of us the chance to speak and be heard, and not holding it gives you the opportunity to listen to your community members. You also have the right to pass, and we can return to you once the rest of the circle has had a chance to speak. Keep in mind that to build our community, we need everyone to have a voice . . . like a democracy!

Questions to Explore Topic of the Circle:

1.

2.

3.

4.

Concluding Statement and Question:

Figure 18.3 Community Circle Template *Sources:* https://restorativeschoolstoolkit.org/sites/default/files/ Community%20Building%20and%20Respect%20Agreements.pdf, www.healthiersf.org/RestorativePractices/ Resources/documents/RP%20Curriculum%20and%20Scripts%20and%20PowePoints/Classroom%20Curriculum/ Teaching%20Restorative%20Practices%20in%20the%20Classroom%207%20lesson%20Curriculum.pdf

CHAPTER 19

Social and Emotional Learning

What Is It?

Social and emotional learning (SEL) refers to the knowledge *beyond* academics that students need in order to be successful in today's global society. Skills most demanded by employers include many that are social and emotional in nature (Beckford, 2018).

In this chapter, we will share content focused lessons that teach two important SEL qualities: growth mindset – the view that skills can be developed through hard work and that problems are opportunities, not obstacles – and empathy – understanding and sharing others' feelings. We have chosen these two traits because we find them to be key in developing lifelong learners and because they fit easily into many social studies topics.

Why We Like It

In our experience, developing SEL skills can greatly improve classroom culture. When we explicitly teach and reinforce growth mindset, for example, the class can develop a common language. This collective understanding can make "teacher moves" like redirecting students or encouraging a positive attitude toward learning more successful. Incorporating these skills into social studies can also help students feel more connected to the content and more supported by teachers. Both of these results can increase engagement (Zins, Bloodworth, Weissberg, & Walberg, 2007, p. 191).

We have found that creating opportunities to make connections between our content and these skills can enrich the classroom experience ("Examples," 2017, p. 2). For example, students who are better able to empathize may develop an increased social awareness. This ability can help them better understand the experiences of people in history such as the victims of Japanese American Internment during World War II or participants of the Selma to Montgomery March during the Civil Rights Movement.

We also like how incorporating SEL into the social studies classroom doesn't have to be time-consuming. It can be easy to make connections between the content and many SEL skills because of the nature of social studies. For example, when examining conflict in history, a teacher may touch on the crucial role of collaboration or effective communication in resolving tensions. Teachers can also embed elements of SEL into daily practice – briefly or in depth.

Supporting Research

A report from the Harvard Graduate School of Education notes that "Because academic and SEL skills develop and operate together, efforts to promote them should be designed to promote both at the same time" (Jones & Bouffard, 2012, p. 9). This report suggests that embedding SEL into content areas, such as social studies, is a good way to reap both academic and SEL benefits.

Extensive research indicates that the benefits of SEL include "greater well-being and better school performance" (Durlak, Weissberg, Dymnicki, Taylor, & Schellinger, 2011, p. 406). Also, including SEL in classroom instruction can improve attendance and support students in developing more positive attitudes toward themselves, others, and challenges they may face (Durlak et al., 2011, pp. 305–432).

Common Core Connections

Though the Common Core standards do not explicitly lay out guidelines, they do note the need for "wide-ranging approaches to learning" – including social and emotional development (Common Core, 2010ee, para. 6).

Additionally, embedded in the standards are "skills critical to each content area" including "problem-solving, collaboration, communication, and critical-thinking skills" (Common Core, 2010r).

Both references highlight how SEL development is necessary to reach the academic goals outlined by the Common Core.

Social Studies Connections

The National Council for the Social Studies Curriculum Standards lists "Individual Development and Identity" as one of the 10 Themes of Social Studies (NCSS, n.d.-a). In its description, this theme acknowledges the importance of students developing identity and incorporating the study of "learning, growth and interaction" (NCSS, n.d.-a).

Application

In this section, we will share two examples of mini-lessons for the explicit teaching of growth mindset and developing empathy as well as how we utilize these skills to deepen understanding in social studies. We will also discuss ideas for how to seamlessly *reinforce* these skills in future social studies lessons to help maximize student benefits.

GROWTH MINDSET MINI-LESSON

We have found that explicitly teaching about growth mindset early in the year can set clear expectations for how students should approach learning in our classrooms. It gives us language to encourage a classroom culture of academic risk-taking, monitoring mindsets, and viewing effort as key to higher achievement (Dr. Dweck, n.d.). This lesson is modified from Larry Ferlazzo's book *Helping Students Motivate Themselves* (2011, p. 7).

We begin this lesson on growth mindset by asking students to choose partners and then passing out Figure 19.1: Overcoming Adversity Matching Activity. We direct students to read through each description and match it to the correct person. After giving students some time to read and work through this task, we review and share the correct answers aloud. Then, we direct students to the prompt at the bottom of the page which asks, "What do all of these people have in common?"

We give students a few minutes to write and then call on several to share with the entire class. We create a list of their responses. Students may say things like, "they didn't give up," "they all had challenges," or "they were all successful." Then, we tell students that today we are going to be exploring something called "growth mindset," which is being demonstrated by the people described in Figure 19.1: Overcoming Adversity Matching Activity.

While our handout features a variety of people from the 1800s to more modern times, teachers could certainly modify the list of figures who overcame adversity to a group of people from a topic or time period currently being studied in their social studies class. We do our best to include people from diverse backgrounds for whatever topic is selected. For example:

- Civil Rights Activists – Martin Luther King Jr., Nina Simone, Cesar Chavez, Rosa Parks, W.E.B. Du Bois, and Malcolm X.

- Athletes – Jackie Robinson, Muhammad Ali, Pelé, Bruce Lee, Serena Williams, and Nadia Comaneci.

- Presidents – Abraham Lincoln, Franklin Delano Roosevelt, Barack Obama, Harry S. Truman, and Jimmy Carter.

After introducing students to the concept of growth mindset with the overcoming adversity matching activity, it's time to delve into the topic further. We distribute Figure 19.2: Brain Graphic Organizer and direct students to read the question at the top, "Can your brain grow?" After reading the question we ask students to choose one of two responses:

- Yes, I think the brain is like a muscle and the more you exercise it, the stronger it gets.
- No, you are born with being however smart you are and that's the way it is.

We direct students to circle the statement they most agree with and then, in two or three sentences, explain their reasoning in the space provided.

After giving students a few minutes to write, we ask them to share with a neighbor. While students are sharing, the teacher can walk around and listen in on the conversations. Then, the teacher can identify a few students with diverse responses to share with the class.

Once students have shared their answers, we show them a quick video about how the brain works. There are many videos available online that cover this idea. Videos can be found by searching for terms like "brain as a muscle" or "how to grow your brain." A couple we have used with success are similarly titled, "How to Grow Your Brain" (www.youtube.com/watch?v=GWSZ1DKjNzY) and "Brain Power" (www.youtube.com/watch?v=6f8NdC9Amhg).

While they watch the video, we ask students to do a quick 3-2-1 notes: writing down three things they learned, two questions they have, and one visual to symbolize the video. It may be helpful to show the video a second time to ensure all students are able to complete the notes.

After the viewing, we ask students to review their notes and revisit the original question "Can your brain grow?" We call on a few students to share an answer and encourage them to refer to their video notes to support their response. This final sharing step helps to solidify the concept of the brain's ability to grow.

Next, we share basic definitions for fixed mindset and growth mindset from Carol Dweck, professor of psychology and pioneer in the mindset field (Dweck, 2015). We ask students to copy down the following definitions onto Figure 19.3: Mindsets Graphic Organizer:

- Fixed mindset is the belief that a person's intelligence is fixed or stays the same.
- Growth mindset is the belief that a person's intelligence can change or develop over time.

After students copy down the definitions, we show a few videos to elaborate on growth and fixed mindset. We ask students to note down ideas they have about each mindset on their graphic organizer (Figure 19.3: Mindsets Graphic Organizer) while they watch the clips. We like to show students at least two or three of these videos which contain examples of people struggling with setbacks and ultimately trying again. A few we have used with success include: "Yoda and Growth Mindset" (www .youtube.com/watch?v=inNMktqIkh0&feature=youtu.be), "Meet the Robinsons – You Failed" (https://youtu.be/AWtRadR4zYM), and "You Can Accomplish Anything" (https://youtu.be/GyhIsFshd1E). There are more resources for growth mindset videos listed in the Technology Connections.

We wrap up the mini-lesson by instructing students to review what they have learned about growth mindset and to respond to three reflection questions:

- "Do you consider yourself a person with a fixed or growth mindset? Why?"

- "Which mindset do you think could help you the most? Why?"

- "How can you practice growth mindset in this class? Give two examples of what you might do."

After considering their own growth mindset, we ask students to return to Figure 19.1: Overcoming Adversity Matching Activity and think about how our world might be different if these people had shown a fixed mindset instead of a growth mindset. A teacher could make this into a prompt and ask students to write about it, or do a quick think–pair–share.

We've extended this activity by adding a twist on "golden lines." These short phrases are typically selections of text that jump out to the reader and are memorable for evoking emotional responses or providing critical details. In our twist, we encourage students to revisit their notes from the video clips and prompt responses, to locate golden lines and share them with the class. We also ask students to consider what a person practicing a growth mindset might say when faced with a challenge. Student phrases like "don't give up easily" and "mistakes are opportunities" may make good motivational statements to refer to during the year.

A teacher could also have students do further research on some famous figures who overcame adversity to find additional "golden lines." These golden lines from students can be put on a growth-mindset poster that can hang in the classroom as a reminder and reference. See more about golden lines in Chapter 5: Writing in Social Studies.

EMPATHY MINI-LESSON

Social studies requires students to take a deeper look at the human experience. In other words, students need to see the value of empathy to be able to apply it and better understand history. Practicing empathy can open up opportunities for better dialogue, helping students to avoid making quick judgments about a historical occurrence (Schwartz, n.d.). For example, when studying Westward Expansion, empathy can help students avoid making a quick judgment about violence committed by Native Americans in response to settlers taking their land. Another example might be to help students have a dialogue about the origin and the effect of the derogatory term *oakie* used in reference to the destitute people coming to California because of the Dust Bowl.

Empathy may also help students understand why people acted the way they did in the past and determine the significance, cause and effect, or continuity and change of historical phenomena over time (Endacott & Brooks, 2013, p. 5). For example, practicing empathy may help students better understand how fear of political and economic instability may give rise to authoritarian regimes, like what occurred in Germany during the 1930s. Helping students understand the feelings of Germans at this time may help students identify the risk of this type of event occurring again. Although it is important to steer clear of justifying authoritarian regimes, empathy can help students understand the context that can give rise to these political extremes. Empathy may also help students in economics classes to better understand the cycle of poverty when studying a concept like "working poor" – people who work but remain in poverty.

The empathy mini-lesson described here takes place after studying the "push" (what pushed people out from Europe) and "pull" (what pulled people into the United States) factors of immigration during the early nineteenth century. Though our lesson focuses on the immigrant experience from Ellis Island during this time period, it could be easily modified to connect to many topics in history by changing the photo in Figure 19.4: Ellis Island 1913. Images of historical figures and events, like the one used in this mini-lesson, can be found at websites like the Library of Congress (www.loc.gov).

We begin our lesson by distributing copies of an image of newly arrived immigrants being inspected at Ellis Island in 1913 (Figure 19.4: Ellis Island 1913). Then, students are directed to create a thought bubble above each person in the image. We direct them to write their best guess of what the person might have been thinking at the time this image was taken. This activity helps students to imagine life from another person's perspective (practicing empathy). It may be helpful for the teacher to model the first thought bubble. For example, above the baby we might draw a thought bubble that says, "I'm so tired. Where am I?"

After giving students a few minutes to complete the thought bubbles, we ask them to share one or two with a partner. Then, we call on a few students to share with the class. We often write a few students' ideas onto our own copy of the image for all to see. Students may generate comments like, "No sign of disease in this person" over the officer inspecting the immigrant's eye or "What have I done?" for the woman with a baby on her lap on the left-hand side of the image. For an example, see Figure 19.5: Ellis Island 1913 Example.

Once we generate a few examples from students, we announce that we will be learning about empathy, an important social and emotional skill, in order to better understand history. We provide students Figure 19.6: Empathy Graphic Organizer. This handout directs students to take notes from a video clip about empathy. There are many short videos about this topic – we have successfully used "Brene Brown on Empathy" (https://youtu.be/1Evwgu369Jw) as well as "The Importance of Empathy" (www.youtube.com/watch?v=UzPMMSKfKZQ&t=53s). The top part of the handout prompts students to define this social and emotional concept and to provide examples of *how* someone might practice empathy.

After watching the video clip(s), we give students time to finish their notes on the graphic organizer. Then, to reinforce the concepts covered, we direct students to share with their neighbor. For accountability purposes, we ask everyone to write down one idea from their partner and denote it with a star. We often ask a few students to share ideas, which we copy down for all to see. This sharing clarifies and reinforces the concept of empathy for students who may have struggled with taking notes on the video.

Once we have reviewed the two boxes on top of Figure 19.6: Empathy Graphic Organizer, we direct students to read and answer the writing prompt on the bottom:

> How might practicing empathy help you to better understand a situation? How might practicing empathy help others understand you?

We give students time to write, usually between 5 and 10 minutes. We then direct students to get out of their seat and share with their designated sharing partner (a partner that has been previously assigned to them). They meet with this same person each time we do this type of sharing. Considering that their designated sharing partner may not be right next to them, this strategy can provide an opportunity to get students out of their seats to practice speaking and listening skills. For more on different ways to organize student sharing, see Chapter 16: Discussions.

While they are talking, the teacher listens and jots down student examples of good ways to show empathy. Once they have returned to their seats, the teacher can share their notes with the class and might say something like, "I heard a lot of good ways to practice empathy like spending time with someone who is upset, or letting a person talk about how they are feeling." Student understanding might be clarified by hearing a variety of examples.

Next, to help deepen their understanding and relevance of the concept, students create a personal empathy map: a graphic organizer that helps students analyze a challenging moment from their own lives. This analysis is done by identifying and describing what their challenging moment looked, sounded, and felt like. We begin by distributing copies of Figure 19.7: Personal Empathy Map.

We direct students to think about a challenge they have faced – an embarrassing moment, conflict, or failure. A teacher may want to let students know ahead of time that they will be sharing this map with peers. We ask them to briefly describe this challenge in the circle placed in the middle of the page titled "My Challenge."

To scaffold this process for students, we share a teacher model Figure 19.8: Empathy Map Teacher Model. While students are working, it may be helpful for the teacher to walk around the room and check in with students, prompting those who may be having difficulty with questions like, "What do you think this event looked like from the perspective of a bystander – someone nearby who saw it?" "What might someone witnessing this event have heard?" or "Think back to when this happened, what do you remember feeling?"

Once they have completed the top portion of the graphic organizer, Figure 19.7: Personal Empathy Map, we ask students to reflect further. We give students a few minutes to write at the bottom of the page describing how others *actually* reacted during their moment of challenge and how they wish those people *would have* responded.

After giving students a few minutes to work, usually no more than five to six minutes, we ask them to turn their desks and form groups of four.

We ask each group member to share their personal empathy map. We remind students to practice active listening skills – eye contact, leaning in, nodding. Once each student has finished sharing, we ask them to respond with an empathy statement. We may provide a few examples like:

- I hear you.
- That sounds like a _____ experience.
- I can understand.
- I'm not sure how to respond, but thank you for sharing.

It is important for the teacher to be aware that some students may choose to share very difficult or even traumatic memories. In these situations, it is important for the teacher to not only support students as they share but also be prepared to follow up with a counselor if necessary.

Once all members of the group have shared, we ask students to return to their seats and again take a look at the photograph of recently arrived immigrants at Ellis Island, Figure 19.4: Ellis Island 1913. We ask them to consider what they have learned about empathy and their own reflection of a challenging experience. Using this inspiration, we have students select a person from the image and create a second empathy map for them by imagining what that person was experiencing at the time.

We provide Figure 19.9: Ellis Island Empathy Map to help guide students through the process. Each box targets the same basic concept as the first empathy map, but has been reworded as a guiding question in order to scaffold student thinking. For example, the section in the first organizer labeled "felt like" becomes "What do you think your selected person might be feeling at this moment in time?"

After giving students a few minutes to select their figure from the photo and create an empathy map, we direct their attention to the question at the bottom of the page. We ask them to take some time and think about how practicing empathy may help us to better understand history, and respond to the prompt in writing. We typically have students pair-share these responses and also call on a few students to share with the class. Students might come up with ideas like, "I never considered what the experience of immigration might be like for children, that must have been really difficult. Parents must have been really concerned about their children's future to take them on a dangerous journey to a new land" or "I realize that a mother must be very desperate to go through all these challenges in order to leave her country. It makes me wonder how bad things were at home for her to want to leave. What was it about the United States that made her want to come? This thought is making me consider modern-day immigration differently." These kinds of responses reinforce how practicing empathy can help us to carefully consider historical phenomena prior to making a judgment.

During the unit, as students learn more about the immigrant experience, they can reflect back on this exercise and compare the empathy map they created for a historical figure to actual diaries and letters from immigrants.

Note: There are many other SEL skills that can be included in social studies lessons. For lists of skills, check out The Partnership for 21st Century Skills created by the National Education Association (NEA) (www.nea.org/tools/52217.htm) and The Collaborative for Academic, Social, and Emotional Learning (CASEL) (https://casel.org/what-is-sel).

TIPS FOR REINFORCING SEL

In order for students to continue to develop SEL skills, it's helpful to reinforce them regularly. Here are a few different ways to embed the skills into any social studies course.

- Monthly themes – Choose an SEL theme for each month of the school year and look for content that may connect to the theme. This structuring can also serve as an opportunity to collaborate with other content areas. During that month, teachers can select texts and writing prompts that reflect the SEL theme. Each teacher can think about ways to incorporate the monthly theme into their classroom giving students a variety of experiences with each skill. For example, teachers could decide on the theme of goal setting for the month of October. Each teacher would then brainstorm different ways to help students to set goals and share examples of goal setting within their content. In a geography class, a student may set a goal to increase the number of countries they can identify and correctly label from 10 to 20.

- Including SEL terms into unit vocabulary lists – We share this tip in Chapter 1: A Fresh Look at Vocabulary. Teachers can discuss a list of SEL terms they would like to cover during the year and then decide which units naturally lend themselves to each SEL skill. Talking with other social studies teachers can help generate ideas for how to connect skills to the content in different ways. For example, we include the term *active listening* in our French Revolution unit for world history. We are able to make multiple connections to it through our discussion of the French citizens feeling unheard by those in power. In a unit about the foundations of American government, we can bring up the organizational and communication skills needed to manage all the different opinions of those crafting the Constitution. In an ethnic studies unit on Indigeneity, the term *empathy* comes up frequently as we read about the treatment of Native people by European colonizers who demonstrated an absence of this quality.

- Recurring structures to revisit SEL – Teachers may have success with dedicating a specific time of the week or month to work on SEL lessons. See the Technology Connections section for sites sharing SEL teaching ideas. Dedicating class time to SEL skills on a regular basis shows students that these skills are a priority. In addition, it provides frequent opportunities to practice and reflect on the growth of our skills. Explicitly pointing out how SEL skills can help students be successful in social studies can increase relevance as modeled in both mini-lessons for this chapter.

- Warm ups and/or tickets out the door – A low-prep way to encourage students to review SEL skills is to make them part of the daily warm-up or ticket out the door. Framing these types of questions through the lens of SEL can help students connect, reinforce, and practice applying SEL skills to the content and themselves. To review these skills, we might use a warm-up question like, "How might perspective taking, or seeing beyond your own point of view, have encouraged earlier involvement of the United States in World War II?" or "How can empathy or lack of empathy affect people's perspectives on US immigration policy?"

DIFFERENTIATION

Picture books can be used to teach SEL concepts in an accessible, fun way. In our experience, even high school students respond positively to this genre. In fact, people of all ages enjoy looking at images (Vercelletto, 2018). Often, children's books are based around skills or life lessons for the reader that directly correspond to the SEL competencies.

For example, teachers could use the book *Rosie Revere, Engineer* by Andrea Beaty to help *show* students growth mindset as the main character experiences multiple failures in an attempt to achieve her goal. Another book to teach growth mindset is *Beautiful Oops!* by Barney Saltzberg. These books can be resources for English language learners (ELL) who can use the images as support for understanding SEL skills. A teacher could share both books by reading them aloud and allowing students to closely view the images. Then, students could write about what happens to the main characters. This process can help students build the background knowledge they need to analyze growth mindset in social studies content. You can find lists of books to help support the teaching of SEL skills by searching online or using a site like Pinterest (www.pinterest.com), which has many lists curated by other teachers.

It could be a fun twist to have all students write their own children's books about an SEL competency using a historical event as the backdrop. For example, students could write the story of a historical figure that overcame adversity like Stephen Hawking – and have them actually read them to students at a nearby elementary school.

ADVANCED EXTENSIONS

Adding SEL components to existing assignments is a way to deepen student understanding of skills like growth mindset, empathy, communication, and collaboration. If students are writing a paper on a historical figure, for example, you could apply SEL to the essay. This may mean an essay on Ruth Bader Ginsburg would incorporate a discussion on how she used a growth mindset to help her overcome discrimination throughout her career. Another idea might be in a world history class during the study of the Indian independence movement. When preparing a presentation on the topic, students might address empathy by researching and incorporating multiple perspectives of those impacted by the movement – British, Hindus, Muslims, children, farmers, and so forth. Including these viewpoints can lead to a richer understanding of the complexity of Indian independence.

Student Handouts and Examples

Figure 19.1: Overcoming Adversity Matching Activity

Figure 19.2: Brain Graphic Organizer

Figure 19.3: Mindsets Graphic Organizer

Figure 19.4: Ellis Island 1913

Figure 19.5: Ellis Island 1913 Example

Figure 19.6: Empathy Graphic Organizer

Figure 19.7: Personal Empathy Map

Figure 19.8: Personal Empathy Map – Teacher Model

Figure 19.9: Ellis Island Empathy Map

What Could Go Wrong?

You may find that students struggle with skills like growth mindset and empathy even after teaching and reinforcing these skills regularly in the classroom. It's important to note that there is more to developing SEL skills than simply teaching them. Multiple studies show that student circumstances and issues like poverty and racism can impact our students' ability to develop cognitively, socially, and emotionally. For more on the research behind these challenges check out Larry Ferlazzo's blog post "The Best Articles About the Study Showing Social Emotional Learning Isn't Enough" (2013, August). Teaching SEL skills is important, but must go hand-in-hand with culturally responsive teaching and assisting our students to understand the social/political/economic challenges they might face and preparing them with the skills to successfully combat them.

Another challenge is not reinforcing SEL consistently. The best way we have found to deal with this is to work with our colleagues to develop a plan. Though we know this isn't feasible at all school sites, when you can, work together with other teachers to support SEL. Developing a common language when talking about these important skills can help students to transfer them from one classroom to another.

Technology Connections

You can use technology to reinforce SEL skill development in various ways. For example, to help students visualize growth mindset, we use multiple video clips from Larry Ferlazzo's blog post "New Video Clips Demonstrating a Growth Mindset in Action" (http://larryferlazzo.edublogs.org/2015/07/02/new-video-clips-demonstrating-a-growth-mindset-in-action).

One thing we make sure to do early on in the year is to have students complete an online self-assessment for SEL. There are many to be found on the web, but we have used the one at Panorama Education (www.panoramaed.com/social-emotional-learning) with success. This kind of self-assessment may help students and teachers see areas that may benefit from more explicit social and emotional-based content lessons.

Another way to incorporate technology is to have students create short videos on different SEL skills that can be posted online and viewed by other students. This can be done by using an app like Instagram. For more on how to use Instagram in the classroom, visit Larry Ferlazzo's blog post "Using Instagram, Bloom's Taxonomy & Student Interest as a Fun Part of A Semester Final" (http://larryferlazzo .edublogs.org/2014/05/11/using-instagram-blooms-taxonomy-student-interest-as-a-fun-part-of-a-semester-final).

Find many SEL lesson ideas at "'Best' Lists of the Week: Social Emotional Learning Resources" (http://larryferlazzo.edublogs.org/2018/04/15/best-lists-of-the-week-social-emotional-learning-resources).

Attribution

Portions of the growth mindset mini-lesson were modified from Larry Ferlazzo's (2011, "Helping") book *Helping Students Motivate Themselves* and portions of the blog posts "A Look Back: My Growth Mindset Lessons Usually Go Well But What I Did Today Was the Best Yet" (Ferlazzo, 2019, August) and "Reading Logs Part Two of How Students Can Grow Their Brains" (Ferlazzo, 2009, September).

Figures

Read the descriptions below of challenges that were overcome by some of the most famous people in history. After reading, choose the famous person that you think matches.

Stephen Hawking	Marie Curie	
Oprah Winfrey		Sonia Sotomayor
	Jesse Owens	

1. After beginning life as child who struggled frequently with illness this person went on to become an Olympic track and field star. A record this athlete set at the Olympic games stood for 25 years. Though winning four gold medals did not protect this athlete from experiencing racism and discrimination at home in the United States, he is celebrated for defying Hitler's theory of Ayran race supremacy during the 1936 games.

2. Today, she's a billionaire and one of the most influential women in the world, but her early life was full of difficulties. These challenges included abuse, running away from home, pregnancy, and the loss of a child at the age of 14.

3. In a time where women in the field of science were often discriminated against, this person went on to have multiple groundbreaking scientific discoveries in the area of radioactivity. Many awards were bestowed to this incredible scientist, including two Nobel Prize awards.

4. After being diagnosed with amyotrophic lateral sclerosis (ALS) and given two and a half years to live by doctors at the age of 21, this scientist went on to defy all odds, contributing to 21 books through the use of a speech synthesizer and spending 30 years as a Lucasian Professor of Mathematics at Cambridge.

5. This person grew up in poverty in the Bronx. Her father died when she was only nine, leaving her single mom to take care of the family. Her mom pushed her in school, encouraging her to become fluent in English. She didn't give up even when she scored low marks on her first midterm paper in college; instead, she took extra English and writing classes. Eventually, she would become the first Latina Supreme Court justice.

Prompt – What do these people have in common?

Figure 19.1 Overcoming Adversity Matching Activity *Sources:* www.biography.com/scientist/stephen-hawking, www.nobelprize.org/prizes/physics/1903/marie-curie/biographical, https://www.biography.com/athlete/jesse-owens, www.oprah.com/own-oprahshow/the-secret-that-oprah-hid-for-years-video, https://www.biography.com/law-figure/sonia-sotomayor.

Brain Graphic Organizer

"Can your brain grow?"

Circle which answer you agree with most and write two to three sentences about *why* you agree.

Yes, I think the brain is like a muscle and the more you exercise it, the stronger it gets.	No, you are born with being however smart you are and that's the way it is.

Brain Video – 3,2,1 Notes

Write three things you learned from the video

Write two questions you have after watching the video

Create a visual to represent the video

Figure 19.2 Brain Graphic Organizer

Mindsets Graphic Organizer

Fixed Mindset is. . .	Growth Mindset. . .
Fixed Mindset – Notes from video	Growth Mindset – Notes from video

Do you consider yourself a person with a fixed or growth mindset?

How can you practice growth mindset in this class? Give two examples of what you can do.

Figure 19.3 Mindsets Graphic Organizer

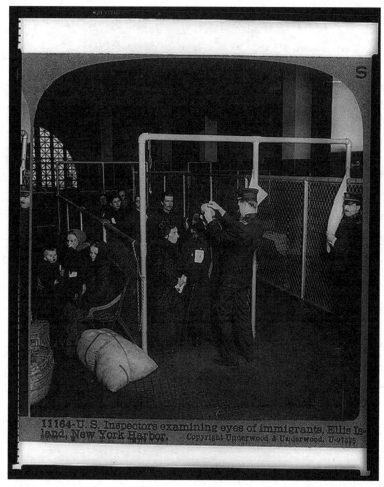

Figure 19.4   Ellis Island 1913   *Source:* www.loc.gov/pictures/item/97501532.

Figure 19.5 Ellis Island 1913 Example *Source:* www.loc.gov/pictures/item/97501532.

"What Is Empathy?"

While watching the video clip, copy down your ideas in the chart below:

Empathy is . . .
To show empathy someone may say/do . . .

Writing Prompt – How might practicing empathy help you to better understand a situation? How might practicing empathy help others understand you?

Figure 19.6 Empathy Graphic Organizer

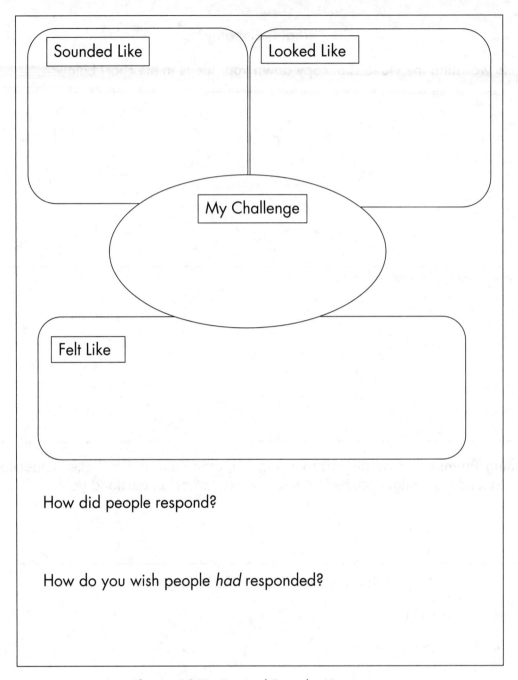

Sounded Like

Looked Like

My Challenge

Felt Like

How did people respond?

How do you wish people *had* responded?

Figure 19.7 Personal Empathy Map

Sounded Like

I was very snappy with my responses and quick with my directions.

Looked Like

My facial expression was not a happy one, I had bags under my eyes, and was not wearing my normal professional clothes.

My Challenge

Not having patience in my classroom due to not sleeping enough because of my new babies (twins) at home.

Felt Like

It felt like everyone was testing my patience on purpose. It felt awful, like I couldn't do anything right. I was exhausted and could only focus on feeling tired instead of thinking about the challenges people around me might be dealing with.

How did people respond?

Many adults were understanding; I assume because many have experienced something similar with their children. Some students were upset by my lack of patience.

How do you wish people *had* responded?

I wish everyone had told me they understood what it's like to be so tired. I also think it might have helped to hear someone say that I wasn't alone.

Figure 19.8 Personal Empathy Map Teacher Model

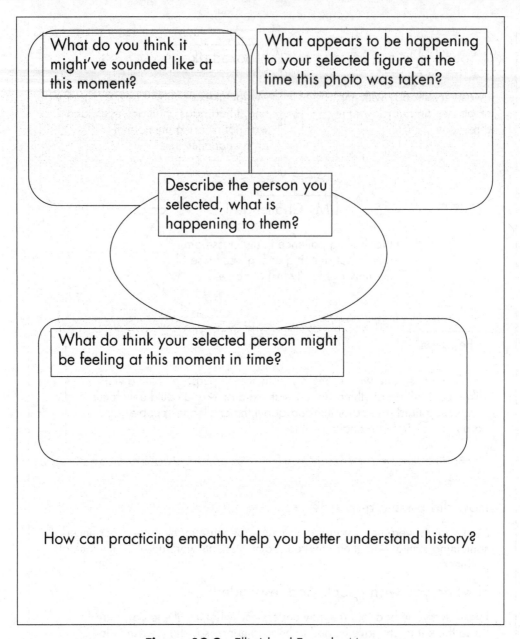

What do you think it might've sounded like at this moment?

What appears to be happening to your selected figure at the time this photo was taken?

Describe the person you selected, what is happening to them?

What do think your selected person might be feeling at this moment in time?

How can practicing empathy help you better understand history?

Figure 19.9 Ellis Island Empathy Map

CHAPTER 20

Assessment

What Is It?

Assessments are tools that teachers and students can use to monitor, evaluate, and judge the progress or comprehension of both skills and content knowledge ("Assessment," 2015). Assessments can provide a heightened understanding of student comprehension, which can be used to guide effective teaching practice.

In this chapter we begin by explaining the difference between formal and informal assessment. Knowing the difference between these two categories of assessment can allow for a teacher to effectively implement evaluation. Then, we share what we have learned about three different types of assessments: diagnostic (helps determine students' prior knowledge), formative (conducted during the learning process to guide teaching), and summative (assesses learning outcomes at the end of instruction). We also provide content examples for employing these types of assessments – in a variety of ways – for any social studies classroom. Further, we explain the importance – and provide examples of – student self-assessment.

Why We Like It

We like how the strategies in this chapter help us to use assessment more effectively. We are better prepared to address the specific needs of our students when we use meaningful assessments on a regular basis. This awareness can lead to higher academic outcomes for students and helps them see the value of assessment beyond just a grade.

Supporting Research

Performing diagnostic or pre-assessments can help teachers to understand what a student's misconceptions, ideas, and beliefs are about a topic of study (Committee on Developments in the Science of Learning, 2000, p. 10).

During instruction, formative assessment provides opportunities for students' thinking to become more visible to teachers and themselves. This information can then be used to provide more effective feedback and improve instruction (Committee on Developments in the Science of Learning, 2000, p. 19).

Common Core Connections

To monitor student progress, the standards encourage assessments that "provide teachers with specific feedback to help ensure students are on the path to success" (Common Core, 2010ff).

Social Studies Connections

The National Council for the Social Studies notes that a range of assessments should be used in order to support college and career readiness (NCSS, 2010, p. 59).

Application

In this chapter, we will discuss two categories of assessment (informal and formal) as well as three different types (diagnostic, formative, and summative). We have also included a discussion on the importance of student self-assessments as well as examples for implementation.

As mentioned previously, assessments generally fall into two categories, formal and informal (see Table 20.1: Types of Assessment). Formal assessments are typically

Table 20.1 Types of Assessment

Informal	Formal
— **Provide ongoing monitoring of student progress** — **Tend to be diagnostic and formative**	— **Analysis of student learning** — **Tend to be summative**
Journaling Exit Slips Four Corners Continuum Thumbs Up/Down Creating a Visual KWL Chart Ranking Think and Ink Concept Map/Web One-Sentence Summary	Test Essay Portfolio Short-Answer Summary Student-Created Tests Answer → Question Debate Creating a Podcast Multisource Analysis Letter to a Future Student Self-Grading

larger stakes and structured, often in the form of tests, quizzes, and projects at the end of a learning segment.

Informal assessments can be embedded into classroom activities, such as a quick thumbs up or down to show understanding of a concept. These assessments show student progress and comprehension at a specific point in time and help teachers make decisions about future instruction ("Formal Assessment," n.d.).

Teachers can use both categories of assessment results to adjust the pace, duration, or focus of classroom activities. In addition to different categories of assessment, there are also different types. There are three common types of assessments: diagnostic and formative assessments (which tend to be informal) and summative (which tend to be formal). The following sections of this chapter will explain each type of assessment and when teachers can use them. To conclude the Application section, we explain student self-assessment, the purpose, and ways to facilitate it.

In our experience, the best time to start thinking about assessment is in the beginning stages of planning a unit. In other words, having clear goals for a unit improves assessment because teachers can thoughtfully craft instruction targeted toward the objectives (Darling-Hammond & Adamson, 2010, p. 24).

By planning assessment ahead of time, evaluation of student progress can be embedded throughout the course of study for both content and skills: the teacher can pinpoint places in the unit to assess student progress and use the results to adjust instruction. Of course, due to time and planning constraints, we may not always preplan *every* assessment in detail.

DIAGNOSTIC

Diagnostic assessments, sometimes called pre-assessments, occur at the start of a unit or topic and determine what a student may already know ("Assessment," 2015).

The purpose of diagnostic assessments is to learn what students know (prior knowledge and skills), in order to plan instruction for what they don't know. It's important to keep in mind that students are not expected to know everything or sometimes even *anything* on a diagnostic assessment.

With any pre-assessment, it is important to be clear with students that the results of these evaluations will only be used to guide learning, not as a judgment or score against the student. Caution must be taken in implementing diagnostic assessments. Some argue that pre-assessments can serve as a failure experience for students, which can impact their attitude toward learning (Guskey, 2018, p. 1). However, pre-assessments can still be a valuable resource when they are carefully crafted and implemented to avoid students walking away with a negative experience.

For example, in our geography classes we used to give a diagnostic world map test. Many students were only able to label two or three countries. They walked away with a very negative feeling about the experience, which tended to carry over into map instruction. Instead, we modified this diagnostic by creating an activity in which a *group* of students are given a blank map and a list of 50 countries. Students then work together using the list to label as many countries as they can. This structure leads to a more positive experience for students, and we still are able to get a basic understanding of their world map knowledge.

Diagnostic Assessment Examples

- KWL Chart – Students are given a topic and begin by writing down what they already <u>K</u>now. Then, students can generate questions for what they <u>W</u>ant to know. We typically ask students to come up with five items for each and then share out create a class list (the "L" or what I <u>L</u>earned section, where students add new information as they study the topic, can be used as a Formative Assessment later on during instruction).

  - For example, prior to teaching about the US Constitution in a government course, we ask students to write what they already know about the document outlining our first system of government, the Articles of Confederation. After writing a few ideas in the K section of their papers, students share with a partner. We ask them to copy one idea from their neighbor, denoting it with a star for accountability purposes. Then, we ask students to generate questions about the Articles of Confederation in the W section of the chart. Before moving on to teaching the Constitution, we make sure to plan instruction that will help address any misconceptions, or provide pertinent information about the Articles of Confederation that is missing in the K section of the chart.

  - Another idea is to have students apply this strategy prior to teaching about a specific country in a geography class. Students could be given the name of the country (Mexico, for instance) and generate a list of five things they already know about the country. Then, students can identify five questions they have about Mexico. Later students add to "what I learned" as they discover key information or answers to their questions, through their study of the country.

  - Students might also use a KWL chart to explore what they know about a skill, like citing evidence in writing. Students can write a list of what they already know about citing evidence, generate questions about the skill, and, after a lesson on the topic, add new information to the last section of the chart.

  - Students could also create a KWL poster as a small group. Prior to starting a unit on a world history topic like the Aztec Empire, they might work together to generate a list of things they already know in the K section of their chart. Then, again working together, they can come up with a few questions for the W section. Later, after reading an article, and viewing related images as a group, students can come back to the chart to add to the L column.

- Ranking – Students are given lists of concepts, people, or vocabulary words from an upcoming unit of study. They rank the concepts by placing a 1, 2, or 3 next to them: 1 means unfamiliar, 2 means some knowledge, and 3 represents good understanding. For those marked 3, we have students write brief summaries of what they know in order to check for misconceptions.

  - For example, before a unit on the Civil Rights Movement, a teacher may ask students to rank some well-known and lesser-known civil rights activists by their level of familiarity with each by ranking them 1, 2, or 3. They may know more about Martin Luther King Jr. than John Lewis, for example. Students can then list what they know about each person they marked as a 2 or 3. This type of ranking can help both students and teachers see which concepts, words, or people students are more familiar with and those they still need to learn.

  - Another idea is to use this strategy prior to teaching about the American Revolution. Students are provided with a list of the causes of the conflict and then asked to rank them. They may know more about taxation without representation than the Boston Massacre (or very little about either). Students can then share with a neighbor what they know about the items they marked a 2 or 3.

  - Students might also use this ranking strategy with economics concepts like *scarcity, want, need,* or *production.* Working with a partner, students can place a 1, 2, or 3 next to each item to show familiarity. Then, students might make a few bullet points to summarize their ideas about each item. For the items ranked 1 (least familiar) students might create a question or make a prediction instead.

- "Think and Ink" – Prior to teaching a unit, present students with guiding or essential questions. These questions about the upcoming topic can help a teacher assess prior knowledge. After selecting two or three questions, we ask students to first "think" and then "ink" (or write about) what they already know. This process could also be done collaboratively with a partner or in a small group.

  - For example, prior to teaching about the growth of transportation in a unit on westward expansion in US history, we may ask students an essential question like, "Should the 'big four' business people behind the transcontinental railroads be considered 'captains of industry' or 'robber barons'? and a guiding question such as "How were Chinese immigrants working on the railroad treated?" See Chapter 11: Questions for Learning for more information on essential and guiding questions.

- In a geography class, prior to teaching about cuisine in France, we could ask students "How might where you live determine what you eat?" or "How might the geography of France impact the regional cuisine?"

- When studying the rise of nationalism in world history, we might ask students "What elements create national identity?" or "What impact did ethnicity, political affiliation, and religion have on national identity in Germany prior to World War II?"

- Concept Web – Students are provided a word bank of terms related to a given topic. Then, students use the provided web to show their prior knowledge about the relationships between the terms. By focusing on making connections between terms, students are given an opportunity to show prior knowledge – without having to provide definitions.

  - For example, Figure 20.1: Scientific Revolution Concept Web shows a concept web for the Scientific Revolution. A word bank has been provided with terms related to the topic. To discover what students already know about the scientific revolution they are directed to place the terms into the circles and connect them with lines. Students write on each line how the items are possibly related. The provided example connects Isaac Newton to the Scientific Revolution by noting on the connecting line that he was a "scientist during this time period."

  - This strategy could also be done in a US history course prior to learning about Reconstruction. Students might be given the concept Reconstruction and the terms *14th Amendment, black codes, carpetbagger, freedmen,* and so on. Then, students can connect words they think are related, writing *how* they are related on the connecting line. This connection might be something like connecting the terms *freedmen* and *black codes* by writing "black codes were placed against freedmen during the period of Reconstruction."

  - In another version of a concept web, students can show what they already know about the causes and effects of a historical event like the Spanish-American War in a world history class. Students are provided with a bank of statements. These statements might be something like "end of Spanish colonial rule in the Americas," "yellow journalism," or "sinking of the American battleship *USS Maine*." Then, students place the statements on a chart divided into two sections, labeled *cause* and *effect*.

FORMATIVE

Formative assessment is an in-process evaluation on student progress toward pre-determined goals ("Formative Assessment," 2014). These types of evaluations are often embedded into instruction frequently during the teaching of a unit. Formative assessment is generally low stakes in terms of impacting student grades.

Teachers can use this type of evaluation to see how students have improved their knowledge of a topic over time. Instead of waiting for a unit test to see that students don't understand what you thought they did, a teacher can assess progress along the way and adjust instruction. For this reason, many education experts see formative as the most powerful of the three types of assessment (Black & Wiliam, 1998).

Formative assessment also helps to inform the *student* of progress made toward learning goals (Garrison & Ehringhaus, n.d.). This means effective formative assessment includes feedback for students to see where they need to improve. Good feedback has three elements, according to researchers Paul Black and Dylan Wiliam, "recognition of the desired goal, evidence about present position, and some understanding of a way to close the gap between the two" (Black & Wiliam, 1998, p. 6). In other words, students need to be aware of the goal, their current standing, and what their next steps should be in order to achieve the learning goal. Formative assessment offers the opportunity to provide this kind of effective feedback and reflection on it.

Formative Assessment Examples

- Thumbs up/down – After asking students a question to check comprehension, students show thumbs up to represent "Yes, I get it" or thumbs down to show "I'm still confused." Then, we take a quick visual poll to determine if the class needs further instruction, or perhaps just a couple of students. Sometimes it is useful to ask all students to first close their eyes, so they are not influenced by the responses of their classmates.
  - We use this technique after showing students how to introduce evidence in an argument in order to see if further scaffolding is necessary. After asking students "How confident do you feel about citing evidence correctly? Give me a thumbs up if you feel confident or a thumbs down if you need more help."
  - Another way to use this type of check-in could be in an ethnic studies class. We might ask students "Do you understand the difference between race and ethnicity?" Students can show their understanding with thumbs up/down to help the teacher know if review needs to be done prior to moving on, or not.

- In an economics course we may ask students, "Do you understand the relationship between supply and demand?" We take a brief poll of thumbs up/down to help us adjust the lesson before continuing.

- Comprehension Continuum – A teacher provides a statement or question that allows students to show their understanding of a social studies concept or skill. Then, students place themselves on an imaginary line in the classroom where each end represents a different response like "agree" and "disagree" or "yes" and "no" to the statement. After considering their response or position, students stand on the line and may be asked to explain their rationale, which can give the teacher information needed to adjust instruction.

  - For example, we might say to students "Freedom of speech means I can say whatever I want." Then, students stand on the line based on agreeing or disagreeing with the statement. After students have arranged themselves, we may ask a few to share out their rationale.

  - After teaching about different types of government, we might state "The United States is an oligarchy." Students then stand on the continuum to represent their response – one end representing "agree" the other "disagree." Students may be selected to offer a rationale for their stance. By listening to the feedback from their peers, students can reflect on their choice and adjust their placement on the continuum.

- Four Corners – In this strategy, the teacher asks a question and provides four responses each represented by a letter: A, B, C, and D. Then, students choose the letter that represents the answer they most agree with and they move to the corner of the room labeled with the letter of their response. Students may be asked to explain their rationale, which serves as another level of formative assessment.

  - For example, during the study of the Bill of Rights we ask students "Which of the following describes the Bill of Rights?" We put the answers on the screen for students to read: A – a document that ensures the basic freedoms of the citizens of the United States, B – a document that limits the powers and controls of the government, C – a document that protects the freedom of religion and speech, or D – all of the above. After reading the choices aloud, we ask students to select the answer they most agree with and to stand in that area of the classroom. Two students from each answer group can be asked to explain their positions. Students may want to reevaluate their answer choice after hearing others justify their choices.

  - Another idea for using this strategy in an economics class would be to present students with a question like "What happens when a market is in equilibrium?" Then, after providing answers: "A" – the price of the product will tend to rise, "B" – quantity demanded equals quantity supplied, "C" – quantity demanded exceeds the quantity supplied, or "D" – quantity supplied exceeds quantity demanded. After selecting the letter that represents the answer students most agree with, we may ask a couple from each answer group to provide a rationale.

- In a US history class, during the study of the women's rights movement, we might provide the following statement to students "A list of resolutions passed at a convention on women's rights in July 1848 included all of the following except for. . ." and provide the following answers: A – demands for improved property rights, B – demands for a role in law-making, C – demands for access to education, or D – demands for the right to vote.

- Think–Pair–Share – Students are asked a question and given time to think about the answer on their own. Then, they talk about their ideas with a partner. Next, we call on a few students to share with the class, which can help the teacher gauge comprehension.

  - For example, after reading a text about the rise of jazz music during the Harlem Renaissance, we might ask students "How was jazz a reflection of the rebirth of African American culture?" After directing students to first think independently about their response for a minute, we direct students to talk with a partner. Then, we call on a few students to share with the class.

  - We might use the question "What similarities do you see between the industrial revolution in China and the United States?" to assess comprehension of the economic development in these countries as part of a world history class.

- One-Sentence Summary – Students write a one-sentence summary of the key ideas of a topic. This task could be done as a quick check-in after reading a text, watching a video, or analyzing a series of images. This summary can give the teacher insight into students' understanding of a concept.

  - For example, after reading a few passages from a thematic data set on weapons used during World War II, we might ask students to write a one-sentence summary of the key advances in weaponry during this time and its destructive effects.

  - In a government course we might ask students to summarize the main role of the legislative branch after reading Article I of the Constitution.

- In a US history course, we might have students watch news footage from the Cuban Missile Crisis in 1962 and then ask students to summarize the event in one sentence.

- 3-2-1 Exit Slips – On a sheet of paper, students write three things they learned today, two questions they have about the material, and a visual representing one of their learnings. Students can compare their 3-2-1 exit slips to provide feedback to one another while teachers can collect them to assess comprehension.

  - For example, after learning about Fidel Castro's guerilla warfare in Cuba, students complete a 3-2-1 exit slip. In the first section they may write something like, "1 – A lot of Castro's men died upon arrival in Cuba, 2 – many locals assisted Castro's men, and 3 – The ship used for transportation was a crowded, old yacht in disrepair." In the next section they may write questions like, "I wonder if any of the soldiers were reunited with their families?" and "I wonder what happened to the soldiers who were injured?" For the last section of the notes, students may draw a small sketch of the ship used for transportation.

  - The same strategy could be applied to reading, or listening to, Malcom X's famous speech "Ballot or Bullet." Students write three things they learned, two questions they now have, and one image to symbolize the speech.

SUMMATIVE

Summative assessments are a way to formally judge what students know at a specific point in time – often at the end of a unit (Garrison & Ehringhaus, n.d.). Summative assessments can be high stakes and directly impact student grades. In contrast to formative assessment, summative *ends* with judgment of content and skill acquisition.

We tend to use performance assessments as summative assessments in our classrooms. In these evaluations, students go beyond multiple choice answers to construct an original response, create a product, or perform an activity to demonstrate knowledge and skill development (Darling-Hammond & Adamson, 2010, p. 7).

Performance assessments can judge students not only on rote learning skills but also on higher-order thinking (Darling-Hammond & Adamson, 2010, p. 42). These types of assessments are more in line with the goals of the Common Core. For example, it may be difficult to assess a student's ability to understand multiple perspectives, a key focus of the Common Core, using a multiple choice exam. This skill, however, can be easily assessed through a performance assessment like a multisource written analysis, which we explain later in this section.

We often use rubrics to score performance assessments. Effective rubrics specify what content and skills are to be assessed as well as what criteria will be used to judge student performance. An added bonus of using rubrics is that they help with grading consistency. For examples of rubrics, see Chapter 9: Genre Study or Chapter 17: Project-Based Learning. For more about creating rubrics, see the Technology Connections section.

Another way to summatively assess students is using multiple-choice exams. Though we prefer other types of summative assessments, we recognize that many teachers use this type of test. There are, however, a few things a teacher can do to improve this type of exam. For example, having students explain why *other* answers are incorrect for a multiple choice question can give a more complete understanding of comprehension. Another idea is to give students partial credit for visibly eliminating choices they know are incorrect even if they end up choosing the wrong answer. See the Technology Connections section for more ideas on improving multiple-choice tests.

Summative Assessment Examples

- Portfolio – Students select three or more previously completed assignments to demonstrate proficiency – skills, content, or both. In this collection of student work, they have the opportunity to show abilities or knowledge with multiple assignments. This portfolio can provide the teacher with a holistic view of a student's comprehension for a social studies concept.
  - For example, in geography class at the end of a unit on China, we ask students to select three assignments to show both their knowledge of China *and* their ability to create evidence-based responses. Often students pick pieces from the unit like a written analysis of Chinese demographics or a prompt response from a text describing the life of a factory worker. This type of assignment provides students an opportunity to actively reflect by reviewing their own work and considering which pieces best represent their knowledge and skills. To hold students accountable for this reflection process, they can be asked to write a short paragraph explaining how each portfolio choice shows their knowledge of China, their ability to create evidence-based responses, or both.
  - Another idea for implementing this type of assessment is to have students create a portfolio after studying imperialism in a world history class. We might have students select assignments from the unit they feel best demonstrates their knowledge of imperialism. Further, students could be asked to write a reflection, in addition to the selected assignments. A reflection question like the following could be used, "What surprised me about what

I learned?" or "What would I do differently on these assignments next time, if given the chance?" These reflection questions add another avenue for the teacher to judge comprehension of imperialism.

- For a US history class, students might make a portfolio to show understanding of religious intolerance in US history. Students could pull assignments from their work that elaborate on the different groups impacted by this discrimination. Then, students might also write a short piece comparing the treatment of one religious group to another.

- Student-Created Tests – Instruct students to use their class materials to create test questions for a given unit of study. Students could be divided into groups and each one assigned to make certain types of questions: multiple choice, matching, short answer, essay response, fill-in-the-blank, and so on. It may help to provide sample questions and sentence starters to scaffold this process for students. This strategy provides two opportunities for assessment. First, teachers can assess the quality of questions produced and second, assess students' performance when taking the student-created test.

  - For example, after reading about the Cold War, students might be directed to create test questions about the topic. Teachers could provide sentence frames like "How did the United States respond to . . . during the Cold War?" or "Describe one result of the . . . that occurred during the Cold War."

  - In an economics course, students might work in groups to make a set of multiple-choice questions about the influence of the federal government on the economy of the United States. Students may benefit from teacher support with creating multiple-choice questions. For example, it may be helpful to instruct students to begin their question with a stem that is as brief as possible like "Which of the following actions by the federal government . . .?" or "How has the economy responded to _____ from the federal government?"

  - After studying institutionalized racism in an ethnic studies class, we ask students to make several True/False statements. We provide tips for crafting these types of sentences: keep statements short, false statements might be only partially wrong, and so forth. Two model statements we provide are, "People of color have historically been restricted from certain neighborhoods" as a true statement, or "Historically, if a person of color can afford a home, they have been allowed to purchase where they please" as a false statement.

- Podcasts – Students research, write, and record a podcast on a given topic or to respond to a question. Both the writing of the script and the final product provide opportunities to show comprehension. Please see Chapter 15: Listening and Speaking Activities for more on student-created podcasts.

- For example, after studying recent efforts to combat racism in the United States, we ask students to analyze key figures from the movement. They write and record a podcast episode about strategies developed by their selected figure to support Civil Rights.

- Students could also write and record a podcast on a government topic like the Bill of Rights. They might develop a series of questions about this important document and interview people to explore misconceptions believed by the general public. For example, they may ask, "What freedoms are protected by the first amendment?" This assessment provides an opportunity to prove what they know about the first amendment by evaluating their interviewees responses for accuracy.

- Multisource Written Analysis – In this assessment, students write extended responses to questions that require analysis of multiple primary sources on the same topic. Students may benefit from employing the evidence-based writing structures discussed in Chapter 5: Writing in Social Studies. We like how this summative assessment shows not only content comprehension, but also literacy skills such as identifying the main point.

  - For example, after studying the independence movement in India led by Mahatma Gandhi, we provide three sources: a painting of the massacre of Amritsar, a description of the Salt March (an act of disobedience against British rule), and a transcript for one of Gandhi's speeches. Then, we ask students to show their knowledge by responding to questions. These range from comprehension questions like "What were the motivations behind the Salt March?," compare/contrast questions like "Identify similar themes in the description of the Salt March and Gandhi's speech," and a synthesis question like "Using all three sources, identify the concerns of native Indians regarding British control of India."

  - In US history, students could write an essay using multiple sources to respond to the question "How did the consequences of World War II impact Germany compared to other countries?" Students might look at casualty statistics for countries involved in the conflict, an image of London after the "Blitz" bombings, and a summary of the discussions that took place at the Potsdam Conference in 1945.

  - After studying the Gay Rights Movement that gained momentum in the 1960s, we ask students, "How did the Stonewall Riots of 1969 serve as a turning point in the Gay Rights Movement?" Students can use newspaper coverage from the time of the riots, images of the riots themselves, and official policies targeting the gay community.

- Answer-Question – In this assessment students are provided with an answer and are challenged to write the question that goes with it. This activity allows students to be creative while keeping them on topic. A teacher could direct more experienced students to come up with multiple questions that could have the same answer. This activity is borrowed from *The ELL Teacher's Toolbox* by Larry Ferlazzo and Katie Hull Sypnieski (2018b, p. 328).

  - For example, after studying US imperialism in the late nineteenth century, we might provide students with the answer "For use as a strategic naval base." This answer might prompt students to create the question "Why did the United States annex Hawaii?"

  - In a US history class after studying political and social movements of the 1920s, students might be given the answer "A movement that argues African Americans could only attain social equality by moving back to Africa" might generate the question "What is one key idea of Marcus Garvey's Back-to-Africa movement?" or "What was one goal of African Nationalism in the 1920s?"

  - After studying landmark Supreme Court cases related to civil rights, the answer provided might be "Established racial segregation in public schools as unconstitutional." The question created by students would likely be something like, "What was the result of the Supreme Court decision in *Brown v. Board of Education*?"

- Debate – Students choose a position on a topic and prepare speaking points that are in favor of their position, against the other side, and counterpoints for their selected position. For more about facilitating this type of activity see Chapter 16: Discussions.

  - For example, after studying the Bill of Rights, students may choose opposing sides on a freedom of speech issue like white nationalists gathering for a rally.

  - Students could also choose sides to argue in a US history course about the United States' entry into World War II. After learning about the events leading up to and including the Pearl Harbor bombing, students could choose to argue that the United States should have entered the war earlier or not.

  - In an economics class, after studying taxes, students might choose a side to argue in a debate about the progressive tax structure. Students may choose to argue that this taxation structure is fair or unfair, citing evidence to support their ideas.

STUDENT SELF-ASSESSMENT

Student self-assessment means providing students opportunities to assess their own learning. Providing these opportunities for self-assessment is an essential part of the cycle of learning (Black & Wiliam, 1998, p. 6). Teaching students the process of self-assessment can help them to better understand what *they* need to do in order to improve, as well as understand the purpose of what they are learning (Black & Wiliam, 1998, p. 7). To this end, we have a few ideas for implementing student self-assessment in any social studies class.

Student Self-Assessment Examples

- Letter to a Future Student – In this assessment strategy, students write a letter to a future student of the same course to share what they have learned about a social studies topic. A teacher may provide guidelines such as length requirement, topics, using a certain number of class resources, and so on.
  - For example, after studying Kenya in a geography class, students may be invited to write a letter to a student taking the course next year, detailing key information about Kenya for the categories of land and climate, culture, economy, and challenges. Students can use their class assignments done throughout the unit as resources to craft their letters.
  - Another idea might be writing a letter after studying personal finance in an economics course. Students could write a letter of advice to a future student outlining smart financial decisions. Some topics that might be included are interest rates, inflation, financial institutions, and so on.
  - In a government course, the letter to a future student might occur after studying the role of media in politics. A student might explain the role and responsibility of the free press as well as how politicians may use media to sway public opinion.
- Student-Created Rubrics – This assessment allows for students to take part in crafting rubrics that determine what is considered proficient for content knowledge or a skill. Students can work to develop criteria for a rubric determining the grading of an assignment. Putting students in the position of creating the assessment can lead to higher levels of critical thinking as they work together to determine what defines success.
  - For example, students might create a rubric for a portfolio where the objective is to show knowledge of the consequences of World War II. Students can work in small groups to develop what might show proficient knowledge of the topic. It might be determined that a proficient student would mention the decline of European colonial empires, the creation of the United Nations, and the Cold War.

- In another student-created rubric, they could determine criteria for evaluating the selection and citation of evidence supporting an argument about the ability to make changes to the Constitution. The criteria might include choosing evidence that supports a main idea, properly introducing the evidence, and providing an accurate citation.

- Self-Grading – Asking students to grade themselves, as well as to provide reasoning for their grade, can provide important insights. A teacher may learn that a student feels they are working hard despite the low quality of their work. Or, on the contrary, that a student feels they are not doing as well as the teacher thinks. For this reason, this assessment strategy can be a good opportunity to help students build confidence as well as other social and emotional competencies, like personal responsibility and agency. This strategy can work for determining a semester grade or for an individual assignment. For cases in which the student grade and teacher grade are vastly different, it may be a good idea to meet with the student to discuss the difference in viewpoints. For more about self-grading forms, see the Technology Connections section.

DIFFERENTIATION

The first consideration teachers should make when assessing English language learners (ELLs) is to determine whether they are assessing content or language. If the goal of the assessment is to determine content knowledge, it's important to craft questions in a way that students can demonstrate their knowledge without unrealistic linguistic demands. A teacher can make these responses possible by allowing beginner and intermediate level ELLs to respond in their home language or by providing sentence frames.

ELLs may perform better on open-ended writing tasks as compared to commercially developed multiple-choice assessments because they can get credit for what knowledge they do have instead of just a right-or-wrong answer (Darling-Hammond & Adamson, 2010, p. 31). For example, a multiple choice question might read "Which of the following terms measures the average amount of money a person makes per year in a given country?" The obvious answer to this would be the letter choice that reads "per-capita income." Instead, we can ask students to write or draw a definition for per-capita income. This task allows a student to demonstrate that they know the variable is related to money, even if they aren't sure about the "per-capita" portion of the term.

Reducing the length of the tasks as well as simplifying language on exams may also help ELLs and/or students who learn differently. Through these modifications, students use less intellectual energy to understand what is being asked and can instead focus on demonstrating what they know (Darling-Hammond & Adamson, 2010, p. 32).

There is likely to be a difference, especially evident in content knowledge, between ELLs and native speakers. Students who have spent the majority of their life in another country may have very little knowledge about the history of the United States. Due to the lack of background information, students may have gaps in their knowledge that no testing accommodation will bridge. For example, a recent immigrant to the United States may not have all the background knowledge needed to respond to questions about the American Revolution. It is important to think through what our common assumptions might be about the prior knowledge of all our students, including ELLs. Provide supplemental materials in advance of assessments to provide needed context, and further support students with visuals and models.

ADVANCED EXTENSIONS

One extension idea is to turn any assessment into a cycle of assessment and reflection. In other words, after completing an assessment and being graded, the students would revise a portion where there is room for improvement. In addition to completing this improvement, students might write about the process of revisiting their own work. They could reflect on the difficulty of redoing their work or new learnings that were achieved.

Student Handouts and Examples

Table 20.1: Types of Assessment
Figure 20.1: Scientific Revolution Concept Web

What Could Go Wrong?

In our experience, there have been times when we thought we clearly defined the goals and tasks on an assessment, and yet, students were unable to show comprehension or proficiency. We have sometimes discovered, after closely reviewing an assessment with a low success rate, that we didn't actually assess what we *taught*. Instead, planning with the end in mind, and checking to make sure each task brings students closer to achieving the predetermined goal, can help to make assessments results more successful. When this type of error occurs, we have found it beneficial to have a "do-over" – rewriting the assessment to actually test what was taught *or* reteaching the content to better align with the original assessment.

Another mistake with assessment might be underutilization of student self-assessment. Recognizing the value of, and prioritizing, this type of assessment can have multiple benefits for students and teachers. In our experience, self-assessment can help students build confidence and see themselves as active participants in their education. Students can also see for themselves when they fall short of the objectives and work to make changes to improve. Bringing this idea to the classroom may help to increase a sense of urgency with student learning.

As new teachers, we often found ourselves spending our weekends grading stacks of student assignments. Our time as teachers can be much better spent by implementing many of the strategies in this chapter, like formative assessment that occurs immediately during instruction with no need to take papers home. Instead, a quick walk around the classroom while students are working can help a teacher determine whether a student is on track. Carefully planning assessments that will take less time to grade may mean simplifying a rubric so that a teacher is only looking at a few items instead of several of them.

Technology Connections

Creating rubrics can be very time consuming, but there are some useful options out there to create them digitally. ForAllRubrics (www.forallrubrics.com) is one site that allows teachers to create rubrics and also has options for students to do self-assessment.

Crowd Signal (https://crowdsignal.com) is an option for creating online polls that can be used as formative assessment with over 14 different types of questions that can be asked. A similar option, an application for smartphones, is MasteryConnect Student (https://itunes.apple.com/us/app/bubblesheet/id413937393?mt=8). This tool allows you to create quick polls, but also has options for short responses, which could be used as a "ticket out the door" as explained in the formative assessments section of this chapter.

For more help about getting the most out of multiple-choice tests check out Larry Ferlazzo's blog post "Intriguing Strategy in Assessing Multiple Choice Tests – Giving Credit for Explaining Which Options Are Wrong" (http://larryferlazzo .edublogs.org/2018/11/17/intriguing-strategy-in-assessing-multiple-choice-tests-giving-credit-for-explaining-which-options-are-wrong).

The website QuizBean (www.quizbean.com/home) allows teachers or students to create an interesting type of quiz called "this or that." In this type of quiz, a student is given a statement and has to choose one of two corresponding answers. For example, if the answer choices are "Declaration of Independence" or "The Constitution," the student might be given the statement "Congress shall make no law respecting an establishment of religion . . ." The student would then need to select one of the given choices that corresponds to the statement. The possibilities for fun quizzes are endless with this site.

Another idea is using a site like ImageQuiz (www.imagequiz.co.uk). It allows teachers or students to create online quizzes using images. Students can be quizzed on geography or people in history. There are many quizzes currently on the site that can give you ideas for other quizzes you could create.

In addition to creating quizzes, students can use self-grading forms like those posted in Larry Ferlazzo's blog post "Here Are Forms My Students Are Using to Evaluate Themselves and Me" (http://larryferlazzo.edublogs.org/2014/10/26/here-are-forms-my-students-are-using-to-evaluate-themselves-me).

Figures

Using words from the bank below, organize a concept map about the Scientific Revolution that shows how these terms may be connected.

Place each word into a circle. Draw lines connecting the circles to the central topic or each other. On the lines, write how the terms are related. See example below.

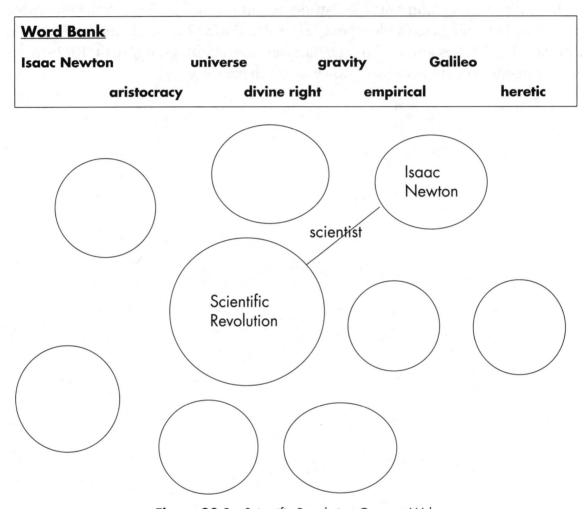

Word Bank

| Isaac Newton | universe | gravity | Galileo |
| aristocracy | divine right | empirical | heretic |

Figure 20.1 Scientific Revolution Concept Web

CHAPTER 21

Getting the Most from Your Textbook

What Is It?

A textbook is, obviously, a comprehensive collection of texts used to study a topic. These books tend to be district or site selected and often teachers are required to use them. Unfortunately, many textbooks aren't very engaging for our students – they are often missing multiple perspectives, may be out of date, and are challenging for students at different levels of English language proficiency. Additionally, while many publishers claim that their textbooks are standards-aligned, new reports are uncovering that these assertions may be untrue. In fact, William Schmidt, a professor of statistics and education at Michigan State University, has shared research that reveals many publishers have done little to actually align newer versions of textbooks to the Common Core standards (Herold & Molnar, 2014).

With these concerns in mind, we will share strategies in this chapter for how to get the *most* out of your textbook.

Why We Like It

A textbook can be a good resource for the social studies classroom. Most of them include a selection of primary sources, which is especially useful for schools with little technology access. Because these books are often mandated by the site or district, there is continuity for students who may move from one class to another. Finally, having textbooks available can sometimes "free-up" teacher time that can be focused on helping students access content instead of developing new curriculum.

Though we may not actually like our textbooks, we *do* like the strategies we discuss in this chapter which make the books more engaging and helpful to our students.

Supporting Research

Research shows that effective instructional strategies used by a teacher can be more important than a "good" textbook (Cheung, Slavin, Lake, & Kim, 2015, p. 1). In other words, the textbook itself is less important to our students than how we use it.

Common Core Connections

Most textbooks claim to be aligned to standards, but a teacher can certainly use good teaching practices to apply the standards to any textbook. For example, students can work to determine the meaning of social studies vocabulary in a textbook as directed in the Craft and Structure strand of the Common Core (Common Core, 2010gg).

Students may also analyze visuals incorporated in a textbook, like charts or graphs, as required by the Integration of Knowledge and Ideas strand of the Common Core (Common Core, 2010hh).

Social Studies Connections

Similar to the Common Core standards, educators can use textbooks to address the standards of the National Council for the Social Studies (NCSS) by implementing good teaching strategies. For example, a teacher can instruct students to analyze primary sources that are included in a textbook to "gather and evaluate sources" as required by the College, Career, and Civic Life (C3) Framework developed by the NCSS (NCSS, 2010, p. 57).

Application

This section describes teaching strategies that can be applied to any textbook in order to promote engagement and increase learning in a social studies classroom. Many of these ideas are explained in detail in other chapters of this book.

USING IMAGES

Apply image analysis strategies, like those described in Chapter 12: Image Analysis, to images included in a textbook. For example, when studying the Protestant Reformation in a world history textbook we have students analyze an image of King Henry VIII. Students begin by writing to set the stage, which helps them to access prior knowledge. They might tap this knowledge by responding to a prompt like "Describe a time when you wanted to feel powerful. What did you do to portray this image to others?" Next, students are directed to look carefully at the image, noting what they see. In this image they may note that the king is dressed in elaborate clothing, which would have been made by hand, denoting wealth. His hand is on his hip in a "power stance." Then, based on their careful observations, students make evidence-based inferences, which can help them evaluate the historical relevance of the painting. Students may infer that, based on his appearance and body language, King Henry VIII must have wanted people to think he was very powerful.

Another idea might be to apply a quick strategy from Harvard's Project Zero called "See, Think, Wonder" (n.d.). This strategy could be applied to any image in a textbook. We begin by asking students to silently look at or *see* an image for a period of time, typically one minute. Then, we ask them to write what they *think* the image is trying to say – the message of the image. Next, we invite students to *wonder*, or develop, questions about the image. These questions may provide an opportunity for further research or simply set up students to read more about the image in the text.

For example, students might employ this strategy when viewing a picture of a "flapper" included in a US history textbook for the study of the Roaring Twenties. While spending a minute looking at the picture (see) students might notice the flapper dancing, appearing to have fun, the dress is above the knee and fringed, and so on. Then, students write what they *think* is the message of the photo (think). To help students use what they noticed in their writing, we may provide a sentence starter like, "Based on (item from the image), I think the message of this image is. . ." For example, "Based on the expression on the woman's face, I think the message of this image is that she seems to be feeling happy and free." Another idea is to ask students to create a hashtag phrase (like those common on various forms of social media) to capture the message of the image. In this case students might come up with something like "#women'sworld" or "#JustWantToDance." Then, students can be invited to generate questions about the photo, sharing one with their neighbor for comparison (wonder). This question might be something like, "I wonder how many women became 'flappers' during this time" or "I wonder what the older generations thought about this woman." While the see and think portions of this activity can help to provide a context for reading the textbook, the questions generated can motivate students to read in order to find an answer.

USING TEXTBOOK EXCERPTS

Use information from a section or chapter of a textbook to create a thematic data set like those described in Chapter 4: Thematic Data Sets. A data set is typically a collection of 10–30 short passages that can be divided into several categories.

When using a data set with students, we apply the following five phases: (1) considering questions (these questions may be provided by the teacher or student to increase relevance), (2) reading for understanding (reading the text while highlighting and making comments in the margins of the text – in other words, annotation), (3) classifying/categorizing (looking for patterns and grouping information), (4) analyzing (developing generalizations for each category), and (5) extending knowledge (apply newly acquired knowledge to a task). Students use the five phases to inductively develop understanding, meaning they analyze the passages for patterns in order to discover the rules of key concepts.

For example, a teacher could create a data set on a given country (like Thailand) or region of the world (like Southeast Asia) by using information about these places from a geography textbook to create short passages. They begin these phases by considering questions, or what they hope to be able to answer after analyzing the data set. For a data set on Thailand, a question may be "How have the Thai adapted to the landscape of where they live?" or "How has globalization impacted Thailand?" Next, students read through the data set while annotating, which can help students to process information as well as hold them accountable.

After annotating, students classify or group related items together into categories that are provided by the teacher or generated by the students themselves. The categories might include land and climate, economy, politics, history, and so forth. Then, students review their categories to determine the rules or main ideas for each category. For land and climate the main ideas might include, "much of Thailand is tropical and experiences monsoons." Finally, students extend their understanding of the topic by applying their newly acquired knowledge. They can do this by making an argument or responding to one of the questions given in phase one of the data set analysis.

In another version of a thematic data set for a US history class, we might profile influential members of the Women's Rights Movement. This data set could include information from a textbook about women like Elizabeth Cady Stanton, Sojourner Truth, Sarah Grimke, Gloria Steinem, and so on. After carefully reading and annotating each item, they could be placed into the following categories: key contributions, challenges faced, and early life. Then, students write key ideas for each category. A key idea for "challenges faced" might be experienced public ridicule. To extend their knowledge of this topic, students might choose a modern-day leader, like Malala Yousafzai, and write an analysis making a comparison between her and a figure from the data set.

DISCUSSIONS

Students can engage in the fishbowl discussion protocol described in Chapter 16: Discussions. This version of a Socratic Seminar begins with students reading a complex text – like a textbook chapter or an excerpt from one. Then, students are divided into multiple groups of five to six – each group taking a turn in the fishbowl or sitting in the center of the class. Students in the fishbowl discuss the given topic while others listen and take notes. Groups rotate through the fishbowl so that each has a turn to discuss. This protocol helps reinforce concepts, as well as provides an opportunity for students to clarify questions with their peers prior to assessment.

For example, before writing an essay, students can engage in a discussion about the major impacts of the American Civil War. After reading a chapter about this topic, students answer four to five open-ended questions that require use of evidence to respond. The responses to these questions are what they discuss in the fishbowl: "How did the enormous loss of life impact the nation after the war ended?" "How was rebuilding the country challenging?" "How did the American Civil War contribute to the rise of the Civil Rights Movement?" "How did the Southern states maintain their system of racial superiority after the end of the war?"

TIMELINES

Use the textbook to gather information about events or people and then place them on a timeline. A teacher may want to give students a certain number of events to incorporate onto this visual organizer in addition to other requirements like visuals. For example, students could create a timeline to track the events leading up to the fall of the Roman Empire using a world history textbook.

In an ethnic studies class, students might create a timeline to track the development of the Latino Civil Rights Movement. This timeline might track important figures and events of this movement. A timeline might also be used to track the life of important figures in US history, like union leaders Cesar Chavez or Dolores Huerta. Timelines are explored further in Chapter 7: Timelines Revisited.

After reading about a key historical event, have students create an "alternative" timeline. These timelines help students to practice critical thinking skills as they analyze how their textbook *could have* been written if things had happened differently. For example, after reading in a history book about the atomic bombs dropped by the United States at the end of World War II, students could create a timeline that imagines the attack had never happened and describe how international relations might be different today.

In another version of this alternative timeline, students in a government class might read about the failure of the Articles of Confederation in a textbook. Then, students create a timeline where they imagine and track the events of a United States that never adopted the Constitution. For more about alternative timelines, see Chapter 7: Timelines Revisited.

VOCABULARY

Teachers can apply a three-phase process to build an understanding of the vocabulary terms in a textbook chapter. In the first phase, students consider what they may already know for a given term – accessing prior knowledge. In phase two, students search the textbook for new information to add to their understanding of the term. Then, students revise this understanding by applying their newly gained information before formalizing their definitions.

For example, teachers might have students write what they already know about the words *the black shirts, charisma,* and *Fascism* before reading a chapter on the rise of Fascism in Italy in a world history textbook. Then, while reading the text, they can add new information to their understanding. After revising their initial definitions, have students make word cards (two different versions are described in Chapter 1: A Fresh Look at Vocabulary) to make that knowledge public.

Another idea might be to have students in a government class make predictions, tapping into prior knowledge, about the protections provided by each of the amendments in the Bill of Rights prior to doing a deeper study. Students may have heard that the First Amendment protects the freedom of speech, for example, but not be aware of the freedom of petition. After noting these predictions on a graphic organizer like Table 21.1: Multiphase Vocabulary – Bill of Rights, students can add notes about each amendment from the textbook. Then, students can create visuals for each amendment based on their new understanding of the terms. Additional columns could be added to the organizer to allow for future revised definitions.

Table 21.1 Multiphase Vocabulary – Bill of Rights

Amendment #	Prediction	Notes from Textbook	Visual
1	EX. Freedom of speech	This amendment protects five kinds of freedoms: religion, speech, assembly, press, and petition.	
2			
3			
4			
5			
6			
7			
8			
9			
10			

READING STRATEGIES

Apply reading strategies like those described in Chapter 2: Reading Strategies while reading the textbook. While reading, a teacher may direct students to summarize, question, clarify, make connections, visualize, and predict in order to develop a deeper understanding of the text. Because students are generally not allowed to write in the actual textbook, have them use sticky notes to place annotations near the text that inspired them. Students can use their notes to help direct them toward evidence they can use in writing or develop a deeper understanding of key ideas. For example, when reading a chapter on prices and decision-making in an economics textbook, students might write questions, quick sketches, and summarize the key points on sticky notes as they read.

A fun extension for this activity might be to have students exchange textbooks with a partner and respond to their neighbor's sticky notes. For example, after reading about the Louisiana Purchase in a US history book, a student might summarize a portion of the text by writing, "Basically, this tells me the United States bought a large area of land from France in 1803." Then, after exchanging textbooks with a partner, the partner might comment on this same sticky note to add "US President Thomas Jefferson bought the land from French Emperor Napoleon." This activity can help students practice critical thinking as well as interact with peers and the textbook.

STUDENT-CREATED TESTS

Students can create questions for a test after reading a section of a textbook. These student-created tests provide an additional review opportunity for students as they reread the text in order to come up with questions for their peers. Often, in our experience, these student-generated assignments increase engagement as discussed in Chapter 11: Questions for Learning and Chapter 20: Assessments.

After reading a chapter on the Watergate Scandal in a US history textbook, students might create several multiple choice or true/false questions about the fallout from the scandal. A question might be something like "True or false, Richard Nixon went to jail for several years following the Watergate scandal," or a multiple-choice question like "How was the Watergate break-in discovered?" and create answers based on information from the textbook like: A – security guard heard weird noises, B – phone call from across the street, C – the door lock was taped, or D – burglars tripped a silent alarm.

PRIMARY SOURCES

Primary source analysis techniques can be applied to documents included in any textbook. For example, students can use a strategy like the In-Depth Analysis of a Primary Source described in Chapter 13: Analysis of Primary Sources. The first step, identification, asks students to identify the genre or type and date of a source. The second step, message, helps students summarize key information in the text in order to determine the message. Then, students are directed to consider the motivation of the author. These three steps help students to analyze any primary source in order to help them understand the historical significance.

This process can be used to study how the American government funded boarding schools to forcefully assimilate Native American children. A US history textbook could contain an official report that includes a letter describing the health of the students written by the superintendent of the school and a chart containing statistics about which tribes students are from, as well as how many have died or remain at the school (Lee, 1887). After guiding students through an initial reading of the document, students can begin a deeper analysis by **identifying** the source. For the assimilation report, students might note the genre or type as an official government document, or as a letter and chart, and the date as September 7, 1887.

In the next step, students determine the *message* of the text by summarizing the key information. In this source, students may note the description of different diseases the students are experiencing along with a glowing report about the school's physician, guiding them to understand that the document is a report about the status of the children, specifically their health, at this boarding facility.

Then, students are directed to consider the *motive* of the author – why was this text created? In this case, after determining the message of the document, students can surmise that the writer wanted to show this school was doing a good job at "reeducating" the Native children sent to it. Perhaps the writer gets paid based on how many children they keep alive, which is why they are focused on the numbers of students. These steps help students gain a deeper understanding of this period of time and how Native children were viewed, which can help them determine historical significance of this primary source.

MNEMONICS

Students can use mnemonics to remember key information from a chapter in a textbook. Using link words to remember key information and incorporating visuals help create mnemonics. For example, after reading about the 13 colonies that eventually became the first 13 states of the United States, a mnemonic device could be created to help students remember the names and locations of the 13 colonies. A teacher might introduce the first part of the mnemonic by providing the following link words:

New (*New York*) Massive *(Massachusetts)* Hamsters (*New Hampshire)* Can get (*Connecticut*) New (*New Jersey*) Pizza (*Pennsylvania*) Deliveries (*Delaware*)

Then, students could be asked to come up with the rest of the mnemonic for the remaining colonies: Maryland, Virginia, North Carolina, South Carolina, and Georgia. It may be a good idea for students to create visuals for each portion of the mnemonic. For example, to represent Pennsylvania, students might draw a sketch of a pizza and a hamster for New Hampshire.

ANTICIPATORY SETS

An anticipatory set (a few questions students answer before reading) could be created to assess prior knowledge and clue students into key information in the text. After reading the textbook, students can review their original responses and correct them, as well as provide evidence from the chapter to support their answers.

For example, prior to reading a chapter, students could be given a series of statements about an economic concept like supply and demand. A statement could be something like "demand refers *only* to the desire to buy something." Students would choose *agree* or *disagree* for each statement. After reading, students could return to the questions and make corrections as well as cite evidence to support their answers (Lent, 2012).

SCAVENGER HUNTS

A fun way to familiarize students with a textbook and/or direct them to key information within it is for teachers to create a textbook scavenger hunt – a list of questions along with clues to where the answers can be found in the book. Students can work individually, in pairs, or small groups to complete the hunt. Activities such as scavenger hunts can "gamify" the use of a textbook (Hammond, 2015). An extension of this type of activity might be for students to create a scavenger hunt for their peers.

JIGSAWS

Assign small groups of students to become experts of a section in a chapter. Then, create new groups that contain one member from each of the first groupings. In other words, the new groups have an expert from each section of a chapter in a textbook. Students can teach their new group about *their* section of the textbook using a poster or presentation. In this way, all students become experts of each section of the chapter. This strategy is commonly referred to as a *jigsaw,* which has been shown to be a particularly effective learning strategy (Schwartz, 2017). This strategy is also discussed in Chapter 15: Listening and Speaking Activities.

For example, in a chapter on the executive branch in a US government textbook, the first grouping could be arranged by the chapter sections: The President and the Vice President, The President's Job, Foreign Policy, and Advisors and Executive Agencies. Then, after becoming experts on their section, new groups would be formed with one member from each section. The new groups work together to create a poster about the executive branch. Students could use a graphic organizer like Table 21.2: Textbook Jigsaw Organizer Example to help them organize, note, and visualize information from the other section experts. For more ideas see Chapter 15: Listening and Speaking Activities.

Table 21.2 Textbook Jigsaw Organizer Example

Group 1 – Becoming an Expert			
Topic _____			
Key Ideas		Visual	
Group 2 – Noting Information from Other Sections			
Topic:		Topic:	
Key Ideas	Visual	Key Ideas	Visual
Topic:		Topic:	
Key Ideas	Visual	Key Ideas	Visual

ANALYZING WHAT'S MISSING IN THE TEXTBOOK

A teacher could have students analyze the textbook for underrepresented perspectives and research and write a supplemental text that provides an additional perspective as described in Chapter 17: Project-Based Learning. This can help to bridge content gaps that may exist in an adopted textbook.

In a world history textbook, the experience of the colonized indigenous populations is often an underrepresented perspective. A teacher has a great opportunity to provide, or have students research and create, supplemental materials on the rich and extensive empires of the populations in the Americas and in other parts of the world prior to European contact.

DIFFERENTIATION

A good strategy for working with textbooks is to chunk the reading by breaking it into smaller sections. Sectioning the reading into smaller tasks and applying a variety of strategies can help to make the reading tasks more accessible.

Prior to reading a chapter, a concept map of its content can be given to students. This map can provide students with prior knowledge helpful to access the content. The map may be a simple chart that outlines the different sections of a chapter, or gives students definitions for key terms prior to reading.

To build context in order to improve comprehension of the textbook, it may be useful to supplement with other text, videos, and/or pictures – especially for English language learners (ELLs). Building on information in the textbook with different mediums can help develop a deeper understanding of the information.

ADVANCED EXTENSIONS

Challenge students to curate a selection of supplemental texts, images, and/or video clips to go with a section of the textbook. In this way, students are showing their understanding of the material while also deepening their knowledge as they comb through related information. Students can then place these supplemental sources on a website or other digital platforms like Google Classroom.

Student Handouts and Examples

Table 21.1: Multiphase Vocabulary – Bill of Rights
Table 21.2: Textbook Jigsaw Organizer Example

What Could Go Wrong?

The biggest mistake teachers can make when using a textbook is relying on the textbook to do the teaching. In other words, a teacher should not expect that assigning a portion to read, and then having students read it, will equate to deep comprehension of the information. Without providing multiple reinforcing lessons, many students are unlikely to carefully consider the information presented in a textbook.

Technology Connections

Many textbooks have online applications including study guides, review, and even audio versions of the textbook. Check with your publisher to see what they may offer.

Using an application from Voice Dream (www.voicedream.com) provides options for students to have the textbook read to them. The Reader application reads uploaded documents aloud. Another application from the same company, the Scanner application, is a new option that allows you to use the camera on your phone to scan text and then have it read to you. Both of these are especially helpful for students who may learn differently. As always, avoid using copyrighted content without permission. However, most major publishers have specific terms allowing distribution of ebooks or audiobooks to accommodate users with disabilities, and they're often glad to help make the necessary files available.

Listening to text while following along has been shown to improve memory over just reading silently to oneself (www.tandfonline.com/doi/abs/10.1080/09658211 .2017.1383434?journalCode=pmem20, p. 4).

For even more ideas about how to maximize the effectiveness of your textbooks, check out Larry Ferlazzo's blog post: "The Best Resources for Adapting Your Textbook So It Doesn't Bore Students to Death" (http://larryferlazzo.edublogs .org/2011/05/14/the-best-resources-for-adapting-your-textbook-so-it-doesnt-bore-students-to-death).

REFERENCES

A defender of the Bastille explains his role (n.d.). *Liberty, equality, fraternity*. Retrieved from http://chnm.gmu.edu/revolution/d/383 (accessed January 22, 2019).

A guide for analyzing historical documents OPCVL: Origin, purpose, content, value, limitation [PDF file] (n.d.). Retrieved from www.commackschools.org/Downloads/OPCVL%20Reference%20Sheet2.pdf

Active listening: Katie Owens at TEDxYouth@Conejo (n.d.). *TED Ed*. Retrieved from https://ed.ted.com/on/KBxwjZ5T#watch

Adams, C. (2013, November 16). Teachers urged to mix it up and use novelty to engage students [web log comment]. *Education Week*. Retrieved from https://blogs.edweek.org/edweek/college_bound/2013/11/teachers_urged_to_mix_it_up_and_use_novelty_in_class_to_engage_students.html

Adichie, C.N. (2009, October 7). The danger of a single story. YouTube. Retrieved from www.youtube.com/watch?v=D9Ihs241zeg#action=share

Alber, R. (2011, July 19). Are you tapping into prior knowledge often enough in your classroom? *Edutopia*. Retrieved from www.edutopia.org/blog/prior-knowledge-tapping-into-often-classroom-rebecca-alber

Albright, L.K. and Ariail, M. (2005). Tapping the potential of teacher read-alouds in middle schools. *Journal of Adolescent & Adult Literacy* 48 (7): 582–591. http://interactivereadalouds.pbworks.com/f/Tapping+the+Potential+of+Teacher+Read-Alouds+in+Middle+School.pdf

Alderman, L. (2015, October 5). Angry workers storm Air France meeting on job cuts. *New York Times*. Retrieved from www.nytimes.com/2015/10/06/business/international/angry-workers-storm-air-france-meeting-on-job-cuts.html

An ode to tartiflette: The "most in demand recipe in France" (2017, December 17). *The Local*. Retrieved from www.thelocal.fr/20171213/an-ode-to-tartiflette-the-most-popular-recipe-in-france

Analyze a photo (n.d.). National Archives. Retrieved from www.archives.gov/education/lessons/worksheets/photo.html

Anderson, R.C., Hiebert, E.H., Scott, J.A., and Wilkinson, I.A.G. (1985). *Becoming a nation of readers: The report of the Commission on Reading.* Washington, DC: Commission on Reading, The National Academy of Education. Retrieved from http://textproject.org/assets/library/resources/Anderson-Hiebert-Scott-Wilkinson-Becoming-a-Nation-of-Readers.pdf

Apkon, S. (2014). *The age of the image: Redefining literacy in a world of screens.* New York: Farrar, Straus and Giroux.

Argument (n.d.). Retrieved from https://writingcenter.unc.edu/tips-and-tools/argument/

Aristotle (330 BCE). *The politics – On slavery.* Retrieved from www.wright.edu/~christopher.oldstone-moore/Aristotleslavery.htm

Assessment (2015, November 10). *The glossary of education reform.* Retrieved from www.edglossary.org/assessment

Associated Press (2013, October 24). Wine's pedigree faked. *New York Times.* Retrieved from www.nytimes.com/2013/10/24/world/europe/wines-pedigree-faked.html

Atrocities against Native Americans (n.d.). United to End Genocide. Retrieved from http://endgenocide.org/learn/past-genocides/native-americans

Aztec social structure (n.d.). University of Texas, Tarlton Law Library. Retrieved from http://tarlton.law.utexas.edu/aztec-and-maya-law/aztec-social-structure

Baer, D. (2014, November 4). Here's why highlighting doesn't actually help you remember anything. *Business Insider.* Retrieved from www.businessinsider.com/highlighting-a-terrible-study-strategy-2014-11

Baker, F.W. (2014, June 27). Close reading and what it means for media literacy. MiddleWeb. Retrieved from www.middleweb.com/15929/close-reading-and-media-literacy/

Baker, F.W. (2016, February 21). Teaching propaganda using political ads. *MiddleWeb.* Retrieved from www.middleweb.com/28053/teaching-about-propaganda-using-political-ads/

Baker, F.W. (2016, November 15). How to help kids be active video viewers. *MiddleWeb.* Retrieved from www.middleweb.com/33351/how-we-can-make-kids-active-video-viewers/

Balonon-Rosen, P. (2016, August 12). *Want to talk about teachers' biases? First, talk about race.* NPR. Retrieved from www.npr.org/sections/ed/2016/08/12/485839561/want-to-address-teachers-biases-first-talk-about-race?utm_medium=RSS&utm_campaign=education?utm_medium=RSS&utm_campaign=education

Baron, B. and Darling-Hammond, L. (2008). *Teaching for meaningful learning: A review of research on inquiry-based and cooperative learning. Book excerpt.* Edutopia. Retrieved from https://backend.edutopia.org/sites/default/files/pdfs/edutopia-teaching-for-meaningful-learning.pdf

Beck, I.L., McKeown, M.G., and Kucan, L. (2013). *Bringing words to life: Robust vocabulary instruction*, 2e. New York: Guilford Press.

Beckford, A. (2018, August 6). The skills you need to succeed in 2020. *Forbes*. Retrieved from www.forbes.com/sites/ellevate/2018/08/06/the-skills-you-need-to-succeed-in-2020/#77b8276f288a

Bekel, J. (n.d.). *Depend on the text! How to create text-dependent questions*. NCTE. Retrieved from www.readwritethink.org/professional-development/strategy-guides/depend-text-create-text-31024.html

Bersh, L.C. (2013). The curricular value of teaching about immigration through picture book thematic text sets. *The Social Studies* 104 (2): 47–56. Retrieved from www.tandfonline.com/doi/abs/10.1080/00377996.2012.720307

Bick, C. and Rabinovich, M.I. (2009). Dynamical origin of the effective storage capacity in the brain's working memory. *Physical Review Letters* 103 (21): 218101. www.ncbi.nlm.nih.gov/pubmed/20366069

Biemiller, A. and Boote, C. (2006). An effective method for building meaning vocabulary in the primary grades. *Journal of Educational Psychology* 98 (1): 44–62.

Billings, E. and Walqui, A. (n.d.). Topic brief 3: De-Mystifying complex texts: What are "complex" texts and how can we ensure ELLs/MLLs can access them? *Bilingual Education & English as a New Language*. Retrieved from www.nysed.gov/bilingual-ed/topic-brief-3-de-mystifying-complex-texts-what-are-complex-texts-and-how-can-we-ensure

Black, P. and Wiliam, D. (1998). *Inside the black box: Raising standards through classroom assessment* [PDF file]. Phi Delta Kappa International Retrieved from www.rdc.udel.edu/wp-content/uploads/2015/04/InsideBlackBox.pdf

Blackburn, B.R. (2018, December 13). Productive struggle is a learner's sweet spot. *ASCD Express* 14 (11) Retrieved from www.ascd.org/ascd-express/vol14/num11/productive-struggle-is-a-learners-sweet-spot.aspx

Blake, C. (2016, January 5). *Metacognition in the classroom* [web log comment]. Retrieved from https://education.cu-portland.edu/blog/classroom-resources/classroom-metacognition/

Bland, A. (2016, October 27). A native plan to restore the winter run chinook. *KCET*. Retrieved from www.kcet.org/shows/tending-the-wild/a-native-plan-to-restore-the-winter-run-chinook

Bloom's revised taxonomy (n.d.). Colorado College. Retrieved from www.coloradocollege.edu/other/assessment/how-to-assess-learning/learning-outcomes/blooms-revised-taxonomy.html

Boaler, J. and Lamar, T. (2019, February 28). There is a better way to teach students with learning disabilities. *Time*. Retrieved from http://time.com/5539300/learning-disabilities-special-education-math-teachers-parents-students/

Bonesteel, M. (2018, July 20). Dopes, not doping, threaten to derail the Tour de France. *The Washington Post*. Retrieved from www.washingtonpost.com/news/early-lead/wp/2018/07/20/dopes-not-doping-threaten-to-derail-the-tour-de-france/?utm_term=.f91ec2a6edb0

Boulware, B.J. and Crow, M.L. (2011, November 9). Using the concept attainment strategy to enhance reading comprehension. *The Reading Teacher* 61 (6): 491–495. Retrieved from https://ila.onlinelibrary.wiley.com/doi/abs/10.1598/RT.61.6.7

Boulware-Gooden, R., Carreker, S., Thornhill, A., and Joshi, R.M. (2007). Instruction of metacognitive strategies enhances reading comprehension and vocabulary achievement of third-grade students. *Reading Teacher* 61 (1): 70–77. Retrieved from https://eric.ed.gov/?id=EJ774540.

Bowen, R.S. (2017). *Understanding by design.* Vanderbilt University Center for Teaching Retrieved from https://cft.vanderbilt.edu/guides-sub-pages/understanding-by-design

Breaking news consumer's handbook [PDF file] (n.d.). Retrieved from https://media.wnyc.org/media/resources/2013/Sep/20/OTM_Consumer_Handbook.pdf

Brooks, A.W. and John, L.K. (2018, May–June). The surprising power of questions. *Harvard Business Review.* Retrieved from https://hbr.org/2018/05/the-surprising-power-of-questions

Bruner, J.S., Goodnow, J.J., and Austin, G.A. (1956). *A study of thinking.* Oxford, England: Wiley.

Build better listening skills (n.d.). National Education Association. Retrieved from www.nea.org/tools/build-better-listening-skills.html

Bunch, G.C., Kibler, A., and Pimentel, S. (n.d.). *Realizing opportunities for English Learners in the Common Core English Language Arts and Disciplinary Literacy standards* [PDF file]. Retrieved from https://ell.stanford.edu/sites/default/files/pdf/academic-papers/01_Bunch_Kibler_Pimentel_RealizingOpp%20in%20ELA_FINAL_0.pdf

Byrd, C.M. (2016). Does culturally relevant teaching work? An examination from student perspectives. SAGE Open: 1–10. Retrieved from https://journals.sagepub.com/doi/full/10.1177/2158244016660744

Canpolat, M., Kuzu, S., Yıldırım, B., and Canpolat, S. (2015). Active listening strategies of academically successful university students. Eurasian Journal of Educational Research 60: 163–180. Retrieved from https://files.eric.ed.gov/fulltext/EJ1076695.pdf

Captives brought on board a slave ship on the West Coast of Africa (1880). Getty Images. Retrieved from www.gettyimages.com/detail/news-photo/captives-being-brought-on-board-a-slave-ship-on-the-west-news-photo/463911399

Caulfield, M. (2017, March 4). *How "news literacy" gets the web wrong.* Hapgood. Retrieved from https://hapgood.us/2017/03/04/how-news-literacy-gets-the-web-wrong

Charlottesville and a "new generation of white supremacists." (2017, August 17). *Fox News.* Retrieved from www.foxnews.com/us/charlottesville-and-a-new-generation-of-white-supremacists

Chen, C.W. (2014, December). *Indigenous rights in international law*. Retrieved from http://internationalstudies.oxfordre.com/view/10.1093/acrefore/9780190846626.001.0001/acrefore-9780190846626-e-77?print

Cheung, A., Slavin, R.E., Lake, C., and Kim, E. (2015, June). Effective secondary science approaches: A best-evidence synthesis [PDF file]. *Best evidence encyclopedia*. Retrieved from www.bestevidence.org/Secondary-Science-07-15-15.pdf

Chu, J.M. (2014, October 21). Supply & dance, man! YouTube. Retrieved from www.youtube.com/user/wetheeconomy/search?query=supply+and+dance+man

Cigainero, J. (2018, April 29). French museum discovers more than half its collection is forged. *NPR*. Retrieved from www.npr.org/2018/04/29/606919098/french-museum-discovers-more-than-half-its-collection-is-forged

Clarke, C. (2016, September 26). Untold history: The survival of California's Indians. KCET. Retrieved from www.kcet.org/shows/tending-the-wild/untold-history-the-survival-of-californias-indians

Coleman, D. and Pimentel, S. (2012, April 12). *Revised publishers' criteria for the Common Core Standards in English Language Arts and Literacy, grades 3–12*. Retrieved from www.corestandards.org/assets/Publishers_Criteria_for_3-12.pdf

Committee on Developments in the Science of Learning (2000). *How people learn: Brain, mind, experience, and school* (Expanded ed.). Washington, DC: The National Academies Press Retrieved from www.nap.edu/login.php?record_id=9853

Common Core State Standards Initiative (2010a). *Common Core state standards for English/Language Arts & Literacy in History/Social Studies, Science, and technical subjects: Appendix A: Research supporting key elements of the standards: Glossary of key terms* [PDF file]. Retrieved from www.corestandards.org/assets/Appendix_A.pdf

Common Core State Standards Initiative (2010b). *English Language Arts Standards >> History/Social Studies >> Grade 11–12 >> 4*. Retrieved from www.corestandards.org/ELA-Literacy/RH/11-12/4

Common Core State Standards Initiative (2010c). *English Language Arts Standards >> Writing >> Grade 11–12 >> 2 >> d*. Retrieved from www.corestandards.org/ELA-Literacy/WHST/11-12/2/d

Common Core State Standards Initiative (2010d). *English Language Arts Standards >> Writing >> Grade 11–12 >> 10*. Retrieved from www.corestandards.org/ELA-Literacy/RH/11-12/10

Common Core State Standards Initiative (2010e). *English Language Arts Standards >> Standard 10: Range, quality, & complexity >> Measuring text complexity: Three factors*. Retrieved from www.corestandards.org/ELA-Literacy/standard-10-range-quality-complexity/measuring-text-complexity-three-factors

Common Core State Standards Initiative (2010f). *English Language Arts Standards >> History/Social Studies >> Grade 11–12 >> 1*. Retrieved from www.corestandards.org/ELA-Literacy/RH/11-12/1

Common Core State Standards Initiative (2010g). *Read the standards.* Retrieved from www.corestandards.org/read-the-standards

Common Core State Standards Initiative (2010h). *English Language Arts Standards >> History/Social Studies >> Grade 9–10.* Retrieved from www.corestandards.org/ELA-Literacy/RH/9-10

Common Core State Standards Initiative (2010i). *English Language Arts Standards >> Writing >> Grade 8 >> 9 >> a.* Retrieved from www.corestandards.org/ELA-Literacy/W/8/9/a

Common Core State Standards Initiative (2010j). *English Language Arts Standards >> Language >> Grade 9–10 >> 4 >> b.* Retrieved from www.corestandards.org/ELA-Literacy/L/9-10/4/b

Common Core State Standards Initiative (2010k). *English Language Arts Standards >> Language >> Language progressive skills.* Retrieved from www.corestandards.org/ELA-Literacy/L/language-progressive-skills

Common Core State Standards Initiative (2010l). *English Language Arts Standards >>.* Retrieved from www.corestandards.org/other-resources/key-shifts-in-english-language-arts

Common Core State Standards Initiative (2010m). Key shifts in *English Language Arts.* Retrieved from www.corestandards.org/ELA-Literacy/RH/6-8/7

Common Core State Standards Initiative (2010n). *English Language Arts Standards >> Writing >> Grade 11–12 >> 9.* Retrieved from www.corestandards.org/ELA-Literacy/RH/11-12/9

Common Core State Standards Initiative (2010o). *English Language Arts Standards >> Language >> Grade 9–10 >> 3.* Retrieved from www.corestandards.org/ELA-Literacy/RH/9-10/3

Common Core State Standards Initiative (2010p). *English Language Arts Standards >> Language >> Grade 9–10 >> 6.* Retrieved from www.corestandards.org/ELA-Literacy/RH/9-10/6

Common Core State Standards Initiative (2010q). *English Language Arts Standards >> Writing >> Grade 11–12 >> 1 >> b.* Retrieved from www.corestandards.org/ELA-Literacy/WHST/11-12/1/b

Common Core State Standards Initiative (2010r). *Frequently asked questions.* Retrieved from www.corestandards.org/about-the-standards/frequently-asked-questions/#faq-2323

Common Core State Standards Initiative (2010s). *English Language Arts Standards >> History/Social Studies >> Grade 11–12 >> 7.* Retrieved from www.corestandards.org/ELA-Literacy/RH/11-12/7

Common Core State Standards Initiative (2010t). *English Language Arts Standards >> Writing >> Grade 11–12 >> 4.* Retrieved from www.corestandards.org/ELA-Literacy/WHST/11-12/4

Common Core State Standards Initiative (2010u). *English Language Arts Standards >> Writing >> Grade 9–10 >> 7*. Retrieved from www.corestandards.org/ELA-Literacy/W/9-10/7

Common Core State Standards Initiative (2010v). *English Language Arts Standards >> History/Social Studies >> Grade 9–10 >> 1*. Retrieved from www.corestandards.org/ELA-Literacy/RH/9-10/1

Common Core State Standards Initiative (2010w). *English Language Arts Standards >> History/Social Studies >> Grade 9–10 >> 2*. Retrieved from www.corestandards.org/ELA-Literacy/RH/9-10/2

Common Core State Standards Initiative (2010x). *English Language Arts Standards >> History/Social Studies >> Grade 11–12*. Retrieved from www.corestandards.org/ELA-Literacy/RH/11-12

Common Core State Standards Initiative (2010y). *English Language Arts Standards >> Speaking & Listening >> Grade 9-10 >> 1 >> c*. Retrieved from www.corestandards.org/ELA-Literacy/RH/9-10/1

Common Core State Standards Initiative (2010z). *English Language Arts Standards >> Speaking & Listening >> Grade 9–10*. Retrieved from www.corestandards.org/ELA-Literacy/SL/9-10

Common Core State Standards Initiative (2010aa). *English Language Arts Standards >> Speaking & Listening >> Grade 9–10 >> 1*. Retrieved from www.corestandards.org/ELA-Literacy/SL/9-10/1

Common Core State Standards Initiative (2010bb). *English Language Arts Standards >> Speaking & Listening >> Grade 9–10 >> 1 >> d*. Retrieved from www.corestandards.org/ELA-Literacy/SL/9-10/1/d/

Common Core State Standards Initiative (2010cc). *Frequently asked questions*. Retrieved from www.corestandards.org/about-the-standards/frequently-asked-questions

Common Core State Standards Initiative (2010dd). *English Language Arts Standards >> History/Social Studies >> Grade 11–12 >> 6*. Retrieved from www.corestandards.org/ELA-Literacy/RH/11-12/6

Common Core State Standards Initiative (2010ee). *English Language Arts Standards >> Introduction >> Key design consideration*. Retrieved from www.corestandards.org/ELA-Literacy/introduction/key-design-consideration

Common Core State Standards Initiative (2010ff). *Frequently asked questions*. Retrieved from www.corestandards.org/about-the-standards/frequently-asked-questions/#faq-2301

Common Core State Standards Initiative (2010gg). *English Language Arts Standards >> History/Social Studies >> Grade 6–8 >> 4*. Retrieved from www.corestandards.org/ELA-Literacy/RH/6-8/4

Common Core State Standards Initiative (2010hh). *English Language Arts Standards >> History/Social Studies >> Grade 6–8 >> 7*. Retrieved from www.corestandards .org/ELA-Literacy/RH/6-8/7

Common Core State Standards Initiative (2019). Retrieved from www.corestandards .org/ELA-Literacy/RH/9-10/

Concept to classroom. Workshop: Inquiry-based learning (n.d.). *WNET Education*. Retrieved from www.thirteen.org/edonline/concept2class/inquiry/index_sub1.html

Cooper, K.M., Haney, B., Krieg, A., and Brownell, S.E. (2017). What's in a name? The importance of students perceiving that an instructor knows their names in a high-enrollment biology classroom. *CBE Life Sciences Education* 16 (1) Retrieved from www.ncbi.nlm.nih.gov/pmc/articles/PMC5332051/

Corcoran, S. (n.d.). *Discussion in the classroom: Why to do it, how to do it, and how to assess it*. Teaching on Purpose. Retrieved from http://teachingonpurpose.org/journal/ discussion-in-the-classroom-why-to-do-it-how-to-do-it-and-how-to-assess-it

Corley, M.A. and Rauscher, W.C. (2013). *TEAL Center fact sheet no. 12: Deeper learning through questioning*. Teaching Excellence in Adult Literacy. Retrieved from https://lincs.ed.gov/sites/default/files/12_TEAL_Deeper_Learning_Qs_ complete_5_1_0.pdf

Cortes describes Tenochtitlan (n.d.). American Historical Association. Retrieved from www.historians.org/teaching-and-learning/teaching-resources-for-histo- rians/teaching-and-learning-in-the-digital-age/the-history-of-the-americas/the- conquest-of-mexico/letters-from-hernan-cortes/cortes-describes-tenochtitlan

Culturally responsive teaching. (n.d.). Brown University: The Education Alli- ance. Retrieved from www.brown.edu/academics/education-alliance/teaching- diverse-learners/strategies-0/culturally-responsive-teaching-0

Daley, S. and Rubin, A.J. (2015, May 27). French Muslims say veil ban gives cover to bias. *New York Times*. Retrieved from www.nytimes.com/2015/05/27/world/ europe/muslim-frenchwomen-struggle-with-discrimination-as-bans-on-veils- expand.html

Darling-Hammond, L. and Adamson, F. (2010). *Beyond basic skills: The role of perfor- mance assessment in achieving 21st century standards of learning* [PDF file]. Stanford, CA: Stanford Center for Opportunity Policy in Education Retrieved from https://scale.stanford.edu/system/files/beyond-basic-skills-role-performance- assessment-achieving-21st-century-standards-learning.pdf

Dean, D. (2008). *Genre theory: Teaching, writing, and being*. Urbana, IL: National Council of Teachers of English www.amazon.com/Genre-Theory-Teaching- Writing-Being/dp/0814118410/ref=sr_1_2?ie=UTF8&qid=1538334057&sr=8- 2&keywords=deborah+dean

Denton, A. (2014). *20 iconic images from alternative perspectives*. Retrieved from https://guff.com/20-iconic-images-from-alternate-perspective

Dewan, P. (2015). Words versus pictures: Leveraging the research on visual communication. Partnership: The Canadian Journal of Library and Information Practice and Research 10 (1) Retrieved from https://journal.lib.uoguelph.ca/index.php/perj/article/view/3137/3473

Digital Public Library of America (2016, September 21). *10 ways to use the primary source sets in your classroom.* Retrieved from https://dp.la/news/10-ways-to-use-the-primary-source-sets

Dougherty, B.K. (2003). Comic relief: Using political cartoons in the classroom. International Studies Perspectives 3 (3): 258–270. Retrieved from https://onlinelibrary.wiley.com/doi/abs/10.1111/1528-3577.00095

Dr. Dweck's research into growth mindset changed education forever (n.d.). Retrieved from www.mindsetworks.com/science

Dunlosky, J. and Thiede, K.W. (1998). What makes people study more? An evaluation of factors that affect self-paced study. *Acta Psychologica* 98 (1): 37–56. Retrieved from www.sciencedirect.com/science/article/pii/S0001691897000516

Durlak, J.A., Weissberg, R.P., Dymnicki, A.B. et al. (2011). The impact of enhancing students' social and emotional learning: A meta-analysis of school-based universal interventions. *Child Development* 82 (1): 405–432. Retrieved from www.ncbi.nlm.nih.gov/pubmed/21291449

Dutschke, D. (1988). A history of American Indians in California. In: *California Department of Parks and Recreation, Five views: An ethnic historic site survey for California.* Sacramento: California Department of Parks and Recreation Retrieved from www.nps.gov/parkhistory/online_books/5views/5views1h90.htm

Dweck, C. (2015, September 22). Carol Dweck revisits the "growth mindset." *Education Week.* Retrieved from www.edweek.org/ew/articles/2015/09/23/carol-dweck-revisits-the-growth-mindset.html

Education Staff (n.d.). *Cartoon Analysis Worksheet.* Washington, DC: National Archives and Records Administration Retrieved from www.archives.gov/files/education/lessons/worksheets/cartoon_analysis_worksheet_former.pdf

Educators want students to ask the questions (2012, August 23). Retrieved from www.wbur.org/hereandnow/2012/08/23/educators-students-ask

El Rafaie, E. (2009). Multiliteracies: How readers interpret political cartoons. *Visual Communication* 8 (2): 181–205. Retrieved from https://journals.sagepub.com/doi/10.1177/1470357209102113

Endacott, J. and Brooks, S. (2013). An updated theoretical and practical model for promoting historical empathy. *Social Studies Research and Practice* 8 (1): 41–58. Retrieved from www.socstrpr.org/wp-content/uploads/2013/04/MS_06482_no3.pdf

Ericcson, K.A., Chase, W.G., and Faloon, S. (1980). Acquisition of a memory skills. *Science* 208 (4448): 1181–1182. Retrieved from www.ncbi.nlm.nih.gov/pubmed/7375930

Evaluation information: Information literacy (n.d.). American Library Association. Retrieved from https://libguides.ala.org/InformationEvaluation/Infolit

Everding, G. (2014, August 8). Expecting to teach enhances learning, recall. *EurekAlert!* Retrieved from www.eurekalert.org/pub_releases/2014-08/wuis-ett080814.php

Examples of social and emotional learning in middle school social studies instruction (2017, August). Retrieved from www.casel.org/wp-content/uploads/2017/08/SEL-in-Middle-School-Social-Studies-8-20-17.pdf

Farming in the gilded age: A simulation (n.d.). *Teaching Channel*. Retrieved from www.teachingchannel.org/video/using-simulation-in-the-classroom

Fergiani, A. (2018, March 9). *Mosaics depicting Roman ports and maritime trade*. Retrieved from www.romanports.org/en/articles/human-interest/334-the-mosaics-depicting-roman-ports-and-maritime-trade.html

Ferlazzo, L. (2009, May 2). The best places to read & write "choose your own adventure" stories [web log comment]. *Larry Ferlazzo's Websites of the Day*. Retrieved from http://larryferlazzo.edublogs.org/2009/05/02/the-best-places-to-read-write-choose-your-own-adventure-stories/

Ferlazzo, L. (2009, September 20). Reading logs – Part Two (or "How students can grow their brains") [web log comment]. *Larry Ferlazzo's Websites of the Day*. Retrieved from http://larryferlazzo.edublogs.org/2009/09/20/reading-logs-part-two-or-how-students-can-grow-their-brains/

Ferlazzo, L. (2010, March 2). The best resources to learn about the U.S. census [web log comment]. *Larry Ferlazzo's Websites of the Day*. Retrieved from http://larryferlazzo.edublogs.org/2010/03/02/the-best-resources-to-learn-about-the-u-s-census/

Ferlazzo, L. (2011). *Helping students motivate themselves*. New York: Routledge www.amazon.com/Student-Motivation-Book-Bundle-Themselves/dp/1596671815/ref=sr_1_1?keywords=helping+students+motivate+themselves&qid=1571404908&sr=8-1

Ferlazzo, L. (2011, April 27). The best resources for learning about the "achievement gap" (or "opportunity gap") [web log comment]. *Larry Ferlazzo's Websites of the Day*. Retrieved from http://larryferlazzo.edublogs.org/2011/04/27/the-best-resources-for-learning-about-the-achievement-gap/

Ferlazzo, L. (2012, May 19). The best resources for teaching "what if?" history lessons [web log comment]. Retrieved from http://larryferlazzo.edublogs.org/2012/05/19/the-best-resources-for-teaching-what-if-history-lessons/

Ferlazzo, L. (2013, June 27). The best tools for making internet "memes" [web log comment]. *Larry Ferlazzo's Websites of the Day*. Retrieved from http://larryferlazzo.edublogs.org/2013/06/27/the-best-tools-for-making-internet-memes

Ferlazzo, L. (2013, August 30). The best resources showing social emotional learning isn't enough [web log comment]. *Larry Ferlazzo's Websites of the Day.* Retrieved from http://larryferlazzo.edublogs.org/2013/08/30/the-best-articles-about-the-study-showing-social-emotional-learning-isnt-enough/

Ferlazzo, L. (2014, April 4). Response: Ways to cultivate "whole-class engagement" [web log comment]. *Education Week.* Retrieved from http://blogs.edweek.org/teachers/classroom_qa_with_larry_ferlazzo/2014/04/response_ways_to_cultivate_whole-class_engagement.html

Ferlazzo, L. (2015a). Creating the conditions for student motivation [web log comment]. *Edutopia.* Retrieved from www.edutopia.org/blog/creating-conditions-for-student-motivation-larry-ferlazzo

Ferlazzo, L. (2015b). *Building a community of self-motivated learners.* New York: Routledge.

Ferlazzo, L. (2015c, July 8). "Culturally responsive teaching": An interview with Zaretta Hammond [web log comment]. *Education Week.* Retrieved from http://blogs.edweek.org/teachers/classroom_qa_with_larry_ferlazzo/2015/07/culturally_responsive_teaching_an_interview_with_zaretta_hammond.html

Ferlazzo, L. (2016, March 24). Collaborative writing, Common Core, and ELLs [web log comment]. *Edutopia.* Retrieved from www.edutopia.org/blog/collaborative-writing-common-core-ells-larry-ferlazzo-katie-hull-sypnieski

Ferlazzo, L. (2017, January 26). Ideas for E.L.L.'s: Finding reliable sources in a world of "fake news." *New York Times.* Retrieved from www.nytimes.com/2017/01/26/learning/lesson-plans/ideas-for-ells-finding-reliable-sources-in-a-world-of-fake-news.html

Ferlazzo, L. (2017, November 28). Response: Students can "own their learning through creating questions." *Education Week.* Retrieved from http://blogs.edweek.org/teachers/classroom_qa_with_larry_ferlazzo/2017/11/response_students_can_own_their_learning_through_creating_questions.html

Ferlazzo, L. (2018, November 5). Response: "Writing frames are the recipes of writing" [web log comment]. *Education Week.* Retrieved from https://blogs.edweek.org/teachers/classroom_qa_with_larry_ferlazzo/2018/11/response_writing_frames_are_the_recipes_of_writing.html

Ferlazzo, L. (2019, January 1). What if? History projects [web log comment]. *Larry Ferlazzo's Websites of the Day.* Retrieved from http://larryferlazzo.edublogs.org/2019/01/01/what-if-history-projects-2/

Ferlazzo, L. (2019, August 18). A look back: My growth mindset lessons usually go well, but what I did today was the best yet (student hand-outs included) [web log comment]. *Larry Ferlazzo's Websites of the Day.* Retrieved from http://larryferlazzo.edublogs.org/2019/08/18/a-look-back-my-growth-mindset-lessons-usually-go-well-but-what-i-did-today-was-the-best-yet-student-hand-outs-included/

Ferlazzo, L. (2019, August 26). Here's the questionnaire my students complete on the first day of school [web log comment]. *Larry Ferlazzo's Websites of the Day*. Retrieved from http://larryferlazzo.edublogs.org/2019/08/26/heres-the-questionnaire-my-students-complete-on-the-first-day-of-school/

Ferlazzo, L., & Sypnieski, K. H. (2012, October 10). Eight ways to use video with English-Language Learners [web log comment]. *Edutopia*. Retrieved from www.edutopia.org/blog/ell-engagement-using-video-larry-ferlazzo-katie-hull-sypnieski

Ferlazzo, L. and Sypnieski, K.H. (2016). *Navigating the Common Core with English language learners: Practical strategies to develop higher-order thinking skills*. San Francisco: Wiley.

Ferlazzo, L., & Sypnieski, K. H. (2018a, March 29). Activating prior knowledge with English language learners. *Edutopia*. Retrieved from www.edutopia.org/article/activating-prior-knowledge-english-language-learners

Ferlazzo, L. and Sypnieski, K.H. (2018b). *The ELL teacher's toolbox*. San Francisco: Wiley.

Finley, T. (2014, February 19). Common core in action: 10 visual literacy strategies. *Edtopia*. Retrieved from www.edutopia.org/blog/ccia-10-visual-literacy-strategies-todd-finley

Finson, K.D., Olson, J.K., and Emig, B. (2015). Navigating visual data literacy and inscriptions in the classroom. In: *Application of visual data in k16 science classrooms* (eds. K.D. Finson and J. Pedersen), 51–84. Charlotte, NC: Information Age.

Fisher, L.A. (2018, September 24). Dancers took over the runway at Dior's spring 2019 show. *Harper's BAZAAR*. Retrieved from www.harpersbazaar.com/fashion/fashion-week/a23398506/dior-spring-2019-show-paris-fashion-week/

Fisher, D. and Frey, N. (2014a). Content area vocabulary learning. *The Reading Teacher* 67 (8): 594–599. Retrieved from https://ila.onlinelibrary.wiley.com/doi/abs/10.1002/trtr.1258

Fisher, D. and Frey, N. (2014b). Close reading as an intervention for struggling middle school readers. *Journal of Adolescent & Adult Literacy* 57 (5): 367–376. Retrieved from https://ila.onlinelibrary.wiley.com/doi/pdf/10.1002/jaal.266

Flavell, J. (n.d.). *Theories of learning in educational psychology* [PDF file]. Retrieved from www.demenzemedicinagenerale.net/images/mens-sana/Theories_of_Learning_in_Educational_Psychology.pdf

Flyvbjerg, B. (2006). Five misunderstandings about case-study research. *Qualitative Inquiry* 12 (2): 219–245. Retrieved from https://journals.sagepub.com/doi/abs/10.1177/1077800405284363

Fordham, N.W., Wellman, D., and Sandmann, A. (2010). Taming the text: Engaging and supporting students in social studies readings. *The Social Studies* 93 (4): 149–158. Retrieved from www.tandfonline.com/doi/abs/10.1080/00377990209599901?journalCode=vtss20

Formal assessment (n.d.). British Council. Retrieved from www.teachingenglish.org.uk/article/formal-assessment

Formative assessment (2014, April 29). *The glossary of education reform*. Retrieved from www.edglossary.org/formative-assessment/

Forrin, N.D. (2018). This time it's personal: The memory benefit of hearing oneself. *Memory* 26 (4): 574–579. Retrieved from www.tandfonline.com/doi/abs/10.1080/09658211.2017.1383434?journalCode=pmem20

Foster, S.J. and Padgett, C.S. (1999). Authentic historical inquiry in the social studies classroom. *The Clearing House: A Journal of Educational Strategies, Issues and Ideas* 72 (6): 357–363. Retrieved from www.tandfonline.com/doi/abs/10.1080/00098659909599425

France beat Croatia to win World Cup 2018 (2018, July 16). *Al Jazeera and News Agencies*. Retrieved from www.aljazeera.com/news/2018/07/world-cup-final-france-beat-croatia-win-russia-2018-180715160625847.html

Frequently asked questions (n.d.). U.S. Department of the Interior, Indian Affairs. Retrieved from www.bia.gov/frequently-asked-questions

Frymier, A.B. and Shulman, G.M. (2009). "What's in it for me?": Increasing content relevance to enhance students' motivation. *Communication Education* 44 (1): 40–50. https://nca.tandfonline.com/doi/abs/10.1080/03634529509378996#.XEDASflKi1t

Ganley, E. and Leicester, J. (2018, December 8). Rioting engulfs Paris as anger grows over high taxes. *Chicago Tribune*. Retrieved from www.chicagotribune.com/news/nationworld/ct-france-paris-riots-macron-20181208-story.html

Garrison, C. and Ehringhaus, M. (n.d.). *Formative and summative assessments in the classroom*. Association for Middle Level Education Retrieved from www.amle.org/BrowsebyTopic/WhatsNew/WNDet/TabId/270/ArtMID/888/ArticleID/286/Formative-and-Summative-Assessments-in-the-

Gittings, P. (2018, July 29). Tour de France 2018: Geraint Thomas wins to make sporting history. CNN. Retrieved from https://edition.cnn.com/2018/07/29/sport/tour-de-france-geraint-thomas-wins/index.html

Glass, G.V. (2002). Grouping students for instruction. In: *School reform proposals: The research evidence, research in educational productivity series* (ed. A. Molnar). Greenwich, CT: Information Age Publishing Retrieved from https://nepc.colorado.edu/sites/default/files/Chapter05-Glass-Final.pdf

Gonchar, M. (2015, September 17). Drawing for change: Analyzing and making political cartoons. *The New York Times*. Retrieved from https://learning.blogs.nytimes.com/2015/09/17/drawing-for-change-analyzing-and-making-political-cartoons/

Gonzalez, J. (2019, July 7). *Think twice before doing another historical simulation*. Retrieved from www.cultofpedagogy.com/classroom-simulations/

Graff, G. and Birkenstein, C. (2014). *They say, I say: The moves that matter in academic writing*. New York: Gildan Media www.amazon.com/They-Say-Matter-Academic-Writing/dp/1469028611

Graham, S., Bruch, J., Fitzgerald, J. et al. (2016). *Teaching secondary students to write effectively (NCEE 2017–4002)*. Washington, DC: National Center for Education Evaluation and Regional Assistance (NCEE), Institute of Education Sciences, U.S. Department of Education Retrieved from http://whatworks.ed.gov/ncee/wwc/Docs/PracticeGuide/wwc_secondary_writing_110116.pdf

Growth mindset feedback (n.d.). Retrieved from www.mindsetworks.com/websitemedia/resources/growth-mindset-feedback-tool.pdf

Guskey, T.R. (2018). Does pre-assessment work? *Educational Leadership* 75 (5): 52–57. Retrieved from http://tguskey.com/wp-content/uploads/EL-18-Pre-Assessments.pdf

Gustin, E. W. (1909). *Election day!* Library of Congress. Retrieved from www.loc.gov/pictures/item/97500226/

Guthrie, J.T., Wigfield, A., Barbosa, P. et al. (2004). Increasing reading comprehension and engagement through concept-oriented reading instruction. *Journal of Educational Psychology* 96 (3): 403–423. Retrieved from www.cori.umd.edu/research-publications/2004-guthrie-wigfield-etal.pdf

Halvorsen, A.-L., Duke, N. K., Brugar, K., Block, M., Strachan, S., Berka, M., and Brown, J. (2012). *Narrowing the achievement gap in second-grade social studies and content area literacy: The promise of a project-based approach*. Retrieved from http://education.msu.edu/EPC/library/papers/WP26/

Hammond, Z. (2013). *Ready for rigor: A framework for culturally responsive teaching* [PDF file]. Retrieved from https://crtandthebrain.com/wp-content/uploads/READY-FOR-RIGOR_Final1.pdf

Hammond, Z. (2014). *Culturally responsive teaching and the brain: Promoting authentic engagement and rigor among culturally and linguistically diverse students*. Thousand Oaks, CA: Corwin.

Hammond, Z. (2015, April 1). 3 tips to make any lesson more culturally responsive. *Cult of Pedagogy*. Retrieved from www.cultofpedagogy.com/culturally-responsive-teaching-strategies

Harvey, G. (1999). *Counterargument*. Retrieved from https://writingcenter.fas.harvard.edu/pages/counter-argument

Hedrick, W.B., Harmon, J.M., and Linerode, P.M. (2004). Teachers' beliefs and practices of vocabulary instruction with social studies textbooks in grades 4–8. *Reading Horizons* 45 (2): 103–125. Retrieved from https://scholarworks.wmich.edu/cgi/viewcontent.cgi?article=1162&context=reading_horizons

Helm, J. (2017, August 14). Recounting a day of rage, hate, violence and death. *Washington Post*. Retrieved from www.washingtonpost.com/graphics/2017/local/charlottesville-timeline/?utm_term=.7adf40bebe53

Herold, B. and Molnar, M. (2014, March 3). Research questions Common-Core claims by publishers. *Education Week*. Retrieved from www.edweek.org/ew/articles/2014/03/05/23textbooks_ep.h33.html

Historians defined (n.d.). Retrieved from https://teachinghistory.org/history-content/ask-a-historian/24120

How the strategic teacher plans for concept attainment (2007). *ASCD Express*. Retrieved from www.ascd.org/ascd-express/vol4/420-silver.aspx

Hymowitz, S., Dikkers, I., and Anderson, A. (2003). *Study guide: The rights of Indigenous peoples*. Minneapolis: University of Minnesota Human Rights Center Retrieved from http://hrlibrary.umn.edu/edumat/studyguides/indigenous.html.

Identifying "fake" news: Common Sense Education (n.d.). *PBS Learning Media*. Retrieved from www.pbslearningmedia.org/resource/nmlit17-ela-idfakenews/identifying-fake-news/

Jones, C. (2018, July 25). Native Americans push schools to include their story in California history classes. *EdSource*. Retrieved from https://edsource.org/2018/native-americans-push-schools-to-include-their-story-in-california-history-classes/600669

Jones, S.M. and Bouffard, S.M. (2012, December 1). Social and emotional learning in schools: from programs to strategies and commentaries. *Social Policy Report* 26 (4): 3–22. www.srcd.onlinelibrary.wiley.com/doi/10.1002/j.2379-3988.2012.tb00073.x

Joyce, B.R., Weil, M., and Calhoun, E. (2017). *Models of Teaching*, 9e. Boston: Pearson www.amazon.com/Models-Teaching-9th-Bruce-Joyce/dp/0134892585/ref=sr_1_3?ie=UTF8&qid=1544390531&sr=8-3&keywords=bruce+joyce

Judkis, M. and Witte, G. (2015, November 13). String of Paris terrorist attacks leaves over 120 dead. *Washington Post*. Retrieved from www.washingtonpost.com/world/europe/paris-rocked-by-explosions-and-shootouts-leaving-dozens-dead/2015/11/13/133f5bc2-8a50-11e5-bd91-d385b244482f_story.html?utm_term=.b448011b7924

Karimi, F. (2018, January 8). Train shooting heroes: The men who helped avert a massacre in Europe. *CNN*. Retrieved from www.cnn.com/2015/08/22/europe/france-train-shooting-heroes/index.html

Kelley, M.J. and Clausen-Grace, N. (2010). Guiding students through expository text with text feature walks. *Reading Rockets*. Retrieved from www.readingrockets.org/article/guiding-students-through-expository-text-text-feature-walks

Kirwan, P. (n.d.). *The emergent land: Nature and ecology in Native American expressive forms* [PDF file]. Retrieved from www.ucd.ie/pages/99/articles/kirwan.pdf

Knight, J. (2018, May 29). *An interview with Zaratta Hammond*. Retrieved from www.instructionalcoaching.com/an-interview-with-zaretta-hammond/

Knowledge lost in information: Report of the NSF Workshop on Research Directions for Digital Libraries [PDF file] (2003, June 15–17). Chatham, MA: NSF Workshop on Research Directions for Digital Libraries. Retrieved from www.digitalpreservation.gov/news/2004/knowledge_lost_report200405.pdf

Korbey, H. (2018, May 23). A history in which we can all see ourselves. *Edutopia*. Retrieved from www.edutopia.org/article/history-which-we-can-all-see-ourselves

Krasnoff, B. (2016, March). *Culturally responsive teaching: A guide to evidence-based practices for teaching all students equitably* [PDF file]. Region X Equity Assistance Center of Education Northwest. Retrieved from https://educationnorthwest.org/sites/default/files/resources/culturally-responsive-teaching.pdf

Kroeber, A.L. (1916). California place names of Indian origin [PDF file]. University of California Publications in American Archaeology and Ethnology 12 (2): 31–69. Retrieved from http://digitalassets.lib.berkeley.edu/anthpubs/ucb/text/ucp012-004.pdf

Lange, J. (2019, June 12). What we lose when we lose political cartoons. *The Week*. Retrieved from https://theweek.com/articles/846560/what-lose-when-lose-political-cartoons

Learning with all the senses (2015, February 5). Max-Planck-Gesellschaft. Retrieved from www.mpg.de/8934791/learning-senses-vocabulary

Lee, J. (1887). Sanitary. In *Reports of Indian schools* (p. 256). Retrieved from www.loc.gov/teachers/classroommaterials/primarysourcesets/assimilation/pdf/report2.pdf

Lehman, C. and Roberts, K. (2013). *Falling in* love *with* close reading: *Lessons for analyzing texts – and life*. Portsmouth, NH: Heinemann www.amazon.com/Falling-Love-Close-Reading-Texts/dp/0325050848

Lent, R.C. (2012). *Overcoming textbook fatigue: 21st century tools to revitalize teaching and learning*. Alexandria, VA: ASCD www.ascd.org/publications/books/113005/chapters/Background-Knowledge@-The-Glue-That-Makes-Learning-Stick.aspx

Leutner, D., Leopold, C., and den Elzen-Rump, V. (2007). Self-regulated learning with a text-highlighting strategy. *Journal of Psychology* 215: 174–182. https://econtent.hogrefe.com/doi/full/10.1027/0044-3409.215.3.174

Linguistic Society of America (n.d.). *Native American language revitalization legislation in the U.S. Congress*. Retrieved from www.linguisticsociety.org/content/native-american-language-revitalization-legislation

Lobrano, A. (2015, October 5). Paris's best new fall menus. *New York Times Style Magazine*. Retrieved from www.nytimes.com/2015/10/05/t-magazine/paris-restaurants-new-fall-menus.html

Lombardi, J.D. (2016, June 14). The deficit model is harming your students. *Edutopia*. Retrieved from www.edutopia.org/blog/deficit-model-is-harming-students-janice-lombardi

Los Angeles, California. Japanese American evacuation from West Coast areas under U.S. Army war emergency order. Japanese American child will go with his parents to Owens Valley (1942). Library of Congress. Retrieved from www.loc.gov/pictures/resource/fsa.8a31170/

Lundstrom, K., Diekema, A.R., Leary, H. et al. (2015). Teaching and learning information synthesis. *Communications in Information Literacy* 9 (1): 60–82. Retrieved from https://files.eric.ed.gov/fulltext/EJ1089165.pdf

Mankiller, W. (2009, March). Being indigenous in the 21st century. *Cultural Survival Quarterly Magazine*. Retrieved from www.culturalsurvival.org/publications/cultural-survival-quarterly/being-indigenous-21st-century

Mark, G.Y. and Allender, D. (2017). *Our stories in our voices*. Dubuque, IA: Kendall Hunt Publishing www.amazon.com/Our-Stories-Voices-MARK-GREGORY/dp/1524923478

Marr, C.J. (n.d.). *Assimilation through education: Indian boarding schools in the Pacific Northwest*. Seattle: University of Washington, University Libraries, Digital Collections Retrieved from http://content.lib.washington.edu/aipnw/marr.html

Marzano, R.J. (1991). Fostering thinking across the curriculum through knowledge restructuring. *Journal of Reading* 34 (7): 518–525. Retrieved from www.jstor.org/stable/40014576?seq=1#page_scan_tab_contents

Marzano, R.J., Pickering, D., and Pollock, J.E. (2001). *Classroom instruction that works: Research-based strategies for increasing student achievement*. Alexandria, VA: Association for Supervision and Curriculum Development.

Mastropieri, M.A. and Scruggs, T.E. (1998). Enhancing school success with mnemonic strategies. *Intervention in School and Clinic* 33 (4): 201–208. Retrieved from https://journals.sagepub.com/doi/10.1177/105345129803300402

Maya social structure (n.d.). University of Texas, Tarlton Law Library. Retrieved from https://tarlton.law.utexas.edu/aztec-and-maya-law/maya-social-structure

McCarthy, J. (2017, March 10). The skills colleges and employers are looking for. *Edutopia*. Retrieved from www.edutopia.org/article/skills-colleges-employers-looking-for-john-mccarthy

McDonnell, M. (2002). Making a case for the case study method. *Social Education* 66 (1): 68–69. Retrieved from www.socialstudies.org/sites/default/files/publications/se/6601/660117.html

McKenna, B. (2014, June 17). *New research shows effectiveness of student-centered learning in closing the opportunity gap*. Stanford Graduate School of Education Retrieved from https://ed.stanford.edu/news/new-research-shows-effectiveness-student-centered-learning-closing-opportunity-gap

McKeown, M.G. and Beck, I.L. (2004). Direct and rich vocabulary instruction. In: *Vocabulary instruction* (eds. J.F. Baumann and E.J. Kame'enui), 13–27. New York: Guilford Press Retrieved from www.learner.org/workshops/teachreading35/pdf/vocab_Instruction.pdf

McTighe, J. and Wiggins, G. (2013a). *Essential questions: Opening doors to student understanding*. Alexandria, VA: Association for Supervision & Curriculum Development www.amazon.com/Essential-Questions-Opening-Student-Understanding/dp/1416615059/ref=sr_1_3?keywords=essential+questions&qid=1559415192&s=gateway&sr=8-3

McTighe, J. and Wiggins, G. (2013b). What makes a question essential? In: *Essential questions: Opening doors to student understanding* (chapter 1). Alexandria, VA: Association for Supervision & Curriculum Development Retrieved from www.ascd.org/publications/books/109004/chapters/What-Makes-a-Question-Essential%A2.aspx

Media theory: How to analyze a photograph (n.d.). Understand Media. Retrieved from https://understandmedia.com/topics/media-theory/111-how-to-analyze-a-photograph

Monte-Sano, C. (2017). Qualities of historical writing instruction: A comparative case study of two teachers' practices. *American Educational Research Journal* 45 (4): 1045–1079. https://doi.org/10.3102%2F0002831208319733

Moss, B. (2005). Making a case and a place for effective content area literacy instruction in the elementary grades. *The Reading Teacher* 59 (1): 46–55. Retrieved from http://citeseerx.ist.psu.edu/viewdoc/download?doi=10.1.1.882.6206&rep=rep1&type=pdf

Moulton, M.R. (1999). The multigenre paper: Increasing interest, motivation, and functionality in research. *Journal of Adolescent & Adult Literacy* 42 (7): 528–539. Retrieved from https://ucenglish4089.files.wordpress.com/2013/10/moulton-mgp.pdf

Museums, libraries, and 21st century skills (n.d.). Institute of Museum and Library Services. Retrieved from www.imls.gov/issues/national-initiatives/museums-libraries-and-21st-century-skills/definitions

National Center for Educational Statistics (2019, February). *Status and trends in the education of racial and ethnic groups. Indicator 6: Elementary and secondary enrollment.* Retrieved from https://nces.ed.gov/programs/raceindicators/indicator_rbb.asp

National Council for the Social Studies (n.d.-a). *National curriculum standards for social studies: Chapter 2 – The themes of social studies.* Retrieved from www.socialstudies.org/standards/strands

National Council for the Social Studies (n.d.-b). *National curriculum standards for social studies: Executive summary.* Retrieved from www.socialstudies.org/standards/execsummary

National Council for the Social Studies (n.d.-c). *National curriculum standards for social studies: Introduction.* Retrieved from www.socialstudies.org/standards/introduction

National Council for the Social Studies (n.d.-d). *Oral and family history: The great Thanksgiving listen.* Retrieved from www.socialstudies.org/tssp/news/oral-and-family-history-great-thanksgiving-listen

National Council for the Social Studies (2010). *College, career & civic life: C3 framework for social studies state standards* [PDF file]. Retrieved from www.socialstudies.org/sites/default/files/2017/Jun/c3-framework-for-social-studies-rev0617.pdf

National Council for the Social Studies (2017). *Powerful, purposeful pedagogy in elementary school social studies.* Retrieved from www.socialstudies.org/positions/powerfulandpurposeful#footnote4_b3pm4hq

National Institute of Child Health and Human Development (n.d.). *Reading and reading disorders: Other FAQs.* Retrieved from www.nichd.nih.gov/health/topics/reading/conditioninfo/faqs#whatis

National Museum of the American Indian (n.d.). *Native knowledge 360°: Essential understandings about American Indians.* Washington, DC: Smithsonian Retrieved from https://americanindian.si.edu/nk360/understandings.cshtml#eublock1

National Reading Panel (2000, April). *Teaching children to read: An evidence-based assessment of the scientific research literature on reading and its implications for reading instruction.* Washington, DC: National Institute of Child Health and Human Development Retrieved from www.nichd.nih.gov/sites/default/files/publications/pubs/nrp/Documents/report.pdf

Neilson, L. (2018, December 6). How Chanel's makeup artist prepped for the brand's New York show. *New York Times Style Magazine.* Retrieved from www.nytimes.com/2018/12/06/t-magazine/lucia-pica-makeup-artist-chanel.html?action=click&module=MoreInSection&pgtype=Article&region=Footer&contentCollection=T%20Magazine

New information is easier to learn when composed of familiar elements (2015, August 13). *EurekAlert!* Retrieved from www.eurekalert.org/pub_releases/2015-08/cmu-nii081315.php

Obenchain, K.M., Orr, A., and Davis, S.H. (2011). The past as a puzzle: How essential questions can piece together a meaningful investigation of history. *The Social Studies* 102 (5): 190–199. Retrieved from www.tandfonline.com/doi/abs/10.1080/00377996.2010.543193

O'Brien, T. (1990). *The things they carried.* Boston: Houghton Mifflin.

O'Connor, T. (2018, September 13). What is France doing in Syria? New U.S. military photos may have shown too much. *Newsweek.* Retrieved from www.newsweek.com/what-france-doing-syria-new-us-military-photos-may-show-too-much-1120332

O'Donnell, C.P. (2004). Beyond the yellow highlighter: Teaching annotation skills to improve reading comprehension. *The English Journal* 93 (5): 82–89. Retrieved from www.researchgate.net/publication/275932276_Beyond_the_Yellow_Highlighter_Teaching_Annotation_Skills_to_Improve_Reading_Comprehension

Onion, R. (2019, May 20). What it felt like. *Slate.* Retrieved from https://slate.com/human-interest/2019/05/history-classroom-role-playing-games-slavery-holocaust.html

Pailliotet, A.W. (1993). Understanding visual information through deep viewing. *Visual literacy in the digital age: Selected readings from the Annual Conference of the International Visual Literacy Association.* Rochester, NY. Retrieved from https://files.eric.ed.gov/fulltext/ED370560.pdf

Parallel histories: Spain, United States, and the American Frontier (n.d.). Library of Congress. Retrieved from www.loc.gov/teachers/classroommaterials/connections/parallel-histories-spain/history2.html

Patall, E.A., Cooper, H., and Robinson, J.C. (2008). The effects of choice on intrinsic motivation and related outcomes: A meta-analysis of research findings. *Psychological Bulletin* 134 (2): 270–300. Retrieved from www.ncbi.nlm.nih.gov/pubmed/18298272

Patterson, N.C., Lucas, A.G., and Kithinji, M. (2012). Higher order thinking in social studies: An analysis of primary source document use. *Social Studies Research and Practice* 7 (2): 68–85. Retrieved from www.socstrpr.org/wp-content/uploads/2013/01/06437_no5.pdf

PEEL paragraph writing (n.d.). Virtual Library. Retrieved from www.virtuallibrary.info/peel-paragraph-writing.html

Peltier, E. (2018, November 3). Migrants bring cricket (and victory) to life in Northern France. *New York Times*. Retrieved from www.nytimes.com/2018/11/03/world/europe/france-cricket-refugees.html

Peters, C.W. (1974–1975). A comparison between the Fraser Model of concept attainment and the textbook approach to concept attainment (abstract). *Reading Research Quarterly* 10 (2): 252–254. Retrieved from www.jstor.org/stable/747186

Pinkerton, P. and Ashworth, J.H. (1898). *The reign of terror: A collection of authentic narratives of the horrors committed by the Revolutionary Government of France under Marat and Robespierre written by eye witnesses of the scenes.* London: Leonard Smithers.

Prince, M.J. and Felder, R.M. (2006). Inductive teaching and learning methods: Definitions, comparisons, and research bases. *Journal of Engineering Education* 95 (2): 123–138. Retrieved from https://onlinelibrary.wiley.com/doi/abs/10.1002/j.2168-9830.2006.tb00884.x

Putnam, A.L. (2015). Mnemonics in education: Current research and applications. *Translational Issues in Psychological Science* 1 (2): 130–139. Retrieved from https://pdfs.semanticscholar.org/8212/c386502bbb57fac01e6676e39e1717b68edf.pdf

Quinn, A. (2018, March 6). After a promise to return African artifacts, France moves toward a plan. *New York Times*. Retrieved from www.nytimes.com/2018/03/06/arts/design/france-restitution-african-artifacts.htm

Radboud University Nijmegen (2014, May 12). How the brain builds on prior knowledge. *Science Daily*. Retrieved from www.sciencedaily.com/releases/2014/05/140512101527.htm

Reiff, M.J. and Bawarshi, A. (2011). Tracing discursive resources: How students use prior genre knowledge to negotiate new writing contexts in first-year composition. *Written Communication* 28 (3): 312–337. Retrieved from http://journals.sagepub.com/doi/pdf/10.1177/0741088311410183

Responding to trauma in your classroom (2016). *Teaching Tolerance, 52*. Retrieved from www.tolerance.org/magazine/spring-2016/responding-to-trauma-in-your-classroom

Reznitskaya, A., Anderson, R.C., and Kuo, L.-J. (2007). Teaching and learning argumentation. *Elementary School Journal* 107 (5): 449–472. Retrieved from https://eric.ed.gov/?id=EJ765988

Rich, M. (2015, April 11). Where are the teachers of color? *New York Times.* Retrieved from www.nytimes.com/2015/04/12/sunday-review/where-are-the-teachers-of-color.html

Richard Feynman – Names don't constitute knowledge (2014, September 17). YouTube [Video file]. Retrieved from www.youtube.com/watch?v=lFIYKmos3-s

Richard Feinman: The difference between knowing the name of something and knowing something (n.d.). Farnam Street. Retrieved from https://fs.blog/2015/01/richard-feynman-knowing-something/

Roan, D. (2018, July 2). Chris Froome: Anti-doping case against four-time Tour de France winner dropped. *BBC.* Retrieved from www.bbc.com/sport/cycling/44679483

Rogers, C.R. and Farson, R.E. (1987). *Active listening* [PDF file]. Retrieved from http://wholebeinginstitute.com/wp-content/uploads/Rogers_Farson_Active-Listening.pdf

Roots of slavery (n.d.). *BBC World Service.* Retrieved from www.bbc.co.uk/worldservice/africa/features/storyofafrica/9chapter1.shtml

Ross, E.W. (2001). *The social studies curriculum: Purposes, problems, and possibilities* (Rev. ed.). New York: SUNY Press https://books.google.com/books?id=Juxsv4h2e4EC&dq=making+social+studies+relevant,+research&lr=&source=gbs_navlinks_s

Rowe, M.B. (1986). Wait time: Slowing down may be a way of speeding up. *Journal of Teacher Education* 37 (43): 43–50. Retrieved from www.scoe.org/blog_files/Budd%20Rowe.pdf

Safir, S. (2016, March 14). 5 keys to challenging implicit bias [web log comment]. *Edutopia.* Retrieved from www.edutopia.org/blog/keys-to-challenging-implicit-bias-shane-safir

Sample, I. (2014, October 2). Curiosity improves memory by tapping into the brain's reward system. *The Guardian.* Retrieved from www.theguardian.com/science/2014/oct/02/curiosity-memory-brain-reward-system-dopamine

Sangillo, J. (n.d.). 5 strategies for using primary source documents in social studies classrooms. *Discovery Education.* Retrieved from http://frontandcentral.com/teaching-and-learning/5-strategies-using-primary-source-documents-social-studies-classrooms/

Santos, R.L. (2014). Yokuts of Stanislaus County [PDF file]. *Stanislaus Historical Quarterly* 7 (1): 602–606. Retrieved from http://library.csustan.edu/sites/default/files/files/pdf/shq/shq-v7-n1.pdf

Schechner, S. (2018, August 13). France takes on cellphone addiction with a ban in schools. *Wall Street Journal*. Retrieved from www.wsj.com/articles/france-takes-on-cellphone-addiction-with-a-ban-in-schools-1534152600

Schwartz, K. (2017, June 14). How do you know when a teaching strategy is most effective? John Hattie has an idea. *KQED News*. Retrieved from www.kqed.org/mindshift/48112/how-do-you-know-when-a-teaching-strategy-is-most-effective-john-hattie-has-an-idea

Schwartz, K. (n.d.). Why intentionally building empathy is more important now than ever. *KQED News*. Retrieved from www.kqed.org/mindshift/54497/why-intentionally-building-empathy-is-more-important-now-than-ever

Scialabba, N. (2017, October 2). *How implicit bias impacts our children in education*. American Bar Association Retrieved from www.americanbar.org/groups/litigation/committees/childrens-rights/articles/2017/fall2017-how-implicit-bias-impacts-our-children-in-education/

Sciolino, E. (2015, August 26). On one Paris street, shopkeepers specialize in only one thing. *New York Times Style Magazine*. Retrieved from www.nytimes.com/2015/08/26/t-magazine/paris-shops-rue-des-martyrs.html

Scruggs, T.E., Mastropieri, M.A., Berkeley, S.L., and Marshak, L. (2010). Mnemonic strategies: Evidence-based practice and practice-based evidence. *Intervention in School and Clinic* 46 (2): 79–86. Retrieved from https://eric.ed.gov/?id=EJ902571

See think wonder: A routine for exploring works of art and other interesting things (n.d.). Harvard University Project Zero. Retrieved from www.visiblethinkingpz.org/VisibleThinking_html_files/03_ThinkingRoutines/03c_Core_routines/SeeThinkWonder/SeeThinkWonder_Routine.html

Seelye, K.Q. and Bidgood, J. (2017, August 18). Protesters flood streets, and Trump offers a measure of praise. *New York Times*. Retrieved from www.nytimes.com/2017/08/18/us/demonstration-race-free-speech-boston-charlottesville.html

Shah, A.K., Mullainathan, S., and Shafir, E. (2012). Some consequences of having too little. *Science* 338: 682–685. Retrieved from https://scholar.harvard.edu/files/sendhil/files/some_consequences_of_having_too_little.pdf

Shernoff, D.J. (2013). *Advancing responsible adolescent development. Optimal learning environments to promote student engagement.* New York: Spring Science + Business Media Retrieved from https://psycnet.apa.org/record/2013-28705-000

Silver, H.V., Dewing, R.T., and Perini, M.J. (2012). Inductive learning. In: *The core six*, 27–36. Alexandria, VA: ASCD www.ascd.org/publications/books/113007/chapters/Inductive-Learning.aspx

Slavery (n.d.). *Ancient Mesopotamian warfare*. Retrieved from http://sites.psu.edu/ancientmesopotamianwarfare/slavery/

Sleeter, C.E. (2011). *The academic and social value of ethnic studies: A research review* [PDF file]. Washington, DC: National Education Association Retrieved from www.nea.org/assets/docs/NBI-2010-3-value-of-ethnic-studies.pdf

Soft skills: Definitions and examples (n.d.). *indeed career guide.* Retrieved from www.indeed.com/career-advice/resumes-cover-letters/soft-skills

Solomon, D., Battistich, V., Watson, M. et al. (2000). A six-district study of educational change: Direct and mediated effects of the Child Development Project. *Social Psychology of Education* 4 (1): 3–51. Retrieved from www.researchgate.net/publication/226827084_A_six-district_study_of_educational_change_Direct_and_mediated_effects_of_the_Child_Development_Project

Songhay (n.d.). *BBC World Service.* Retrieved from www.bbc.co.uk/worldservice/specials/1624_story_of_africa/page83.shtml

Soter, A.O., Wilkinson, I.A., Murphy, K. et al. (2008). What the discourse tells us: Talk and indicators of high-level comprehension. *International Journal of Educational Research* 47 (6): 372–391. Retrieved from www.sciencedirect.com/science/article/pii/S0883035509000020

Sousa, D.A. (2010). *Mind, brain, and education: Neuroscience implications for the classroom.* Bloomington, IN: Solution Tree Press www.amazon.com/Mind-Brain-Education-Neuroscience-Implications-ebook/dp/B0046W6UDY

Sparks, S. (2015, June 18). Can sorting teach students to make better connections among subjects? [web log comment]. *Education Week.* Retrieved from http://blogs.edweek.org/edweek/inside-school-research/2015/06/sorting_improves_science_transfer.html

Staats, S. (2015). Understanding implicit bias: What educators should know. *American Educator* Winter 2015–2016: 29–43. Retrieved from www.aft.org/ae/winter2015-2016/staats

Stein, L. and Prewitt, A. (2009). Media literacy education in the social studies: Teacher perceptions and curricular challenges. *Teacher Educator Quarterly* 36 (1): 131–148. Retrieved from www.jstor.org/stable/23479205?seq=1#page_scan_tab_contents

Stereotypes and Tonto (n.d.). *Teaching tolerance.* Retrieved from https://sharemylesson.com/teaching-resource/stereotypes-and-tonto-248423

Storch, N. (2005). Collaborative writing: Product, process, and students' reflections. *Journal of Second Language Writing* 14 (3): 153–173. Retrieved from www.sciencedirect.com/science/article/abs/pii/S1060374305000172

Story sequence (n.d.). *Reading Rockets.* Retrieved from www.readingrockets.org/strategies/story_sequence

Street, F. (2018, July 11). The Louvre launches Beyoncé and Jay-Z tour. *CNN.* Retrieved from www.cnn.com/travel/article/louvre-beyonce-jay-z-tour/index.html

Strong, R., Silver, H.F., and Robinson, A. (1995). Strengthening student engagement: What do students want. *Educational Leadership* 53 (1): 8–12. Retrieved from www.ascd.org/publications/educational-leadership/sept95/vol53/num01/Strengthening-Student-Engagement@-What-Do-Students-Want.aspx

Swan, K., Barton, K.C., Buckles, S., Burke, F., Charkins, J., Grant, S.G., . . . Wiesner-Hanks, M. (2017). *College, career & civic life C3 Framework for social studies state standards* [PDF file]. Retrieved from www.socialstudies.org/sites/default/files/2017/Jun/c3-framework-for-social-studies-rev0617.pdf

Synthesis (n.d.). *Cambridge dictionary*. Retrieved from https://dictionary.cambridge.org/us/dictionary/english/synthesis

Taba, H. (n.d.). Think inductively. Retrieved from www.csus.edu/indiv/m/mcvickerb/imet_sites/fundamentals/inductive/

Taba, H. (1967). *Teacher's handbook for elementary social studies*. Boston: Addison-Wesley.

Teachers as learners and leaders: Advancing literacy for ALL students in California (n.d.). University of California San Diego, California Reading & Literature Project. Retrieved from http://crlpstatewideoffice.ucsd.edu/

Teaching with primary sources: Professional development [PDF file] (2010, December 9). TPS Direct. Retrieved from www.loc.gov/teachers/professionaldevelopment/tpsdirect/pdf/Analyzing-Political-Cartoons.pdf

TeachThought Staff (2017, October 28). *28 critical thinking question stems for any content area*. Retrieved from www.teachthought.com/critical-thinking/28-critical-thinking-question-stems-content-area/

TeachThought Staff (2019, May 13). *A giant list of really good essential questions*. Retrieved from www.teachthought.com/pedagogy/examples-of-essential-questions/

The 6 C's of primary source analysis (n.d.). University of California, Irvine, The History Project. Retrieved from https://historyproject.uci.edu/files/2016/11/6Cs_PSAnalysis.pdf

The Industrial Revolution: The assembly line simulation [PDF file] (n.d.). Retrieved from www.ucis.pitt.edu/esc/system/files/resources/documents/Assembly%20Line%20Simulation_0.pdf

The Revolutionary Tribunal's use of the guillotine (n.d.). *Liberty, equality, fraternity*. Retrieved from http://chnm.gmu.edu/revolution/d/552 (accessed January 22, 2019).

The Room 241 Team (2018, January 11). *Essential Trauma-Informed Teaching Strategies for Managing Stress in the Classroom*. Concordia University-Portland Retrieved from https://education.cu-portland.edu/blog/classroom-resources/trauma-informed-teaching-tips/

The story of . . . smallpox – and other deadly Eurasian germs (n.d.). *PBS Guns Germs and Steel*. Retrieved from www.pbs.org/gunsgermssteel/variables/smallpox.html

Tracey (2011, January 19). *Native American stories: A tradition of storytelling.* Prairie Edge & Sioux Trading Post. Retrieved from https://prairieedge.com/tribe-scribe/native-american-tradition-storytelling/

Traynor, I. (2018, April 23). France approves controversial immigration bill. *BBC.* Retrieved from www.bbc.com/news/world-europe-43860880

Understanding DBQ's & primary resources (n.d.). Franklin D. Roosevelt Presidential Library and Museum. Retrieved from www.fdrlibrary.org/documents/356632/390886/dbqs.pdf/eef70122-da3a-4580-91fc-7afd33122ac5

University of Waterloo (2016, April 21). Need to remember something? Better draw it, study finds. *Science Daily.* Retrieved from www.sciencedaily.com/releases/2016/04/160421133821.htm

van Woerkom, M. (2018, March 12). Building community with restorative circles. *Edutopia.* Retrieved from www.edutopia.org/article/building-community-restorative-circles

Vega, V. (2012, December 3). Project-based learning research review: Evidence-based components of success. *Edutopia.* Retrieved from www.edutopia.org/pbl-research-evidence-based-components

Vercelletto, C. (2018, February 23). Never too old: Embracing picture books to teach older students. *School Library Journal.* Retrieved from www.slj.com/?detailStory=never-old-embracing-picture-books-teach-older-students

Viscusi, G. (2015, November 15). Paris killings mark escalation from Charlie Hebdo attack. *Bloomberg.* Retrieved from www.bloomberg.com/news/articles/2015-11-16/paris-killings-mark-major-escalation-from-charlie-hebdo-attack

W.E.B. (William Edward Burghardt) Du Bois, 1868–1963 (1919). Library of Congress. Retrieved from www.loc.gov/pictures/item/2003681451/resource/cph.3a53178/?sid=3e650091222fc676bd991edf0936a04b

Wallingford Public Schools. (2007, October). *Social Studies K–12 enduring understandings and essential questions.* Retrieved from www.wallingford.k12.ct.us/uploaded/Curriculum/SOCIAL_STUDIES_K-12/SS_K-12_EUs_&_EQs.pdf

Wang, J., Liu, R.-D., Ding, Y. et al. (2017). Teacher's autonomy support and engagement in math: Multiple mediating roles of self-efficacy, intrinsic value, and boredom. *Frontiers in Psychology* 8 (1006) Retrieved from www.frontiersin.org/articles/10.3389/fpsyg.2017.01006/full

Washington, B.T. (n.d.). Library of Congress. Retrieved from www.loc.gov/pictures/resource/hec.16114/

Wells, I. B. (2016, June 10). *It's more than achievement gap. It's opportunity gap. Segregating most marginalized students more than test scores* [Twitter post]. Retrieved from https://twitter.com/nhannahjones/status/741281352079835136?ref_src=twsrc%5Etfw%7Ctwcamp%5Etweetembed%7Ctwterm%5E74128135

2079835136&ref_url=http%3A%2F%2Flarryferlazzo.edublogs.org%2F2011%2F04%2F27%2Fthe-best-resources-for-learning-about-the-achievement-gap%2F

Wiggins, G. (2013, May 17). *On close reading, part 2*. Retrieved from https://grantwiggins.wordpress.com/2013/05/17/on-close-reading-part-2/

Wilhelm, J. (2012). *Improving comprehension with think aloud strategies: Modeling what good readers do*, 2e. New York: Scholastic.

Williams, T.R. (2013). Examine your LENS: A tool for interpreting cultural differences. *The Interdisciplinary Journal of Study Abroad* 22: 148–165.

Willis, J. (2018, July 13). The value of active listening. *Edutopia*. Retrieved from www.edutopia.org/article/value-active-listening

Willsher, K. (2018, May 29). "Spider-Man" of Paris to get French citizenship after child rescue. *The Guardian*. Retrieved from www.theguardian.com/world/2018/may/28/spider-man-of-paris-to-get-french-citizenship-after-rescuing-child

Woods, A. (2018, December 7). Eiffel Tower, Louvre close over "significant violence" during protests. *New York Post*. Retrieved from https://nypost.com/2018/12/07/eiffel-tower-louvre-close-over-significant-violence-during-protests

World population projected to reach 9.8 billion in 2050, and 11.2 billion in 2100. (2017, June 21). United Nations, Department of Economic and Social Affairs. Retrieved from www.un.org/development/desa/en/news/population/world-population-prospects-2017.html

Write Institute (2019). *Writing redesigned for innovative teaching and equity*. Retrieved from https://writeinstitute.sdcoe.net

Yue, C.L., Storm, B.C., Kornell, N., and Bjork, E.L. (2014). Highlighting and its relation to distributed study and students' metacognitive beliefs. *Educational Psychology Review* 27 (1): 69–78. Retrieved from https://sites.williams.edu/nk2/files/2011/08/Yue.Storm_.Kornell.Bjork_.inpress.pdf

Zins, J.E., Bloodworth, M.R., Weissberg, R.P., and Walberg, H.J. (2007). The scientific base linking social and emotional learning to school success. *Journal of Educational and Psychological Consultation* 17 (2–3): 191–210. Retrieved from www.tandfonline.com/doi/abs/10.1080/10474410701413145?journalCode=hepc20

Zusak, M. (2005). *The book thief*. New York: Alfred A. Knopf.

Zwiers, J. (n.d.). *Research*. Retrieved from www.jeffzwiers.org/research

Zwiers, J. and Crawford, M. (2009). How to start academic conversations. *Educational Leadership* 66 (7): 70–73. Retrieved from www.ascd.org/publications/educational-leadership/apr09/vol66/num07/How-to-Start-Academic-Conversations.aspx

Index

Page numbers followed by f and t refer to figures and tables, respectively.

3-2-1 exit slips, 404

A

ABC answering strategy guide, 98f
ABC model questions/ responses, 99f
ABC strategy, student sample, 100f
ABC writing structure, 87–89
Acronym mnemonics, 113
Active listening, 278–280; graphic organizer, 280t
Advanced extensions: assessment, 411; concept attainment, 185; current events, 150; discussions, 315; genre study, 167; image analysis, 221; listening/speaking activities, 288–289; mnemonics, 113–114; primary sources, analysis, 245–246; project-based learning, 345; questions, 199; read-aloud protocol, 48; reading strategy, 29; social and emotional learning, 383; social studies writing, 93; synthesis charts, 273; textbook, 425; thematic data sets, 64; timelines, 132; vocabulary instruction, 14
Advanced modifications, culturally responsive teaching, 368
Adventure, selection (PBL idea), 344–345
Alternative timelines, 131
Analyzing (data set usage teaching protocol), 62–63
Animal noise line up, 279
Annotation: examples, 33f, 35f; prompts, 52f; usage, 42–43
Answer-question, 408
Anticipatory sets, 423
Argument: extending argument writing, 90–91; making, 196; organizer, 102f; prompts, examples, 90; writing, sentence starters, 103f
Article blizzard, usage, 148
Assessment: 3-2-1 exit slips, 404; advanced extensions, 411; answer-question, 408; application, 396–411; Common Core connections, 396; comprehension continuum, 402; concept web, 400; debate, 408; diagnostic assessments, 397–400; examples, 398–400; differentiation, 410–411; formative assessment, 401–404; four corners, 402–403; Know-Want-Learn (KWL) chart, 398–399; Letter to a Future Student, 409; multisource written analysis, 407; one-sentence summary, 403–404; podcasts, 406–407; portfolio, 405–406; preference, reasons, 395; problems, 411–412; ranking, 399; Scientific Revolution concept web, 414f; self-grading, 410; social studies connections, 396; student-created rubrics, 409–410; student-created tests, 406; student self-assessment, 409–410; summative assessments, 404–408; examples, 405–408; supporting research, 396; technology connections, 412–413; "Think and Ink," 399–400; Think-Pair-Share, 403; thumbs up/ down, 401–402; types, 396t

At a glance primary source analysis, 234–235, 248f; student example, 250f; teacher copy, 251f

Attributes, hypothesizing, 180–181

Attribution: culturally responsive teaching, 369; discussions, 316; genre study, 168; listening/speaking activities, 290; mnemonics, 115; primary sources, analysis, 247; read-aloud protocol, 49; reading strategy, 31; social and emotional learning, 385; social studies writing, 95; synthesis charts, 274; thematic data sets, 66; timelines, 133

Authentic texts, finding/preparing (read-aloud protocol), 39–40

Author purpose (analysis), questions (usage), 195–196

B

Bastille Soldier (read-aloud protocol example), 50f

Beginning of the Year Questionnaire, 359, 370f

Benchmark, completion, 333

Bias: awareness/research, 143–147; implicit bias, education, 354–355; media bias chart example, 152f

Bill of Rights, multiphase vocabulary, 420t

Binder clips, usage, 302

Blind drawing, 280

Bollywood movie script starter, 169f–171f; annotation, 171f

Bollywood script assessment rubric, 159t

Brain Graphic Organizer, 387f

Brainstorm, 124t–125t. *See also* Questions; questions, 122

Brazil synthesis chart, 261t, 267–269; example, 263t–264t

C

Cartoons. *See* Political cartoons: creation, 215

Categorization chart, 242t–243t

Category graphic organizer (thematic data sets), 65t; example, 66t

Caution (practice), simulations (usage), 366–367

Census education campaign (PBL idea), 343

China response, teacher model, 163t

Claim, upstream following, 147

Clarifying (reading strategy), 27–28

Classifying (data set usage teaching protocol), 61–62

Classroom: community, building (process), 358–361; cultural lens: awareness/reflection, 353–356; exploration, ideas, 354–356; culturally responsive classroom, promotion, 367–368; current events ideas, inclusion, 148–149

Collaboration (tracking), online surveys (usage), 330

Comment: commenting, 298; making, 59

Common Core Standards for Social Studies and History, connections: assessment, 396; concept attainment, 178; culturally responsive teaching (CRT), 352; current events, 138; discussions, 296; genre study, 154; image analysis, 202; listening/speaking activities, 278; mnemonics, 108; primary sources, analysis, 232; project-based learning, 324; questions for learning, 190; read-aloud protocol, 38; reading strategies, 20; social and emotional learning, 374; social studies writing, 82; synthesis charts, 258; textbooks, 416; thematic data sets, 56; timelines, 120; vocabulary acquisition, importance (description), 4

Community: challenges, incorporation, 363; problem/solution (PBL idea), 344

Community Circles (Restorative Circles), 360–361; templates, 372

Comprehension continuum, 402

Concept attainment: advanced extensions, 185; application, 178–185; attributes, hypothesizing, 180–181; Common Core connections, 178; defining, 177; democracy concept attainment, 179–182; example, 181t; dictatorship paragraph, example, 186f; differentiation, 185; examples: list, making, 179; study, commonalities, 179–180; "Hooks" concept attainment, 184t; hypotheses (testing), student-created examples (usage), 181–182; nonexamples, list (making), 179; preference, reasons, 178; problems, 186; social studies connections, 178; student expectations, 179; supporting research, 178; technology connections, 186; usage, 182–185; source citation function, 183t

Concept web, 400

Conclusion, writing, 185

Connecting (reading strategy), 23

Connections. *See* Social studies connections; Technology connections: making, 149

Content-focused guiding questions, 220

Critical analysis (practice), paintings (usage), 211

Culturally relevant writing prompts, 364–365

Culturally responsive classroom, promotion, 367–368

Culturally responsive literature, students (connection), 368

Culturally responsive mindset, reflection: ideas, 357–358; names, practice, 357; name tents, usage, 357–358; people, referring process, 358; words, impact, 356–358

Culturally responsive teaching (CRT): advanced modifications, 368; application, 352–368; attribution, 369; Beginning of the Year Questionnaire, 359, 370f; classroom, cultural lens: awareness/reflection, 353–356; exploration, ideas, 354–356; Common Core connections, 352; community challenges, incorporation, 363; Community Circles (Restorative Circles), 360–361; template, 372f; differentiation, 367–368; diverse primary sources, inclusion, 361–362; preference, reasons, 351–352; problems, 368–369; questions, 352–353; reflective questions, 353–367; Senior Year History Community Circle, 371f; social justice issues, approach, 362; social studies connections, 352; students: learning capacity, building, 364–367; lives, social studies content choices (relationship), 361–363; relationships/ classroom community, building, 358–361; supporting research, 352; teachers: observation, 355; reflection

structures, usage, 355–356; teaching strategies, culturally responsive analysis, 363–367; technology connections, 369; victimization, examination, 362–363; Warm Demander, role, 360

Current events: advanced extensions, 150; application, 138–150; article blizzard, usage, 148; bias awareness/ research, 143–147; case study, 137; Common Core connections, 138; connections, making, 149; daily news, analysis, 148–149; differentiation, 149; explainer videos, usage, 149; full text (out of order), usage, 139–140; headline, writing, 148; inclusion, ideas, 148–149; information literacy, 146–147; building, 147; media bias chart example, 152f; one-minute presentation, 149; precut passages, usage, 140; predictions, usage, 149; preference, reasons, 137–138; problems, 150–151; questions, development, 141–143; examples, 142; research guide, 145t; example, 146t; sequencing, 139–141; social studies connections, 138; supporting research, 138; technology connections, 151; text: preparation methods, 139–140; reading/ sequencing, 140–141; selection/preparation, 139–140; timeline: example, 152f; organizers, examples, 141t; weekly articles, usage, 148; written analysis, 147–148

Cut-up data set, examples, 78f

D

Daily news, analysis, 148–149

Data sets. *See* Thematic data sets: analysis chart,

241t–242t; analyzing (teaching protocol phase), 62–63; building, 57–58; classifying (teaching protocol phase), 61–62; Cut-up data set, examples, 78f; extending (teaching protocol phase), 63; France headlines data set, example, 71f–75f; indigeneity data set, 67f–70f; primary source data set, usage, 240, 253f–256f; questions, consideration (teaching protocol phase), 59; reading/understanding (teaching protocol phase), 59–60; student-created data sets, 79f; types of government data set, 76f–77f; usage, teaching protocol phases, 59–63

Debate, 408; evidence, 314t

Definitions, revision/formalization (vocabulary instruction), 11–12

Democracy concept attainment, 179–182; example, 181t

Designated sharing partner, 298

Details, impact, 83

Diagnostic assessments, 397–400; examples, 398–400

Dictatorship paragraph, example, 186f

Differentiation: assessment, 410–411; concept attainment, 185; culturally responsive teaching, 367–368; current events, 149; discussions, 313, 315; genre study, 166; image analysis, 220–221; listening/speaking activities, 288; mnemonics, 113; primary sources, analysis, 245; project-based learning, 345; questions, 199; read-aloud protocol, 48; reading strategy, 28; social and emotional learning, 383; social studies writing, 92–93; synthesis charts, 273; textbook, 425; thematic data sets, 63–64; timelines, 131–132; vocabulary instruction, 13

Digital slide presentation, 287

Digital timelines, 130

Discussions: advanced extensions, 315; application, 296–315; attribution, 316; comment, commenting, 298–299; Common Core connections, 296; debate, evidence, 314t; designated sharing partner, 298; differentiation, 313, 315; facilitator card: example, 318f; usage, 302; fishbowl, 306–312; discussion, 307, 309–310; evidence, 308t, 309t; insights chart, 311t; post-fishbowl writing, 312; preparation, 306–307; teacher control, advice, 309–310; formal discussion strategies, 300–312; group discussions: norms, 320f; starters, 347f; informal discussion strategies, 297–300; norms, review, 304; popsicle sticks: facilitator selection, 303; usage, 302; preference, reasons, 295; problems, 316; question strips (Terrorism in Paris), 317f; response frames, 299t; sharing rotations (speed dating), 298; small-group discussion materials, 319f; small-group discussion protocol, 300–305; deconstruction, 304; modeling, 300–303; post-writing prompt, 305; student attempt, 304–305; social studies connections, 296; strategies, 312–313;

supporting research, 296; teacher cheat sheet, 320f; technology connections, 316; textbook discussions, 418–419; think-pair-share, 297; values continuum, 312–313; volleyball debate, 313; weekly discussions, 329–330; whole class sharing, no-hands policy, 299–300

Document-based questions (DBQs), usage, 240, 243

E

Economics, topics/questions, 307, 312

Economic systems (social studies concept), 182

"Election Day" political cartoon, example, 228f

Ellis Island 1913 (photograph), 389f; example, 390f

Ellis Island Empathy Map, 394f

Email template (PBL), 348

Emotional responses, evocation, 83

Empathy Graphic Organizer, 391f; usage, 379

Empathy mini-lesson, 378–381

Empathy statement, response examples, 380

Essential question, 192t, 193–194; example, 195t

Events. See Current events

Evidence: analysis, 184; evidence-based inferences, 206–207, 213–214, 218–219

Explainer videos, usage, 149

Extended argument writing, 90–91

Extending (data set usage teaching protocol), 63

F

Facilitator card. See Discussion

Feedback, usage, 365–366

Fishbowl, 306–312; discussion, 307, 309–310; evidence, 308t; example, 309t; insights chart, 311t; post-fishbowl writing, 312; preparation, 306–307; teacher control, advice, 309–310

Follow-up writing activities, 129

Formal discussion strategies, 300–312

Formative assessment, 401–404; examples, 401–404

Four corners, 402–403

France headlines data set, example, 71f–75f

Full text (out of order), usage, 139–140

G

Genre study: advanced extensions, 167; applications, 154–167; attribution, 168; Bollywood movie script starter, 169f–171f; annotation, 171f; China poem, student example, 172f; China response, teacher model, 163t; Common Core connections, 154; differentiation, 166; genre cheat sheet, 174f–175f; genre rating, 165t; genres station activity, exploration, 164; movie script, 158; assignment directions, 158–161; Bollywood script assessment rubric, 159t; examples, studying, 155–158; possibilities, 160–161; project, 155; preference, reasons, 153–154; problems, 167; project extensions, 166; project genre study, 330; prompt/project, introduction, 162–164; scene: diagram example, 175f; dissection, 157t; social media, student example, 173f; social studies connections, 154; student choice genre: assessment rubric, 163t; project, 161–166; supporting research, 154; technology connections, 168; video clips, 155–156; work time, 164, 166

Geography, topics/questions, 306, 312

Get out the vote campaign (PBL idea), 344

Golden lines: identification process, 84; writing, kick starting, 83–84

Government: topics/questions, 307, 312; types (social studies concept), 182

Grading rubric. *See* Timelines

Graphic organizer: creation, 284; usage, 329

Group discussions: norms, 320; starters, 347f

Group timelines, 130

Growth mindset: mini-lesson, 375–377; promotion, feedback (usage), 365–366

Guest speakers: impact, 280–283; listening, 282; post-listening, 282–283; preparation, 281–282; suggestions, 291f; thank-you template/example, 292f, 293f

Guiding questions, 192t, 194–195, 219; content-focused guiding questions, 220; example, 195t

Guillotine (read-aloud protocol example), 51f

H

Headline, writing, 148

Historical figure: commonality, 129; research, 128t; timeline, 126–127; items, review/reflection, 129

Historical narrative, 92

Hook questions, 192t, 196

"Hooks" concept attainment, 184t

Hypotheses (testing), student-created examples (usage), 181–182

I

Ideas, generation (problems), 15

Identity synthesis chart, 265t, 269, 272–273; teacher model, 270t–271t

Identity timelines, 121–129; life events, description/significance, 123; student example, 135f; student identity timelines, 122–123; teacher identity timelines, 121–122; teacher model, 134f

Image analysis: advanced extensions, 221; application, 203–221; chart, 223f; Common Core connections, 202; differentiation, 220–221; Japanese-American evacuation photograph, 224f; observations, usage, 209; preference, reasons, 201–202; problems, 222–223; slideshow, creation, 208–209; social studies connections, 202–203; supporting research, 202; technology connections, 223; Word Cloud, creation, 208

Image analysis, paintings, 209–211; activism, 211; evaluation, factors, 210; protocol, 210–211; strategies, 211; usage, 211

Image analysis, photographs, 203–209; analysis chart, teacher model, 225f; essay, creation, 209; evidence-based inferences, 206–207; notations, 205–206; prewriting, 204–205; protocol, 204–208; relevance, evaluation, 207–208; strategies, 208–209; Word Cloud, DuBois/Washington images, 226f

Image analysis, political cartoons, 212–215; analysis chart, 227f; creation, 215; "Election Day," example, 228f; evidence-based inferences, 213–214; literary devices, identification, 215; memes, engagement, 214; notations, 212–213; prewriting, 212; protocol, 212–214; relevance, evaluation, 214; strategies, 214–215; teacher model, 229f

Image analysis, video, 215–220; analysis chart, 215t; content-focused guiding questions, usage, 220; evidence-based inferences, 218–219; footage, analysis, 216; notations, 217–218; notes, passing, 220; online choices, criteria, 216; prewriting, 216–217; prompts, provision, 216; protocol, 215–219; relevance, evaluation, 219; strategies, 219–220; student-created videos, 220; summarizing/predicting, pauses (usage), 219–220; teacher model, 217t

Image slideshow, graphic organizer, 208t

Images, usage, 416–417

Implicit bias, education, 354–355

Indigeneity data set, 67f–70f

Inferences: evidence-based inferences, 206–207, 213–214, 218–219; making, 196

Informal discussion strategies, 297–300

Information: connection, 110; literacy, 146–147; processing, usage, 364

Initial questions, impact, 195
Insights chart, usage, 311t
Introduction, writing, 184

J

Japanese-American evacuation photo, 224f
Jigsaws, 423–424; organizer, example, 424t; student presentation method, 286, 287t

K

Key ideas: highlighting, 59; recognition, reading strategy, 24
Know-Want-Learn (KWL) chart, 398–399
Know-Want-Learn (KWL) graphic organizer, usage, 197

L

Letter frame, examples, 96f, 97f
Life events, description/significance, 123
Link word, saying aloud, 112
Listening/speaking activities: active listening: graphic organizer, 280t; mini-lesson, 278–280; advanced extensions, 288–289; animal noise line up, 279; application, 278–289; attribution, 290; blind drawing, 280; Common Core connections, 278; differentiation, 288; guest speakers: impact, 280–283; listening, 282; post-speakers, 282–283; preparation, 281–282; suggestions, 291f; thank-you template/example, 292f, 293f; podcasts, 283–286; graphic organizer, creation, 284; listening, 284–285; post-listening, 285–286; preparation, 283–284; serial podcast listening graphic organizer, 285t; preference, reasons, 277; problems, 289; social studies connections, 278; student interview, 279; student presentations, 286–288; digital slide presentation, 287; jigsaw, usage, 286, 287t; Pechakucha presentation, 287; supporting research, 278; technology connections, 289–290; Telephone (game), playing, 279; two truths and a lie, 280
Literary devices, identification, 215
lives, social studies content choices (relationship): marginalized groups, thematic teaching, 361

M

Map story guide, examples, 111t, 116f–117f
Map visual, student examples, 116f, 117f
Marginalized groups, thematic teaching, 361
Media bias chart example, 152f
Memes, engagement, 214
Mindsets Graphic Organizer, 388f; usage, 376
Minidocumentaries (PBL idea), 344
Mnemonics, 107; acronym mnemonics, 113; advanced extensions, 113–114; application, 109–114; attribution, 115; Common Core connections, 108; differentiation, 113; map story guide, examples, 111t, 116f–117f; map visual, student examples, 116f, 117f; preference, reasons, 107; problems, 114; social studies connections, 108; story: review, 112; story, introduction, 109–111; story mnemonics, 109–113; supporting research, 108; technology connections, 114–115; textbook mnemonics, 422–423
Model answer frame, creation, 44
Modified vocabulary graphic organizer, 13t; answer sheet, 14t
Monthly themes (SEL), 382
Movie script, 158; assignment directions, 158–160; Bollywood script assessment rubric, 159t; examples, studying, 155–158; possibilities, 160–161; project, 155; scene, dissection, 157t
Multisource written analysis, 407

N

Name tents, usage, 357–358
News story (validity), guide/criteria (provision), 147

O

One-minute presentation, 149
One-sentence summary, 403–404
Overcoming adversity matching activity, 386f

P

Paintings: activism, 211; evaluation, factors, 210; image analysis, 209–211; protocol, 210–211; strategies, 211; usage, 211
Passage, reading, 59
Pechakucha presentation, 287
Peer-to-peer presentations, 286
Personal connections, 129t; identification, 127–129
Personal Empathy Map, 392f; teacher model, 393f

Photographs: analysis chart, teacher model, 225f; historical significance, analysis, 207; image analysis, 203–209; notations, 205–206; prewriting, 204–205; protocol, 204–208; purpose, analysis, 207; relevance, evaluation, 207–208; Word Cloud, DuBois/Washington images (example), 226f

Pictionary, playing, 112

Podcasts, 283–286, 407–408; listening, 284–285; PBL idea, 344; post-listening, 285–286; preparation, 283–284; questions: chronological listing, 284; mix, selection, 284; serial podcast listening graphic organizer, 285t; time stamps, placement, 284

Point Example Explain (PEE): answering strategy guide, 101f

Point Example Explain (PEE) writing structure, 898

Political campaign ads, accuracy/fallacy (student analysis), 147

Political cartoons: analysis chart, 227f; creation, 215; "Election Day," 228f; image analysis, 212–215; literary devices, identification, 215; memes, engagement, 214; notations, 213–214; prewriting, 212; protocol, 212–214; relevance, evaluation, 214; strategies, 214–215; teacher model, 229f

Politifact, student introduction, 147

Popsicle sticks. *See* Discussions

Portfolio, 405–406

Post-writing prompt, 305

Precut passages, usage, 140

Predicting (reading strategy), 22–23

Predictions: making, 59; usage, 149

Pre-reading, 22

Primary sources: diverse primary sources, inclusion, 361–362; secondary sources, differences, 182; textbook primary sources, 421–422

Primary sources, analysis: advanced extensions, 245–246; annotation strategies, 236; application, 232–246; attribution, 247; categorization chart, 242t–243t; Common Core connections, 232; data set: analysis chart, 241t–242t; example (slavery, roots), 253f–256f; differentiation, 245; document-based questions (DBQs), usage, 240, 243; at a glance analysis: student example, 250f; teacher copy, 251f; post-analysis reflection, 239–240; preference, reasons, 231; primary source data set, usage, 240; primary source engagement activity, 232–234; problems, 246; reflection prompts, 239; scaffolding strategies, 239t; secondary sources, fact checking, 244; slavery, roots (primary source data set), 253f–256f; social studies connections, 232; source, at a glance analysis, 234–235, 248f; source, in-depth analysis, 236–240; teacher copy, 238t; strategies, 240–245; supporting research, 232; technology connections, 247; Tenochtitlan, Cortés account, 249f; teacher copy, 253f; transcribing, 244–245; unit/topic introduction, 244; written source, in-depth analysis, 252f

Prior knowledge, access (vocabulary instruction), 6–9; splashed vocabulary, 8–9; stations activity, 9; vocabulary graphic organizer, 7–8

Prison reform: fishbowl, evidence (example), 309t; questions, 312

Progressive classroom timeline, 131

Project-based learning (PBL): advanced extensions, 345; adventure, selection, 344–345; application, 324–345; assessment, 331, 333, 340; benchmark, completion, 333; Census education campaign, 343; collaboration (tracking), online surveys (usage), 330; Common Core connections, 324; community problem/solution, 344; differentiation, 345; email template, 348f; expert, contact, 330; get out the vote campaign, 344; group discussions, starters, 347f; ideas, 343–345; minidocumentaries/podcasts, 344; planning, 325, 334–335; planning/progress form, 328t, 338t; preference, reasons, 323–324; presentation, 330–331, 340; problem, introduction, 325–327, 335–337; problems, 346; project: genre study, 330; introduction, 325–327, 335–337; questions, 326–327, 336; reflection, 333–334, 340–341, 343; ideas, 333–334; research: chart, 329t; graphic organizers, usage, 329; rubric, 332t–333t;

social studies connections, 324; steps, 325–334; structured work time, 327–330, 337–339; student-created unit, 343; student questions, 336–337; supporting research, 324; teacher planning form/checklist, 326t; textbook insert, 334t–335t; technology connections, 346–347; textbook insert project, 334–343; rubric, 341t–343t; textbook insert structure, 349f–350f; weekly discussions, 329–330; younger student education, 344

Prompts: culturally relevant writing prompts, 364–365; example, 50f–52f; introduction, 162–164; post-writing prompt, 305; reflection prompts, 239; usage, 259

Publishing Online, 92

Q

Questioning (reading strategy), 25–26

Questions: advanced extensions, 199; application, 191–199; brainstorming, 198; chronological list, 284; Common Core connections, 190; consideration (data set usage teaching protocol), 59; creation, academic starters/frames (usage), 198; development, 141–143; student support, 197–198; differentiation, 199; document-based questions (DBQs), usage, 240, 243; essential questions, 192t, 193–194; example, 195t; follow-up assignment, 198; generation, 197–198; guiding questions, 192t, 194–195, 219; example, 195t; hook questions, 192t, 196;

initial questions, impact, 195; Know-Want-Learn (KWL) graphic organizer, usage, 197; mix, selection, 284; preference, reasons, 189–190; problems, 200; reflective questions, 353–367; social studies connections, 190; strips (Terrorism in Paris), 317f; strips, usage, 301; student-generated questions, 196–198; subquestions, generation, 336; supporting research, 190; teacher-generated questions, 192–196; advice, 192–193; technology connections, 200; text-dependent questions, 195–196; categories, 195–196; types, examples, 192t; usage, 195–196; "What If?" history project, 198

Quick Writes, 91

R

Ranking, 399

Read-aloud protocol, 37; advanced extensions, 48; annotation, prompts, 52f; application, 38–48; attribution, 49; authentic texts, finding/preparing, 39–40; Common Core connections, 38; differentiation, 48; phases, 41–44; preference, reasons, 37; problems, 49; prompts, examples, 50f–52f; social studies connections, 38; student-created read-alouds, 45–48; supporting research, 37–38; technology connections, 49; text revision, annotations (usage), 42; writing prompts, answering, 43–44

Read-alouds: attributes, 53f; searching, questions (usage), 46; series, additions, 46;

student-created read-alouds, 45–48; success, factors, 41

Reading aloud (read-aloud protocol phase), 41

Reading, improvement (strategies), 47

Reading strategies: advanced extensions, 29; annotation, examples, 33f, 35f; application, 21–29; attribution, 31; clarifying, 27–28; Common Core Initiative, connections, 20; connecting, 23; differentiation, 28; handout, 21t; key ideas, recognition, 24; predicting, 22–23; preference, reasons, 19–20; pre-reading, 22; problems, 29–30; prompts, example, 52f; questioning, 25–26; sentence starters, 32f; social studies connections, 20; summarizing, 24–25; examples, 34f; supporting research, 20; technology connections, 30–31; textbook reading strategies, 421; text selection, 22; visualizing, 26–27

Reading/understanding (data set usage teaching protocol), 59–60

Reflection: prompts, 239; questions, responses, 377; structures, usage, 355–356

Reflective Learning Logs, 92

Reflective questions, 353–367

Reign of Terror (read-aloud protocol example), 52f

Research guide, 145t; example, 146t

Response frames, 299t

Restorative Circles, 360–361

Resumés: concept attainment, 183t–184t; writing, 183–184

Right-there questions, think-about questions (differences), 197

S

Scaffolding strategies, 239t
Scavenger hunts, 423
Scientific Revolution concept web, 414f
Secondary sources: fact checking, 244; primary sources, differences, 182
Self-grading, 410
Senior Year History Community Circle, 371f
Sentences: frames, 84–86, 93; usage, 273; one-sentence summary, 403–404; resonance, 83; starters, 84, 103f; provision, 123; starters (reading strategy), 32f; usage, 43
Sequencing activity (timelines), 131
Sharing (timelines), 125–126
Sharing rotations (speed dating), 298
Simulations, usage, 366–367
Small-group discussion materials, 319f
Small-group discussion protocol, 300–305; deconstruction, 304; modeling, 301–303; post-writing prompt, 305; student attempt, 304–305
Social and emotional learning (SEL): advanced extensions, 383; application, 375–383; attribution, 385; Brain Graphic Organizer, 387f; Common Core connections, 374; differentiation, 383; Ellis Island 1913 (photograph), 389f; example, 390f; Ellis Island Empathy Map, 394f; Empathy Graphic Organizer, 391f; usage, 379; empathy mini-lesson, 378–381; empathy statement, response examples, 380; growth mindset mini-lesson,

375–377; Mindsets Graphic Organizer, 388f; usage, 376; monthly themes, 382; overcoming adversity matching activity, 386f; Personal Empathy Map, 392f; teacher model, 393f; preference, reasons, 373–374; problems, 384; reflection questions, response, 377; reinforcement, advice, 381–383; social studies connections, 374; structures, recurrence, 382; students, response selection, 376; supporting research, 374; technology connections, 384–385; terms, inclusion, 382; topic diversity, 376–377; warm-ups/tickets out the door, 382–383
Social justice issues, approach, 3262
Social media, student example, 173f
Social studies: classes, topics/questions, 306–307; concepts (teaching), 182; PBL questions, 326–327
Social studies connections: assessment, 396; concept attainment, 178; culturally responsive teaching (CRT), 352; current events, 138; discussions, 296; genre study, 154; image analysis, 202–203; listening/speaking activities, 278; mnemonics, 108; primary sources, analysis, 232; project-based learning, 324; questions for learning, 190; read-aloud protocol, 38; reading strategies, 20; social and emotional learning, 374; synthesis charts, 258; textbooks, 416; thematic data sets, 56; timelines, 120; vocabulary instruction, 4–5

Social studies writing: ABC answering strategy guide, 98f; ABC model questions/responses, 99f; ABC strategy, student sample, 100f; ABC writing structure, 87–89; activities, 91–92; advanced extensions, 93; application, 82–93; argument organizer, 102f; argument writing, sentence starters, 103f; attribution, 95; Common Core connections, 82; differentiation, 92–93; extended argument writing, 90–91; golden lines, writing (kick starting), 83–84; letter frame, examples, 96f, 97f; Point Example Explain (PEE): answering strategy guide, 101f; writing structure, 89; preference, reasons, 81; problems, 94; social studies connections, 82; structures, 86–89; supporting research, 81–82; teacher argument model response, 104f; technology connections, 94–95; word bank paragraph, example, 105f
Sources. *See* Primary sources: citing, concept attainment (usage), 183t; in-depth analysis, 236–240; teacher copy, 238t; written source, in-depth analysis, 252f
Speaking activities. *See* Listening/speaking activities
Speed dating, 298
Splashed vocabulary, 8–9; example, 16f
Stations activity, 9
Stations, creation, 112
Sticky note, usage, 112
Story: introduction, 109–111; map story guide, example, 111t; mnemonics, 109–113; review, 112; student telling, 112

Strip Stories, 92

Structured work time, 327–330, 337–339

Students: choice genre: assessment rubric, 163t; project, 161–166; classroom community, building process, 358–361; culturally responsive literature, connection, 368; hypotheses (testing), student-created examples (usage), 181–182; identity timelines, 122–123; information literacy, building, 146; interview, 279; learning capacity, building, 364–367; Letter to a Future Student, 409; lives, social studies content choices (relationship), 361–363; perspectives, encouragement, 368; presentations, 286–288; jigsaw, 286, 287t; methods, 286–287; relationships, building: assessment, questions, 359; process, 358–361; self-assessment, 409–410; student-created data sets, 79f; student-created rubrics, 409–410; student-created tests, 406; student-created texts, 421; student-created unit (PBL), 343; student-created videos, 220; student-generated questions, 196–198; support, question development, 197–198; synthesis charts, implementation, 266–273; words, sharing, 367; younger students, education (PBL idea), 344

Stylistic imitations, 366

Subquestions, generation, 336

Summarizing (reading strategy), 24–25; examples, 34f

Summative assessments, 404–408; examples, 405–408

Synonyms, dissection, 43

Synthesis charts: advanced extensions, 273; application, 258–273; attribution, 274; Brazil synthesis chart, 261t, 267–269; example, 263t–264t; Common Core connections, 258; creation, 259–266; differentiation, 273; identity synthesis chart, 265t, 269, 272–273; teacher model, 270t–271t; implementation, 266–273; preference, reasons, 257–258; problems, 274; prompts, usage, 259; resources, 262; sentence frames, usage, 273; social studies connections, 258; summary/synthesis, 266; supporting research, 257; technology connections, 274; template, 260t; topics, 262; usage, examples, 259

T

Teachers: argument model response, 104f; identity timelines, 121–122; observation, 355; reflection structures, usage, 355–356; teacher-generated questions, 192–196

Teaching strategies, culturally responsive analysis, 363–367

Technology connections, 15; assessment, 412–413; concept attainment, 186; culturally responsive teaching, 369; current events, 151; discussions, 316; genre study, 168; image analysis, 222; listening/speaking activities, 289–290; mnemonics, 114–115; primary sources, analysis, 247; project-based learning, 346–347; questions, 200;

read-aloud protocols, 49; reading strategy, 30–31; social and emotional learning, 384–385; social studies writing, 94–95; synthesis charts, 274; textbook, 426; thematic data sets, 65–66; timelines, 133

Telephone (game), playing, 279

Tenochtitlan. See Primary sources

Text: drama, reduction, 47; evidence, finding, 43–44; main point, 83; preparation methods, 139–140; reading/sequencing, 140–141; revision, annotation usage (read-aloud protocol phase), 42; selection (reading strategy), 22; selection/preparation, 139–140; structure (analysis), questions (usage), 195–196; student-created texts, 421; text-dependent questions, 195–196; categories, 195–196

Textbook: advanced extensions, 425; anticipatory sets, 423; application, 416–425; Common Core connections, 416; differentiation, 425; discussions, 418–419; excerpts, usage, 417–428; images, usage, 416–417; jigsaws, 423–424; organizer, example, 424t; mnemonics, 422–423; multiphase vocabulary (Bill of Rights), 420t; preference, reasons, 415–416; primary sources, 421–422; problems, 426; reading strategies, 421; scavenger hunts, 423; social studies connections, 416; student-created texts, 421; supporting research, 416; technology connections,

426; text, absence (analysis), 425; timelines, 419; vocabulary, 420

Thematic data sets, 55; advanced extensions, 64; application, 57–64; attribution, 66; category graphic organizer, 65t; example, 66t; Common Core connections, 56; differentiation, 63–64; preference, reasons, 55–56; problems, 65; social studies connections, 56; supporting research, 56; technology connections, 65–66

Themed timelines, 130

Think-about questions, right-there questions (differences), 197

"Think and Ink," 399–400

Thinking process, modeling, 336

Think-pair-share, 297

Think-Pair-Share, 403

Thumbs up/down, 401–402

Timelines: activities, 130–131; advanced extensions, 132; alternative timelines, 131; application, 120–132; attribution, 133; brainstorm, 124t–125t; questions, 122; Common Core connections, 120; comparison, 130–131; differentiation, 131–132; digital timelines, 130; events: content, comparison, 131; impact/ranking, 130; example, 152f; formats, 131; grading rubric, 123t; group timelines, 130; historical figure: research, 128t; timeline, 126–127; identity timelines, 121–129; student example, 135f; teacher model, 134f; items, review, 131; organizer, examples, 141t; pattern, possibility, 130; personal connections, 129t;

identification, 127–129; preference, reasons, 119–120; problems, 133; progressive classroom timeline, 131; prompts, follow-up writing activities, 129; sequencing activity, 131; sharing, 125–126; social studies connections, 120; student identity timelines, 122–123; supporting research, 120; teacher identity timelines, 121–122; technology connections, 133; textbook timelines, 419; themed timelines, 130

Time stamps, placement, 284

Topics (synthesis charts), 262

Topic, writing, 197

Two truths and a lie, 280

Types of Government data set, 76f–77f

U

Understanding, building (vocabulary instruction), 10–11

Understanding/reading (data set usage teaching protocol), 59–60

Unit vocabulary graphic organizer, 7t

Unit vocabulary lists, SEL terms (inclusion), 382

V

Values continuum, 312–313

Victimization, examination, 362–363

Video: analysis chart, 215t; content-focused guiding questions, usage, 220; evidence-based inferences, 218–219; footage, examination, 216; guiding questions, 219; image analysis, 215–220; notations, 217–218; notes, passing, 220; online choices,

criteria, 216; prewriting, 216–217; prompts, examples, 216; protocol, 215–219; relevance, evaluation, 219; strategies, 219–220; student-created videos, 220; summarizing/ predicting, pauses (usage), 219–220; teacher model, 217t

Visualizing (reading strategy), 26–27

Visual, showing, 112

Vocabulary: acquisition, importance (Common Core Standards for Social Studies and History description), 4; graphic organizer, 7–8; modified vocabulary graphic organizer, 13t; answer sheet, 14t; multiphase vocabulary (Bill of Rights), 420t; splashed vocabulary, 8–9; example, 16f; textbook vocabulary, 420; unit vocabulary graphic organizer, 7t; word, usage, 46

Vocabulary instruction, 3; advanced extensions, 14; applications, 5–14; Common Core connections, 4; preference, reasons, 3–4; problems, 15; social studies, connection, 4–5; supporting research, 4; technology connections, 15

Volleyball debate, 313

W

Warm Demander, role, 360

Weekly articles, usage, 148

Weekly discussions, 329–330

"What If?" history project, 198

Whole class sharing, no-hands policy, 299–300

Word: card, examples, 17f; choice (analysis), questions (usage), 195–196; link word, saying aloud, 112; list, building, 5–6

Word bank, 92; paragraph, 105f
Word Cloud: creation, 208; DuBois/Washington images, example, 226f
Words: impact, 356–358; linking, 110; student sharing, 368
Work time, 164, 166; structured work time, 327–330, 337–339
World history, topics/questions, 307, 312

World religions (social studies concepts), 182
Writing: ABC writing structure, 87–89; culturally relevant writing prompts, 364–365; follow-up writing activities, 129; frames, 84–86; improvement, concept attainment (usage), 182–185; PEE writing structure, 89; post-fishbowl writing, 312; prompts: answering (read-aloud protocols), 43–44; student generation, 198; resumé writing, 183–184; structures, 86–89
Writing, kick starting, 83–84
Written source, in-depth analysis, 252f

Y

Younger students, education (PBL idea), 344